D1547718

ADVANCED PRAISE FOR *NURTURING LANGUAGE AND LEARNING*

"From their rich history in early work with babies and their families, Spencer and Koester have identified *the* area where the field is failing children; that is, providing support to practitioners and families of very young babies who are deaf or hard of hearing. This book doesn't just dabble in the area, it dives head-first into the breach between the rarified air of the research camp and the hardscrabble struggle of real parents and their babies. This book is a *must* on the shelf of all early interventionists."
—**Susan Easterbrooks, Regents' Professor of Educational Psychology, Special Education and Communication Disorders; Program Coordinator, Deaf Education Program, Georgia State University**

"At last! Parents of deaf and hard-of-hearing children now have a book that puts all the information about their child's development during the first three years of life in one tidy place. Spencer and Koester repeatedly reassure parents: you can do this! And then tell them how. You will meet all kinds of families and their deaf and hard-of-hearing children—children with hearing parents, children with deaf parents, deafblind children, children with multiple disabilities, families of diverse cultures and diverse languages, children with CIs and those without—and all are accorded the same respect. Spencer and Koester not only know their stuff, but they write from the heart."
—**Linda Risser Lytle, Professor, Department of Counseling, Gallaudet University; co-author of *Turning the Tide: Making Life Better for Deaf and Hard of Hearing Schoolchildren***

"How do parents respond to their infant's unique personalities and gifts when the infant is deaf or hard of hearing? This timely, well-written and comprehensive book provides insights gleaned from parents and professionals who have been successful in detecting, accepting, and learning how to communicate with these infants. This book is an essential and long-awaited guide to understanding the normal developmental stages of infants who have hearing challenges, providing parents and caregivers with the intervention resources and best practices that they need for early identification and fostering of optimal development in this population of infants."
—**Alan Fogel, Professor Emeritus, Developmental Psychology, The University of Utah**

"Anyone involved with deaf and hard-of-hearing infants and toddlers—parents, early interventionists, health care professionals, students—will value Spencer and Koester's clearly written and unbiased presentation of developmental advances across domains. Drawing from their own interactions with deaf and hard-of-hearing infants and toddlers, they explain in a reader-friendly tone how advances in one domain propel development in others, and provide evidence-based strategies to support positive early interactions with and a positive developmental trajectory for these young explorers."
—**Janet R. Jamieson, Professor and Co-Director, Program in Education of the Deaf and Hard of Hearing, The University of British Columbia**

DISCARD

Porter County
Library System

Valparaiso Public Library
103 Jefferson Street
Valparaiso, IN 46383

PROFESSIONAL PERSPECTIVES ON DEAFNESS: EVIDENCE AND APPLICATIONS

Series Editors

Patricia Elizabeth Spencer

Marc Marschark

Social Competence of Deaf and Hard-of-Hearing Children

Shirin D. Antia and Kathryn H. Kreimeyer

Mental Health and Deafness

Margaret du Feu and Cathy Chovaz

Auditory (Re)Habilitation for Adolescents with Hearing Loss

Jill Duncan, Ellen A. Rhoades, and Elizabeth Fitzpatrick

Literacy Instruction for Students Who Are Deaf and Hard of Hearing

Susan R. Easterbrooks and Jennifer Beal-Alvarez

*Nurturing Language and Learning: Development of Deaf
and Hard-of-Hearing Infants and Toddlers*

Patricia Elizabeth Spencer and Lynne Sanford Koester

Introduction to American Deaf Culture

Thomas K. Holcomb

Evidence-Based Practice in Educating Deaf and Hard-of-Hearing Students

Patricia Elizabeth Spencer and Marc Marschark

*Early Intervention for Deaf and Hard-of-hearing Infants, Toddlers, and their
Families: Interdisciplinary Perspectives*

Marilyn Sass-Lehrer (Ed.)

Nurturing Language and Learning

Development of Deaf and Hard-of-Hearing Infants and Toddlers

Patricia Elizabeth Spencer
Education and Research Consultant, Bethesda, Maryland

Lynne Sanford Koester
Professor Emerita, University of Montana-Missoula

OXFORD
UNIVERSITY PRESS

Porter County Public Library

Valparaiso Public Library
103 Jefferson Street
Valparaiso, IN 46383

vabnf   VAL
371.912 SPENC

Spencer, Patricia Elizabeth
Nurturing language and learning
33410013776101   02/16/16

OXFORD
UNIVERSITY PRESS

Oxford University Press is a department of the University of Oxford. It furthers
the University's objective of excellence in research, scholarship, and education
by publishing worldwide. Oxford is a registered trade mark of Oxford University
Press in the UK and certain other countries.

Published in the United States of America by Oxford University Press
198 Madison Avenue, New York, NY 10016, United States of America.

© Oxford University Press 2016

First Edition published in 2016

All rights reserved. No part of this publication may be reproduced, stored in
a retrieval system, or transmitted, in any form or by any means, without the
prior permission in writing of Oxford University Press, or as expressly permitted
by law, by license, or under terms agreed with the appropriate reproduction
rights organization. Inquiries concerning reproduction outside the scope of the
above should be sent to the Rights Department, Oxford University Press, at the
address above.

You must not circulate this work in any other form
and you must impose this same condition on any acquirer.

Library of Congress Cataloging-in-Publication Data
Spencer, Patricia Elizabeth.
Nurturing language and learning: development of deaf and hard-of-hearing infants and toddlers /
Patricia Elizabeth Spencer and Lynne Sanford Koester.
pages cm. — (Professional perspectives on deafness: evidence and applications)
Includes bibliographical references and index.
ISBN 978–0–19–993132–3
1. Deaf infants—Language.   2. Deaf infants—Education (Early childhood)   3. Hearing impaired
infants—Language.   4. Hearing impaired infants—Education (Early childhood)   5. Language
acquisition.   6. Oral communication.   7. Early childhood education.   I. Koester, Lynne
Sanford.   II. Title.
HV2391.S64 2016
371.91'2—dc23
2015022369

9 8 7 6 5 4 3 2 1

Printed by Webcom, Canada

We gratefully acknowledge the mentors who taught us so much about infants, toddlers, and their parents, Kathryn P. Meadow-Orlans and Hanuš and Mechthild Papoušek.

And with love and gratitude, we want to thank our own very first teachers, Margaret and Walter Spencer, Robert and Lillian Golden, Essie Mae Spencer Foster, Elizabeth and Gilbert Sanford, Vonnie Gaulding, and Walter Edward Sanford.

CONTENTS

PREFACE: OR, WHY THIS BOOK WAS WRITTEN

The idea for this book has been incubating for some time—decades, actually. It stems in large part from the work we were privileged to do as members of the research team headed by Dr. Kathryn P. Meadow-Orlans in the Center for Studies in Education and Human Development at the Gallaudet University Research Institute. Lynne brought to this work a background in developmental psychology, one enriched by her previous collaboration with Professors Hanuš and Mechthild Papoušek, who pioneered creative ways of studying infants. They developed the concept of "intuitive parenting," which has had significant application to the early experiences of deaf and hard-of-hearing infants, as well as those with typical hearing. Pat came to the research team with extensive background in early language development and in both assessment and programming for young children who were deaf or hard of hearing. Dr. Meadow-Orlans, who gave us the opportunity to participate on her team, was already a leading researcher on topics related to the social-emotional and psychological development of deaf and hard-of-hearing infants and children. With her colleague Hilde Schlesinger, she was among the first to bring a truly developmental perspective to this field of study—a perspective that went beyond a focus on the child to include family and cultural influences. Not at all incidentally, Dr. Meadow-Orlans was one of a small group of researchers in the 1960s and 1970s to draw attention to the developmental advantages experienced by deaf and hard-of-hearing children whose parents were deaf—and to provide data showing that using signs was beneficial in supporting social-emotional and cognitive abilities as well as building language skills.

In the 1980s, when we (first Pat and Lynne soon thereafter) joined Dr. Meadow-Orlans's team, research with mothers and infants had already begun. The focus was on ways in which variations in hearing, across infants and between mother and infant, were reflected in patterns of early interactive behaviors and, in turn, infant and toddler developmental achievements. As these investigations were expanded and extended, some mother–infant pairs were seen as early as the baby's third month, others at 6 months, and all by 9 months. They were followed through at least 18 months of age—some until age 3 in "add-on" investigations. These babies, for their time, received very early identification of their hearing levels and early intervention support. Uniquely (perhaps to this day), the research included four groups of infants and mothers: deaf and hard-of-hearing babies with hearing mothers; deaf and hard-of-hearing babies with deaf mothers (primarily using sign language); babies with typical hearing who had deaf, signing mothers; and a group of babies and mothers in which both had typical hearing. Because we believed that characteristics of the baby, like temperament and special abilities, affect interaction and communication as much as do those of the mother, we expected to see a number of patterns of different interactive strengths and strategies. And we did. Those strategies and patterns of interaction, and the data and analyses that support their description, are provided in detail in a book entitled *The World of Deaf Infants* (Meadow-Orlans, Spencer, & Koester, Oxford University Press, 2004). We recommend that anyone involved in intervention programming for families with deaf or hard-of-hearing infants and toddlers read and study the unique trove of information in that in-depth report of the research.

We make no effort to replicate that information in this book, although we are confident that not a single chapter has escaped reference to it. We have each had a variety of experiences working with infants, toddlers, and their families since the completion of that project, and, as we recently recalled with more than a little amazement, those experiences have taken place in a variety of locations and across a variety of cultures over several continents. They have included investigations, observations, and consultation for programs and families including toddlers and young children with early cochlear implant use, those in oral (spoken language) programs as well as in programs in which the emphasis was on signing and sign language, and those with multiple developmental challenges.

We have, as well, continued to study and interact with families and infants-toddlers with typical hearing. A burgeoning research literature of reports and analyses of the newly recognized competencies of infants and toddlers, as well as bookstores (both the physical and electronic variety) stuffed with "how-to" and "when-does-it-happen" guidebooks for parents of young children with typical hearing, have impressed us with the amount of information available about early development. Equally impressive was the relative lack of such references for parents of infants and toddlers who are deaf or hard of hearing. We reasoned that the story of development has been told often enough regarding babies and toddlers who have typical hearing. Why not produce such a story for those whose parents find out, often within weeks of giving birth, that their babies will have added challenges due to limited hearing abilities? How will these babies be similar to those with typical hearing, and how might they differ? What kinds of parenting attitudes and activities will be especially supportive? What kinds and levels of development can be expected when these babies reach 3 years of age and their early intervention services (if available at all) have ended? We envisioned weaving a rich tapestry of all the available strands of information; instead, we must confess that our efforts have produced something a bit more like a jigsaw puzzle—with more than a few of the pieces yet to be located.

HOW THE BOOK IS ORGANIZED

We had more than a few discussions about how to organize this book. Should we discuss each topic in depth but separately, such as (for example) having a chapter only about social skills from the earliest age through 3 years? Or should chapters be age-based, with social skills being discussed as they typically emerge at each increasing age level? The second approach was finally adopted because we wanted to illustrate the way that theoretically different areas of development actually overlap and are mutually influential. Social development cannot really be understood, for example, without knowing how it affects and is in turn affected by language development, increasing abilities to think and to remember, and even physical abilities to move around and manipulate things. Also, we reasoned that if books about babies and toddlers with typical hearing are organized to allow a parent to say, "Hmmm, my baby is about 6 months old, I wonder what we might expect he will be learning to do next?", then wouldn't the same be helpful for the parent of a deaf or hard-of-hearing baby? Yes, we do recognize the danger in this. Any individual baby may or may not be following along the theorized developmental path at the age rate described as "average" or "to be expected" in such books or found on the ubiquitous (but often oddly disagreeing) online charts portraying these developmental steps. Readers need to know that some deviation from the path is actually expected, regardless of a baby's hearing level; however, we thought it would be helpful for the steps along that path to be laid out so there would be a kind of "roadmap" to provide some expected guidelines. We have even gone so far as to intersperse throughout the book charts based on "expected achievements" at given ages, with occasional asterisks provided when children with limited hearing often show different patterns. We sincerely hope that the ages indicated for developmental advances will be used by readers to learn what to expect next and not to indicate any written-in-stone age at which something must appear—or else.

Of course, there can be special problems when relating the development of a baby or toddler with limited hearing to guidelines developed for those with typical hearing. Some differences can logically be expected—for example, anything on a developmental chart or guideline that specifies reaction to various types of sounds or to the production of various types of vocalizations after about 6 months of age will be suspect and should be treated with caution. However, we are convinced from research, reading, but mostly observation and hands-on practice that the general developmental paths of babies with various hearing levels are more alike than different. This is becoming more obvious as identification of hearing levels, provision of early family-focused intervention support, adoption of communication and language approaches fitting the baby's and family's strengths, and use of newly available technologies to increase access to sound have all become more available in the industrialized world. When observing the development of deaf and hard-of-hearing children, the focus has turned from what they are missing toward how to assure that nothing is missed.

Differences in the most effective learning strategies are beginning to be identified for deaf and hard-of-hearing students in middle childhood and adolescence (see, for example, Marschark & Hauser, 2012). However, such differences are not as obvious during the early years. From our observations, deaf and hard-of-hearing infants and toddlers can be expected to generally follow the same developmental steps as have been identified for hearing infants and toddlers. Nevertheless, optimally *supporting* those steps will require some "tweaking" of early sensitive parenting behaviors and carefully focused intervention support. Some of these appropriate adaptations can be seen by observing the early interactive behaviors used by deaf parents with their own babies. Living in a highly visual world themselves and relying primarily on their eyes to receive communication, they seem to intuitively accommodate and strengthen their babies' attention to visual information while demonstrating the added benefits of sensitive use of touch. We will refer to deaf parents and professionals as models for various kinds of support for babies' development throughout the book. The increasingly recognized value and status of natural sign languages has opened up further opportunities for deaf and hard-of-hearing babies, regardless of their parents' hearing status, to have access to visually based language from birth.

At the same time, opportunities for developing auditory-based speech and language have increased impressively over the past decades as improving technologies (introduced at ever-earlier ages) have increased so many infants' access to the sounds of language and of their surrounding environment. We are fortunate to have had direct experience with children using modern hearing aids and cochlear implants to learn spoken language—sometimes with and sometimes without the addition of signs or sign language—and we have worked hard to consider the range of language options while writing here about stages of development. Because of our experiences in places around the world where neither technologies nor wide acceptance of sign languages has been common, we are unable to ignore the experiences of deaf and hard-of-hearing children in less fortunate circumstances. However, our focus has been on what happens when conditions are optimal, in part to establish the idea that limited hearing need not set limits on a child's developmental potential. It is nonetheless critical that the child's environment provide appropriate kinds of support.

THIS IS *NOT* THE ONLY BOOK YOU NEED TO READ

We started out hoping to write "the" book about the development of deaf and hard-of-hearing infants and toddlers only to discover that to cover all of the areas of development in sufficient detail, with sufficient theoretical background, and to incorporate as much as possible about the specific patterns and strengths of deaf and hard-of-hearing children was a massive task. Nevertheless, we hope we have given enough information so that specialists working with deaf and hard-of-hearing infants and toddlers can not only gain new information about them, but can also see how their development fits in the larger theoretical picture of child development in general. At the same time, we sincerely hope the book will be useful for early intervention specialists and other professionals who already know the "big picture" but are unclear about how the relative presence or absence of hearing affects—or does not affect—development.

You may find that this book goes into seemingly excessive detail about some topics, but inevitably skims over or sometimes even skips others that you hoped to read about. We have done our best to identify the areas of development and existing information that will be most useful, but we have become increasingly aware that the "egocentrism" that so strongly influences the perspective of human infants does not necessary disappear fully even in older adulthood. We have not escaped it ourselves in picking our topics. You may well want to follow up on reading this book with a careful look at one of the more generally focused books on early child development—where deaf and hard-of-hearing children's growth barely rates a footnote—but where theories and processes of development in general are far more deeply, broadly, and fully explained.

Furthermore, if your goal is to provide early intervention services for deaf and hard-of-hearing children, this book is probably only one of several you will need. Our goal has been to provide the basic information on which early intervention programming (in our opinion) should be based. Despite having sometimes followed our inclinations to give suggestions for activities and approaches to use, that is far from our primary goal. A book that focuses on the ways in which early intervention can and should be implemented will probably be another necessary addition to your reading. For example, *Early Intervention for Deaf and Hard-of-Hearing Infants, Toddlers and Their Families: An Interdisciplinary Perspective* (edited by Dr. Marilyn Sass-Lehrer, 2015, Oxford University Press) may be especially helpful.

ONWARD

There's a lot more we'd like to say, but we are eager for you to get started on the book itself. As usual in such books, you will be treated to a general introductory chapter about the issues to be addressed, background information about how differences in hearing levels interact generally with development, and different methods to support language development. This information is followed by our attempt to fit what is known about the development of deaf and hard-of-hearing infants and toddlers into the theoretical frameworks that have been proposed to explain development in general. In the second chapter, the focus will be on hearing—how it is measured, supplemented, and described. We have done our best to provide this information in a less technical way than in more specialized publications. This will be an important chapter for those new to the area of hearing, but undoubtedly will be redundant for some other readers.

Having thoroughly dampened your feet in the first two chapters, you can then paddle into the main current of the book. Age by age, stream by stream, different areas of development will be illustrated and discussed, and their interactions as they merge with and alter what has come before will be addressed. Just as rocks in a river may appear to be more prominent at different water levels, some areas of potential developmental challenge may be more prominent at different ages and with different hearing levels. Skillful paddling and having a good idea of how and where the river is going will help to set a course around those rocks. Similarly, skillful negotiation around potential barriers to optimal development and knowledge of strategies to help overcome them will keep development flowing smoothly onward. We hope this book can provide some helpful guidance for navigating this process.

AND WITH SPECIAL THANKS

As with all efforts such as this, many people—babies, toddlers, parents, and scholars—have contributed enormously to the development of our book. Although they are too numerous to list here individually, we especially want to extend our thanks to the families who participated in our earlier research, to those (and their schools) who generously provided photographs of their children, to Dan the "photo doc" who helped refine the images, and to Royce the "computer doc." We are grateful to Dr. Barbara Cone and to Ms. Debra Nussbaum for guidance and assistance on issues related to hearing, hearing assessment, and intervention. Finally, and most importantly, we thank members of our own families who have given us their full support, have continuously piqued our interest in child development, and have provided us with years of fascinating observational experiences and insights!

Notes on formatting and about terminology:

1. We have not followed the convention of using all capital letters to represent signs, in part because we have often "translated" adults' sign language productions into English form to focus on the content and level of expression instead of its exact form. We have taken care to indicate what has been signed or spoken, however, in accompanying sentences.

2. We have used the terms "limited hearing" and "deaf and/or hard of hearing" instead of "hearing loss" (which is not entirely accurate in many cases in which a baby did not have hearing to begin with) or "hearing impairment" (which many people feel has an unwarranted negative tone).

1 Great Expectations

AN INTRODUCTION

QUESTIONS TO CONSIDER

- What developmental achievements and challenges can be expected for infants and toddlers who are deaf or hard of hearing?
- What conditions are needed to support their optimal developmental progress?
- What are the potential benefits of early, family-focused intervention?
- What special knowledge and skills are needed for early intervention team members working with families with deaf and hard-of-hearing infants and toddlers?
- What approaches are available for supporting language development when hearing is limited, and how can the "best" approach be identified for a particular child and family?
- What theories and observations about development of infants and toddlers with typical hearing can be applied to those who are deaf or hard of hearing?
- In what ways might early development of young children be similar—or potentially different—based upon hearing status?

Amy is a bright, happy, deaf 19-year-old with deaf parents who has grown up using sign language. Many personal and family friends are deaf or hard of hearing. She attended special classes for deaf students during elementary school, but decided to go to a mainstream high school. Using interpreters for classes, Amy repeatedly made the honor roll, was Student Council representative, and made many hearing friends. She is now an undergraduate in a college where most students are deaf. Sign language is used during classes, although, like Amy, many of the students have some spoken language skills. With high grades and strong recommendations from her professors, she hopes to go to graduate school.

Stan is a tall, athletic 22-year-old with hearing parents. Stan's identification as profoundly deaf when 6 months old surprised them. (Six months would be considered "late" for identification in the United States now, but it was considered "early" when he was born.) However, Stan's parents, with help from an early intervention team, learned sign language and began to meet deaf adults and families nearby. Stan started signing at age 12 months, but, despite speech/ language therapy emphasizing listening and speaking—and using two hearing aids—Stan was not babbling or speaking at 2 years. At age 3, he received a cochlear implant and continued to sign and to have speech and listening therapy. At 5 years, his speech was understandable, his sign language communication skills remained excellent, and he could read at first- or second-grade level. Stan went through elementary and high school in a mainstream setting where most classmates had typical hearing. Because his family maintained contacts with deaf adults and children, Stan had hearing and deaf friends and role models. He plans to attend law school.

Why does a book about babies and toddlers begin with stories about two young adults? We start with their stories to remind us of several important things. First, we need to remember that the baby or toddler of today will grow and change before our eyes. How often do parents of grown children say "It's almost like yesterday that he was just a tiny little thing"? Indeed, although parents' priority is to enjoy their children as they are right now, assuring opportunities for them when they are older must also be a priority. Second, although being deaf or hard of hearing causes challenges to language, learning, and social development, Amy and Stan are just two examples of the success that can be attained with early and continuing support from family, community, and school.[1]

The successful developmental paths of these two young people differ from typical or "average" language and educational attainments reported for children with limited hearing. There have been long-standing and repeated reports of low levels of literacy (reading and writing) and other academic skills upon graduation from high school (Qi & Mitchell, 2012); more frequent social, emotional, and behavioral problems than are expected for children with typical hearing (Antia & Kreimeyer, 2015); and ongoing delays in learning to understand and use language, whether in spoken or signed form (Moores, 2010). Given these discouraging reports, how did Amy and Stan "beat the odds"? They clearly had many advantages, including opportunities to learn language early in life. They were able to interact socially with many people and to use their language skills to benefit from daily life experiences and activities: Amy learned sign language from her parents through naturally occurring daily experiences; Stan's parents faced the challenge of learning enough sign language to be able to communicate with him, but both were fairly successful with this. They also made sure Stan had frequent experiences with other signing adults, as well as with those who provided spoken language experiences. His excellent spoken language skills were promoted through weekly, often daily, sessions with speech-language specialists, and he received a cochlear implant at a relatively early age. (See Chapter 2 to learn more about cochlear implants and what they can and cannot do.) His early development of signed vocabulary and communication skills also supported his learning spoken language. Both Amy and Stan shared another important advantage: their achievements were not complicated by cognitive delays, social-emotional problems, sensory problems (other than hearing), or motor difficulties. Furthermore, during their school years, neither of them gave any evidence of specific learning disabilities; these can greatly complicate the academic achievement of deaf and hard-of-hearing students just as they do for some of those with typical hearing. An estimated 40% of children with significant limits to their hearing are thought to have one of these challenges to learning (Holden-Pitt & Diaz, 1998; Knoors & Vervloed, 2011).

Rob has just turned 20. He is quick with a confident smile and has many friends who are deaf, hearing, and hard of hearing like himself. Rob was actually born with typical hearing and was using some spoken words before he became ill as a toddler. The illness resulted in his having a moderately severe hearing loss in both ears. Using two hearing aids and with strong support from family and early interventionists, Rob regained his physical skills, like walking, and began to speak again about 6 months after his illness. However, his balance remained weak, and spoken language progress was slow. Through junior high, he attended mainstreamed schools where few of the students had limited hearing, but he was given extra individualized sessions with speech-language as well as physical therapy specialists. Reading and writing posed special challenges for him, and Rob was identified as having a learning disability (not stemming directly from his loss of hearing) when he was 8 years old. After that, he also received services from a specialist in learning disabilities. When he reached high school, Rob and his parents decided that he should learn some sign language, and he transferred to a special program for deaf and hard-of-hearing students. It required an adjustment, but he received more intensive learning support and eventually became comfortable there. He graduated from high school and considered attending a 2-year-associate program that provides support for students with limited hearing and/ or with learning challenges. However, he applied for and got a job in a local specialty grocery store, and, during the summer there, he moved beyond stacking and bagging groceries and was trained to be a checker. His spoken language skills, using powerful hearing aids, made it possible for him to communicate with hearing co-workers and customers. He also showed that, despite some continuing difficulties with reading and writing, he is a quick and efficient learner in a work setting. He is

*so happy with his progress that he is temporarily postponing further
education. Rob and his parents are learning that he has more options
than they previously thought, although those options will continue to
be limited by his literacy difficulties.*

Like Stan and Amy, Rob is another successful young adult with limits to his hearing ability. Like them, he has a highly supportive family.
His intervention services began soon after his hearing loss was identified.
Unlike the other two, who would be considered "deaf" because they cannot hear the sounds of spoken language without use of advanced technology (like Stan's cochlear implant), Rob is considered to be "hard of
hearing." That is, although his hearing is limited, he is able to hear some
of the louder sounds of spoken language without using a hearing aid,
and he can hear much more when using his aids. Rob faces more challenges to learning despite the fact that he can hear more than either of the
other students. However, early and consistent intervention and support
for academic progress, communication, and language helped him build
his skills very successfully.

It is important to remember that the three young people just
described had access to highly positive family and educational supports. They had, in fact, close to "ideal" experiences. Of course, early
support for education and overall development is not always available
to families of young children with limited hearing. In many parts of the
world, and even in some relatively isolated or impoverished areas of the
United States and other industrialized countries, services can be limited, difficult to access, or even unavailable. In addition, worldwide patterns of immigration result in many deaf and hard-of-hearing children
moving to countries where services are available—but only after years
of growing up without services. We in no way want to minimize the
challenges facing families and children in such situations, and we will
address these issues where information is available. However, our focus
is on the possibilities for development when optimal supports are in
place. The progress that infants and young children can make when appropriate services are available should set our expectations for development. In fact, both research and personal experiences have convinced

us that "limited hearing" does not mean that the growth and achievements of deaf or hard-of-hearing children must also be limited. More importantly, there is now evidence that the achievements of "stars" of past generations of children with limited hearing can now be attained by many more children born in the current and coming decades.

For deaf and hard-of-hearing children to achieve their potential, though, certain characteristics of their environment and their experiences need special attention and sometimes modification. To provide this, we must know what to expect about their development during their earliest years. Little was actually known about the early development of deaf or hard-of-hearing infants until the 1980s, when it became possible to measure hearing abilities during the early months of life. Before then, many deaf and hard-of-hearing children were not identified and therefore did not receive special intervention services until they were 2 or 3 years old—or even older. They typically reached their preschool and school years already having significant delays in communication and language skills. Those delays often continued, affecting other aspects of learning and social experiences and resulting in the generally discouraging statistics that have been historically reported about their language, academic, and even social-emotional development.

Fortunately, information about what babies know, what they can do, and how they develop various skills and abilities has increased significantly over the past few decades. Because our ability to identify hearing levels during infancy and toddlerhood has increased dramatically during those years, more is also being learned about the development of babies and toddlers with limited hearing. This allows parents (as well as professionals who work with them and their babies) to provide effective early support for increasingly "on-time" achievement of important developmental milestones.

EVERY BABY IS A GIFT AND A CHALLENGE

Even in families that already have several children, the arrival of a new little one causes changes in daily life and, sometimes, in the way that the parents think about future plans and goals. These challenges are complicated by the fact that every baby is also a mystery. He or she seems to be born with highly individual preferences—some like to be held closely, and others may be happier when free to move around. Some look around sooner than others. Some are easily upset, whereas others seem calmer and easier to soothe. Part of every parent's challenge is to begin to solve the mysteries of the family's particular baby, one who undoubtedly differs in important ways even from other children in the family. Responding to a baby's unique preferences, needs, and behaviors requires careful observation and trying different approaches to see what happens next, as we will explore further in subsequent chapters. This process takes time, and because the baby will change as time passes and new developmental levels are reached, finding ways to best meet each child's needs is a long-term commitment of parenting—one that continues far beyond the infant and toddler years.

Babies who are deaf or hard of hearing are no more "all the same" than are hearing babies. They bring their own personalities and their own preferences into the world. In addition, their own particular profiles of what they can hear and what they cannot hear differ from baby to baby. If anything, in learning how to respond most effectively to their baby's individual patterns of behaviors, the parents of deaf and hard-of-hearing babies face an even more complex task than those whose babies have typical hearing. (This task will be even more complex, of course, if the baby has some other complicating factor, such as visual or motor difficulties.)

For the small (4–5%) proportion of parents who are deaf themselves (Mitchell & Karchmer, 2004), meeting the needs of a baby with limited hearing may not seem to be especially complex or daunting. Parents who are deaf or hard of hearing and use sign language can naturally provide rich visual communication experiences as soon as their babies are born (Meadow-Orlans, Spencer, & Koester, 2004). Even deaf adults who do not use sign language use more gestures with their deaf babies than do most hearing parents (deVilliers, Bibeau, Ramos, & Gatty, 1993). Deaf parents can also share with their children their own learned ways of living successfully as deaf or hard-of-hearing people. Given these advantages, it may not be surprising that, despite the fact that their first language is usually in signed instead of spoken form, young deaf children with deaf parents usually develop language at a rate very much like that of hearing children.

The needs of a deaf or hard-of-hearing baby often seem more complex and more challenging to the majority of parents who are hearing and have little, if any, experience with deaf or hard-of-hearing children or adults. Grandparents, close friends, and those extended community members who are especially involved in caring for young children in traditional cultures may also lack experience with the effects of limited hearing. Similarly, most of the "baby books" used by many parents to learn about developmental milestones and how to respond to infant and toddler behaviors are written without much detail about development when hearing is limited (if this is even mentioned at all). Finally, many medical specialists have rarely, if ever, worked with a baby who is known to be deaf or hard of hearing. This general lack of experience is due to the fact that, until recently, limited hearing was rarely identified during infancy. For example, in the recent past, only 1 or 2 of every 1,000 babies born in the United States or United Kingdom (Fortnum, Summerfield, Marschall, & Bamford, 2001; Vohr, Carty, Moore, & Letourneau, 1998) was identified as having significantly limited hearing.

More recently, better and earlier testing has shown that number to be closer to 4 per 1,000 if limited hearing in only one ear instead of both is considered (www.infanthearing.org). That number increases somewhat by school age because a small number of babies and toddlers born hearing lose this ability over their first few years of life. Most children, whether identified soon after birth or somewhat later, have what is considered to be milder or lesser hearing limits. Although even mild, recurring hearing difficulties because of repeated ear infections can delay or interfere with language development, young children with more severe hearing losses usually face greater challenges. (In the United States, somewhere between 4 and 11 children out of 10,000 who have limited hearing are so deaf that they have essentially no functional hearing during their early years; www.asha.org.) As limited hearing is identified earlier and in more children, efforts have accelerated to provide support for early development, especially in communication and language areas. However, many professionals and members of the general public continue to have little experience (or information) about how deaf and hard-of-hearing infants and toddlers develop—or what kinds of experiences most readily promote their development. This is even more strongly the case in many less-industrialized countries where health and education services are more limited, but where, unfortunately, the incidence of hearing loss is high due to higher rates of maternal illness during pregnancy and high rates of illness during early childhood (Leigh, Newall, & Newall, 2010).

The general lack of knowledge about and experience with deaf and hard-of-hearing children can leave hearing parents puzzled, worried, and feeling as if they have no expert to turn to—even in fairly optimal situations. This might especially be the case when an early screening of a baby's responses to sound (in industrialized countries, usually before the baby and mother leave the hospital or birthing center) raises questions about hearing abilities. Parents' initial concerns can be eased somewhat when they are informed honestly that the early screening typically overestimates potential hearing difficulties (Young & Tattersall, 2005, 2007). In-depth, follow-up assessment is much more accurate, and many babies who are referred for further testing on the basis of the initial newborn screening turn out to have no limits at all. However, taking the baby for follow-up testing is critical for determining whether special services and assistance are needed to help baby and family make the best possible start. Because early intervention services can make a real difference in how quickly a baby will learn language, develop social skills, and acquire information about the world, it is important to allow this early start to happen (Bodner-Johnson & Sass-Lehrer, 2003).

BEGINNING EARLY, BEGINNING RIGHT

Although information about the development of babies with limited hearing tends to be scattered in bits and pieces across books and articles—many of them highly technical and written for researchers—such information is increasingly available. The information presents an increasingly hopeful and positive picture of achievement when families are aware of their babies' needs and when babies can get early help for their development. In many places around the world, early intervention services are available to assist parents who are not familiar with the special needs—as well as the potential strengths—of deaf and hard-of-hearing babies. More positive expectations for the development of deaf and hard-of-hearing children are emerging as we observe the advances made by children with access to such programs.

The need for "intervention," that is, special medical, language, and educational support for the development of children with limited hearing, has been accepted for many years. However, there have been changes over time in how early services are provided, the relative focus on serving the family as a whole instead of focusing only on the child, and the actual content of the activities or services provided. Examples of these positive changes include: (1) Intervention efforts now occur earlier in a baby's life—often very soon after limits to hearing have been identified. In the United States, for example, identification of babies born deaf or hard of hearing is expected to take place by 1 month of age; intervention is to begin no later than age 6 months (www.asha.com; Joint Committee on Infant Hearing, 2007). (2) Intervention specialists traditionally worked directly with the child. However, parents, grandparents or other family members, and occasionally other caregivers are acknowledged to be the primary supports for an infant or toddler's development. Therefore, early intervention specialists now work primarily with parents and family members to increase their knowledge and confidence in supporting their child's development. (3) Intervention specialists usually work as a team that includes professionals knowledgeable about general cognitive and social-emotional development, language, hearing, and education, and often also includes social work, psychology, or other fields as needed by an individual child and family. For example, a specialist in vision or motor development may be part of the team when needed. There is typically a "case manager" or "coach" who is the primary person interacting with the family (Sheldon & Roush, 2010) and bringing them information and ideas from the whole team, and this is supplemented by individual visits from other team specialists as needed. It can be particularly helpful to have team members who are themselves deaf or hard of hearing and who thus can bring practical as well as "academic" knowledge to the intervention efforts (Sass-Lehrer, 2015). There is also increasing recognition that members of the intervention team need to know about the expectations, family and community roles, and social traditions of a variety of cultures and subcultures in the environment they are serving. Practices for providing family-focused assistance in early intervention are constantly being modified as more experience is gained, so it can be expected that new ways will continue to be found to provide families with the most effective intervention services.

Intervention specialists must also be able to help families evaluate the effects of their participation in early intervention activities. Since 2007, the Office of Special Education and Rehabilitation Services in the United States has emphasized that schools providing early intervention services must report outcomes: do they really promote and accelerate children's development? Do they increase the effectiveness of parents' and other family members' efforts to support the child's development? This has required new scales or tests to measure early developmental progress. In addition, intervention specialists must be knowledgeable about ways to include parents and other family members as integral members of the evaluation "team."

The skills required of intervention specialists are therefore numerous and varied. They extend to areas often thought of as "people skills," as well as to more traditional areas of language, hearing, and learning. It is a challenging role, but the provision of specialized early intervention services has already proved to be the lynchpin for helping families give their deaf and hard-of-hearing babies the best start possible.

Making the Case for Early Intervention

There are several reasons why early intervention *should* be of special importance for deaf and hard-of-hearing children. First, without effective early identification of and intervention for limited hearing, children are likely to experience significant delays across developmental areas by 2 or 3 years—historically, the age when identification usually occurred in the United States. In the past, when intervention was finally provided, deaf and hard-of-hearing children would be required to develop *faster* than their hearing age-mates if they were to "catch up" with age-appropriate language skills. That was, understandably, rarely accomplished.

A second, related argument for early intervention is based on the idea of "critical" or "sensitive periods"; that is, ages during which various abilities develop best and perhaps easiest. The idea of sensitive periods has been investigated especially for language learning (Lederberg & Spencer, 2005). For example, recognizing similarities and differences between sounds of speech develops most rapidly and strongly during the first 12 months after birth. Understanding the grammar (or "syntax") of language seems to develop most easily in naturally occurring conversations (instead of planned lessons) during the first several years of life (Rubin, 1997). Therefore, giving a child language experiences during the early months and years of life—whether from seeing sign language and/or using technology such as advanced hearing aids—can support development most effectively and efficiently. This will prevent initial delays in language development as well as the probability of slowed and somewhat more difficult development in later years. However, the possibility for learning certainly does not stop after a certain age. In most cases, more formal instruction or therapy becomes increasingly necessary for learning to occur in a specific area if that initial "window of maximum opportunity" for optimal learning has passed. A range of ages during which various skills and abilities are most easily required without special remedial work extends beyond the language area and has been proposed for a number of social and psychological areas (Fogel, 2009; Lamb, Bornstein, & Teti, 2002). Although the optimal age ranges differ among various types of abilities, underlying foundations for later developments are almost always best built during the earliest years. For most areas of development, this is before the age of 3 years. (And, as we will discuss in later chapters, the optimal age for some of the foundations of language is especially early.) A third argument for positive expectations from early intervention is that it often allows synchronous development across different areas (Robbins, Koch, Osberger, Zimmerman-Philips, & Kishon-Rabin, 2004). This refers to the fact that certain accomplishments tend to occur at approximately the same age and, as they occur, become mutually supportive of further development. For example, as babies begin to label objects, that labeling helps them to remember and recall those objects. Remembering an action they have done with an object, in turn, may "bring to mind" the verbal label for it and help to build a stronger memory for it. In addition, understanding language influences social-emotional development. We watched a deaf toddler in our research lab become worried about why her Daddy had gone away: "*Where daddy?*" she signed to her mother[2], "*Where daddy?*" Her mother explained, "*Daddy at work. Goes to work. Works, works. Then comes back.*" The little girl then smiled and signed back to her mother, "*Daddy work,*" and settled down to play. In this case, the matching levels of the toddler's language skills and her thinking skills allowed the mother to give her an answer appropriate to her age and overall developmental level. Deaf and hard-of-hearing babies and toddlers (unless they have fluently signing parents and/or early access to the sounds of speech through the use of a particularly effective hearing aid or cochlear implant) usually develop language skills more slowly than they do general cognitive or thinking skills. This difference or *asynchrony* between the two developmental areas interferes with the ability to learn through natural, routine experiences of daily life. A major goal of early intervention is to prevent this asynchrony or unevenness in development across language and other abilities. This can be expected to "normalize" the child's experiences and support overall learning.

A final argument in support of early intervention is that it allows the family as well as the baby to benefit from early information and support. Drs. Rosemary Calderon and Mark Greenberg (Calderon & Greenberg, 2011; Greenberg, 1983) found that parents can best support their child's growth when they feel comfortable and confident about their abilities to do so. Furthermore, the quality of parents' relationships with early intervention providers was found to relate to feelings of confidence in providing what their deaf or hard-of-babies need and having realistic but hopeful expectations about their children's abilities. When parents understand the challenges and potential strengths of their child with limited hearing, they can be more natural, more "intuitive," and therefore more supportive of the child's development than if they are confused and unsure about how to interact and best support learning (Koester, 1992). In general, parents' involvement with their children contributes very significantly to the children's progress. This is no less true of deaf and hard-of-hearing than of hearing children (Moeller, 2000; Spencer, 2004).

Evidence has been available for more than a century that early support promotes better overall development of young children with limited hearing, but much of that evidence was based on individual stories or reports of small numbers of children. It became possible to assess the developmental progress of larger numbers of deaf and hard-of-hearing infants and young children only after ways to measure hearing abilities in early infancy became widespread. As this occurred, support grew for early hearing testing followed by early intervention.

Influential reports of progress with early identification plus early intervention became available in the United States in the late 1990s and the early years of the 21st century. For example, a team in Colorado was able to compare information about the development of a relatively large number of children born before and after their state began screening hearing abilities during the newborn period. More than 90% of babies determined to have limited hearing were then provided comprehensive, team-based, family-focused early intervention. Parents had the option of choosing to use spoken language along with or without signing. They had access to specialists in the selected language approach, including fluent deaf or hard-of-hearing signers. Families could also access a supportive network of other parents and families with deaf or hard-of-hearing children.

In a series of studies, the researchers found that when families had access to high-quality early intervention services, parents' stress was lower than in past reports of hearing parents with children with limited hearing (Pipp-Siegel, Sedey, & Yoshinaga-Itano, 2002). Furthermore, children's understanding and production of language progressed better than in the past (Yoshinaga-Itano, 2003). In fact, when limits to hearing were identified by 6 months, children's later average language achievements fell within the low-average range compared to scores of hearing children (Yoshinaga-Itano, Sedey, Coulter, & Mehl, 1998). Although still not optimal, this is a great improvement over past results, and it occurred whether the children and their families were using speech only or speech plus signing. Children's cognitive skills influenced language development, with higher levels of thinking and problem-solving skills associated with better language skills. However, benefits of early intervention were also noticed in the development of children who had disabilities in addition to being deaf or hard of hearing. The researchers concluded that the first 6 months of life is a "sensitive period" when the groundwork for language learning can be most effectively provided.

Other researchers have reported similarly improved results for children provided early intervention, although the age of 6 months has not always been identified as critical. For example, Dr. Mary Pat Moeller (2002) at Boys Town National Medical Research Hospital in Nebraska measured language skills of 112 5-year-old children with limited hearing and found that age of first intervention (plus a measure of parent involvement with the child and program, as well as the child's cognitive abilities) predicted language progress. Again, this held regardless of the language modalities or approach used: children in intervention by 11 months of age outperformed, on average, those who did not begin until later. Drs. Rosemary Calderon and Susan Naidu (2000) similarly found that children in Washington state beginning intervention by 1 year achieved higher-level skills than those beginning later. These and other research-based reports, plus strong advocacy by parents and professionals, led to increasing efforts to provide early identification of limited hearing and prompt, family-focused early intervention—nationally and internationally. Of course, the challenges faced differ by location, and the way in which early intervention is provided will necessarily vary depending on cultural expectations and traditions.

Delivery of early intervention services is challenged in industrialized as well as still-industrializing countries by a general lack of trained specialists with experience related to deaf and hard-of-hearing children, especially during the early years of life. Specialists need to be knowledgeable about early development, fluent in a variety of language approaches, and unbiased in helping families choose among communication options (including both signing and nonsigning approaches) and then learn to effectively use the selected communication system(s). As technological advances in hearing aids and cochlear implants increase deaf and hard-of-hearing children's access to sounds of spoken language, specialists as well as parents are continually faced with learning how to best use these technologies. Multiple options make matching language method with child and family strengths and needs possible; however, they can also make parents' early decisions about language approaches more complex.

OPTIONS FOR SUPPORTING COMMUNICATION
AND LANGUAGE DEVELOPMENT

A child who does not hear many of the sounds of spoken language will have great difficulty learning it. Because spoken language is usually the primary language method of the family and community, hearing families will naturally be inclined to support its development. However, it is now widely recognized that babies whose parents (usually these are deaf parents) are fluent signers learn sign language at least as early in life as hearing children begin to learn spoken language (Meadow-Orlans et al., 2004). Thus, over the centuries, there have been two major reactions to supporting language development of deaf and hard-of-hearing children: one has been to try to boost a child's ability to hear and/or to increase attention to sound; the other has been to increase visual communication to supplement or to substitute for spoken language (Moores, 2010). A number of options have been developed over time for the language development of children who are deaf or hard of hearing, with varied emphasis placed on visual versus auditory (spoken) language. Discussion of these options is often rife with controversy, and arguments about the "best" method to use have often interfered with making effective matches between methods and child and family characteristics. Some argue, for example, that using sign language interferes with learning to speak and is detrimental to development and social participation—despite the fact that there is no firm research-based information to support this belief (see Spencer & Marschark, 2010; see also Tang & Yiu, 2016, for more details and references). Others suggest that sign language is a necessity for all deaf and hard-of-hearing children in order to give them access to language during the earliest months of life and to assure that they can interact with other children and adults with limited hearing. Although this may be optimal, many individual and family factors sometimes make it difficult to accomplish. Strengths and abilities, as well as differences in home, school, and cultural environments, need to be taken into account when language methods are chosen (see Knoors & Marschark, 2012).

Options midway between using only speech or only sign language are available, although their use is similarly controversial. Among these communication systems are signing combined with spoken language, cued speech (a system using visual signals to represent speech sounds), and "fingerspelling," in which visual signals represent the alphabetic letters to "spell out" words. The descriptions given here begin with the most strongly visually oriented approaches and move toward those that are most auditory-oriented (that is, dependent on listening to the sounds of language):

Natural Sign Language

Many different natural sign languages exist around the world: American Sign Language (ASL), British Sign Language (BSL), South African Sign Language, Swedish Sign Language, and so on. Natural sign languages are expressed by hands, postures, facial expressions, and body movements; they have developed over time in communities of deaf people just as spoken languages developed over time in communities of mostly hearing people. Unlike spoken words, signs in these languages represent meanings, not sounds. A sign sometimes has a physical resemblance to the thing it represents. For example, the sign *cat* is made in ASL by moving the hands away from each other in the general shape and location of a cat's whiskers (Sternberg, 1987). However, across languages, the signs representing a specific meaning (or word) are often quite different. Natural sign languages tend to share many characteristics, however, especially related to how signs are made in the space around the signer, the direction of movement of signs as they are made, and other aspects of "grammar." These affect the way concepts like plurals, possession, and verb tenses are shown—in ways and orders different from the way they are usually managed in spoken languages. (For example, past tense in ASL is usually indicated by making the specific tense indication—with a specific hand/arm movement—at the beginning of a sentence. In contrast, past tense is usually indicated in spoken English by attaching a specific ending sound ["-ed"] to the verb itself.) Because of these different ways of handling grammar (or syntax), it is almost impossible for a person to produce a message using a natural sign language and to speak that message at the same time.

Natural sign languages, because they developed to precisely fit the way that visual communication can be produced and received, are as easy for deaf and hard-of-hearing infants and toddlers to learn as sound-based language is for hearing babies to learn. Using a natural sign language can support "on-time" language learning when hearing is limited. This will only be the case, however, if the young child is immersed in a world in which fluent sign language is used in naturally occurring daily activities and conversations. Like any other language, sign language is learned best when it is learned early and in meaningful, everyday situations. Parents who use a natural sign language with their babies and toddlers often also want them to learn spoken language. But speech and spoken language will be used (and learned) separately from the signing.

Natural sign languages form the "heart" of communities of people who identify themselves as culturally *Deaf*—that is, as a group that shares certain values, patterns of social interactions, and a sign language. Actual hearing abilities of members of a Deaf cultural community vary from those who can hear no or almost no sounds to those who are able to hear some sounds and are therefore sometimes called "hard of hearing." Even some people who have complete hearing but come from families who have Deaf members—usually parents—and who learned a natural sign language as their first language may consider themselves to be part of the culturally Deaf community. Researchers and other professionals have reported social-emotional advantages for deaf and hard-of-hearing people who can communicate with and identify with others who have similar levels of hearing. Many hearing as well as deaf parents want their children to learn a natural sign language and increase potential interactions with others who share their hearing levels.

Sign-Bilingual (or Bilingual-Bimodal) Approach

Using this approach, a natural sign language is expected to be the "first" language for a deaf or hard-of-hearing child. The second language, that used by the hearing people in the surrounding community, is typically learned through reading and writing—often after fluency in sign language has been achieved (Bailes, 2001; Delk & Weidekamp, 2001; Evans, 2004). Hearing children who learn two spoken languages are said to be "bilingual," and the same is true for children who learn a natural sign language plus a spoken language. Although the emphasis in the early years in the sign-bilingual approach is usually on sign language, most deaf and hard-of-hearing children will also have frequent interactions with people using spoken language. In addition, many have individual or small-group spoken language instruction.

Fingerspelling

The signs and grammar of a natural sign language are sometimes supplemented by specific finger or hand shapes representing each letter in the alphabet, and these are produced in order to actually spell words (Padden, 2006). (A system was popular in the past in which all words in a message were fingerspelled. This is referred to as the *Rochester method* and is rarely used today.) Signing deaf mothers fingerspell short words to their babies (often in exaggerated, enlarged, and rhythmic patterns) to have fun, to keep the babies' attention, and perhaps even with an unconscious thought that it's never too early to learn to read! Fingerspelling is used more often in some natural sign languages than others, but it is fairly common during adult-to-child ASL conversations.

Signing Systems

Many signs from natural sign languages, plus some newly created signs, are used in signing systems (Signed English [SE], Signed French, Signed Dutch). The term "system" is used instead of "language" because they were developed to mimic the word order and other grammar rules of an existing spoken language (i.e., Bornstein, 1990; Gustason, Pfetzing, & Zawolkow, 1980). The main signs used in each system are usually the same as used in the local natural sign language—sometimes with a few changes. In some forms of SE used in the United States, for example, the sign for "cat" would be made in the same location and with the same movement as in ASL;

however, some SE signers would change the shape of the hands to copy the "C" shape using in fingerspelling. They might also form the handshape for the fingerspelled letter "s" after making the sign to indicate that there is more than one cat—that is, to make the plural form. This is different from the way plurals are shown in natural sign languages.

Signing systems were created for several reasons. One was a belief that learning the grammar or word order and sentence structure of the hearing community's spoken language would help children learn to read that language. It was also thought that hearing parents new to signing would learn to use these systems quickly because of similarities to their existing spoken language grammar: There would be less "new" language information to learn. It was assumed that adults could speak and sign words and sentences simultaneously using these systems and that this would help children learn both spoken and signed forms. Unfortunately, most researchers have found that using the created signing systems has not accomplished the original goals (Johnson, Liddell, & Erting, 1989; Wood, Wood, Griffith, & Howarth, 1986; Wood, Wood, & Kingsmill, 1991).

There are reports that hearing parents, as well as educators and other professionals, neither learn nor use the sign systems consistently and in their complete form. (Indeed, this is not surprising given the time and attention required during the adult years to learn a new way to represent language.) Often, hearing learners of sign systems produce signs only for the main words in a sentence. Signs for grammatical terms like "to be" verbs, plural and verb tense markers, prepositions, and articles (like "a" and "the") are omitted. Johnson, Liddell, and Erting (1989) at Gallaudet University have referred to this kind of production as "sign-supported speech," with the emphasis placed on the spoken, not signed, part of the message. Some researchers have argued that producing signs with the hands to exactly match the order and pattern of speech is simply not possible. They propose that the grammar and forms of spoken and signed languages developed to match either visual or auditory processing—so that forms used in one modality do not transfer easily to another. However, a few researchers who have studied children in schools where the teachers (and parents) were strongly committed to using a sign system, such as

SE, found much better language development than has otherwise been the case (Luetke-Stahlman & Nielsen, 2003; Schick & Moeller, 1992). Furthermore, Dr. Linda Spencer and her colleagues have reported that older children who are deaf but use cochlear implants to increase their access to speech sounds are able to mentally "combine" information from visual signing systems and sound-based language (Spencer, Tye-Murray, & Tomblin, 1998). This information suggests that signing systems (or sign supported speech) may deserve another look, especially now that technologies are making more information about sound available to more deaf and hard-of-hearing children (see Knoors & Marschark, 2012, for an expanded discussion).

Cued Speech

Cued speech is another system that was developed to give deaf and hard-of-hearing children visual information about language that they can combine with whatever sounds they can hear (LaSasso, Crain, & Leybaert, 2010). This system does not use signs; instead, special hand-shapes, movements, and positions represent spoken language sounds, not the meanings of words. Seeing these hand signals, and also paying attention to mouth shapes and movements, will allow a listener to know what sounds have been made and to identify the language spoken.

Cued speech has not been used widely in the United States, but versions have been created for use in languages other than English. More success has been reported for older than younger children (Spencer, 2000), and research is available about children in French-speaking communities. After an extensive review of available information, LaSasso, Crain, and Leybeart (2010) concluded that cued speech provides strong support for reading and writing skills, in part because it gives information about the sounds of spoken words that can be used to build phonics skills. They suggest that children learning a natural sign language as their first language might also use cued speech to build knowledge of spoken/written language as a second language. They have also suggested that cued speech can be an effective aid for children who are using cochlear implants to learn spoken language (Leybaert, Bayard, Colin, & LaSasso, 2016).

Traditional Oral

This approach emphasizes learning to understand and produce spoken language without use of signs or cues or fingerspelling. Sometimes called "auditory-oral," the approach includes a number of variations (Beattie, 2006). Practice in listening and speaking, plus the use of the best available technology to improve the quality of sound an individual receives, are combined with instruction in speechreading ("lipreading"), attention to gestures, and noticing the context of the conversation. Although reliance on oral approaches decreased in the 1970s (at least in the United States), use of modern hearing aids and cochlear implants has brought about a resurgence of use as more children have at least partial access to the sounds of speech. In many parts of the world, this is the primary approach used in schools and for spoken language therapy.

Auditory-Verbal

The auditory-verbal approach to developing spoken language and listening skills differs from the "traditional oral" approach in emphasizing hearing without reliance on visual information (Rhoades & Duncan, 2010). Similar approaches in the past were called "unisensory" or "acoupedics." The auditory-verbal approach is often practiced as a "therapy" involving intensive sessions early in life with a highly trained specialist and with reinforcement from family members. (Parents are seen as the primary language models and are expected to reinforce listening skills throughout daily activities.) The goal is for children to learn to make maximum use of available hearing during infancy, toddler, and preschool years. The approach assumes the use of the best technology (hearing aids, cochlear implants, etc.) to increase and improve the quality of sound received. It is expected that children will learn spoken language and be able to participate in regular classrooms by elementary school years. Therapy sessions can be resumed later if and when a child begins to have difficulty, for instance, in developing vocabulary or in hearing in a classroom with a lot of background noise.

The "Best" Language Approach

The decision about which language method or methods to use should take into account not only the child's abilities but also the desires, culture, and resources of the entire family. In making choices, families benefit from consultation with early intervention professionals and from communication with other families with deaf or hard-of-hearing children and with older children and adults who are deaf or hard of hearing themselves. All other things being equal, a child with more ability to hear speech, even if only by using advanced hearing aids or other modern technology, can be expected to have an easier time learning spoken language than one who has less access to sound. However, even when a child has a significant amount of hearing ability, the presence of learning or other disabilities can increase the benefits attained from more visual language approaches.

Although parents have often been told that they must pick a communication approach early in their deaf or hard-of-hearing child's life and stick with that approach, this is not always the best tactic. Especially with identification of limited hearing early in the first year of life, an individual child's language potential using various approaches can only be estimated. In addition, a child's actual hearing level can change over time; some experience additional hearing loss with age. On the other hand, some babies and toddlers will show more effective use of their hearing abilities with time and experience than was predicted. Frequent, periodic measurement of advances in language and related development of babies and toddlers is critical for decisions about continuing or changing the approach used and whether increased resources and supports are needed.[3] It is most important to notice and document the degree to which real, satisfying communication takes place between parents (and other family members) and their children during daily activities. Opinions and attitudes toward one method or another should take second place to consideration of the growth of communication skills that a particular child is demonstrating. There is more than one path leading to successful language development.

Although the focus on the development of babies and toddlers who are deaf or hard of hearing inevitably leads to an emphasis on supporting growth of language, no aspect of development occurs in isolation. Intricate patterns of mutual influences are woven among communicative, physical, cognitive, social, and emotional experiences and achievements. This is at least as true during infancy and the early years as at any other stage of life. Communication and language can be areas of potential "difference" (or at least differences in the degree of challenge) for deaf and hard-of-hearing children and their families compared to hearing children and their families. However, there are more similarities than differences among children in the foundations underlying language development and ongoing social, emotional, physical, and cognitive development, regardless of their ability to hear. Because special challenges in one area will affect other areas, it is important to look beyond language when considering the successful development of a deaf or hard-of-hearing baby or toddler.

A Baby Is a Baby Is a Baby...

In the not-too-distant past, many people thought that babies and young children with limited hearing could not develop learning and thinking abilities like those with typical hearing. Deaf and hard-of-hearing children were expected to face limits not just in language skills but in most other areas. This attitude led to an emphasis on *differences* related to hearing levels. However, evidence countering this bias is readily available in studies of the development of deaf and hard-of-hearing children with deaf parents and, increasingly, those who have hearing parents. The basic procedures and requirements for early learning do not appear to be affected strongly by hearing status when other aspects of the growing child and his or her environment are supportive. Many of the same factors influence the development of deaf or hard-of-hearing babies and toddlers and those with typical hearing. Similarly, theories about child development, often based on observing hearing babies and toddlers, are just as viable when the baby is deaf or hard of hearing.

The psychologist Jean Piaget (1936/1952) described ways in which learning occurs through early experience as babies and toddlers "act" on or with objects. When their actions, sometimes accidental at first, get an interesting response (for example, perhaps excited kicking starts an object swinging), babies tend to repeat that movement again and again, producing modifications in their actions and thus in the reactions to them with time and experience. They are learning how to make things happen. Limited hearing does not interfere with babies' tendency to be interested in what is around them and, using their own natural actions, learn about those things and how they move and work. However, it goes without saying that the visual and tactile (or "touch") characteristics of the objects will be especially important in getting these babies' attention and motivating their actions.

Similarly, being able to see the faces and feel the touch of parents and others will be especially important as babies who are deaf or hard of hearing learn to interact and play with the people who care for and communicate with them. Fortunately, most babies (regardless of hearing abilities) are born with tendencies to pay attention to people. For example, although a newborn infant certainly does not really understand what another person is or what a "face" is, those who can see show a preference for looking at pictures and images that resemble faces. And because young infants only see clearly things that are fairly close to them, an adult's tendency to put her face close to the baby's gives extra chances to be seen as they communicate or play. Furthermore, adults' apparently intuitive (or "natural") tendency to communicate and play with babies through the use of several modalities or senses at the same time provides plentiful opportunities for babies with limited hearing to be aware of and react to their parents' behaviors (Papoušek & Papoušek, 1987). Dr. Michael Tomasello (1999) proposed that in-born tendencies to pay attention to and respond to other people's behaviors, as well as adults' tendencies to respond to those behaviors, are foundations for learning to communicate effectively with other children and with adults. Again, these processes appear to be very similar for children regardless of hearing abilities. In the case of babies who do not hear and alert to sounds, however, there is a need for adults to be especially sensitive to the fact that it is what the babies see and feel that will most effectively get and hold their attention.

Yet another psychologist, Lev Vygotsky (1978), emphasized the importance of learning through social experiences. For example, although a baby is born with the potential for learning in a special area (such as learning how to use a spoon or to make a toy move in a specific way), that potential may not fully develop without some interaction or communication between the young person and an older, more accomplished one. Learning occurs most effectively when there is a skilled person who can guide the child by helping to set up a focus of attention that they can share and then providing information about it. It is particularly helpful if the "guide" understands what the child already knows or is capable of doing and can then support the child's efforts to accomplish the next level. Being an effective guide takes skill in order to neither bore the child nor try to move her along too quickly, thus possibly leading to frustration. Parents and daily caregivers of babies and toddlers are most likely to have this kind of understanding of what the children know and can already do, and caregivers can therefore be most effective in helping to build knowledge and skills.

Parents and caregivers have another advantage when it comes to being a baby's developmental guide: the emotional aspects of early experiences affect learning as well as the baby's social and psychological development. Warm, close relationships with adults who are especially responsive to a young child's needs and interests help to build a positive sense of self and of trust in others (Bowlby, 1958, 1969). Strong emotional development in turn encourages exploring and learning and helps the child become increasingly resilient to the ups and downs of daily life. Such resilience can be best supported when the family itself feels comfortable and parents and caregivers feel confident in their abilities to meet the child's needs. Roles and attitudes in the family itself will be affected by forces both within and beyond the family unit and will change over time as the child also changes. Early intervention efforts should result in parents recognizing their own competencies, recognizing their own and their babies' accomplishments, and finding support beyond as well as within the family unit.

Just like children with typical hearing, those with limited hearing learn more readily when they have warm, loving relationships with parents and other adults, when they have a variety of social and object-play experiences, when they have opportunities to engage in different and varied activities, when they are able to communicate meaningfully with other children and adults, and when their entire family (sometimes their whole community) feels directly involved with and supportive of their development. Infants and toddlers who have physical, cognitive, or social-emotional disabilities in combination with limited hearing face extra and more daunting challenges. However, their general developmental needs are like those of all children and are similarly dependent on family and community support for language and learning about their world (Jones & Jones, 2003). Overall, common factors influence the development of all babies and toddlers, but those with specific challenges will benefit from a greater emphasis on some specific types of experiences. For example, as we have already pointed out, babies with limited hearing will benefit from increased visual and tactile input, babies who generally learn more slowly often benefit from more repetition in their experiences, and those with limited sight may respond especially well to increased tactile experiences and to having a more structured and predictable environment and increased experiences in manually exploring toys. In general, the modifications required to support individual children's learning differ more in degree than in basic type from those that are generally available to hearing children with no disabilities. Confident, empowered parents (with assistance from early intervention specialists who focus on the characteristics and strengths of individual families as well as of their babies and toddlers) are capable of making adjustments in the ways that they interact with their babies and toddlers and to give strong support for their development.

SUMMARIZING KEY IDEAS

Limited hearing does not necessarily result in limited accomplishments, although the challenges faced are increased. For an individual to be able to achieve his or her potential, it is *not* necessary to be able to hear. However, it is essential that language (signed, spoken, or both) is learned

early and well. Other kinds of experiences (for example, those supporting using visual attention effectively and those promoting thinking and
problem-solving skills) are also especially important when a child is deaf
or hard of hearing. The following are some key ideas that we hope will be
useful to readers:

- All babies respond to "messages" received by all their available
  senses. They receive and respond to multisensory or multimodal
  inputs. The senses include feelings from touch (tactile), sensations
  from being moved around or moving their own bodies (kinesthetic),
  things that they can see (vision), and sounds that they can hear
  (audition), even if hearing is not complete. Most adults, even when
  they know a baby can hear them, tend to present all of these sensory
  messages to babies in a "bundle." A mother will often touch or hold
  the baby while she talks. She may bounce or rock the baby gently.
  Perhaps the most important part of such a bundled (multimodal or
  multisensory) message is the expression of physical closeness and
  care for the baby—a message that, even when no language is used,
  stimulates and prompts the baby's earliest development of social,
  thinking, and language skills.

- There are a number of effective approaches to communication
  and language development for deaf and hard-of-hearing children.
  Options include use of sign language plus speech, use of sign language without speech, use of speech only (accompanied by use of
  technology such as hearing aids and cochlear implants), and use
  of other systems such as cued speech that give visual clues about
  sounds. The critical questions are whether and with how much
  ease the baby or toddler can actually receive and understand communications directed to him or her. Advocates of the different language approaches used with deaf and hard-of-hearing children can
  boast about successful users, but no single approach has proved to
  be the one and only best way for every child. Each child's responses
  to the different approaches—and the ability of the child's family
  to provide good communication and language models with that
  approach—must be determined over time. It is clear, however, that

language (whether signed, cued, or spoken) must be learned and used early in life if a child is to reach his or her potential.

- A number of hearing parents have reported positive impacts from getting to know deaf and hard-of-hearing adults and children (Hintermair, 2000; Sass-Lehrer, 2011). For families learning sign language, this can be a critical ingredient in successful language learning. But even families using a strictly oral (spoken language without signs) approach gain from engaging with adults with limited hearing who use a variety of communication methods and have had a variety of life experiences. Including deaf as well as hearing professionals on early intervention teams gives hearing parents an opportunity to get to know successful deaf adults.

- Use of sign language or signing systems is now frequently supported in early intervention programs, and parents can even receive training online if it is difficult to attend classes in person (see www.familysigns. org). Expressing and receiving language-based communication during the first years of life provides a critical foundation for later skills: the communication modality (spoken, signed, or cued) does *not* seem to matter when child and family characteristics are considered.

- A large proportion of children who are deaf or hard of hearing have learning challenges in developmental areas not necessarily related to hearing. These difficulties may or may not be evident in early infancy. When learning or other developmental challenges are suspected, careful assessment and extra attention to the child and his or her opportunities to learn are required. The good news is that intervention beginning in infancy can help ease the effects of these difficulties. Early intervention teams should include professionals who understand the needs of children with specific constellations of developmental challenges beyond those typically resulting from limited hearing.

Expectations are much more positive for the quality and rate of development of deaf or hard-of-hearing children born in the 21st century. Beginning a family-focused intervention program before the child reaches 6 months of age can have significant positive effects on rates of development of language, social, and academic skills. However, missing that 6-month deadline does not mean that all is lost. *High-quality inter-vention as early and consistently as possible will always help.*

The years from birth to age 3 are perhaps the most important of the child's entire life when communication and learning are considered. The rapid and dramatic changes in behaviors and skills are mind-boggling! Learning can happen at what seems to be lightning speed when experiences that are developmentally appropriate occur in a warm and support-ive environment that is tailored to the special needs and abilities of each child and family.

The concepts and information introduced in this chapter will be dis-cussed in greater detail throughout the book. In the next chapter, we focus on basic information about hearing, how it can be assessed, and some interventions to promote the effective use of available hearing. After this basic background information is presented, subsequent chapters will focus on development as an integrated process. Development involves drawing from all sensory input available, on rapidly increasing physical (motor) abilities, on social and emotional experiences (especially with parents and caregivers), and on increasingly sophisticated cognitive abili-ties. Fasten your seatbelts—a lot happens in just 3 years!

NOTES

1. We will give many examples in the book drawn from our experiences in observing and working with children and families. To protect their identities, names and some details may be changed.
2. As we noted at the end of the Preface, we have deviated from standard prac-tice in that we have not used small capital letters to indicate signs. Instead, we have stated in the text whether an expression was signed, spoken, or both. Especially with language of mothers who are deaf, we have often translated their sign language expressions to English form, in order to focus on the meaning and function of the message they are transmitting instead of its modality or structure.
3. Although a few tests are available for assessing the early development of nat-ural sign languages like ASL or BSL, they are still being refined. The most up-to-date instrument with which we are familiar is the *Standardized Visual Communication and Sign Language Checklist for Signing Children* (VCSL) (Simms, Baker, & Clark, 2013). Assessments often continue to rely on informal assessments by teams including highly fluent signers (see Mann & Haug, 2016).

2 What Can My Baby Hear?

QUESTIONS TO CONSIDER

- Can we tell what a young baby can and cannot hear just by watching everyday behaviors?
- How do specialists use technology to test hearing without relying just on observing the baby's behavior?
- After a baby or toddler is identified as deaf or hard of hearing, why are frequent reassessments of hearing necessary?
- What does an audiogram tell us about what a baby or toddler can hear?
- How do the baby's ears and brain develop and work together?
- How can technology (like hearing aids, cochlear implants, and other devices) benefit a deaf or hard-of-hearing baby or toddler?

Little Gregory was 7 days old. He rarely responded to sounds around him—not to his two sisters running through the room and yelling, not to their mother loudly reminding them to be quiet, not even to the dog barking. However, when his father sat near him and pulled the ring-top off a soft drink can, Gregory startled and moved his arms and legs up and down quickly.

Carlos, a 2-month-old, was reclining in his infant chair, which was sitting on the hardwood floor of his living room. He was looking occasionally at a toy his sister was swinging in front of him while she sang a little song. When his older brother ran through the door and slammed it shut, Carlos looked quickly toward the door, jumped a bit, and began to cry.

It is notoriously difficult to tell just by watching a baby, especially a very young one, what he or she can hear.[1] For example, little Gregory has typical hearing, but Carlos has significantly limited hearing and was probably responding to vibrations caused by the door slamming. Because it is difficult to identify a baby's hearing status just by observing his or her behavior, in the past many children were 2 or 3 years old or even older before limited hearing abilities were discovered. In fact, one of us (back in the late 1970s) documented the language growth of 3-year-olds who were just beginning intervention programming (Spencer Day, 1986). Several of the children had lost hearing due to illness (meningitis) at about 1 year or so of age. Two other children were apparently deaf when they were born, but this was not identified until one was older than 6 months and the other older than 17 months of age. The parents of both children were upset and embarrassed that they had not noticed their babies' limited hearing abilities earlier, but, in fact, identification of the one baby at six months was considered extremely early at that time. The second child's identification was more typical in that parents only began to suspect limited hearing after he failed to begin speaking when expected. Although their initial concerns were discounted by well-meaning medical professionals, the parents had persisted. Otherwise, this little boy's significantly limited hearing would not have been discovered until even later. This story was all too common throughout most of the 20th century, even in highly industrialized and technologically developed countries. It undoubtedly remains the case in many parts of the world today.

The difficulty in identifying what babies can hear is due, in part, to the fact that they respond to things they see and things they can feel as well as to what they can hear—as in the case of Carlos. In contrast, like Gregory, many young babies with typical hearing often seem unaware of sounds around them, especially if they are in a sleepy state or if they are concentrating on looking at something interesting. Audiologists, the professionals who specialize in assessing and measuring hearing, are specially trained to recognize when a young baby's behaviors indicate that he or she has heard a sound. But even after intensive training to recognize a specific baby's behaviors, just observing behaviors doesn't give consistent (or "reliable") evidence of hearing levels until a child reaches about 3 months of age. Consistently earlier identification of hearing levels had to wait for technological advances that make it possible to test hearing *without* relying on observations alone (see Ackley & Decker, 2006; Cone, 2011; Northern & Downs, 2002, for more in-depth discussions of testing issues).

ASSESSING INFANT AND TODDLER HEARING

By the 1990s, two major methods had been developed to assess the hearing of newborns and young babies without relying on observations of behaviors. Babies do not have to be paying attention for these assessments to be effective; in fact, it is better if the baby is asleep. One method (evoked otoacoustic emissions testing [OAEs]) painlessly measures faint sounds that the inner ear itself produces as an "echo" when a sound is heard. These inner ear echoes are far too soft to be heard by someone who is merely listening. A special tiny microphone is placed in the baby's ear canal, sounds are played in fast repetition, and the echoes produced by the inner ear are recorded using a computer. If there are no echoing sounds, the baby's ear probably did not process (or "hear") the sounds: limited hearing can be suspected. Using the second method (auditory evoked potentials [AEPs]), sounds are again played in fast repetition. Small sensor disks are put at specific places on the baby's head; the sensors pick up tiny waves of electrical energy that the brain produces when a sound is heard. This information is transferred to a computer-based system that processes them for interpretation by an audiologist. The strength and timing of the waves gives information about how loud the sounds had to be for the baby's hearing system to respond. This information is compared to what would be expected from a baby of that age with typical hearing.

One and sometimes both of the above methods are typically used in the process of initial hearing "screening." These first screening measurements taken soon after birth do not in fact "identify" whether a baby is deaf or hard of hearing. Instead, if these preliminary screening measures suggest that a baby may not hear sounds as expected, parents are asked to return to the hospital (or go to a local hearing clinic) within a specified time period for another screening or for more in-depth testing (Figure 2.1). In the United States and many other countries, the goal is for screening to be completed by 1 month of age, for any hearing-related issues be identified by 3 months, and for the family to be receiving intervention services by the time the baby is 6 months old (American

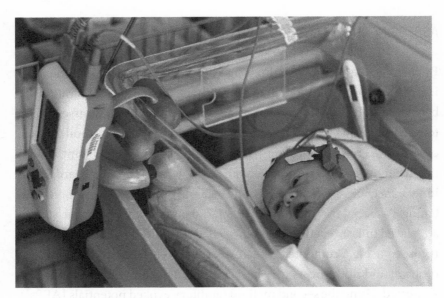

Figure 2.1 Hearing screening within first 24 hours. (Photo courtesy of Torin Koester. Reprinted with permission.)

Academy of Audiology, 2011; American Speech, Language, & Hearing Association, 2008a; Joint Committee on Infant Hearing, 2007).

Screening test procedures are largely automated, with sounds being presented and responses from the baby's ear or brain recorded by computer-based software. Such screening tests may be given by a technician. Although professionals who manage the screening tests and oversee the technicians are given special training, they are typically not hearing specialists or audiologists. In contrast, follow-up assessments are usually conducted by highly trained audiologists experienced with infants and toddlers. These assessments use more detailed, in-depth methods and are more sensitive versions of the general kinds of tests used in screening. For example, the AEP approach can be used in complex and detailed ways to assess responses from different places in the hearing system (including the inner ear, the hearing nerve, and various parts of the brain involved in hearing) and using a variety of types of sounds. These extensive tests will give a more complete and accurate picture of what the baby can or cannot hear. Only after such in-depth follow-up can deaf and hard-of-hearing infants be "identified" with confidence. In a study conducted in a number of centers in the United States, researchers found that the more extensive follow-up testing was highly accurate (Norton et al., 2000).

This system only works, of course, if parents bring the baby back for follow-up testing. Unfortunately, it is estimated that approximately half of the babies in the United States referred by screening tests as needing follow-up do not receive it (American Speech, Language, and Hearing Association, 2008b; Centers for Disease Control and Prevention, 2010). Families may fail to return for in-depth testing because they are so busy and often so tired after a baby is born—and the baby gives them no clear signals of problems hearing. Other families have problems making appointments, getting transportation to follow-up appointments, and finding care for their other children while taking the baby to an appointment. Also, some parents have reported that the person explaining the screening to them emphasized so strongly that the screening results might be misleading that they felt little pressure to return.

Even when both screening and follow-up testing indicate typical hearing (and no limited hearing is suspected), it is still important to be alert to behaviors that suggest any lack of sensitivity or response to sounds. For example, newborn screenings are not designed to detect mild hearing difficulties even though these can also affect development, putting a child at higher than average risk of language and learning difficulties. In addition, not all children who become deaf or hard of hearing have limited hearing at birth. Hearing can be affected by illnesses and even by the medications that must be used to treat some severe illnesses during infancy, early childhood, or later in life. Even repeated ear infections can affect hearing significantly. We know of one instance in which a child who was born with typical hearing developed a condition that resulted in his becoming significantly hard of hearing after 2 years of age. His daycare teacher first noticed the change and reported it to parents: the little boy, who had previously been quite responsive to communication and usually complied with her requests, suddenly seemed to be "ignoring" communications.

Loss of hearing during the first years of life can also occur due to genetic causes. That is, a baby can be born with typical hearing but become deaf or hard of hearing during the early months or years of life—not due to any illness. Although this does not happen very often, it does occur. In one case, the baby of a deaf mother we knew was initially found to have typical hearing abilities but gradually became deaf by the time he was 3 years old. Looking back, his mother began to suspect that she herself had been born with typical hearing and had become deaf during her preschool years. Of course, hearing screening within the first days of life or testing in the early weeks or months cannot detect a loss that has not yet occurred.

It is important, therefore, that family members as well as professionals who work with families and children know about behaviors that suggest any decrease in hearing during infancy and the early years. The behaviors listed in Figure 2.2 should be watched for and, if noticed, they should be immediately reported to the baby's primary care physician who can assess any medical condition that might be responsible. From there, referral should be made for audiological testing. Of course, because babies seem to respond to sounds inconsistently during typical home and small-group

- Infants (approximately birth to 1 year):
  1. Does not startle when a loud noise occurs—or having done this at an earlier age, stops jumping at or looking toward noises. (Babies can be expected to turn toward sound by about 6 months of age. This often occurs *much* earlier but is less consistent.)
  2. Doesn't say things like "mama" or "dada" or "uh-oh" at about a year of age.
  3. Reacts to some sounds but not others.
  4. Turns head toward you when you are in his or her visual field—but not reliably in response to voice.
  5. May watch movements of objects, but does not turn toward their sounds.
- Toddlers (approximately 1–3 years of age):
  1. Does not respond to whispers; seems to hear and respond better if you are facing each other.
  2. Usually does not sing or dance, but attends carefully to and often imitates songs that use gestures (e.g., "Itsy-Bitsy Spider" song).
  3. Seems to understand fewer words than other children of the same age, and either does not say many words or those that are spoken are harder to understand than those of playmates.
  4. Often turns one specific ear (left or right) toward you when you are speaking.
  5. Changes in behavior—becoming noticeably quieter or more active than earlier; seems to "ignore" when told things to do or spoken to from more than a few feet away.

Source: Modified from http://www.whattoexpect.com/grooming/toddler-earinfo/hearing-loss-in-toddters.aspx, and http://www.dcd.gov/ncbddd/hearingloss/facts.html)

Figure 2.2 Behaviors suggesting limited or decreasing hearing during infancy and toddler years

situations, the behaviors on the list may not actually mean that hearing is being lost. Still, it is important to get a professional assessment of hearing if there is any doubt.

When it is discovered that an infant or toddler is deaf or hard of hearing, frequent reassessments of hearing are required to check for any changes in response to sound over time and to determine exactly which sounds he or she can hear. Special assessments may be conducted to measure how much help a hearing aid provides and, when necessary, to modify the way the aid is programmed. These assessments become more reliable as the baby continues to grow and develop cognitive and motor skills. Especially after babies reach about 6 months of age (although the exact age differs among children), audiologists can more confidently identify their behaviors in response to sounds. For assessments based on babies' behaviors, the baby usually sits on the caregiver's lap in a quiet "sound booth." In this quiet environment, babies can be taught to look at an interesting toy (for example, a dancing puppet) when a sound is played. After the baby learns to look at the toy when and only when a sound is heard, sounds that differ in loudness (soft-to-loud) and pitch (low-to-high) are played while the audiologist watches through a one-way window.

With increasing age and maturation, babies and toddlers can participate more directly in the assessment. For example, a 1-year-old baby may learn to make a specific action, like dropping a block in a bucket, when she hears a sound. When this kind of ability is achieved, hearing assessments can become even more accurate and give a better picture of the level of hearing at different pitches. Of course, if a baby has a visual disability, a motor or physical disability, or is perhaps just developing slowly overall, testing methods have to be adapted to match those abilities. It will usually take longer for children with any of these extra challenges to learn how to respond consistently to sounds when they hear them, and it may take longer for the audiologist (and parents and other adults) to learn to recognize the responses the child is giving.

The need to assess hearing abilities continues throughout childhood and even beyond for deaf or hard-of-hearing individuals who want to make the best use of available hearing. As assessments continue, the effectiveness of various listening experiences or devices like hearing aids and cochlear implants (CIs) can be determined. Although hearing levels may stay the same, the ability to make use of any available hearing can increase over time as language and thinking skills mature.

The Hearing System: Ear and Brain

The parts of the body that make hearing possible work together in a complex system (see Figure 2.3). This system includes:

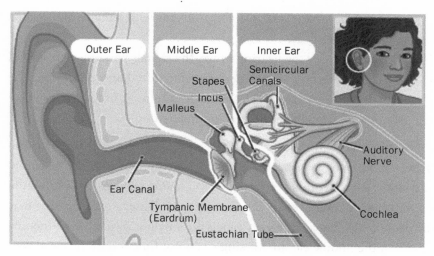

Figure 2.3 Parts of the auditory (hearing) system. (Copyright The Nemours Foundation/ KidsHealth. Reprinted with permission.)

- the outer part of the ear (the *pinna*—from which an earring can dangle) and the ear canal through which sound waves pass to get to the eardrum (which is also called the *tympanic membrane*).
- the middle ear (the space behind the eardrum), which contains a series of small bones (called the *stapes, incus,* and *malleus*) that strengthen the sound waves and send them to the inner ear. (The Eustachian tube connects this part of the ear to the throat cavity; although it can play a role in ear infections, it is not directly related to hearing.)
- the "inner ear," which includes the fluid-filled cochlea and its hairlike nerve endings ("hair cells"). As sound waves reach the hair cells, they move: those in some parts of the cochlea respond to highpitched sounds and others respond to lower pitched sounds. As the hair cells move, they cause electrical signals to be sent to the auditory (or "hearing") nerve. The auditory nerve transmits these signals to other parts of the brain.

The inner ear also contains the *semicircular canals* that control balance. Although these structures are not directly involved in hearing, children whose hearing is limited because of inner ear functioning are at higher than usual risk for problems with balance and related abilities.

- Once sent on by the hearing nerve, the signals pass through several parts of the brain, where they are reorganized and processed. The signals eventually reach the cortex, or outermost brain layers, where sounds are actually interpreted or understood.

Hearing can be limited when there is interference with information from sound being transmitted by any one part of the auditory system to any other part. Decreased hearing due to malformations or dysfunction in the outer or middle ear is called *conductive*. For example, hearing may be decreased when a child's ear canals are small or blocked or if the tiny bones in the middle ear are missing or do not function in the usual way. In such cases, sound waves may not be conducted (that is, not sent on) to the more internal parts of the hearing system—or they may not be sent onward with enough strength. Limited hearing that is conductive usually results in a person being hard of hearing—that is, he or she can hear some things but not all. Conductive hearing difficulties can often be corrected, at least to some extent, through surgery or other medical interventions. When the hearing difficulties are permanent, hearing aids are often beneficial.

When portions of the inner ear—like the hair cells or the auditory nerve—are missing, malformed, or nonfunctioning, the resulting limit to hearing is called *sensorineural*. This is usually permanent and cannot be corrected by medication or surgical reconstructions. However, cochlear implants, which are implanted surgically, can provide information about sound in many cases in which the hair cells are damaged or missing. CIs in effect substitute for the hair cells and send electrical information about sounds directly to the fibers of the hearing nerve.

CIs can sometimes (but not always) help with another type of difficulty in which signals from the hair cells become disorganized or lose "synchrony" as they are transmitted to the hearing nerve. This type of dysfunction is called *auditory neuropathy*, and it may or may not occur along with generally decreased hearing. Auditory neuropathy is not a common condition (or group of conditions); however, it can make understanding spoken language more difficult than would ordinarily be the case because the signals are not clear.

Hearing can also be affected by difficulties at any of the other places within the brain where the signals usually travel and are organized. Anything that affects these parts of the brain may result in a *central hearing dysfunction*. Again, this is not a common occurrence, but the ability to recognize and make sense of incoming information from sound can be compromised if central processing difficulties exist.

It is important to recognize that "hearing" involves more than just structures of the ear itself. To serve as a foundation for language development and for learning, it is necessary that information from sound be transmitted to all parts of the ear–brain system so that sounds can be organized, recognized, and eventually interpreted as meaningful. This is typically referred to as sound *perception*. In the early months and years of life, however, hearing testing focuses not on what is understood by the baby but on determining how loud (or intense) specific sounds must be to activate his hearing system.

Audiogram: Creating a Picture of What Your Baby or Toddler Hears

Determining the types of interventions and other assistance that will be most beneficial for an individual baby or toddler requires knowing exactly what the child can hear—that is, knowing how loud sounds at different pitches need to be before the child is aware of them. The results of hearing testing, whether from using the AEP approach or behavioral testing of toddlers and older children, are displayed in a graph called an *audiogram* that gives a picture of what a child can hear.

The chart in Figure 2.4 is an audiogram from Bobby, a young child with typical hearing.[2] The audiogram illustrates how loud (intense) sounds must be at different *frequency* levels (pitches) for Bobby to hear them. Different pitches (measured in units called Hertz [Hz]) are shown on the horizontal line at the top of the audiogram. Just as on a piano keyboard, lower pitched sounds are toward the left side of the chart and higher pitched sounds are toward the right of the chart. Hz numbers increase from left to right. Examples of very low-pitched sounds include

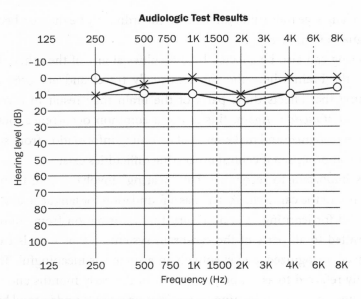

Figure 2.4 Audiogram for Bobby, a child with typical hearing.

thunder, a bass drum, or even some deep male voices. Hearing the melody or intonation of speech (and many of the vowels of English) requires the ability to hear lower pitched sounds. High-pitched sounds include the twittering of birds, some "high" female voices, and (importantly) many of the consonant sounds of spoken languages such as English. It is necessary to hear consonant sounds to be able to *discriminate*, or tell the difference between, many spoken words. Sensorineural hearing difficulties (caused in the inner ear) often limit the range of high pitches that can be heard—no matter how loudly those sounds are made (www.nidcd.nih.gov/health/hearing/pages/neuropathy.aspx).

Sound energy, or loudness levels, are measured in units called *decibels* (dB).[3] Loudness levels are marked on the left vertical line of the audiogram: the softest or quietest levels are at the top, and increased loudness is shown toward the bottom of the chart. The sound made by a dripping faucet is usually a very soft, quiet sound (about 15 to –20 dB). In contrast, the sound made by an ambulance siren or a lawnmower is usually very loud (at about 100 or higher dB). Because Bobby has typical hearing, sounds do not need to be very loud for him to notice them. But his audiogram shows that there are some slight differences in the loudness needed for him to hear different pitches. This is usually the case even when hearing is in the typical range overall.

Like most audiograms, Bobby's shows two lines (one for each ear). Hearing in each ear can be measured separately by having the child wear headphones; sounds are then played to one ear at a time. One line on Bobby's audiogram connects a series of X's and the other connects a series of circles. The X's show how loud a sound must be for Bobby to hear it in his left ear; the circles indicate hearing levels for the right ear. (One way to remember which ear is shown by the X's and O's is that "Round = Right." And, of course, the other line is the left ear.) Also, many times, the line for the right ear will be drawn in red (so "round" = "red" = "right" ear); the line for the left ear will be indicated by the color blue.

The dB scale used to indicate loudness has some characteristics that might seem puzzling at first.[4] For example, the audiogram shows 0 dB at one level. This does not, however, mean that there is no sound. Instead, this is the usual loudness level at which a person with typical hearing would be aware of a sound about half the time. So, it is possible for an audiogram to show a "minus" or below-zero decibel hearing level for some sounds. This would mean that the person being tested could hear that particular pitch when a sound was even softer than required for an "average" hearing person. Another oddity about the dB measure is that loudness levels increase more rapidly than the numbers suggest. In fact, every increase of 10 dB actually means the loudness (or sound energy) has increased by 10 times. This means that if a particular sound can be heard by one child when it is 40 dB loud but cannot be heard by a second child until it is 50 dB loud, the sound must be 10 *times* stronger for the second child to hear it.

Bobby's audiogram in Figure 2.4 shows results for testing without use of a hearing aid, of course, because his hearing is not limited and he does not use one. If hearing had been tested with a hearing aid, different symbols would have been used on the lines. An "A" often indicates testing with a hearing aid. An "S" indicates that no headphones were used: instead, "soundfield" testing was done in which the child could use both ears at the same time to listen to the sounds. Other symbols are used to indicate when the testing was performed using special equipment to test only the inner ear and not the outer and middle ears or when testing was done with the child using a CI. It is important to read the *key* (or legend), which should be shown on each audiogram to explain the meaning of the symbols used, because they can vary across testing locations. And, *it is important for a parent or nonaudiologist professional working with a family to ask the audiologist for detailed explanations of anything that shows up on the audiogram that is not clearly understood.*

Figure 2.5 shows an audiogram for a toddler named Jennifer. Her audiogram shows that she has very significant limits to hearing. In fact, her hearing level would be called "severe," and she has serious difficulties hearing all but very loud sounds (like rumbling trucks or perhaps very loud shouting) without the use of a powerful hearing aid (see the next section for a more detailed explanation of hearing levels). As Jennifer's audiogram shows, she hears a bit better with her left than with her right ear. In addition, she can hear low-pitched sounds at somewhat softer levels than she can hear higher pitched sounds. This kind of "sloping" ability to hear low-pitched better than high-pitched sounds is fairly common.

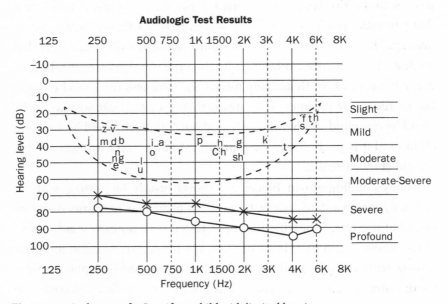

Figure 2.5 Audiogram for Jennifer, a child with limited hearing.

Some things appear on Jennifer's audiogram that are not always shown. For example, the shape outlined by dashes stretching across the middle or so of the chart is often called the "speech banana." This outlined area shows the pitch and the loudness in decibels of various speech sounds of English. Jennifer's audiogram indicates that, without using assistance from listening technology, she cannot hear any of these sounds spoken at normal conversational loudness levels unless the person speaking is quite close to her. Hearing aids using current technologies allow most children with hearing like Jennifer's to hear some speech sounds, but the aids are not always very effective. In Jennifer's case, it would be important to obtain her responses to sound using a hearing aid as well as her responses without the aid.

Loudness and Levels

Although the exact loudness needed for an individual to hear every specific pitch is important, professionals have traditionally described *hearing levels* (sometimes called "levels of hearing loss") by calculating the average of the loudness necessary to hear pitches at 500 Hz, 1,000 Hz, and 2,000 Hz. (This is usually called the *pure tone average.*) These pitches include most of the sounds of spoken language. (Loudness necessary to hear sounds at the 4,000 and 8,000 Hz levels is also usually measured.)

Jennifer's audiogram shows (along the right side) "hearing levels" based on the approximate range of loudness necessary for a child to hear sounds at each pitch. Her pure tone average in each ear shows hearing at the "severe" level. Each overall hearing level, based on the pure tone average, is described in more detail here, beginning with the level "slight" that indicates the least limited hearing.

15 to 25 dB (slight—sometimes called "minimal or slight hearing loss"). Researchers have recently focused on the needs of children with relatively small decreases in hearing ability (Moeller et al., 2007a, 2007b). On average, children who need sounds to be this loud before they can be heard are at a higher than average risk for some difficulties with spoken language and classroom learning. Some speech sounds like /s/ and

/th/ may be difficult to hear, and it is often more difficult to hear clearly in a noisy situation (for example, in a large-group child care setting or some classrooms). Children with this hearing level are estimated to miss hearing up to 10% of the spoken conversations that occur in a classroom (Cole & Flexer, 2010). They will find it harder than hearing children to follow conversations not directed toward them but occurring between other people around them. That is, they often may be unable to "overhear" information that would be available to children without limited hearing. This can limit the amount of information they learn "incidentally," or without actively trying. Children with even this minimal limit to hearing can become tired more quickly than children with typical hearing do when they are in a situation requiring careful listening. Adults should pay special attention to these children over time, watching for any additional loss of hearing sensitivity that might occur. Attention should be given to their developing language skills and their ability to understand in different settings in order to make sure that they are not in need of additional help or different environmental accommodations (for example, a smaller or quieter classroom). Hearing aids are usually not needed by children with this hearing level, but other assistance such as sitting near the teacher or making sure the child is attending before spoken language is addressed to him or her might be considered as older children begin regular classes.

26 to 40 dB (mild hearing level or "mild hearing loss"). Again, researchers are still learning about the development of children with mild decreases in hearing ability. However, a child with this hearing level faces all the difficulties as do those with minimal hearing loss—but to a greater degree. Those whose hearing is at the "mild" level will have more difficulty hearing clearly when there is noise in the background or when there is a greater than the typical 3- to 4-foot distance between the child and a person speaking. Because many of the sounds of conversational language are produced in the "mild" loudness range, children with this hearing level may miss hearing some speech sounds and therefore have problems learning to speak them. (Refer back to the "speech banana" on Jennifer's audiogram in Figure 2.5: sounds like English /f/, /s/, /th/, /p/, and some others are usually produced in this loudness range and can be totally missed by a child like Jennifer.) Listening fatigue is also common, and children with this hearing level may be unfairly thought to be inattentive. They often acquire less information than expected through naturally occurring situations because, unlike children with typical hearing, they are unable to "overhear" what is being said around but not directly to them. Children with this hearing level are typically considered candidates for using hearing aids and may benefit from them. Children with hearing at the mild hearing level need frequent attention to assure that more hearing is not being lost over time, that they are able to understand spoken language in various social and school-related settings, that they are able to pronounce speech sounds clearly, and that they are not falling behind in language and academic skills. Speech and language therapy, as well as therapy aimed at increasing attention to spoken language and instruction in how to watch a speaker's lips to get "speechreading" (lip-reading) information can be helpful.

41 to 55 dB (moderate hearing level or "moderate hearing loss"). With hearing at this level, a child can usually hear sounds of conversational speech only if the person speaking is within 3 or 4 feet and directly in front of him or her. In most everyday communication situations, more than half of the sounds of spoken language will be missed. This interferes with the child being able to pick up information from spoken language occurring around him or her and will also directly affect the ability to learn to recognize and express the sounds of speech. Consonant sounds that help a child tell the difference between one word and another are especially difficult to hear and can be entirely missed. This makes it difficult to know when one spoken word ends and another begins. It also interferes with the ability to tell the difference between words that have the same number of syllables. Any noise in the background will make it much harder to hear and understand speech clearly. Modern hearing aids are often very helpful for a child who has this level of hearing, but specialized training that focuses on skills in listening and producing spoken language are almost always required. Signing or other visual language systems (like cued speech) can also be of assistance in language learning or in difficult listening situations.

56 to −70 dB (moderately severe hearing level or "moderately severe hearing loss"). Without using a hearing aid or some other technological device, all but very loud conversations will be difficult if not impossible to follow. Spoken classroom conversation and instruction can be impossible to understand. Group communication settings are especially difficult, and spoken language development is usually quite delayed. Although there is much individual variation, children with this hearing level can usually acquire spoken language if provided hearing aids as well as speech/language and other therapies (including training and experience with speechreading). Devices such as frequency modulation (FM) systems can be very helpful, especially in noisy situations like classrooms. In many cases, the use of sign language has been shown to support language development for children with this hearing level.

71 to –90 dB (severe hearing level or "severe hearing loss"). This is the hearing level at which even modern hearing aids may fail to allow the child to hear spoken language clearly. Specific listening and speechreading (lipreading) training as well as speech-language therapies can improve some children's understanding and production of spoken language, but language development is almost sure to be delayed unless sign language (or another visual language system) is used. Although children with this hearing level were not provided CIs in the past, that is being reconsidered in some cases, and there is some evidence (Leigh, Dettman, Dowell, & Sarant, 2011) that CIs can significantly increase the ability of these children to receive and understand spoken language.

91 dB or greater (profound hearing level or "profound hearing loss"). Even when children with this hearing level use hearing aids, the sounds of spoken language are not received clearly. At this hearing level, visual language information (from sign language or a combination of signing, speechreading, and other visual information) is almost always necessary for them to understand language. Where CIs are available, they have mostly been provided to children with this level of hearing and have proved, on average, to very significantly boost their ability to hear and learn spoken language and academic skills (Spencer, Marschark, & Spencer, 2011). CIs usually provide access to sounds at levels within the "speech banana" and are often most effective when obtained and used during the early years. There are some reports that use of a CI during the first two years of life can support early spoken language development at typical rates (Dettman & Dowell, 2011). There is also emerging evidence that early use of signing plus spoken language with children using CIs has positive effects (Knoors & Marschark, 2012), although this remains a topic on which there is much disagreement. Outcomes in language and other developmental areas for children with profound hearing levels have significantly improved, largely due to wider use of sign language, earlier identification of hearing levels plus early high-quality intervention services, and the availability of powerful hearing aids and CIs.

Knowing the *average* loudness level an infant or young child needs in order to be aware of various pitches of sound—that is, knowing his or her averaged hearing level as described above—is useful for parents, caregivers, and professionals working with family and child. However, the averaged hearing level measure is oversimplified and can be misleading. There are many other factors to consider. One is whether there is a difference between hearing abilities in each of an individual child's ears. In the past, it was often assumed that one ear was "enough." However, we now know that when hearing is limited in just one ear (or even when hearing is limited in both ears but more so in one than the other), the child will be required to use more attention and energy to understand spoken language. This will be especially true in noisy environments, when multiple people talk at once and when there is a greater than usual distance between the child and the speaker. Because these complications can affect the rate of a child's language development, children with limited hearing in one ear are also at higher than average risk for academic and even social difficulties. Differences between hearing levels in the two ears also affect the ability to tell what direction a sound comes from. Difficulty in locating the source of a sound will interfere with the child's ability to follow conversations involving more than one speaker, and it also raises specific safety risks. For these reasons, a hearing aid (or, occasionally, a CI) may be used in the ear with limited hearing to increase listening abilities.

Looking only at a child's averaged hearing level can tempt us to ignore the differences in loudness required for the child to hear different pitches from the low-to-high spectrum. One child with a 50 dB average hearing level may hear most or all of the pitches that occur in spoken language when they are increased enough in loudness. This child, with a "flat" or non-sloping hearing level, can typically get good results in picking up both low- and high-pitched sounds when using a hearing aid. However, another child might have the same average level but have a "sloping" profile of hearing abilities. A child with this kind of hearing profile might hear lower pitched sounds (like most vowel sounds) at fairly soft levels, but higher pitched consonant sounds would require vastly greater boosts in loudness to be heard. Modern hearing aids can be tuned to account for this kind of sloping hearing level more successfully than in the past; however, even with the best hearing aids, it may still be difficult if not impossible for some children with severe-to-profound sloping hearing levels to hear high-pitched sounds well enough to allow understanding of spoken language. The sounds that must have their loudness boosted the most may remain especially fuzzy or indistinct. Even two children whose audiograms look essentially the same may differ in their ability to hear speech sounds clearly because of differences in various parts of the ear and the brain that process sound. Therefore, it is critical to understand a child's specific ability to respond to different pitches at different loudness levels as shown on his or her audiogram. However, it is only through careful observation of the child's behaviors and changes in those behaviors over time and in different circumstances that an individual's unique hearing characteristics and abilities can be measured with confidence.

What Technology Can (and Cannot) Do

When hearing levels are identified at or near birth, it is typical for deaf or hard-of-hearing babies to be fitted with hearing aids as soon as possible. Scientists have shown that gaining the ability to hear sounds, even imperfectly, during the early months prompts the brain to develop efficient pathways to receive and understand sounds better than if access to sound only occurs later. (We discuss this in more detail in Chapter 5.)

Hearing Aids

In the somewhat distant past, hearing aids were fairly simple devices. They increased the intensity, or loudness, of sounds so that a deaf or hard-of-hearing person might hear them. However, the increase in loudness tended to be the same across pitches, and often the sounds of some pitches were too loud while the sounds of other pitches still could not be heard. In addition, distortion or blurring and fuzziness of pitches was common. Well before the end of the 20th century, however, audiologists were able to "tune" hearing aids to boost different pitches in whatever amounts best matched an individual child's hearing profile. The technology has continued to evolve, and both the quality of sound and the "fit" between an individual's needs for amplifying (or increasing the loudness) at specific pitches has improved. Accomplishing this match is not a simple process. It requires multiple visits to the audiologist to tune the aid as well as ongoing follow up to make sure the settings continue to be a good match for a child's hearing needs. In addition, hearing aids will not make it possible for a person to hear sounds if there are problems with the inner ear hair cells, the hearing nerve, or parts of the brain that process sounds. Not infrequently, people with profound or even severe hearing levels cannot understand spoken language even with the most powerful hearing aids.

Hearing aids come in different forms. Some fit just inside the ear canal, but this design is more useful for older people than for infants and toddlers. Behind-the-ear hearing aids are more commonly used for babies and young children. Although the programming or individualizing of hearing aids is much more specific now than in the past, aids still have the same basic parts. There is a tiny microphone that takes in sounds and sends them to an amplifier. The amplifier will be set (or programmed) by the audiologist to make the various pitches of sounds louder, matching as closely as possible a specific child's hearing needs. These now-louder sounds are sent through the ear hook (sometimes called a *tone hook*) to the earmold that fits into the child's ear canal; this earmold is made to fit each individual child. Through the earmold, the sounds travel toward the middle ear, which transmits them to the inner ear.

Hearing aids also have volume controls, and some can be set to increase the loudness levels to different extents depending on the situation. The microphone on hearing aids can also be set to be directional (focused, for example, on picking up mostly sound from directly in front of the head or, instead, to pick up sounds from all directions). There is even a type of hearing

Figure 2.6 Comfortable and alert with her hearing aid. (Photo courtesy of Dorothy Goldbar. Reprinted with permission.)

aid called a *bone conduction aid* that can help when a child's middle ear does not function but the inner ear does. These aids send the sounds more directly to the inner ear through the bone that lies behind the ear lobe itself. Given the speed of technological advances in the 21st century in general, we can be sure that more advances will be made in hearing aid technology over time. However, these advances will only be effective for babies if hearing aids are kept in good working condition and are worn consistently (see Figure 2.6).

An early intervention specialist (usually an audiologist or a trained teacher of deaf and hard-of-hearing children) should be sure that parents understand how to insert the hearing aid correctly and check daily to assure it is working. Batteries need to be replaced periodically. And, as a baby grows, so does the ear canal. The earmold will therefore need to be re-made and replaced as often as every 2 to about 4 months. Feedback, or a ringing sound, is one indication that an earmold is no longer fitting right. The audiologist may also change the settings on the amplifier (changing the relative loudness of the sounds the baby receives) as more testing is done and detailed measures of hearing with and without the aid are obtained.

A major challenge for many parents is keeping the hearing aid in the baby's ear. This can become especially difficult during the second half of the first year and the second year of a baby's life. Curiosity and a natural tendency to explore objects may tempt the baby or toddler to pull the aid out of the ear, or the baby may simply not like the feeling of wearing the hearing aid. The possibility that the aid is not fitting correctly or is actually uncomfortable should always be investigated. Early intervention specialists and audiologists who work with babies can give a number of suggestions to parents, who are ultimately responsible for helping the baby tolerate the hearing aid. Sometimes parents will need to gradually increase the time during the day when the aid is worn. At other times, parents may find it necessary to put a soft, thin cloth bonnet on the child when he or she is first wearing the aid to prevent its removal. (However, some audiologists object to this practice.) Over time, most babies and toddlers learn to leave the aid alone. Some babies learn fairly quickly that their parents really want them to wear the hearing aid and, depending on the circumstance, this may increase or decrease the baby's willingness to wear it. We once watched a clever little 12-month-old boy who was placed in a high chair "threaten" to remove his hearing aid because he wanted out of the chair. When his mother did not let him out of the chair, he gave her a meaningful stare and a little grin as he moved his right hand up to his ear, clearly indicating that he would pull out the hearing aid if he wasn't allowed out. We, along with the baby's mother, had to smile at this behavior—and his mother (who had clearly seen it before!) was able to distract him with one of the toys we had brought so they could continue the play activity.

An audiologist's tests will reveal how much the child benefits from using a hearing aid, but careful observation at home can also provide important information about how a baby or toddler responds to sounds in real life. There are several often-used scales asking parents to report how their young child responds to sounds in the home. The Infant-Toddler

Meaningful Auditory Integration Scale (IT-MAIS; Zimmerman-Phillips, Osberger, & Robbins, 1997; see www.advancedbionics.com for free access to the scale) requires that a professional (usually an early intervention or deaf education specialist or audiologist) interview the parents and pose questions about how their child reacts to sounds at home in both quiet and noisy environments. This scale is for children from birth to 2 years of age and can be used for children with any hearing level. It was based on an older scale, the Meaningful Auditory Integration Scale (MAIS; Robbins, Renshaw, & Berry, 1991) for toddlers and preschoolers older than 25 months of age. A scale called the *Functional Auditory Performance Indicators* (FAPI; Stredler-Brown & Johnson, 2003; see www.tsbvi.edu for free access to the scale) can generate scores on a variety of listening abilities, including recognizing sounds and remembering them. The scores can be based on parents' reports or on interventionists' observations of the child's behavior. The Early Listening Function (ELF) scale (Anderson, 2002; see www.phonakpro.com for a free copy) is designed for children with minimal or mild hearing levels or for children with limited hearing in only one ear. Scales like these, whether they are filled out by parents directly or by an interviewer who records their responses to items, allow parents to be directly involved in the assessment of their child's use of hearing. Parent reports can provide information in an organized way for professionals working with them and their child. Perhaps as importantly, this information can be reviewed by parents as they decide whether to continue current practices, intensify them, or consider using different approaches or technologies.

Cochlear Implants

Since the 1980s, increasing numbers of young children around the world who are profoundly deaf (and more recently those with severe-to-profound hearing levels who receive little or no benefit from hearing aids) have been provided cochlear implants (CIs). Some children with severe hearing levels have also received CIs, and, overall, they are reported to have gained significant hearing abilities from their use (Dettman & Dowell, 2010). However, the usual effect of using a CI is to help a child with hearing in the profound or severe-to-profound range hear those things that can usually be heard by a child who has a moderate hearing level and uses a hearing aid. (For example, young children using CIs can understand an average of about 80% of the sounds in one-syllable words and about 50% of a list of the whole words themselves just by listening [Dowell, Dettman, Blamey, Barker, & Clark, 2002].) Therefore, a CI can provide great advantages for a child who hears little or nothing when using only a hearing aid. But, because parts of a CI must be surgically implanted, and because they do not restore complete hearing, CIs are usually not provided to children who can hear many of the sounds of spoken language when using a hearing aid.

Like hearing aids, CIs receive sound through an external microphone that is part of a behind-the-ear unit. The sounds are changed to electrical signals in a *processor* or small computerized unit that is worn externally. The processor must be programmed or *mapped* for each individual child by the audiologist to get the right level of electrical signal for various pitches. These signals are then directly sent to a string of tiny electrodes that has been inserted into the inner ear. These electrodes in effect substitute for the hair cells in the inner ear; they "fire" or send electrical signals in complex sequences to the hearing nerve. If the hearing nerve is functioning correctly, it then sends electrical messages on to other parts of the brain that process sound. (Technologies related to cochlear and other kinds of implants to increase access to sound are continuing to be developed at a rapid rate.)

The surgery to insert the electrodes and some other parts of the CI can take about 3 hours.[5] As with other surgeries, there is a recovery period, and occasionally a child will experience some short-term postoperative swelling, minor bleeding, and even some balance problems. However, these problems tend to be temporary, and the complication rate is very low even though surgery is now performed on babies at about 1 year of age or even younger (Dettman & Dowell, 2010).

For the parents of most children who receive a CI, the primary goal is to help the child hear enough to learn to understand and produce spoken language. An enormous amount of research has been done in multiple countries to identify factors or conditions that predict the effectiveness of CIs. One factor is the type of technology used in the processor or software of the CI itself. As technologies have advanced over the years, outcomes have improved for most children. Another important factor is the age at which the CI is first used, with 2 years of age being an apparently important boundary beyond which there is an overall gradual reduction in benefits. (Although there are reports that using a CI by the age of about 1 year makes spoken language development faster and easier, other researchers report that the difference between 1 and 2 years of age is not significant [Dettman, Pinder, Briggs, Dowell, & Leigh, 2007; but see Holt & Svirsky, 2008]). Because of effects of improved technology and decreases in age of first use of CIs, it is important when reading reports of their effects to consider which "generation" of users is being discussed. Children who received CIs in the 1980s or early 1990s tended to receive them only after age 3—and the technology was not as sophisticated as in CIs developed later. Children who first used CIs in the mid-1990s generally received more sophisticated devices and began using them as early as about 18 months of age. By the 2000s, the technology had continued to improve, and CIs could be used by 12 months of age—earlier in some countries outside the United States. The results of using a CI have, in general, improved across these generations.

Other factors affect CI outcomes, however. For example, if a child is not born deaf but loses hearing later, less time without hearing predicts better spoken language development. Children who have used hearing aids successfully and have developed some spoken language skills before using a CI also generally have good spoken language outcomes, even if they get the CI after 2 years of age. It also appears that, for children who have limited hearing in both ears, either using two CIs (if hearing is at the profound level in each ear) or using a CI in one ear and a hearing aid in the other can give increased benefits (Boons et al., 2012). Because CIs give more information about high-pitched sounds while hearing aids tend to give better information about lower pitched sounds, they may complement each other.

Characteristics of the child and the child's environment can also affect the rate of development when using a CI. A few children receive little or no benefit, but some are able to develop spoken language at the same or similar rates as hearing children (Dettman & Dowell, 2010). Most children, however, perform somewhere in between. One characteristic that affects outcomes from using a CI is an individual child's overall speed of learning. We saw this in research we conducted with 13 children who began using a CI by the age of 2 years (Spencer, 2004). Children in this group who had some neurological disabilities that caused learning problems did not gain as much benefit from the CIs—at least not during the first few years of use. A number of other researchers have drawn similar conclusions: benefits from using a CI are likely to be more limited and more slowly gained for children who have multiple disabilities (Edwards, 2010; Fortnum, Stacey, Barton, & Summerfield, 2007; Palmieri et al., 2012). Also, children whose hearing (or auditory) nerve is less developed than usual, either narrower or unable to transmit electrical signals in a rhythmic way, tend to gain less from CIs. Similarly, although rarely, there can be damage or difficulties in other parts of the brain that prevent the CI's signals from being understood even when thinking skills and learning abilities are not limited.

Not surprisingly, there is another factor that influences a child's development of language when using a CI: the amount of spoken language taking place around the child. But, to date, we have no real information to guide parents who are trying to decide whether signs should be used along with spoken language. Some researchers have concluded that spoken language develops more quickly when signs are not used (Dettman & Dowell, 2010; Geers, Brenner, & Davidson, 2003). Others have reported that learning signs before CI use supports spoken language development *after* a CI is used (Connor, Heiber, Arts, & Zwolen, 2000; see also Knoors & Marschark, 2012, for a recent summary). There is some evidence, moreover, to support continuing to sign to a baby after the CI is received and turned on. Many hearing parents seem to do this intuitively—without being advised to do so—often gradually decreasing use of signs as their toddler starts responding to sounds. We have personally observed several families in which a transition from using primarily sign language to predominant use of spoken language (on the part of both child and parents) occurred. One such experience was with Ian, a little boy in Australia:

Ian's hearing parents learned that he was profoundly deaf before he was a month old. This came as a surprise, because no one else in the family was deaf or hard of hearing, and they did not have any friends or neighbors who were deaf. But they sprang into action. After discussions with early intervention professionals and the speech therapists at the clinic where Ian received therapy (as well as what they read on the Internet), they decided to learn and use Auslan, the natural sign language in Australia, with Ian. Although the parents learned sign language pretty slowly, Ian picked it up quickly from them and from deaf parents and older children whom his therapist helped the family meet. Although Ian took to signing quickly and naturally, his parents wanted him to have every opportunity available to interact comfortably with hearing as well as deaf people. After more research and discussion, they decided to get a CI for him a few months before his second birthday. We first saw him at age 3 years, and he was still signing words and sentences consistently, but he had also begun to speak words. (To our American ears, Ian's emerging "baby-Aussie" accent made him difficult to understand, but his parents assured us that they could understand him.) We asked Ian's parents to update us on his progress a year later, and another year after that. By age 5, Ian's parents reported that he was "able to talk just like his hearing friends" and that they had stopped signing to him "except when he needs to learn a new word or when something is unclear." At those times, they used signs to clarify and to explain but used the spoken word afterward. And, they reported, "(Ian) talks without signing almost all the time—except when he is playing with a deaf friend—or when he gets angry. Then you should see his hands fly!"

Like Ian, many other children who could not have heard the sounds of spoken language have gained the ability to do so using a CI. Not surprisingly, the use of CIs is continuing to expand—and there continues to be a strong focus on improving the technology used and conducting research on the best ways to take advantage of the sound-like information that a CI can provide. Some researchers have reported that, all other things being equal, children with CIs who are in programs focusing totally or very intensely on spoken language advance more quickly in *expressive* speech skills than do those in programs where there is a shared or sole focus on signing (e.g., Geers et al., 2003). Our personal observations, however, are consistent with a number of other research reports of children learning sign language who also develop spoken language using a CI. In general, children who are learning two languages (whether both are spoken or one spoken and one signed) tend to learn both of them a bit more slowly than if they were focused on only one language; however, their eventual mastery and use of both languages tends to be strong. Bilingual children also often gain social and cognitive benefits from knowing and using two different languages (Adesope, Lavin, Thompson, & Ungerleider, 2010).

And More...

Hearing aids and CIs, although they receive the most attention, are not the only listening technologies that parents who have spoken language as a goal for their child can investigate (Harkins & Bakke, 2010). For example, Frequency Modulation (FM) devices that are used in conjunction with a child's hearing aid or CI make it possible for a child to hear a person speaking more clearly even from a distance and with a lot of background noise. The speaker wears a microphone that sends radio signals to a receiver connected to the child's hearing aid or CI. This kind of system has been used for many years, especially in classrooms, where it can help the child hear the teacher.

Some parents use FM systems at home with their young children. This can be of benefit, for example, when the baby is riding in the back seat of a car and parents are sitting in the front. There is often background noise (perhaps from the car motor or wind or other children talking), and a baby in a back seat safety chair cannot even see the face of the driver speaking to him or her. With an FM system, these difficulties can be overcome. They can also be helpful when a toddler is playing in a park or when in a child care situation. As the toddler or slightly older child acquires language skills, she can report when the level or quality of sound needs adjustment, and use of an FM device may become even more effective. Other wireless technologies, such as systems using several wireless microphones, continue to emerge and can help to include a deaf or hard-of-hearing child in spoken conversations at family dinnertimes and other situations (see Harkins & Bakke, 2010, for more information about communication technologies). For older children, mobile texting on smartphones and portable computer devices that allow video and print messages as well as sound are increasingly widespread in parts of Asia, Africa, and the Middle East, as well as in Europe and the Americas. Such devices can help deaf and hard-of-hearing individuals stay in contact with family and friends. To make full use of these devices, however, the abilities to read, write, and understand technology will be increasingly important.

SUMMARIZING KEY IDEAS

Great strides have been made in understanding hearing, its assessment, and its supplementation over the past several decades. Early identification of hearing levels, along with high-quality early intervention programs, have actually increased the degree to which many children can make use of their available hearing even when it is limited. However, there is also increased recognition that even slight or mild hearing levels (or "levels of hearing loss") can challenge development of listening, language, and learning. Identification of hearing levels is not a one-time activity but should be an on-going part of the services provided to children and their parents or caregivers. It is important that parents, who are the true experts on their child's day-to-day behaviors, be integral to the assessment process. These are some of the key ideas presented in this chapter:

- Based on behaviors alone, it is difficult to know whether a young baby hears a sound; identifying deaf and hard-of-hearing newborns and babies up to about 3 months of age depends to a great degree on the use of modern assessment innovations and technologies.
- Preliminary screening procedures do not identify a baby as deaf or hard of hearing, but they can alert professionals to the need

for further testing. It is important that parents return with their infants for follow-up assessment when the screening results indicate a need. Without this follow-up, precise hearing levels cannot be determined.

- With increasing age, older babies and toddlers can actively participate in hearing assessment procedures, and the results become more definitive.
- Hearing is not only affected by the structures and functioning of parts of the ear itself but also involves functioning of nerves and parts of the brain.
- For almost all children with limited hearing, some sound pitches must be louder than others to be received. An audiogram gives a picture of how loud different sounds must be to be heard by an individual child. Parents and caregivers should be well versed in "reading" and understanding their child's audiogram—and in asking questions whenever needed.
- Digital, programmable hearing aids can increase hearing for many but not all babies and toddlers. When the nerve endings (hair cells) of the inner ear are not functioning adequately to transmit complete information from sound to the auditory (hearing) nerve, CIs can often be of great benefit. Early use of these technologies tends to provide more long-term benefit than delaying their use.
- Many factors influence the degree to which available hearing abilities—even using hearing aids or CIs—support listening and spoken language skills. There is evidence that well-developed thinking or cognitive skills are important; there is also some evidence that use of visual language (like signing or cued speech) can support spoken language abilities, but this remains controversial.
- Families are wise to revisit and perhaps sometimes revise decisions about use of various technologies and approaches to support language learning over time.

Effective intervention for babies and toddlers who are deaf or hard of hearing requires understanding what they hear—and what they cannot hear. But hearing ability is far from the only factor influencing their development. In the next chapter, we begin to consider in more depth some of these other important influences—including abilities and behaviors during the earliest days and months of life and the world of social experiences in which a baby is immediately and deeply immersed.

NOTES

1. Readers should be warned that neither of us is an audiologist, although Dr. Spencer has had both classwork and practical experience reading and interpreting audiograms. This chapter is our attempt to explain ideas about hearing and results of hearing testing to provide a basic foundation for understanding how hearing affects—and in some ways does not affect—other areas of development. We have taken some liberties to simplify terms, and we have tried to express major ideas instead of details.

   We received expert assistance in preparing this chapter, however, and want to express great appreciation for the time and advice given so freely by Dr. Barbara Cone (CCC-A), a professor in the department of speech, hearing, and languages sciences at the University of Arizona. She has extensive clinical as well as teaching and research experience. Dr. Cone has received numerous awards and fellowships internationally in recognition of her work in pediatric audiology and serves on the Board of the American Speech-Language-Hearing Association. Debra Nussbaum, MA (CCC-A) also gave us extensive advice and assistance with the writing of this chapter. She has worked at the Laurent Clerc National Deaf Education Center at Gallaudet University since 1977, first as a pediatric audiologist, then as Coordinator of the Cochlear Implant Education Center, and currently as Manager of Projects—Language Development and Communication Support. She has been chair of DC HEAR's Intervention Committee since 2001, supporting early intervention initiatives in the District of Columbia's newborn infant screening program.

   Audiology is a field that has become increasingly sophisticated over the past decades, especially in the technology used. It is critical that a pediatric audiologist be a member of the team serving a family. Many experienced teachers of deaf and hard-of-hearing children are also highly knowledgeable about hearing and its assessment, so they often can provide a "first level" of response to parents' questions.

2. Audiograms usually include more information than we discuss here. For example, results of tympanometry (assessment of the flexibility of the ear drum) will usually be shown for babies older than about 6 months of age. Among other things, these results can indicate whether there is fluid in the middle ear that could be influencing responses to sounds.

3. The B is capitalized in honor of Alexander Graham Bell, who not only invented the telephone but who also had a lifelong interest in advancing deaf persons' development of spoken language.

4. Notice that this average dB level is *not* a percent. When people talk about a "50% hearing loss" or a "78% hearing loss," they are probably confusing the idea of percent with the dB measure. In fact, because of the complicated (at least to us) way that the dB scale measures sound energy, it requires extremely sophisticated math to convert the dB number to a percent. Our recommendation? If a professional quotes a "percent" hearing loss to you, ask to see the audiogram and look at the dB loudness levels that were necessary for the child to react to each pitch that was tested. Then ask for a more in-depth description of what the child can and cannot hear.

5. We were able to observe the surgery on a 3-year-old child some years ago. We are still in awe of the careful, detailed, dedicated work of the surgical team as they focused on making sure not to damage nerves and other structures while making room for and inserting the CI.

Chart 1: *Behaviors to Watch For**

At or near Birth

Physical and Motor Abilities	• Reflex movements (e.g., grasping, sucking, startle response)
	• More time sleeping than awake
	• Cannot hold head up without support
Getting Information from the Senses	• Notices differences in flavors—prefers sweet tastes
	• Recognizes differences between smells
	• Feels pain
	• Sees shapes, edges, strong contrasts if object or display close to the face[V]
	• Prefers to look at faces
	• "Tracks" or follows slowly moving objects
	• Hears relatively loud noises in "pitch" range of human voices; recognizes mother's voice[H]
Mental Abilities ("Cognition")	• Remembers songs or words heard often before birth[H]
	• Tires of looking at same thing after some time, showing use of memory[V]
	• "Alerts" and attends briefly to things seen, heard, or felt
Social-Emotional and Communication Behaviors	• Expresses discomfort by crying, body movements
	• Cries, makes "natural" sounds like coughing, breathing
	• Calmed by gentle touches, rocking, being held closely

Sources: Information on this and all charts to follow is compiled from many sources. Many items are from Eliot (1999), Fogel (2009), Meadow-Orlans, Spencer & Koester (2004), Northern & Downs (2002), and Slater & Lewis (2007).

[H] may be delayed or require different circumstances if hearing is limited; [V] may be delayed or require different circumstances if vision is limited.

Chart 2: *Advances to Watch For**

By About 3 Months

Physical and Motor Abilities**	• Some reflexes disappear, others become more refined and intentional
	• Sleep/wake periods more predictable
	• More time awake
	• Can lift head
	• (If sighted) Reaches toward hanging toys, may grasp or kick at them
	• Sits with support
Getting Information from the Senses	• More accepting of new tastes
	• Develops favorite smells
	• Increased sensitivity to pain
	• Better perception of shapes and colors^V
	o Begins to detect dimensions and distances^V
	o Tracks moving objects more smoothly^V
	o Stares intently at faces and objects^V
	• Turns head consistently toward sounds^H
Mental Abilities ("Cognition")	• Recognizes familiar faces^V
	• Remembers, repeats actions with interesting results
	• Recognizes groupings of objects with similar features
	• Pays attention to objects for longer times, but prefers social interactions
Communication/ Language	• Produces "coo's" "goo's," and vowel sounds
	• Waves arms, kicks legs when excited
	• Stays engaged with adult's activities and takes "turns"
	• Quiet and alert when attending to something
Social-Emotional	• Positive response to social interactions
	• Smiles at familiar faces^V or voices^H
	• Calmed by close contact, rhythmic rocking

*See Chart 1 for partial list of sources for information.

**On all charts advances in motor abilities assume no physical disabilities.

^{H} may be delayed or require different circumstances if hearing is limited; ^{V} may be delayed or require different circumstances if vision is limited.

3 Welcome to the World

THE PRENATAL PERIOD TO 3 MONTHS

QUESTIONS TO CONSIDER

- When do the sensory systems—hearing, vision, taste, smell, touch, and vestibular (awareness of position and movement of the body)—begin to function?
- How do hearing and vision work together?
- Why do most babies enjoy the sensation of being moved rhythmically by rocking, or riding in a stroller or on someone's back?
- What role does touch and the feeling of physical contact play in early parent–child interactions? Why is this sense especially important for deaf and hard-of-hearing babies and toddlers?
- How can you know when a baby is alert and awake, or drowsy and no longer receptive to your communications?
- How do newborns learn to regulate (or control) their emotional responses, and what role do caregivers play in this process?

PRENATAL DEVELOPMENT AND THE FIRST 3 MONTHS AFTER BIRTH

Even before birth, during what is called the *prenatal period*, babies receive some information from the outside world through their senses.
The senses of taste, smell, touch, the orientation (or position) and movement of the body—even hearing and limited vision—operate during the
last 3 months (trimester) of a full-term pregnancy. For example, in the
months before birth, sounds of the mother's voice, her heartbeat, even
loud talking from others who are close by (like siblings in the home) can
be heard indistinctly by a baby with typical hearing. Over time, especially after birth, the information from each of the senses is combined
and integrated and begins to form meaningful "wholes" for the baby. For
example, the aroma specific to her mother's milk and body is associated
with the feeling of being cuddled and with the sight of the mother's face.
Even at the time of birth, it is evident that newborns without hearing limitations can recognize (and will actively seek) their own mother's voice—
probably as a result of having heard it and felt the rhythmic vibrations
when she spoke or sang during the 9 months of pregnancy (DeCasper &
Fifer, 1980). These sensations gradually blend together so that, after some
time, the baby will easily recognize this special person as well as others
who provide comfort and loving care.

How long *before* birth can a fetus receive sensory information, and how
can we know this? Sensory responses begin in the mother's womb, and
they can be noticed by changes in fetal heart rate, activity level, changes
in position, and more. However, the rate and timing of this development
varies according to each specific sensory system. The following sections
give a few examples of how this occurs both prenatally and soon after
birth. We begin with the auditory sense and then provide an overview
of vision, vestibular/kinesthetic perception, tactile perception, taste, and
the sense of smell.

The Auditory Sense

Parts of the *hearing* (or auditory) system start developing as early as 4
weeks after a baby is conceived and begins to grow in the womb. Between

10 and 20 weeks, the cochlea or inner ear and the hair cells (discussed in Chapter 2) are developing. In fact, after about 6 months in the womb, small brain wave responses can be observed using the auditory evoked potential (AEP) method described in the previous chapter. To get a response, the sounds must be quite long-lasting and within only a "middle" range of pitches—not too high and not too low. By about this time, fetuses with typical hearing abilities developing begin to respond to speech, especially from the mother, and to other loud sounds.

"Response" is shown by changes in the baby's heart rate, in movement, or by eye blinks (that can be seen on ultrasound recordings) when loud noises occur. Noises from outside the mother's body must be quite loud to be transmitted through the mother's skin and organs and the fluid surrounding the fetus, however, and they will be muffled and indistinct. Remember that the womb is really quite a noisy place—there are the rhythmic sounds of mother's heartbeat, the swooshing flow of blood through her veins, her digestive processes, her voice, and possibly other sounds from her environment. The sounds that are heard best are those that are low in pitch or frequency, and it is probable that much of what the baby receives as "sounds" while in the womb are sequences of rhythms—the rhythm of music and of intonations as mother talks, for example—as well as differences in the pitch and duration of sounds. (These rhythms may be available as touch-like vibrations to a fetus whose hearing is not developing.) As the baby continues to mature in the womb, if hearing is developing, she begins to hear more higher pitched as well as lower pitched sounds than before. The range of sounds that can be received is expanding even before birth. By 35 weeks or so, very near the expected time of birth, the baby can hear differences between sounds like "bah" and "bee" and can even remember them!

By 39–40 weeks, when babies are considered "full term" (Fogel, 2009), a typically hearing baby will already have had about 10–12 weeks of listening experience. The *experience* of hearing has already been influencing the connections among nerve fibers sending information about sound to various parts of the brain. Like other aspects of brain development, this works in a cycle. As the fetus (still in the womb) and then the newborn is exposed to more auditory information, the brain is stimulated to develop more efficient ways of processing that information. In turn, sensitivity to sounds increases, auditory experiences continue to occur, and the brain continues to develop more efficient processing of them. Assuming there is no hearing limitation, this cycle continues after birth and, in fact, well into adolescence. It is most efficient, however, during the early years.

At birth, sounds are only heard if they are relatively loud. (They must be about 40–50 dB louder than those an adult would be able to hear.) The baby is able to perceive softer sounds as the next months pass, but even preschool children cannot reliably hear sounds as well as can young adults. High-pitched sounds are heard less easily by newborns than are lower pitched ones, although this ability develops rapidly over the first 3 months after birth.

At several days of age, babies with typical hearing often turn their head to the right or the left, toward the source of a sound. This ability to localize sound becomes very helpful over time if the baby is to associate a particular sound with its location and then attend to the person or object causing it. But, initially, this ability has its limits. By the time they are 2–3 months old, most babies who have typical hearing can find the source of a sound and follow it visually—such as a dog barking, a car engine starting, or the voice of someone approaching—but this skill requires time and experience to develop. Remember that one of the most important hearing skills in terms of overall development is the newborn's ability to recognize, respond to, and be comforted by her mother's voice. Not surprisingly, young infants with typical hearing recognize and turn to their own mother's voice.

Eventually, this skill will be important in helping the child who can hear become an active participant in conversations with others. Imagine, for example, Daddy entering the room as Heather awakens from her nap; he calls out cheerfully, "Hey there sweetie! How's my little pumpkin today?" Heather alerts to Daddy's voice, turns to look at him, and thus encourages his continued chatter. A dialogue has begun, even though the baby is primarily communicating with body language at this stage. For the child with limited hearing, this social skill may depend more on other sensory channels such as vision and touch in order to develop sufficiently. When a baby's hearing system does not develop, or when limited hearing prevents the baby from having hearing experiences while in the womb (or soon after birth), other sensory experiences such as vision can be emphasized for compensation.

The Visual Sense

By the seventh month of prenatal life, nerves have begun to connect the visual region of the brain with the eyes, allowing primitive visual functioning, such as when the fetus responds (by moving or a change in heart rate) to very bright lights shining on Mom's abdomen (Hepper, 2007). However, vision is the last sensory channel to fully develop and, of course, the one that receives the least stimulation in the womb. At birth, most newborns are best at perceiving changes in light or shadows but not much visual detail. In addition, newborns can focus best on objects within close range, at approximately the typical face-to-face distance used intuitively by someone who is holding or feeding a young infant. Perhaps it should not be surprising then, that infants are especially attracted to the human face or to other face-like images they might see in pictures, dolls, stuffed animals, and the like. How fortunate that most adults enjoy interacting in close proximity with babies, and most babies reciprocate by showing us that they like this, too!

Early Visual Experiences After Birth

For deaf and hard-of-hearing children, the visual system may have to help take the place of or compensate for decreased auditory input. The newborn's visual capacities are not as refined or well-focused as they will be somewhat later in development. Nevertheless, this is one of the infant's more complex senses, and the visual perceptions which it makes possible are quite varied. Let's take a look at a few more examples based on findings from careful scientific studies.

Newborns can use vision to detect and respond to differences in shapes, their locations in space, and certain features such as bold colors and textures. However, perceiving the finer distinctions among colors (e.g., pink vs. violet) does not usually occur until somewhat later, between 4 and 7 months of age. Although the newborn infant probably sees the world as somewhat blurred and out of focus, she can nevertheless track large movements within the visual field, such as the shadowy image of a caregiver entering the room. It will take several months, however, before the infant can track moving objects with much accuracy.

Scanning the Environment

Watch closely as a newborn's eyes trace around the edges of a visual image such as someone's face, a stimulus to which they are especially attracted. The newborn seems to find it so much more interesting to look at a round shape with all those moving parts (shining eyes, fuzzy eyebrows, and a mouth that seems to be in constant motion) rather than simply at an apple or a basketball! When observing this, you may notice the baby's small, quick eye movements from one point on the image (e.g., Dad's hairline) to another (such as Dad's glasses or beard). As the child studies the parameters and features of the visual stimulus, she gradually builds up a reliable mental representation of *Dad* that is different from the image the infant has of Mom or Uncle Nathan.

Visual Preferences

Newborns seem to especially enjoy looking at images that have clearly defined boundaries; they prefer circles over straight edges; and they will gaze longer at symmetrical than at "scrambled" or random features. Does this help explain why they will gaze at faces longer than at geometrically or randomly organized patterns (think of a Picasso painting, for example)?

In the examples mentioned here, as during the prenatal period, visual development is not inevitable but depends on stimulation from the environment to help the immature brain become "wired" correctly. Think of the physical surroundings for most infants, regardless of culture or background: in the course of any 24-hour period, there are ample opportunities to be moved to various heights and locations, to see objects fall or be thrown and eventually drop to the ground, to observe people and things coming closer and then disappearing into the distance. How puzzling this must be for newborns, before these repeated exposures to proximity, distance, and gravity begin to become predictable and even something that they can perhaps influence by their own behavior!

How does the newborn child make sense of the jumble of new, unfamiliar lines, shapes, colors, and textures that make up her visual world, a world that confronts the neonate almost immediately after birth? Detecting patterns, another important aspect of visual perception, is a skill that must gradually become refined as the newborn accumulates day-by-day experience in visually exploring the world. These repeated and varied experiences with the visual world allow the infant to become better able (by around 3 months) to pick out meaningful patterns and to discriminate among familiar and unfamiliar people, faces, objects, places, family pets, and more.

Despite newborns' relative immaturity, they actively use their visual abilities to begin to make sense of and construct meaning from the world around them. However, other senses may be even more available to most infants at birth and may not require a "motor component" the way vision does; that is, visual tracking or following often requires movements such as head-turning, focusing of the eyes, maintaining head and neck control, and so forth.

The Vestibular Sense

Within the first 10–12 weeks of gestational age (that is, the time since conception), the fetus begins to respond to sensations of body movements and rotations through the vestibular sense. This sense arises from the semicircular canals in the inner ear (discussed in Chapter 2) and is important for the later development of balance and postural control (Eliot, 1999). At the time of a full-term birth (roughly 36–40 weeks), the vestibular system is already well developed, so that bouncing and other forms of motion convey sensations that are not only enjoyable to most infants, but are also beneficial for early brain development. In fact, these kinds of sensory experiences are thought to play a role in developing emotional, perceptual, and cognitive or learning abilities (Eliot, 1999). When children are deaf or hard of hearing due to differences or dysfunction in the inner ear, they have a somewhat increased risk of having some vestibular-based balance difficulties that can delay early motor skills like walking. Both parents and professionals have wondered whether providing supplementary vestibular stimulation might be advantageous for children who have any developmental delays, and there is some reason to believe that this could be the case. Increased opportunities for experiences that stimulate the vestibular sense seem to be particularly helpful for babies born prematurely. In some neonatal intensive care units, for example, tiny waterbeds that move and rock the infant whenever he moves are used to simulate the womb-like experience the premature baby might otherwise be missing. But benefits of experiences that stimulate the vestibular sense are not limited to babies who have some kind of birth or developmental difficulties. Almost all newborns usually cry less or can be calmed more readily if they are rocked, jiggled, or bounced—especially when they are in a state in which their behavior seems "disorganized" and difficult to interpret. (And such disorganized states are not uncommon during infancy.) Sometimes, the simple act of putting a baby to your shoulder in a semi-upright position has the same effect because, in addition to the physical contact, it is also stimulating to the vestibular system (Korner & Thoman, 1970, 1972). Consider the following example, as described by Dr. Lise Eliot (1999):

> Parents will do just about anything to stop the crying, and when Anna picks Timothy up, holds him over her shoulder, and gently jiggles him, he soon becomes "organized" again; his crying stops, his body relaxes, and for a brief time, he is highly alert—looking intently at the lamp behind Anna's back, then at the bright picture on the wall, and finally, when she moves him to a cradling position, straight into Anna's eyes. Indeed, infants who are comforted through vestibular stimulation show greater visual alertness than babies comforted in other ways. It's during these periods of quiet alertness that babies do their best learning, when they can most effectively absorb information about the world around them. (Eliot, 1999, p. 156)

Closely related to the vestibular system is *kinesthetic feedback*, which helps us to know where our body parts are located. This also begins in the womb, as can be illustrated by the familiar ultrasound images of the fetus sucking its thumb, but is a process that continues into later development (Slater, Field &, Hernandez-Reif, 2007). For example, as the older baby (around 4–5 months old) begins to reach for objects, she will use not only her vision but also her kinesthetic sense of where her arm is positioned in order to guide her hand movement. According to Slater and colleagues, essentially all physical-motor development during infancy relies on information from both of these senses: vestibular to provide a sense of balance and kinesthetic to inform the child about the positioning of specific body parts such as the limbs (Slater et al., 2007).

The Tactile Sense (Touch and Physical Contact)

This sense begins to develop within around 10 weeks after conception, when nerves on the skin start to convey information about touch; a short time later, the areas of the brain that receive and interpret sensations from various parts of the body begin to react to tactile contact. By the time of birth, most newborns can tell the difference between soft and rough textures, and they generally prefer those that are soft. They display reflexes that are elicited by touching certain areas of the body, such as stroking the sole of the foot (causing the toes to spread apart and then curl back inward). Another common reflex in newborns is grasping tightly with the fist and fingers—often to the delight of the father or sister whose own finger is being held. Again, this newborn is basically responding to the stimulation (touch, in this case) of the palm of the hand; with increasing pressure, the baby's grip seems to tighten even more.

For most babies, the mouth and hands are especially sensitive to touch, as can be seen when soft or hard objects are placed nearby or are touching the newborn. On a more social level, many babies respond well to skin-to-skin contact and gentle, repetitive touch, both of which often have a calming effect. For example, it has been found that gentle massage of the baby's limbs and torso can reduce stress and provide comfort (Drebohl & Fuhr, 2000; Field, 1995). Carrying or allowing very premature newborns to sleep nestled against the warm skin of an adult's chest—known as "kangaroo care"—is a practice often used in neonatal hospital nurseries to help soothe, promote growth, and enhance bonding. And, in many cultures around the world, almost constantly carrying or holding a baby is simply the way things are done—no one would think of putting a newborn down on a dusty desert floor or directly on the ground where the rest of the family and animals congregate! Therefore, babies in these cultures may experience more tactile contact (particularly with other humans) in their early lives than do those in many industrialized nations. (Notice that being carried also provides vestibular or movement stimulation.) It may be true that strollers and car seats also offer a certain amount of tactile stimulation for infants, but it is of a more "mechanical" nature rather than the result of direct skin-to-skin contact with other people.

Why Is Tactile Contact So Important?

As most parents quickly learn after their baby is born, gentle and repetitive touch can be very effective for soothing a fussy baby, but it also serves several other important functions. The skin, which receives all forms of touch the child may experience, is the largest sensory system of the human body and the first to fully mature. Tactile contact therefore plays an important role in early parent–child interactions and serves many functions such as comforting, calming, soothing, and even maintaining the child's alertness.

Although we may not normally think of touch as being an aspect of communication, it clearly does have a part to play in that system. Not only is the sense of touch already highly developed at birth, but the newborn also has more sensory nerve endings than adults, which means that, regardless of hearing ability, infants are especially receptive to touch as a form of communication. In many cultures, babies are carried, held, bounced, and passed from person to person almost constantly throughout the day, regardless of whether they are asleep or awake. We assume that this amount of tactile contact is not only a source of warmth, security, and social bonding, but that it also fosters the newborn infant's sense of being an important part of her community. In addition, those who are holding or carrying her (ranging from older siblings to much older grandparents) are also learning about little Mamitu's preferences, her soothability, her hunger and sleep cycles—simply by perceiving her activity level, vocalizations, and body movements. Touch is therefore a mutual event when it involves two *people* (as opposed to just touching a tree or the side of a crib), and both parties give and receive the sensations and create their own awareness of what this feeling means.

Being the recipient of tactile contact helps the young child learn about boundaries between self and others, thus contributing to the development of reciprocity when interacting and to effective social communication skills. This is particularly true for caregiver–infant pairs involving a deaf or hard-of-hearing baby: touch in these cases eventually becomes very important for attracting the infant's visual attention, letting her know that signs or gestures are forthcoming, and maintaining contact or reassuring the child that a caregiver is still present even when the baby is looking away. Interestingly, hearing as well as deaf parents of deaf or hard-of-hearing infants have been found to increase their use of touch during interactions, thereby compensating for the child's limited hearing (Paradis & Koester, 2015). Mothers and fathers commonly use tactile stimulation (touch) during face-to-face interactions with their babies, and this can facilitate the infants' alertness and desire to continue the interaction, as long as it is done in a sensitive manner.

In the industrialized world, it is not uncommon to observe the following sequence of behaviors when parents are interacting in a face-to-face position with their infant: first, the adult's gentle, playful touch leads to an infant's gaze or smile; this in turn leads to the parent's wide-eyed facial expression and vocalizations; this reaction is followed by the infant's eager visual attention; and so on. Parents naturally respond to these signals or "body language," which are the preverbal infant's earliest forms of expressive communication. This, in essence, sets the stage for *turn-taking*, a very important skill that promotes communication, language development, and early social exchanges. For deaf children in particular, their parents' use of the important sensory channel of touch helps in the process of learning to communicate in a visual-gestural modality, one step along the path to becoming an effective social partner.

Remember, however, that this pattern may not be observed as frequently in parts of the world where adults rarely engage in such efforts to communicate directly (i.e., face-to-face) with babies. Try to visualize a West African marketplace for example, where children are carried in a sling strapped to someone's back. In this case, it will most likely be other villagers of all ages who stop to admire the baby, stroking and patting but mostly talking to the mother or sibling who is carrying the infant. There is no lack of stimulation in this scene because the baby is clearly being exposed to constant touch, movement (requiring an early awareness of balance and muscle control), colorful sights, and lively sounds of the busy communal marketplace. This example serves as an important reminder that sensory stimulation rarely occurs in just one modality at a time—sights are often accompanied by sounds and even by vibrations (think of a car driving by the infant in a stroller and all of the senses that may be stimulated by this event). Thus, regardless of culture, home or family setting, hearing status, or other individual differences, infants are typically bathed in a variety of sensory stimulation that helps them to understand the world into which they are born.

The Sense of Taste

The sense of taste may begin to develop as early as 7 weeks after the baby is conceived, when taste buds on the tongue first appear. For the newborn, this sense is well enough developed that the mother's milk may be rejected after she's eaten a particularly spicy or pungent meal. However, it seems that when a mother eats a varied diet before the child is born, her baby is more likely to have varied taste buds and to accept new foods more readily after birth. (Of course, if the pregnancy causes a sensitive stomach or frequent queasiness, this may not be possible for some women.) Even in the last few weeks before birth, sweet tastes seem to be preferred by the fetus, and newborns can respond to differences between sweet, salty, sour, or bitter substances placed on the tongue. Their reactions are most vividly shown by their facial expressions (seen on ultrasound images), but certain tastes may also later induce relaxation and calming in the infant.

The Olfactory Sense (Smell)

As early as the 24th week of prenatal development, the fetus can detect odors in the surrounding fluid of the mother's womb, and, by the time it is born, the infant has a well-developed sense of smell (or olfaction)—including being able to recognize the smell of her own mother and preferring this, as associations are made between Mom's body and experiences of pleasure and comfort. Within the first 2 months after birth, the newborn expands her repertoire and learns to distinguish many more types and intensities of smell. Again, her active brain is making connections between pleasant/unpleasant aromas and pleasant/unpleasant experiences, thus creating long-term memory traces.

EXPANDING, FINE-TUNING, AND INTEGRATING EARLY SENSORY EXPERIENCES

After birth, the senses continue to develop and be refined through interactions with others and through stimulating experiences within the infant's environment. This is particularly important during the first 3 months, when the brain is most active in areas involved in processing sights, sounds, and touch. In recent decades, neuroscience researchers have made tremendous strides in advancing our understanding of how the human brain grows and develops both before and after birth. Much of this development depends on the child's experience, although genetic background admittedly plays an important role, too. Crucial to these experiences are interactions that take place within the context of the infant's social sphere—typically, within the family unit or surrounding community and culture. One of the most remarkable characteristics of the brain is its "plasticity," which allows it to adapt as the demands of the environment change or to different cultural expectations (Hawley & Gunnar, 2000). (See Chapter 5 for further details about brain development in the early years.)

Dr. Lawrence Rosenblum (2013) summarized research indicating that many of our senses actually work together in the human brain much more than had earlier been thought. Previously, scientists often described the brain as having distinctly different areas, each of which seemed responsible for specific tasks—seeing, hearing, tasting, and so forth. More recently, we have come to realize that the brain is actually much better integrated than this and that information from the various senses is constantly being merged and processed to form meaningful impressions. Perhaps there are important implications here for understanding and assisting individuals with various sensory challenges. For example, we know that the process of learning a language typically involves not only the ears, but also the eyes. In fact, the brain is more multisensory than previously thought, and there is a great deal of "cross-talk" among the senses, so that the brain's sensory regions are magnificently intertwined! Or, as Rosenblum says, it may be that "Our senses are always eavesdropping on one another and sticking their noses in one another's business" (p. 74). This is wonderful news for parents with deaf or hard-of-hearing babies: if the brain gives equal weight to sensory information coming in from touch, vision, physical movement, and from audition, then, clearly, there are advantages to providing stimulation or communication by relying on multiple sources of input rather than focusing exclusively on the sense that is not working efficiently.

Surely, direct experiences involving physical manipulations or contact with objects play an important role in the child's emerging ability to make sense of the world around him. However, another factor is equally if not more important: the role of *people* in the infant's social environment, their reactions to these events, and the messages they communicate to the infant about whether or not something should be approached or avoided, enjoyed or feared.

Sensing and Perceiving

The terms "sensation" and "perception" are often used interchangeably, but psychologists sometimes like to make a distinction between the two. Essentially, *sensation* refers to the process by which stimulation is received in the brain via the various sensory regions: in other words, brain cells are stimulated by sounds, sights, tastes, and so forth. But this is just the beginning of a much more complex process, one that involves interpreting, processing, or making sense out of these various inputs. This next step is called *perception* and is the more advanced or sophisticated part of the process. This will become more important as we discuss infants at somewhat older ages. To help clarify the difference, we offer the following example:

Two-week-old Rhula is happily lying on a blanket on the floor when her brother Omar bounds into the room, laughing and calling her name. With him is his best buddy, Nizar, who has not met little Rhula before. At first Rhula is startled by the sudden entrance of two rather boisterous preschoolers, as shown by her reflexive physical response: arms and legs are extended and then rapidly withdrawn as if clutching at something—Mom? big sister? the blanket?—for safety. Even her little fists are clenched, and her eyes are opened wide. Rhula's brain has registered the presence of Omar and Nizar by visually sensing their physical shape, feeling the vibrations of their footsteps, possibly hearing some sounds of their laughter and voices, and maybe even smelling their slightly damp socks. But she has not yet put all of these sensations together, maybe because she simply hasn't experienced them often enough in her short life. In other words, she cannot make the brain connections required to understand that Omar's voice belongs to her brother Omar, or that his rapid footsteps and the look of this tousled hair go together to form one complete "whole" person whom she'll learn to refer to as "Omar." This latter part of the process is called perception, and involves more of the brain's interpretation and creating meaning out of these innumerable sensory experiences.

Multimodal Communication

Within a short time after birth, infants change dramatically as they adapt to their new postnatal environment, regardless of their hearing status. They arrive already prepared to become part of their own social and linguistic environment and to be effective communicators. Similarly, parents are predisposed to support their infant's early developing skills, even though these efforts may be largely unconscious. Parents the world over use subtle, almost automatic behaviors to guide their infants in the processes of learning language, dealing with emotions, and participating as social partners in ways that are accepted in their culture (Koester, Papoušek & Smith-Gray, 2000; Papoušek & Papoušek, 1987).

One aspect of these behaviors that we have not yet addressed is that of *rhythmicity*, or the ways in which rhythms are incorporated into so many caregiving behaviors—talking, singing, rocking, bouncing, carrying, and, of course, *signing*. (When a deaf adult signs to a very young baby, the signs are likely to appear unusually large, slow, and rhythmic; this is actually quite appropriate given the infant's limited visual capacity that we described earlier.) In many cases, coordinated rhythmic patterns can be detected when an adult is engaging in a variety of behaviors simultaneously, such as walking at a certain pace while carrying the newborn, all the while patting the baby's back and gently bouncing her in a very soothing way. The voice may or may not be included, but if it is, then one may notice that the rhythm of the language is also well matched to that of the physical, nonverbal behaviors. Perhaps rhythmicity plays an important role in tying together this "bundle" of multimodal stimulation so that the newborn can make sense of it as readily as possible (Field, 1978; Koester & Lahti-Harper, 2010).

Thus, a crucial aspect of development in a deaf or hard-of-hearing child involves learning how to effectively understand the visual, tactile and vestibular features of communication, rather than relying primarily on auditory information. It follows logically then, that a crucial aspect of parenting a child with limited hearing involves effectively incorporating these sensory features into communication, either to supplement or substitute for auditory input. Consider, for example, the role that the various senses may play in early interactions and especially in prompting the visual attention of a young baby with limited hearing:

> *Tabitha, identified soon after birth as profoundly deaf in both ears, is becoming acquainted with her parents who both have hearing and little prior exposure to people who are deaf or hard of hearing. As a newborn, she seeks the warmth and protection provided by her parents*

when they hold her close for feeding, carrying, or playful interactions. With this physical contact comes soothing tactile stimulation as well as a connection with the rhythms of her caregivers' voices and heartbeats through the vibrations she can feel. What is missing, of course, are the melodies, pitches, and specific sounds in their vocalizations which she is unable to hear. In many instances, therefore, merely speaking to Tabitha will not prompt her visual attention. How do her parents get Tabitha's attention so that she will look at them and eventually smile in recognition and delight?

During these early weeks, they are likely to automatically rely primarily on vocal patterns such as calling her name when they enter the room, or referring to themselves and others similarly ("Hi, Tabitha! Can you look at Mommy? What do you see there in your crib? Do you see your Teddy Bear?"). Such narratives are only natural, and are in fact good indicators of parents who are making an admirable effort to engage with, entertain, and get to know their newborn. But the difficulty in this scenario should be obvious when Tabitha's hearing level is taken into account.

Gradually then, her parents will need to supplement their vocalizations with increased amounts of intentional tactile contact, visual and vestibular (movement and balance) stimulation. These may include waiting to vocalize until after they have gained Tabitha's attention by gently stroking her arm, moving close to her, and exaggerating their facial expressions. Each of these actions helps ensure that the gestures and other behaviors that so often occur along with vocalizations are easily seen by the infant.

Through many similar interactions with their caregivers, infants learn how to express their interests, take turns, and maintain mutual interest or focus on topics with others. For parents and other caregivers, it is therefore important to use as many sensory channels as possible when communicating with a deaf or hard-of-hearing child; as discussed in the previous sections, even if a child cannot hear, she can probably receive messages through a variety of other senses that are available from birth.

Observations of deaf mothers have shown that they often incorporate exaggerated facial expressions as well as close physical and tactile contact into their parent–infant interactions—and that their babies love this!

> These exaggerated and happy facial expressions, plus gestures or signs, make the mothers very interesting for babies to look at—and the babies begin to learn that it is important and pleasant to watch their mothers. If hearing parents increase these kinds of communication behaviors, they will make their own communications more interesting to their deaf or hard of hearing baby, thus making it easier to keep the baby's attention. (Spencer, 2001, p. 7)

"BUT WHAT IS MY BABY TRYING TO TELL ME?"

The rhythm and pacing of behaviors also play an important role in early interaction, in addition to the use of various modalities. Being responsive to an infant means following the child's lead, being tuned into her signals, and interpreting them accurately, as illustrated in the following examples:

Where is baby Trevor looking? Maybe he's staring with great concentration at Grandma's shiny, dangling earrings, even wrinkling his brow as if curious about the light being reflected in such interesting ways when Grandma moves her head. When Grandma's face becomes animated with a broad smile and lively expressions, Trevor's gaze suddenly focuses more on her mouth and eyes. Compared to the baby whose drowsy gaze is slowly cycling around the room as his eyelids begin to open and close—sure signs of approaching sleep—Trevor's patterns of looking at specific features of his environment indicate interest and mental activity, his way of exploring both the physical and social world around him.

Next, let's consider the baby's own physical activities: Are Trevor's arms and legs moving back and forth rhythmically in excitement? If so, this might mean either that he's interested or that he's overwhelmed by too much stimulation. Or is this an early, primitive effort at matching Dad's peek-a-boo or "The Wheels on the Bus" hand movements? (In our own research, we were somewhat surprised at the different ways in which deaf and hard-of-hearing babies' rhythmic hand and arm movements were interpreted by either deaf or hearing parents: the hearing mothers often reported being concerned that their baby was "hyperactive," whereas the deaf mothers were more likely to see this as a positive indication of their baby's eventual sign language skills!)

It's important to pay attention to these physical activity signals in case Trevor is becoming agitated, anxious, or overstimulated. By removing him from the sources of noise, visual, or social activities around him, caregivers may be able to avoid a complete "meltdown" and help Trevor settle back into a state of calm alertness. On the other hand, if his excitement escalates, and he begins thrashing around or fussing, parents may find that rhythmic stimulation such as rocking, swaddling to prevent Trevor's arms and legs from flailing around and adding to his agitation, or providing a pacifier or feeding may all be helpful interventions. In such a situation, what does Trevor's facial expression say about whether he's happy or on the brink of tears?

Many babies in the first few months seem to be perpetually serious, carefully studying this strange new world into which they've been born. Smiles that result from pleasant social interactions don't usually occur until a few months after birth, but other facial expressions can give us important clues about what the newborn is feeling: Is his face puckered up in a grimace, indicating pain, discomfort, or fear? Is it relaxed, and are the facial muscles smooth, with open eyes and an alert expression? If so, you can take this as a sign that he's in a state of readiness to learn, to interact, and to participate.

Has Trevor been given time by other people around him to "set the topic" or to express his own interest in objects and activities? In general, sensitive parents frequently respond to and follow the child's interests, rather than redirecting or always being in "teacher mode." These responsive parenting behaviors facilitate language development, but will also help Trevor form positive emotional attachments to his caregivers, as will be seen when we describe social-emotional development in later chapters. Is he looking away, letting you know that he needs time to regroup? Again, this may be Trevor's way of saying "slow down—there's too much going on for me right now!," so it's important to watch for and respect this. Remember, babies need "down time," too!

Now that we have described the various sensory systems of the newborn and how they develop pre- and postnatally, let's consider some of the variability seen in individual babies and their responses to stimulation and to their social environment. Of course, we all have periods of time, cycling throughout each day, when we are alert and awake as compared to drowsy and less receptive to outside stimulation or events. The same is true of infants, but the length of these awake phases tends to be much shorter for the young baby who needs lots of sleep; therefore, the variability during a given day may seem to be greater. These alternating "states" of rest and activity can even be detected in the movements of the fetus, beginning as early as 26 weeks (Fogel, 2009). Those who study infant development like to think of these states as reflecting an infant's internal arousal or physical activation level, but it's also easy to describe these in terms that are more familiar to most parents and caregivers:

- *Quiet sleep*: regular breathing, little movement, eyes closed and still
- *Active sleep*: eyes closed, but maybe flickering (rapid eye movement or REM sleep), irregular breathing, and occasional startles or jerky body movements
- *Drowsy*: eyes may open and close, physically more active than in sleep states, breathing is faster
- *Quiet and alert*: little physical activity, but eyes are open and scanning, showing interest in people and surroundings
- *Active and alert*: body may be moving, baby is less attentive or responsive to environment, eyes aren't focused as well on things in the environment or on people
- *Crying*: may be overtired or overstimulated, body is moving actively, breathing is rapid, vocal and facial expressions of distress/discomfort

There are several important points to be made regarding these infant states. First, there is a great deal of variability among individual babies in terms of how long they remain in each state (on average), how often they cycle through some or all of these within a typical day, and whether they tend to prefer one state over another. These individual differences can be influenced by culture or inherited tendencies, by gender and health status (for example, infants with digestive problems such as colic may spend more time in the crying state, to the dismay of all around them), and by the ways in which their caregivers respond to these signals. Even the child's position—constrained in a car seat, carried on big sister's back in a cloth sling, put down for "tummy time" on the floor—may play a role, depending on the baby's own comfort and need to either rest or be active.

Another message here, as anyone who has spent much time with infants knows, is that the simple matter of an infant's state of alertness or arousal can have a powerful effect on other people who happen to be nearby. Sometimes we wait eagerly for the baby to wake up in a playful, interactive mood so we can see that big smile and inquisitive eyes; other times, we will do almost anything possible to get him to quiet down and fall asleep, especially after a long period of fussiness. How is a parent to know what these signals mean? Although reading parenting books may provide some useful tips, it's going to largely be a matter of trial and error before a parent figures out exactly what a particular baby's body language, eye gaze, activity level, and vocalizations mean—and how he responds to the parent's behaviors as well. (Some infants, for example, begin to gnaw on their own fists when they're hungry, whereas others may develop specific signals such as pulling at their ears when they're becoming tired.) There is no evidence, by the way, that the amount of time spent in various states by deaf or hard-of-hearing babies differs on average from that of hearing babies.

As we will explore further in the next chapter, the early parent–infant relationship is a kind of "dance" in which each partner influences the other, and each one gradually becomes better able to read the other's signals and respond appropriately. In these early months, it is usually the caregiver who must take the initiative or be responsible for observing the baby's state, his interests, and indications of his needs and then make the appropriate adjustments to meet these needs. The good news is that this process is not affected very much by whether or not a child has limited hearing, and most parents do just fine in detecting and interpreting their baby's signals accurately over the first few months—even though it may sometimes feel like it takes much longer than that!

"GET A GRIP, PLEASE!" HELPING INFANTS REGULATE THEIR EMOTIONAL RESPONSES

One of the most important tasks in terms of infants' social-emotional development is to find ways of managing emotional reactions to the many exciting, joyful, or disturbing events in their daily lives (Koester & McCray, 2011). Caregivers play an important role in this process by demonstrating strategies for *self-regulation* that can later be used by the developing child. Infants need these important messages and feedback if they are to learn effective ways of dealing with their own emotions and of regaining equilibrium when they become overly excited, tired, or upset. In the first few months (as well as later), newborns observe and experience the many ways in which their parents react to both difficult and positive experiences. Through body language, touch, vocal and facial expressions, and other overt parental behaviors, the infant learns about appropriate emotional displays that are acceptable in her family and in her community. Of course, this is a process that will continue well past the first months and years of the child's life. With increasing development, language skills will be important aids in this aspect of learning.

Like most other aspects of an infant's early experiences, this ability to modify and regulate emotions develops within the context of parent–infant interactions, such as when parents help babies reduce their negative emotions by soothing or offering a distraction. Caregivers also reinforce positive emotions, model culturally appropriate ways of expressing emotions, and influence how infants interpret situations. By paying attention to infants' emotion-related behaviors (such as the muscle tone, facial expressions, and quality of vocalizations described earlier), parents help infants learn to regulate their reactions to experiences. This is a reciprocal process—a two-way street—in which parental reactions contribute to the intensity of signals that the infant must produce in order to get her needs met. Some adults respond to an infant's signals only when they reach a particular intensity, while others have a lower tolerance for crying and respond as soon as they detect distress. Infants then learn which signals (and at what level) they can use most effectively to get their needs met.

WHAT MAKES UP A HUMAN INFANT?

It's an interesting exercise to imagine what you would need if you wanted to "build" a human infant. What do you think would be essential to include, and what might be simply desirable? Are all of the senses we have described necessary, or can some of them compensate for decreased functioning in another area? In the context of this book, the answer should be clear: the absence (or limitation) of hearing may diminish the infant's responsiveness to a caregiver's voice, but the same baby is likely to have visual skills that will help him identify and respond positively to Mom and Dad. Other sensory functions, such as sensitivity to touch and motion, also benefit an infant with limited hearing. Drs. Roberta Golinkoff and Kathy Hirsh-Pasek have commented about this, noting that an infant's ability to recognize and respond to its mother's voice is "only an advantage, not a necessity. Babies born to deaf parents haven't been given much verbal stimulation as fetuses. Babies who are adopted hear a different voice after they are born from the one that they heard in the womb....Babies are known for their versatility and adaptiveness to any number of different environments. When nature builds a baby, she builds in multiple routes the baby can use for later growth and success" (Golinkoff & Hirsh-Pasek, 1999, pp. 22–23).

This last point is vital, and it is one reason for including all the sensory channels and their early developmental patterns in this chapter. Most children, whether deaf, hard of hearing, or hearing, exhibit preferences for certain kinds of stimulation (for example, liking lots of bouncing and touch) or will respond more to certain sensory experiences (perhaps being more reactive to strong tastes than to smells). Regardless of hearing levels, the important fact to remember is that each baby is an individual—we must learn to read each child's unique behaviors and cues, just as he must eventually learn to read the signals of his caregivers, family members, and peers and to communicate his needs effectively to others.

SUMMARIZING KEY IDEAS

A newborn's senses have been developing while she is still in the womb, and, at birth, she has already experienced the stimulation of almost all sensory channels including taste and smell, touch and movement, hearing (if it is developing), and vision (to a very limited degree). The following key ideas presented in this chapter relate to early sensory functioning and ways that parents and caregivers can best reinforce babies' early sensory, communication, and social-emotional development:

- The development and refinement of sensory capacities occur rapidly in the early months, but this does not happen in a vacuum. Biological maturation in the sense organs is reinforced and promoted by stimulation and experiences during the early days and months of life.
- Babies receive information from all available senses, and that information is rapidly combined and integrated. When one or another sense is limited, information from others can supplement and, in some instances, substitute for it. Visual, tactile, and vestibular senses may be especially important avenues of interaction and communication when a baby has limited hearing.
- At least as important as inborn sensory functioning is the way in which caregivers respond to an individual child's needs and abilities to use various senses. In the early months, physical contact, touch, rhythmic movement—cuddling—are important for the development of all babies. But individual preferences and sensitivities are noticeable even at birth.
- Parents and other caregivers are involved in a learning process just as the infant is, and they are also adjusting to many unknowns about their baby's unique behaviors. Parents' ability to accurately "read" and interpret their baby's signals is influenced by characteristics of the baby as well as their own experiences. Some babies are easier

to "read" than others. In general, hearing status does not affect this characteristic, although health and related difficulties may do so.

- Because adults tend to communicate with babies using multiple sensory modalities, parents of deaf and hard-of-hearing babies can meet their early needs for security and positive interactions. Parents and other caregivers should be alert, however, to the benefits of gently boosting visual, tactile (touch), and vestibular stimulation in supporting these babies' development.

In the next chapter, our focus shifts a bit more toward parent and caregiver behaviors that effectively support the development of babies and toddlers during these earliest months of life. It is important to keep in mind that parent and baby act as a *system*. That is, the characteristics of each one influence the behaviors of the other in a spiraling, mutually reinforcing manner.

4 Early Parenting Goals
NURTURING AND SUPPORTING DEVELOPMENT IN THE FIRST 3 MONTHS

QUESTIONS TO CONSIDER

- What behaviors give us clues that newborns are already tuned into their social environment and ready to interact and communicate with others?
- How does the ability to communicate effectively influence the development of deaf and hard-of-hearing babies and toddlers?
- How might parental stress and hearing parents' concerns about their ability to communicate with their child affect early parent–infant interactions?
- What are some examples of responsive and sensitive caregiving that is often intuitive rather than consciously planned?
- How might a child's tendencies to respond in unique ways (for example, activity level, sociability, excitability, and predictability) affect the behaviors of caregivers?
- What characteristics of parents are particularly responsive when interacting with deaf or hard-of-hearing infants?
- What kinds of parenting behaviors contribute to the development of communication, social skills, and emotional attachments of infants with limited hearing?

Infancy is a distinctive period, a major transition, and a formative phase in human development. Infants assume few responsibilities and are not at all self-reliant. Rather, parents have central roles to play in infants' survival, social growth, emotional maturity, and cognitive maturation. With the birth of a baby, a parent's life is forever changed. The pattern that these changes assume, in turn, shapes the experiences of infants and, with time, the people they become. Parent and child chart that course together. Infancy is a starting point of life for both infant and parent. (Bornstein, 1995, p. 30)

As we saw in Chapter 3, many significant changes occur within the infant's first few months after birth—changes that profoundly affect both parents and infants, regardless of their hearing status. When infants first greet the world outside the mother's womb, they are already prepared to pick up cues about their social and physical environments and to learn how to communicate with others. Similarly, most parents are prepared to assist the newborn in developing these early skills, although they may not always be aware that they are doing this. Of course, even while a child is developing prenatally, the parents have already contributed significantly to their fetus's innate, genetically determined characteristics. It may be less apparent during those prenatal months, but many environmental influences (for example, the mother's nutrition, her health, her level of stress, or her intake of medications) are also already profoundly influencing the developing child.

Following birth, the child continues to be exposed to innumerable external influences, such as the quality of air and diet, stimulation from others, and exposure to bacteria or toxic substances. Each of these in its own way, either positive or negative, can play a major role in determining the individual child's health and development in all realms—physical, mental, social, and communicative. If either the parent or infant is ill, has special learning styles or perceptual needs, or is under extraordinary stress, the normally expected course of development may be altered. Therefore, the developmental charts we provide in this book, along with those often seen in pediatric clinics, portray primarily what we expect to see in those cases in which there are no especially exceptional circumstances, and in which development is likely to proceed along fairly predictable pathways. Nevertheless, the focus of this book in general is on infants and toddlers with limited hearing; in this chapter, then, we will explore in greater depth the characteristics of parents who interact with deaf and hard-of-hearing children in particularly sensitive and responsive ways. Our hope is to provide examples that might be useful for those involved with caring for deaf and hard-of-hearing infants. We will also describe characteristics that may be evident in any child but that can exert a strong influence over the ways in which others respond (for example, the baby who is particularly sensitive to changes, the one who is easily excited or frightened, or the one who is typically easy-going and calm).

Universal Newborn Hearing Screening (UNHS) in the United States and other countries has led to a significant change in the age at which an infant's limited hearing is now typically detected, as discussed in Chapters 1 and 2. As part of these advances, early intervention professionals need to be more knowledgeable than ever about the dynamics of interactions when the infant partner is deaf or hard of hearing. Of course, there is still much to be learned about the development of communication, social skills, emotional attachments, and effective socialization of infants in these situations.

Most would agree that "normal" development in early childhood depends a great deal on the ability to communicate effectively. In the case of deaf or hard-of-hearing infants, as well as those who have typical hearing, evidence indicates that those who become the most competent socially and cognitively are those who are able to participate actively in language-based exchanges early on. It is within these interactions that infants gain knowledge and objective facts about their surroundings; they observe and eventually imitate the behaviors of people in their social environment, and they gradually develop a sense of who they are in relation to these others (Vaccari & Marschark, 1997). The process remains the same with deaf and hard-of-hearing babies whose parents are deaf, those with hearing parents who are learning to sign, or those whose parents use primarily spoken language and visual signals like facial expressions and gestures to communicate with them. In the earliest stages of postnatal life, both parents and infants gradually become "attuned" to each other, developing a sense of synchrony and reciprocity in their interactions. These interactions do not necessarily need to involve vocalizations (although they often do, even with deaf and hard-of-hearing infants) because caregivers typically incorporate other sensory modalities such as visual cues, tactile contact, and rhythmic movement.

If an infant is identified as deaf or hard of hearing soon after birth, the news may be received by hearing parents as upsetting (and, of course, by far the majority of deaf and hard-of-hearing children *are* born to hearing parents). The stress that can result from this identification can lead to parent or caregiver feelings of helplessness, concern, and inadequacy about their ability to communicate with a deaf child. These feelings, in turn, can lead to interactions that appear to be less "fluent" and smooth between caregivers and the deaf or hard-of-hearing infant. For example, hearing parents have sometimes been described as less flexible in their interactions with an infant with limited hearing, and their well-intended efforts to guide the infant's learning may even be seen by others as overly intrusive. In some cases, parents who are simply trying very hard to accommodate to their infant's needs may appear to others to be too directive, particularly in this early postnatal period. Increasingly, however, there are reports that contradict these earlier ones, and hearing mothers are more often described as showing "emotional availability" (Biringen & Robinson, 1991; Easterbrooks & Biringen, 2000; Pipp-Siegel & Biringen, 1998) and being responsive to babies regardless of their hearing status. This is one indication that early intervention services are playing a truly supportive role for families.

Following the birth of a deaf or hard-of-hearing baby, hearing parents may find that they are faced with many unexpected decisions that complicate the joys of welcoming a newborn into the family. Some are decisions that can be delayed until the child is older, but some are more urgent. For example, these might include considerations regarding the use of spoken versus signed communication in the home, when the child should be fitted with hearing aids, and what kind of child care will be most appropriate if needed. It should be remembered, however, that these decisions may be revisited frequently, revised, or even reversed altogether as the child grows and the parents become more aware of his capabilities in terms of language and communication. Later decisions regarding the type of educational environment parents prefer for their deaf child and exposure to or integration into available deaf communities may be influenced greatly by popular opinion and media coverage of the controversies surrounding them. Thus, for hearing parents, the time following identification of limited hearing in their newborn may be difficult and confusing, especially if they have had little or no previous experience or interactions with people who are deaf.

For deaf parents, the situation can be strikingly different: knowing that their infant shares their own hearing status sometimes leads to a sense of relief and of feeling well-equipped to relate to a child who shares their communicative style. Perhaps as a result of this, and as a result of their own sensitivity to visual communication, many deaf parents have been shown to easily foster their infant's visual needs from birth onward by incorporating more strategies involving vision and touch rather than relying primarily on vocalizations and hearing. Of course, like hearing parents, those who are deaf vary in attitudes, skills, and parenting behaviors from person to person and family to family—so it is never appropriate to expect certain kinds of parenting approaches based on hearing status alone.

RESPONSIVE CAREGIVING: WHAT IS SENSITIVE PARENTING?

As discussed in the previous chapter, human newborns are already very social creatures. They may show surprisingly strong preferences from birth onward, as seen in the contrast between baby Adam, who loves to be held close and snuggled, and baby Kim, who simply prefers to have her limbs free and unrestrained—even pajamas or a soft jacket will set her off in a frenzy of kicking and bawling! Both of these newborns are ready and eager to be social partners, however, as shown by their response to the faces, voices, and many other forms of stimulation they encounter every day in their social world. These important behaviors help the so-called helpless newborn become a participating member of his or her family;

however, support from caregivers is also needed to allow these competencies to develop and become more advanced.

The Concept of Intuitive Parenting

Through those seemingly endless repetitions of peek-a-boo, bedtime stories, labeling objects, and mimicry, parents help the infant learn to maintain emotional stability, take part in interactions with others, and participate as a social partner. The notion of *intuitive parenting* is useful for understanding many of the processes that take place during interactions between parents and infants (Papoušek & Papoušek, 1987). That is, many caregiving behaviors that occur quite naturally between most parents and their infants actually serve very important functions: they support the early development of the immature infant and increase the likelihood that the child will have positive outcomes. Other than feeding, changing diapers, bathing, and putting an infant to sleep, what are some of these important parenting behaviors that we so often overlook? How do caregivers adjust their own behaviors and ways of communicating so that they are appropriate for a newborn with so little prior experience in the world of human beings? Here are a few examples to help illustrate how this often occurs in general. These will be followed by a more detailed description of how this applies in the case of deaf or hard-of-hearing infants:

- *Infant-directed communication*: If you have ever had a chance to visit newborns and their parents soon after birth, you probably noticed that, even during these earliest interactions, parents seem to want to create a dialogue with an as-yet totally nonverbal being. Adults seem ready to interpret any of the newborn's behaviors (yawning, stretching, opening or closing the eyes) as indications that the baby is already participating in that dialogue. And even though the infant is clearly not expected to contribute vocally at this immature stage (except perhaps for crying), adults nevertheless adjust the pitch, tonality, and rhythms of their own vocalizations in ways that show us just how well they are already tuned in to the needs and sensory abilities of a newborn infant. This increased variability helps the newborn pick out language that is directed toward him rather than to someone else in the room, and it also helps him know when to pay attention to this "infant-directed" communication (sometimes called "motherese" or "parentese"). And of course, modifications in sign language are also seen when fluent adults use this visual-gestural communication with infants or young children. We will return to this point in greater detail later in this chapter.

- *Imitation*: Caregivers also seem to love to reproduce or "mirror" the baby's actions, whether these are gestures or vocalizations, waving the arms, or making funny faces. Again, this is thought to facilitate infant learning on a variety of levels. This kind of imitation helps the infant understand, in a very basic way, how relationships work, how their own actions are interpreted, and what those actions might mean to others. By imitating the infant, responding to those behaviors we find amusing, appealing, or evidence of the baby's growing skills, we can therefore reinforce them. The message to the child is that his or her behaviors have been noticed (not ignored) and that someone else thinks they are important or entertaining enough to respond to with similar actions. An infant who is growing up in an environment lacking this kind of responsiveness from others may fail to develop the appropriate social skills expected in his or her family and culture. Fortunately, this occurs only rarely; when it does seem to be occurring, professionals who are trained to watch for such patterns can bring them to the parents' attention, sensitively modeling more responsive behaviors and supporting the parents' efforts to interact with their newborn more effectively.

- *Visual aspects of early interactions*: Another important intuitive parenting behavior can be seen by noticing how adults modify the visual distance between themselves and a very young infant with whom they are interacting. It would be highly unusual in most situations for two adults to interact face-to-face in such close proximity as we usually do with newborns! Although we tend to stand back at a greater distance when simply watching a baby, particularly if the child is not watching us in return, the picture changes dramatically when we want to "engage" with or communicate with a newborn. In that case, most adults will use a much closer "dialogue distance" (as close as 8–10 inches from the baby's face) to communicate with an infant who is alert and indicates he's ready to interact. Interestingly, it just so happens that this is exactly within the newborn's visual range until he or she becomes able to focus on objects at greater distances—usually by around 6 months (Eliot, 1999). Some researchers (e.g., Prendergast and McCollum, 1996) have found that deaf mothers are particularly responsive to their infant's eye contact, which is often a signal that the baby is ready for interactions to begin.

Infants learn, even through these earliest interactions with their caregivers, that they can initiate topics (by letting others know their interests, their likes and dislikes), they can keep these activities going, they can begin to take turns, and they can influence their caregivers in many different ways. For infants with severe to profound hearing levels, developing effective interactive skills early in life may depend on their caregivers' sensitivity to the infant's visual attention and needs and the use of a variety of sensory modalities when communicating with the infant.

It is important to recognize that parenting behaviors are also influenced by the infant's own signals indicating alertness, attention, emotional state, and tolerance level. (For example, recall our discussion in Chapter 3 about infant states of alertness.) What can we tell by watching the baby's muscle tone, the direction of his eye gaze, or the rhythmic pumping of his arms and legs? Is the message one of excitement or fatigue, of calmness or becoming upset? How we interpret these signals will greatly influence how sensitively we respond to the infant's body language—his primary way of communicating at this early stage. Of course, supportive caregiving continues to be found in situations in which the child is ill, premature, undernourished, born with a disability, and so forth. Parents who are deaf often provide good models of intuitive behaviors that are well-suited to the special perceptual and developmental needs of an infant with limited hearing. Remember, though, that it is also entirely possible for *hearing parents* of deaf and hard-of-hearing children to develop alternative interaction patterns that are just as well-suited to the needs of their child—including increasing their physical contact, visible gestures, eye contact, and lively facial expressions.

Infant-Directed Signed or Spoken Communication

As we have seen, most adults seem to make an effort to initiate a "dialogue" even when interacting with the tiniest of newborns; almost any response by the baby is readily interpreted as a potential contribution to that social event. A sneeze, a burp, a turn of the head—all may result in commentary by the caregiver or a humorous exclamation about the infant's state and capabilities. True, the newborn clearly is not expected to respond in kind at this immature stage. Nevertheless, adults frequently adjust their vocalizations or their signed language in ways that indicate just how well they are already tuned in to the needs and abilities of their baby. When speaking to or commenting on a newborn's behavior, for example, hearing adults using "babytalk" or "motherese" incorporate patterns that would be considered quite strange and bizarre if they were directed to another adult. For example, speech to an infant is typically slower than other communication, its form is greatly simplified, and it involves higher pitch and greater variability than heard in most other human dialogues.

Imagine the following scene in which 4-week-old Devin has just awakened from a nap; his mother hears him moving in his crib, and, as she approaches, he opens his eyes as if to greet her. Mom's vocal response has a dramatic sing-song quality, with many words emphasized and repeated, and she uses a much higher pitch than if she were talking to an older child:

> *"Well, HI THERE! Did my sweetie have a good nap? Did you have a good nap? Yes you did, you had a GOOD nap, didn't you? You slept a LONG, long time! Yes, my sweetie slept and slept and SLEPT, didn't he? And your Teddy was right there with you—right next to Devin—both of you sleeping and sleeping and SLEEPING, such a long, long time!"*

Striking parallels can be found in the ways in which signing deaf parents modify their signed communication to an infant. For example, deaf parents have been shown to include many highly expressive visual, tactile, and facial components, particularly when signing to an infant. Deaf parents using sign may also tap on or stroke their babies when starting to sign to them, beginning early to help the baby know when and where communication will be happening. Such strategies, used so often without conscious thought by deaf parents, help to ensure that the child does not miss part of the message. Other features of infant-directed signed "motherese" involve:

- much repetition (similar to vocal "motherese")
- highly animated facial expressions (also like vocal "motherese")
- larger than usual hand movements
- making the signs directly on an object and within the infant's visual field
- producing signs slowly and holding them longer than usual
- physically orienting the infant for better visual attention
- often signing directly on the infant's face or body

(Erting, Prezioso, & Hynes, 1994; Maestes y Moores, 1980; Meadow-Orlans, Spencer, & Koester, 2004; Spencer, Bodner-Johnson, & Gutfreund, 1992).

For interactions with most deaf or hard-of-hearing infants to be successful, shared visual attention must be established. Although deaf parents may seem to accommodate to this need almost automatically, for hearing parents, the task is likely to be less intuitive; therefore, guidance from professionals and from deaf parents and other deaf adults can be very beneficial. Hearing parents should be reassured, however, that this is mostly just a matter of becoming more conscious, more aware of their baby's perceptual needs, and then practicing the strategies that are most useful when communicating with deaf and hard-of-hearing children. When multiple caregivers or family members interact with a baby on a regular basis, they can all benefit from being "coached" about getting attention and using multiple modes when interacting and communicating with the baby.

Supporting Optimal Social-Emotional Development in Infants

Now let's return to the imitations—mimicking a child's own behaviors, facial expressions, vocalizations and gestures—so often observed when adults interact with babies regardless of hearing status. During these exchanges, the infant receives feedback that the other person is paying close attention to him, that the partner is engaged and responding to his actions, and that by continuing to behave in this way more interactions are likely to follow. Without this kind of give-and-take—one person behaving in a certain way and the other person imitating—the infant could be left in a social and emotional vacuum with no one to provide that "mirror" that says "I like what you're doing—you're funny and cute, and I'd love to see you make that face again!" Imitation can therefore reinforce or enhance certain infant behaviors as the caregiver responds and lets the baby know which sounds or sights are most appealing and appropriate in the eyes of others. In addition, some researchers (Carpenter, Uebel, & Tomasello, 2013) have found that when adults mimic a toddler's behaviors (as long as it's not done in a teasing way), the child is more likely to respond in a prosocial manner—for example, a toddler may help the adult pick up something that has dropped. Although this relates primarily to older children, it is nevertheless an indication of the important role that imitation plays in the socialization of the very young. (We have also found that older infants and toddlers who initially refuse to engage in an activity—such as an assessment, for example—often join in happily if the adult begins to imitate the child's actions.)

Another key aspect of a deaf or hard-of-hearing child's development is learning through the visual features of the environment (Spencer, Swisher, & Waxman, 2004). Even from the early days of life, deaf or hard-of-hearing infants face the challenge of needing to include in their visual attention both caregivers' communications and objects or events in the environment. Deaf parents have been found to be particularly responsive to their infant's eye gaze, and, similarly, by around 1 year of age, their infants have been shown to spend longer than usual periods of time gazing at their parents. These mothers and fathers sometimes appear to be "instructing" the child about where to look and when to watch for communication that's meant for him. For example:

> *Two-month-old baby Lucas is staring at the cuddly brown teddy bear in his crib and seems intrigued by its large eyes and upturned mouth. Dad, standing beside the crib, notices this and picks up the teddy bear, slowly bringing it toward his own face so that Lucas follows it with his eyes. As soon as the two make eye contact, Dad smiles broadly, makes the sign for "bear," shakes the toy to maintain Lucas' attention, and then moves the teddy bear slowly in an arc past the baby's face to elicit more visual following.*

In this example, not only has Dad given a basic lesson in vocabulary by signing "bear" while Lucas is looking at the object being labeled, but he has skillfully used social signals and emotional responses to reinforce Lucas' attention to both the object and parent. Again, it is important to note that this scene (and others of a similar nature) is one that can very easily be replicated by deaf and hearing parents alike. Once a hearing parent becomes aware of and tuned in to a baby's special need for visual and/or tactile input during communication, these kinds of interactions will become more natural and more frequent—all of which will be to the advantage of the baby.

What Message Is My Baby Sending when She Turns Away?

One important indication of an infant's attention is the simple act of turning away from the social partner or from an object of interest. What is the result of this when the baby has limited hearing? By turning his gaze away from another person, the deaf infant essentially cuts off or eliminates access to that person's social responses. Because flexible switching of visual attention cannot be expected to occur until later in the first year of life, at this early stage parents must learn to accommodate the infant's attention while beginning to provide guided experiences (like that of Lucas's dad in the example above) that will promote eventual establishing of shared attention. Most hearing parents are accustomed to vocalizing simultaneously while demonstrating or drawing attention to objects, which is effective if the infant has sufficient ability to hear the vocalizations (Vaccari & Marschark, 1997). When hearing is significantly limited, however, different approaches must be used.

There are several ways in which caregivers respond to this unique situation with a deaf or hard-of-hearing infant. In many cases, parents wait a bit—allowing the baby or toddler to turn back to them when ready. In other cases, we have observed behaviors such as signing/gesturing within the child's field of vision or holding the baby in a position so that his face is turned toward the parent, thus ensuring that both the object or event of interest and the visible language about that object are in close physical proximity. We have also seen sensitive deaf and hearing parents move their own bodies so as to be within the baby's existing visual attention focus.

> Swisher . . . argued that hearing parents of deaf children need to do more than just learn to sign; they need to adapt their habitual communication behaviors to meet the vision-related needs of their children. Early on, mothers need to take the responsibility for "orchestrating" such interactions, waiting for the child's attention before beginning to sign and trying to maintain visual attention for the duration of the message. (Vaccari & Marschark, 1997, p. 794)

It is true that hearing parents with deaf or hard-of-hearing infants face special (but certainly not insurmountable) challenges: they must use communication behaviors that both parent and child can understand and use effectively. This will be the foundation upon which the child's later social, emotional, and intellectual skills will be built. Regardless of hearing status, any parent–infant dyad that lacks an effective means of mutual communication will experience ongoing struggles as they search for a satisfying and emotionally secure relationship. The sense of touch may be of special importance in building such a relationship with babies with limited hearing.

"I Like It when You Hold and Cuddle Me, Mommy!"

Of all the sensory systems in the human body, the sense of touch (as discussed in Chapter 3) matures the earliest. Tactile contact therefore plays important roles and serves many developmental functions, particularly during the early months of life. It is an important component of many parental efforts to comfort, calm, soothe, or even to maintain the infant's alertness. In addition, tactile contact helps the newborn become aware of the boundaries between self and other, of the difference between "touching" and "being touched," and of the emotional messages that can be conveyed by tactile contact that is either gentle or rough (Figure 4.1).

One aspect of touch that has not been adequately explored or explained is its role in communication, which is of particular relevance when thinking about deaf and hard-of-hearing infants. For example, caregivers can use this highly salient sensory channel to help the baby learn to attend, respond to, and eventually use visual and gestural (or signed) communication effectively. Often, rhythmically patterned taps and strokes are used by deaf parents to serve the same functions as variations in child-directed vocalizations—that is, to express emotions and to redirect or obtain visual attention. Understanding that touch is an important component of visual-gestural communication may come

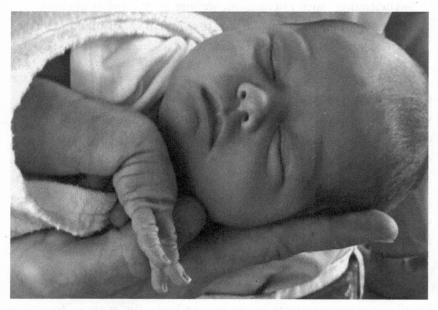

Figure 4.1 Touching and being touched can be calming and reassuring. (Photo courtesy of Lonsdale Green. Reprinted with permission.)

quite naturally for a deaf parent but may require more conscious effort on the part of a hearing one. For example, just as hearing parents exaggerate the pitch of their voice when speaking to an infant in "motherese," deaf parents may emphasize the ways they touch the infant's body to alert her that signed communication is forthcoming. Another important function of touch with a deaf or hard-of-hearing child is to maintain contact, providing reassurance that the caregiver is still there even when the child has looked away. Hearing parents often can accomplish this with a hearing baby simply by continuing to talk when the baby has turned away. But they, too, are likely to spontaneously keep a hand on a baby's tummy to signal "I'm still here."

Even early communications are two-way. The infant will, although not consciously, send subtle cues back to the parent about which forms and intensities of touch are most appreciated and pleasurable, most soothing and reassuring. In the first 3 months, parents are actively learning about their new baby, their relationship, and which behavior strategies are most effective given their child's temperament and preferences. In other words, as part of this *bidirectional* nature of social interactions (the idea of a *two-way* street), babies do in fact train their parents: the infant's behavior influences how the parents respond, and the baby then learns how to successfully initiate and prolong enjoyable interactions. Hearing is only one aspect of this complex system, and, although it is an important one, there are many other factors that contribute to the emergence of a smoothly running interaction system between baby and parents. When parents and infants are interacting well together, there is indeed the flow and turn-taking and sensitivity to one's partner that resembles a fluid and graceful dance (Brazelton, 1982, 1984; Brazelton, Koslowski & Main, 1974; Nugent, 2011).

It is important to remember, however, that each individual child comes into the world with certain biological predispositions or tendencies to respond to stimulation, change, or discomfort in distinct and unique ways. Infants' individual characteristics, which are sometimes referred to as "temperament," will affect the infant's caregivers, just as caregivers' ability to recognize and respond to those characteristics will promote positive emotional bonding and the development of social behaviors.

Individual Reactions to Stimulation: "He's Just Like His Uncle Eddie!"

The term *temperament* is used to refer to differences in infant tendencies toward reactivity, the ease with which they can be soothed, or the regularity of their biological rhythms (Chess & Thomas, 1996; Kagan & Snidman, 2004; Thomas & Chess, 1963). This is similar to what we call "personality" in older children and adults. Regardless of terminology, there seem to be several easily identified behavioral patterns in babies that often elicit different caregiving responses.

Some infants arrive in the world with reactions that appear to be both hypersensitive and somewhat fearful compared to their peers: the world simply seems to be more intense, more overwhelming from the start. For the caregiver, more effort is needed to calm such an infant, to anticipate activities that might trigger anxious reactions, and to protect the child from unnecessary exposure to such situations. These children may take a bit longer to adapt to new situations, people, foods, or routines, but, over time (and with patience from others), they are typically able to make the necessary adjustments.

By contrast, the same child's brother or sister or playmate might be a risk-taker from day one—always in motion, showing little impulse control and even less fear of possible consequences. In this case, parents may feel that they are always doing double-duty just trying to keep up with and anticipate the possibilities of actual danger, although this may be less apparent in the very early stages of development.

Another pattern sometimes seen is an infant who is under-reactive. Such children show little interest in exploring the world and seem more passive than responsive. Although they may rarely complain or express their needs, they also do not seek interactions with others and may therefore miss out on important opportunities for cognitive, social, and language development. The inattentive child is one who may later have difficulty following simple directions, sequencing things in time, or following multistep instructions. And, finally, there are those who, from early on, seem to be characteristically defiant and difficult to manage. Even as babies, these children seem to have a strong need to control their world, leading often to power struggles with far-reaching consequences.

(A word of caution: to avoid the somewhat negative overtone of the label "difficult," some psychologists today prefer to use the term "exuberant child" to describe those who tend to greet the world with a great deal of intensity, but who may also be more challenging for their parents.) Again, this will be observed more in the later months, although some of these temperament characteristics are also obvious soon after birth.

Although most of these descriptions appear to focus on negative characteristics, it is important to remember that the majority of infants and young children—regardless of hearing status—are actually quite easy-going, respond well to instructions and limits, develop appropriate social and communicative skills, and, in general, are a delight to be around! As with all aspects of development, there are many natural variations in the ways that individual babies respond to the world around them—both the physical world and the social world. In other words, vast individual differences are to be expected regardless of an infant's hearing ability, so that one baby may be an eager explorer and ready to engage with others, while his cousin may be entirely the opposite: shy and wary from the outset and hesitant to venture beyond the safety of his father's lap.

These behavior patterns may have either a positive or negative effect on interactions between parent and infant—in other words, they can be either a risk or a protective factor. Biologically based characteristics are evident soon after birth and are usually fairly stable as the individual develops, although the social environment also influences how they are later displayed. That is, predispositions the child is born with interact with the caregiving environment to form relatively predictable patterns of behavior as the child grows.

Infant temperament can be seen by observing a newborn's typical levels of agreeableness, cooperativeness, activity, sociability, and how effectively the baby is able to manage excitement or responses to stimulation. It is easy to imagine the effect that such behaviors may have on the developing relationship between parent and child. For example, how might parents' feelings of competency change as a result of the feedback they receive about whether newborn Jason likes the way he is being held, fed, or left alone to sleep? If Jason is normally calm and easy-going, he will let his parents know that he can accept and adapt to most caregiving situations, even if they involve change or something unfamiliar. The parents then feel comfortable leaving him with a baby-sitter, changing the feeding schedule, or introducing a new pet into the family. However, imagine a different scenario in which any slight modification of what is familiar (a different blanket, being carried by someone different, or a new stuffed animal in the crib) results in wails and protests from daughter Sally, who has a less flexible behavioral style. Sally is difficult to soothe because of a more sensitive temperament, which might lead her parents to feel frustrated, unsure of their parenting strategies, and incompetent. In both of these cases—Jason and Sally—caregivers might try a strategy such as swaddling in an effort to put the infant to sleep, prevent her startle reactions, or calm him down. Temperament alone may not predict just how effective this will be because each individual child reacts in his or her own way to having the legs or arms restricted. For some, this creates a secure "cocoon" that indeed may lead to calmness or sleep; for others, however, the feeling of being constrained is highly aversive and may lead to even greater distress. Once again, the parents' ability to "read" the baby's signals and respond appropriately will help determine whether or not a practice such as swaddling is effective and useful.

Remember, however, our important message about the parent–child relationship: taken by themselves, the infant's behavioral patterns probably will not have a direct effect on the child's eventual adjustment or personality. Rather, the *match* between these characteristics and the way in which the caregiving environment responds to them seems to play a much larger role in determining later outcomes. This is sometimes referred to as "goodness of fit," a term that reminds us to consider how the infant's behaviors affect the parents and vice versa. In other words, the family should be viewed as a "system"; within this system, the dynamics can be altered by the behaviors or characteristics of any one individual, as well as by the subtle ways in which each person interacts with the others.

Systems are not static; they change as circumstances change. So, there may be multiple factors influencing and changing these dynamics at any given time, within any given situation. Has a parent just come home from a difficult day at work? Is a sibling sick and irritable, demanding more attention than usual? Is the infant teething and not easily soothed today? Or is it simply a matter of some external factor, such as unpleasant weather keeping everyone indoors, that seems to be contributing to an increased level of tension in the family? Of course, more positive examples can also be used, such as the baby's new-found social skills and interests, her smiles and coos when a favorite person enters the room—these influence the family system as well, making the challenges of early parenting suddenly seem all the more rewarding!

As seen in the earlier examples, "goodness of fit" is influenced by how parents interpret their infant's behaviors; it may be particularly important to remember this when considering the case of deaf or hard-of-hearing infants. With all infants, early efforts to communicate must be inferred from their body language, facial expressions, gestures, or nonlinguistic vocalizations. These inferences may be influenced by the adult's expectations as well as by differences in infant behaviors, which is one reason that early identification of limited hearing is so important. If a baby does not respond to vocalizations as might be intuitively expected, it can "throw off" the adult's behavior; however, if the adult is aware that the baby does not necessarily hear what is being said or sung, the adult can more easily modify communicative behaviors. This can lead to more responsiveness from the baby and therefore better understanding of what the baby is communicating. Remember, these social interactions are a two-way street, with each partner influencing the other either by overt behaviors or by the lack of certain behaviors or responses.

When infants become frustrated as a result of not being able to communicate their needs effectively, emotions and negative behaviors may escalate and lead the parents to think that their child is difficult or even unmanageable. The risk of this becoming a negative spiral is more easily minimized if the parents can communicate effectively with their infant, thus helping the child develop a means of expressing and regulating emotions effectively. It is probably the case that both temperament and limited hearing will affect how readily an infant's signals can be understood; similarly, the parents' own personalities and behavioral styles clearly influence how they interpret and respond to the infant's behaviors. Remember, however, that these patterns can just as well be positive, as in the case of an easy-going and adaptable infant. In other words, if the child's behaviors generally elicit positive and nurturing responses from others, this can provide a buffer against the inevitable stressors that accompany caring for any young infant.

WHAT IS "ATTACHMENT"?

One of the most fundamental tasks an infant undertakes is determining whether and how he can get his needs met in the world in which he lives. He is constantly assessing whether his cries for food and comfort are ignored or lovingly answered, whether he is powerless or can influence what adults do. If the adults in his life respond predictably to his cries and provide for his needs, the infant will be more likely to use these adults as sources of safety and security. With his safety taken care of, he then can focus his attention on exploring, allowing his brain to take in all the wonders of the world around him. If, however, his needs are met only sporadically and pleas for comfort are usually ignored or met with harsh words and rough handling, the infant will focus his energies on ensuring that his needs are met. He will have more and more difficulty interacting with people and objects in his environment, and his brain will shut out the stimulation it needs to develop healthy cognitive and social skills. (Hawley & Gunnar, 2000, p. 5)

As this quote implies, one of the most important accomplishments during the first few years of life is the development of secure attachments—close and rewarding relationships with those in the social environment who are invested in protecting and nurturing the infant. This emergence of early social bonds, a process known as *attachment formation*, is perhaps one of the most well-studied aspects of infant socioemotional development and one thought to have long-term implications even into adulthood. Being securely attached as an infant—"falling madly in love" with one's caregivers—is a tremendous asset, although it does not necessarily guarantee healthy relationships and a positive emotional life later on. Establishing this secure attachment during the early years seems to give children a protective head start, laying the foundation for healthy emotional development in later life (Hawley & Gunnar, 2000). And the process begins at birth, even though it may not be apparent until some time in the second year of life. Although we will revisit this topic in later chapters, it is important to describe some of the factors present soon after birth that may already begin to influence the development of healthy emotional attachments.

In many species, infant survival depends on the ability to maintain close proximity to the mother or attachment figure so as to receive nourishment and protection. Human newborns are somewhat unique, however, in that they are not physically mature enough to be able to voluntarily move themselves close to others or even to cling to them for protection; they will not have the strength and coordination to do this until several months after birth.

How, then, do infants let others know of their desire to be held or carried, comforted or entertained? Many signals may be available even to the human newborn (such as grimacing, agitated body movements, or cuddling when being held), but by far the most prevalent for the first several months is *crying*. However, it is not necessarily the case that "a cry is a cry is a cry"! In other words, as the infant learns that some signals are more effective than others, and begins to associate different bodily sensations (hunger, wetness, rough textures of clothing) with different emotions, his cries will also begin to be more differentiated. According to some researchers (e.g., Eliot, 1999), most babies do use certain kinds of cries when they are hungry (a rhythmic and repetitive pattern), angry/upset (louder and more prolonged crying), or in pain (this tends to start suddenly and may include bouts of breath-holding).

Although most adults can actually discriminate among a baby's cries that indicate pain, hunger, or tiredness, it may take some time before they can recognize the more subtle characteristics and the message their infant is trying to communicate. (This is also true of deaf parents, who respond to signals such as the baby's facial expression, body tension, or motor activity, and may even use electronic devices in the infant's crib to alert parents in another room when the baby starts to cry.) Thus, during the first 2 months of life, one of the helpful developmental changes is the emergence of a greater variety of cry signals that more effectively communicate an infant's desires and responses to caregiving behaviors.

It is usually not until the second or third month that smiling will be added to this repertoire, much to the delight of everyone in the child's social world. When an infant first begins to smile in response to pleasant events or people, adults and others are compelled to approach, stay close, and interact with the infant in playful and positive ways. The effect is just as powerful as that of crying, but in quite a different direction. Now, instead of trying to do whatever possible to terminate the infant's behavior (crying), the adult is much more likely to try to prolong the smile and to encourage even more positive interactive behaviors. In this stage of development, the newborn is clearly not dependent on the use of language to communicate his needs. Although the adult must become an expert reader of "body language," this is not affected by the baby's limited hearing. The sensitive parenting that comes from being able to accurately read and interpret an infant's cues helps set the stage for later secure relationships between the baby and his parents.

Which Early Parenting Behaviors Lead to Positive Attachments?

Responsive parents are aware of and respond promptly to their infant's signals, are flexible in their expectations and behaviors, set appropriate limits, and are able to navigate around the sometimes conflicting goals of their infants. If we observe parents who are considered responsive, we notice that their actions are generally sensitive and child-focused both in daily care routines and during more playful social interactions. Such parenting behaviors are evident even in the first few weeks or months of life and provide the foundation that allows children to feel secure, to develop trust in others, and, later, to explore their environments with curiosity and confidence.

For parents to be sensitive to their infant's own needs and abilities, it is necessary for them to accurately understand their child's skills, interpret their behaviors, and take pleasure in each child's unique attributes.

Factors such as the parents' own personality types and how effective and rewarded they feel when interacting with the infant, as well as situational factors like stress and social support may all influence parental responsiveness (Hintermair, 2000, 2006; Meadow-Orlans, 1994; Meadow-Orlans & Steinberg, 2004). In addition, infant characteristics discussed earlier (temperament, readability, predictability) have been shown to influence how responsive parents are to the infant's cues and behaviors. As mentioned earlier, the "goodness of fit" between a caregiver's style and the infant's behavior patterns may be more important than the characteristics of either individual alone. Sometimes a baby who is deaf or hard of hearing, especially if there is a disability in an area such as vision or motor abilities, does not provide the types of responses that a parent intuitively expects. In this case, early intervention specialists can be particularly effective in helping parents detect the baby's signals of specific needs and preferences and, in turn, assisting these parents in matching their behaviors with those that seem to work best with their child. These things are sometimes more easily noticed by someone who is not directly involved in the interaction and has special training or experience in the development of infants with varied sensory and behavioral needs.

It is generally true that parents who respond to an infant with sensitive and nurturing interactions during the first year of life foster the development of a secure attachment. On the other hand, parents who tend to be highly directive or even intrusive with their babies may find that their infants will later have less secure attachment patterns. One aspect of sensitivity that has particular relevance to interactions with a deaf or hard-of-hearing child is that of skillfully modifying one's behaviors in response to the infant's visual attention, which we have mentioned before and will elaborate on in later chapters. This is true of interactions with hearing infants (Langhorst & Fogel, 1982) but can be of special significance when the infant is deaf or hard of hearing.

Another important consideration has to do with how emotionally "available" the parents are when interacting with their infant (Biringen, 2000; Biringen, Robinson, & Emde, 1998; Pipp-Siegel & Biringen, 1998). This implies a reassuring, supportive presence that spurs the child on to explore the world. The idea of emotional availability expands our understanding of attachment formation by including the child's own con-tribution to the relationship. In other words, when observing emotional availability, researchers make a point of noting the individual child's responsiveness to the caregiver and of ways in which the child involves the partner in their interactions—not just the caregiver's behaviors. This is consistent with the idea that the family should be viewed as a "system" in which one person's behavior is constantly affecting the other's during an interaction and vice versa.

Emotional Availability

Through both verbal and nonverbal interactions with parents, infants learn to understand and identify their feelings. In terms of emotional availability, sensitive and responsive parenting creates a positive foun-dation both for social-emotional well-being and for language develop-ment, regardless of hearing status. It was sometimes reported in the past that hearing parents have a tendency to be more rigid and controlling toward their deaf or hard-of-hearing children when compared to hearing parent–child dyads. For example, hearing mothers with deaf or hard-of-hearing infants have been described previously as being more physically directive, playing "a far more active, if not intrusive role in their children's day-to-day behaviors than mothers of hearing children" (Marschark, 1993, p. 15).

A word of caution is now in order: these observations were done approximately two decades ago, before early identification of limited hear-ing and early intervention efforts were as widespread as they are now. In addition, two later research groups found no such difference (Lederberg & Prezbindowski, 2000; Pressman, Pipp-Siegel, Yoshinaga-Itano, & Deas, 1999; Pressman, Pipp-Siegel, Yoshinaga-Itano, Kubicek, & Emde, 1998). Drs. Lederberg and Prezbindowski concluded from reanalyses of existing data that, in fact, hearing mothers with higher levels of education were highly sensitive to the cues of their deaf and hard-of-hearing toddlers. The reason for this is not clear, although this might indicate that more resources were available to them, leading to decreased stress. Parents' feel-ings of competence and confidence in their parenting skills also appear to promote more sensitive and responsive behaviors, so those with more information about what to expect from their babies may tend to be more comfortable and thus responsive. High-quality, family-focused intervention practices can support parent and caregiver confidence, help parents be more sensitive to their infant's communicative signals, and lead to better social-emotional as well as cognitive and communicative outcomes.

How Might Parental Depression Interfere with Early Interactions?

Even with high-quality early intervention services, positive parenting experiences are not necessarily assured. Regardless of a baby's hearing status (or that of its parents), difficulties may arise. One that occurs quite frequently and is worthy of attention is parental depression (Bernard-Bonnin & Canadian Paediatric Society, 2004). Short-term "blues" (with symptoms including crying, anxiety, and depressed mood) are not uncommon in the week after giving birth, but this typically subsides after several days. Episodes like this have not been found to have any long-term effects on the baby's development. However, longer-term depression (which can be accompanied by eating and sleep disorders, excessive feelings of guilt and anxiety, severely depressed or variable moods and even occasionally suicidal thoughts) extending for a month or more after a baby's birth hinder the playful, carefree, and animated behaviors so important when interacting with an infant. The baby may begin to mimic these parental behaviors, showing a similar lack of affective responses, disinterest, and inability to explore the environment (Tronick, 1989; Tronick & Field, 1986). Babies whose mothers have suffered from such difficulties for extended periods of time are at risk for delays in cognitive (learning and problem-solving skills) and communicative development and may experience problems in social-emotional development during the infancy and toddler years—perhaps even beyond.

New mothers who have experienced periods of depression before the baby's birth, as well as those who face significant challenges in finding resources and support for parenting, are at increased risk for postpartum depression. Some researchers have concluded that parents of babies with special needs or disabilities are at higher risk of depression, but this is not a consistent finding. Because extended parental depression can have devastating effects on the person experiencing it, on the baby, and on other family members, intervention specialists and parents themselves need to be sensitive to any indications that this is occurring. In such circumstances, family-focused intervention approaches are especially important. Parents experiencing depression (and this includes fathers as well as mothers) need to understand that help can be obtained and that this help can greatly ease their emotional distress, thus leading to gains for both their baby and themselves.

Are Infants with Limited Hearing at Risk for Disruptions in Attachment?

Although severe post-birth parental depression can interfere with bonding or attachment between parent and baby, careful and repeated research has found no overall negative effect on early baby–parent attachment based on the baby's hearing status (see Meadow-Orlans, Spencer & Koester, 2004, for a summary). On average, deaf and hard-of-hearing infants and toddlers are as likely to be securely attached to parents (deaf or hearing) as are their age-mates with typical hearing. In fact, most parents (and babies) are quite psychologically resilient. If given adequate support from their families, communities, and workplaces, hearing as well as deaf parents are likely to adjust to their infant's identification as deaf or hard of hearing without significant adverse effects on the emerging parent–child relationship. However, it is true that, in some cases, as with all parent–infant relationships, this process can take somewhat longer and may require caring support from others. If anxious or conflicted attitudes toward their child's limited hearing affect a caregiver's or parent's ability to respond sensitively to a baby, difficulties in achieving secure attachment can result.

It can be especially helpful for intervention specialists (as well as family members and friends) to focus on reinforcing the positive aspects of the parent–infant interactions they observe. Having someone else point out examples of effective, successful interaction episodes can help build the adults' confidence as well as appreciation of their own—and their baby's—unique skills and behavior patterns. In fact, it is often very helpful to have a third person observe, especially a professional knowledgeable about deaf and hard-of-hearing babies' communication needs, and identify positive patterns of stimulation and infant responses. Contributions of deaf and hard-of-hearing professionals (as well as deaf parents) on the intervention team can be of special importance in helping parents and caregivers identify and appreciate their baby's current strengths and preferences, as well as his or her developmental potential. Interactions with deaf and hard-of-hearing adults can benefit hearing parents by providing positive models of communication strategies as well as reassurance about the abilities and achievement potential of babies who have limited hearing.

SUMMARIZING KEY IDEAS

Hearing parents may need extra support and guidance in adapting to a deaf or hard-of-hearing baby's unique perceptual, learning, and communicative needs. However, it is worth repeating that the identification of limited hearing changes relatively little in terms of the emerging parent–infant relationship in the early months. The parent–child relationship that unfolds in the early years is founded on the many subtle, specific interactive behaviors that can be observed soon after birth. As infants and caregivers become acquainted with each other during the first 3 months, as they become attuned to each others' styles and preferences, they will each gradually learn which behaviors are most effective and most satisfying in this early "dance." Thus, the stage is set for the infant's increasingly sophisticated social, communicative, cognitive, and motor development as he or she moves into the next period of development.

The following are some key ideas discussed in this chapter:

- Most parents respond to infant behaviors in ways that are "intuitive" or nonconscious but that reinforce and assist young babies in developing their budding interaction and communication skills.

Even when babies have typical hearing, parents tend to produce communicative behaviors that are multimodal and include visual, tactile, and even kinesthetic input, as well as auditory information from spoken language.

- Deaf parents can provide especially effective models for early multimodal communications with deaf and hard-of-hearing infants—emphasizing the tactile and visual stimuli that are so easily received by the babies. Hearing parents can learn to boost the levels of these kinds of communications to supplement their vocal behaviors.

- Early interactions and communications are bidirectional (as are those occurring later), and infants' tendencies, preferences, and behavior patterns influence parents' feelings and behaviors—and vice versa. A "match" or the "goodness of fit" between parents' expectations and behaviors and their babies' tendencies and preferences for various types of stimulation helps to promote successful infant development.

- Babies differ in characteristics such as attention to others, excitability, and ability to regulate their changing emotional states. In addition, those who are deaf or hard of hearing will also differ in their relative attention and responsiveness to sound. Each baby is a unique bundle of abilities, feelings, and behaviors!

- There have not been any consistent differences identified in the ability to form early emotional attachments or the quality (sensitivity) of caregiving behavior of parents based on infants' hearing abilities.

- Support from high-quality early intervention programs can reduce stress that might otherwise be experienced after a baby is identified as deaf or hard-of-hearing (Lederberg & Golbach, 2002; Meadow-Orlans, 1994; Pipp-Siegel, Sedey, & Yoshinaga-Itano, 2002). This, in turn, has important implications for the child's social-emotional as well as communication development.

- Early intervention is most helpful when the focus is on serving and supporting the family as a whole; this will have significant benefits for the baby or toddler as development proceeds.

In this and the preceding chapter, the spotlight was on development and experiences during the first few months of life. In the next chapter, we turn to changes that typically occur as development proceeds. We will begin by addressing why the entire period from birth to 6 months of age seems to have such strong and often enduring impacts on a baby's achievements.

Chart 3: *Advances to Watch For**

By About 6 Months

*Physical and Motor Abilities***	• Rolls from tummy to back, sometimes back to tummy
	• May still need support, but begins to sit alone
	• Reaches out with one hand
	• Reaches for and grasps nearby objects[V]
Getting Information from the Senses	• Explores objects with hands, eyes, and/or mouth
	• Visual clarity almost as good as adults'[V]
	○ 3-D vision functions well[V]
	○ Looks back and forth between person and object, focus of interaction[V]
	• Discriminates between low- and high-pitched sounds[H]
	○ More easily localizes sounds[H]
	○ Begins to recognize speech sounds used in the home language[H]
Mental Skills (Cognition)	• Focuses on objects, their characteristics, what they do
	• Recognizes objects from different perspectives
	• Recognizes, remembers different shapes or patterns
	• Recognizes some differences in quantity
	• Recognizes some nursery rhymes in sign or speech
	• Recognizes differences in simple melodies[H]
	• Remembers, learns from pictures, labels[V]

(continued)

Chart 3 *Continued*

Communication and Language	• Makes wider range of sounds and likes to explore them (e.g., "raspberries", shrieks, extended vowels)
	• If exposed to sign language, may produce simple, gesture-like signs or manual babbles
	• Responds to words or signs for "Mama" and "Daddy" by looking at a picture of the correct parent
Social-Emotional	• Detects emotion in spoken language or on face
	• Smiles to positive, approving voices or faces
	• Waits for adult pauses to take turns with actions, vocalizations
	• Participates in social "games" with partners
	• Developing a sense of "self" as able to do things, cause things to happen

*See Chart 1 for partial list of information sources.

**On all charts, advances in motor abilities assume no physical disabilities.

[H] may be delayed or require different circumstances if hearing is limited; [V] may be delayed or require different circumstances if vision is limited.

5 Why Is Early Learning So Important?
3 TO 6 MONTHS

QUESTIONS TO CONSIDER

- Why are early sensory experiences (vision, hearing, etc.) particularly effective for supporting learning and later achievements?
- What is the difference between an age range being considered a "critical period" compared to a "sensitive period?"
- When experiences to support learning in a particular area are delayed beyond an early sensitive period, what differences in the processes of learning can be expected?
- What changes in visual abilities can typically be expected by about 6 months of age?
- What gains are typically made in hearing abilities by 6 months or so, when babies have sufficient access to sound?
- How do sensory experiences and growth in brain structures and functions work together and reinforce each other?
- How does a baby's experience of the world around her change as her motor and sensory abilities develop and are refined?

Four-month-old Will is strapped in his infant carrier seat, sucking on his pacifier and looking around. He pulls the pacifier out of his mouth, holds it with his left hand, and stares at it. Using both hands, he then turns the pacifier around the other way—so that he is looking at the colorful circular handle instead of the bulbous part that usually goes in his mouth. He seems to study it visually, then turn it around again. After another period of looking at it intently and a bit of fumbling, he pops it back in his mouth and begins to suck again.

Will, a baby with fully-functioning vision, has been exploring one of his favorite things. He is learning that it looks different when he turns it—but it is still the same thing! Two months ago, Will might have used only his mouth to explore his pacifier, but now he is combining that with the use of his hands and, most importantly, his eyes as he learns more about this object.

If Will could not see clearly during his first 6 months of life, would it affect his ability to use vision later in life? And because Will's hearing abilities are limited—and he is not yet using a hearing aid—might his lack of hearing during the first months of life interfere with his abilities to understand spoken language later in life? Studies that have been conducted in many places around the world suggest that early sensory experiences—or the lack of them—can have long-lasting effects on development. In an earlier chapter, we discussed research that indicates that starting intervention programming by 6 months of age rather than at later ages usually results in higher levels of achievement in communication, language, and social abilities. This is thought to occur because early use of visual language, like signs, or of devices like hearing aids to increase hearing, provide a foundation for later learning. Why is this so?

A large number of high-quality research studies have shown that a baby's brain is still developing after birth and that the sensory and social experiences she has will help the brain to set up "pathways" for transmitting information from one part to another more efficiently during early life than later. Different age ranges have been found during which the brain is especially sensitive and responsive to a specific kind of input.

These age ranges, early in life, are sometimes referred to as *critical periods*. However, the concept of a critical period is more specific than the general notion that "early is better than later." To say that a certain age range is critical for a specific ability implies that if the ability is not developed during that age range, it *cannot* be developed to the same extent or the same level later. It implies that, beyond those ages, the brain will no longer be "plastic" or able to reorganize itself to learn that kind of skill.

There are clearly times when a child's brain structures and behavioral tendencies are likely to be most receptive to the influence of certain experiences (Bornstein, 1995). However, this fact should not be overinterpreted. "Critical period" age boundaries have been arrived at by statistical calculations combining information from many children, not by the detailed observations of individuals. There is no automatic cutoff date for different kinds of learning, and it remains clear that, despite averages, there is great individual variation. Instead of using the term "critical period," therefore, we prefer *sensitive period* for the age windows during which various abilities can develop to their optimal level most easily and most naturally through experiences that typically occur in the natural home environment. This is not to argue at all against the imperative for intervention efforts to begin by 6 months. In fact, we are hopeful that they will already be under way at that age because clear advantages have repeatedly been demonstrated for intervention by the middle of the first year of life. However, we think it is important that parents not be led to believe that if any specific age has been passed, their baby's or toddler's opportunity to develop a particular ability is forever blocked. Many factors can cause an infant to miss these most sensitive periods for developing one or another ability. These might include a lack of availability of diagnostic or intervention services or the presence of additional more "visible" disabilities that may seem to have greater priority in the minds of parents and/or professionals. Experiences that are not provided within the general age ranges considered most sensitive for learning in a certain area will mean that progress will probably be slower and may require extra effort, extra practice, and more structured programming. But skills can still be increased and achievements attained.

In this chapter, we focus attention on the development of three of the basic senses—vision, hearing, and touch—during the first 6 or so months of life and use them as examples to explain what is happening in the brain during particularly sensitive periods for acquiring abilities. As you will see, the combination of "nature" and "nurture"—that is, the biological readiness of the brain to organize itself plus having appropriate experiences at appropriate ages—work together to optimize developmental achievements.

VISION IMPROVEMENTS AND CHALLENGES DURING THE FIRST HALF YEAR OF LIFE

Although babies can receive information from their senses before they are born, that information is fairly limited. This is especially true for the important sense of vision. It is, after all, very dark in the womb—and there's just not much to see! As a result, even though the brain structures develop to allow a fetus to see a bit prenatally, this is usually the least well-developed sense at birth. This begins to change once the baby is exposed to the big, bright world and experiences more and more through the eyes. But it takes a long time before babies develop visual abilities that even come close to matching those of older children and adults. Although a newborn can see contrasting edges and the shapes of things (especially if they are drawn in black and white—or perhaps colored bright red contrasted with bright green), they will appear indistinct and "fuzzy." They also need to be close to the baby to be seen because a newborn can only focus on objects and people who are between about 8 inches and 1–2 feet away. (Review Chapter 3 for a further discussion of the visual skills at and around birth.)

People's faces meet both of these criteria: They have lots of sharp contrasting lines and shapes. In addition, adults holding or caring for a baby tend to place their heads close to the baby's face, putting themselves (perhaps unconsciously or "intuitively") where they can best be seen. This results in lovely experiences in which a young baby seems to, at least briefly, "look deeply into the eyes" of her mother or father. In fact, these early eye-to-eye events may be more reflexive (or "automatic") than actual intentional behaviors on the part of the baby.

However, these early experiences, combined with changes in the brain that seem to be "preprogrammed" to occur as the baby grows older and stronger, are important foundations for the visual skills that develop after birth. By about 3 months of age (or a bit later), babies are gaining more control over what they look at, and their face-to-face visual exchanges with parents and others can last a much longer time than earlier. They continue to also be especially attracted to motion and will focus on objects that move across their field of vision. This is helped by the fact that their neck muscles are growing stronger, allowing them to lift, turn, and begin to control their heads more easily. And, although at birth babies are able to see what is on the edges (or periphery) of their field of vision better than what is in the center, they become increasingly able to focus on the center as they mature.

Between 3 and 6 months, babies make great strides in their visual abilities. They remain, as at birth, quite sensitive to motion and get better at visually following (or *tracking*) moving objects. They begin to see in much more detail: what they see is less fuzzy and more refined, they can see things that are farther away from them, and they see differences between colors in very much the same way as adults see them. In fact, researchers have discovered that by 6 months of age, babies can recognize that slightly different colors are similar and can even remember when they see the same color again. Like Will in the example given at the beginning of this chapter, they learn to recognize objects when looked at from different angles or perspectives. Importantly, although babies at first see only in two dimensions (so that objects and people look the way flat drawings look to an adult), they begin to see in three dimensions (3D) before they reach 6 months of age. This allows them to see differences in object thickness, as well as shapes and outlines, and to tell when one object is farther away than another. The ability to see in 3D can be permanently affected, however, if a baby's two eyes don't work together well—for example, if the baby has crossed eyes or a "lazy" eye—during the first 6 months or so of life. Furthermore, by about 6 months of age, problems such as cataracts (which limit the amount of light going into the eye and therefore affect visual clarity) can permanently limit vision if not corrected soon.

STRENGTHENING BRAIN CONNECTIONS AND PATHWAYS

How can something like the ability to see clearly be affected by early visual experiences? Just as with other aspects of brain development, experience matters: seeing things impacts the way that connections develop to send messages between the relevant brain cells. Babies are born with essentially all of the brain cells (called "neurons") they will ever have.[1] Those brain cells have begun to communicate with each other, to receive as well as to send messages to other brain cells, long before the baby is born. These messages allow the baby to move and allow the senses to function at least to some degree in the womb.

There are three basic parts to a brain cell. On one end of the cell are *dendrites*, structures that look a bit like the roots of a plant; they receive signals from other brain cells. In the middle is the *cell body*. At the other end is a sometimes very long branch-like structure called an *axon*. Signals received by the dendrites pass through the middle of the cell and travel down the axon. The end of the axon comes close to but doesn't actually touch the dendrites of other brain cells. To communicate with other brain cells, special chemicals are produced in the axon that travel through the tiny gap (called a *synapse*) between it and the other cell's dendrites. When these chemicals are received, they are changed by the cell into slight electrical charges. These electrical charges can be measured by electroencephalograms (EEGs) and by evoked response tests used to assess hearing. In response to a sound, the charges mean that information about the sound has been received by one brain cell along the message route and is being sent on to another. The same kind of process happens when other kinds of information, perhaps about vision or touch or balance, are communicated from one brain cell to another—although the particular cells involved will be different depending on the type of information being sent (Figure 5.1).

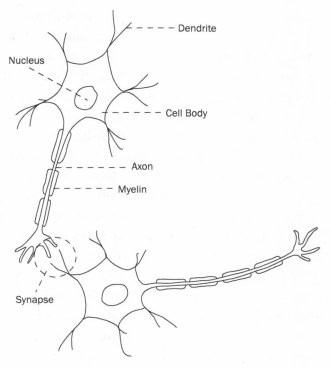

Figure 5.1 Basic Components of Brain Cells.

The directions in which axons first stretch or develop and the specific cells' dendrites that they approach are determined by the "pre-wiring" of the brain. The axons of brain cells in certain regions of the brain seem programmed to grow toward certain other areas and so begin to form a circuit or pathway that will send information from specific sensory organs, for example an eye, to the part of the brain where the cells will be most ready to receive and pass it on. But experience—that is, the more often messages are sent along this route—results in these pathways becoming better established and able to send messages more quickly and efficiently. This process of growing stronger is rather like what happens when a muscle is exercised repeatedly: using it makes it stronger. But just as a muscle weakens when for some reason it is not used, a particular path between brain cells weakens when it is not sufficiently exercised. The process by which some paths become weaker and even deteriorate is called *pruning*. It is through these processes of strengthening paths being used and pruning those not used that efficient message pathways are established in the brain. And, these pathways tend to be established most rapidly and most efficiently for different kinds of abilities at specific ages. The age range within which a specific area of ability develops most rapidly and effortlessly is particularly important for laying the foundation for the optimal functioning of that ability later in life.

The concept of a critical period for developing various visual skills in kittens was described back in the 1950s (Hubel & Wiesel, 1959). That idea has been expanded and investigated for other types of abilities and with human babies (as well as with different kinds of animal babies). The early investigations showed that kittens failed to develop normal vision if either one or both of their eyelids were surgically closed for a certain period of time soon after birth. The researchers found that if the eyes had remained open for a few months after birth, however, keeping them closed for a period of time at a later age did not permanently damage vision. The axons and dendrites in the parts of the brain that take in and interpret visual information had already hooked up correctly and developed strong message pathways based on the earlier experience of seeing. From this and associated studies, researchers decided that there was a period of time when typical development of the kittens' visual systems was most dependent on their being able to receive visual input. Interfering with receiving information from the visual sense either before or after this age range did not affect the development of visual skills as greatly. During this special age range, however, the parts of the kittens' brains that were most involved in sight were the most "plastic." That is, the establishment of connections between axons and dendrites of brain cells controlling vision was highly sensitive to the input received from the kittens' eyes during that time. Pruning of unused pathways—and strengthening of those often used—occurred rapidly and efficiently within these age ranges. It was necessary for the kitten to see things in order for these messaging pathways to develop normally.

Similar periods—ages when the developing brain is most sensitive to various kinds of experiences—have been identified for many different kinds of skills and abilities in human babies. As we stated earlier, however, we believe that most research on human babies and toddlers suggests that such periods should be considered to be "most sensitive" instead of critical. That is, in humans, many abilities can be developed to some degree at later than typical ages. However, it becomes increasingly difficult to develop those abilities completely at later ages, and it will require different kinds of activities, specific interventions and therapies, and much practice to support development that would have occurred naturally and easily during earlier ages.

Even within a single sensory system such as vision, different kinds or subsets of skills have slightly different ages at which optimal development occurs. Furthermore, some of these specific skills will be more "plastic," that is, more able to be developed at later ages than others. When only vision is considered, for example, we have already said that a human baby's ability to combine information from both eyes and to see in 3D (depth, breadth, and distance) begins to develop by about 2 months of age and is usually well in place by 5 months. Anything that interferes with the baby's using both eyes equally during this period can disrupt the eventual level of skill attained in this area. And it is difficult to overcome this lack of early development. However, the ability to see details clearly (called *acuity*) enters its most sensitive period for development slightly later, and there is considerable plasticity in the brain pathways involved in this ability until about 2 years of age. As a result, there is a longer period of time during which successful interventions can be provided to support this aspect of visual development.

Because vision is so important for deaf and hard-of-hearing children, it is especially important that assessment of visual abilities occurs during early infancy. Some causes of limited hearing, for example prematurity, some illnesses, and some genetic causes, tend to affect vision as well. As a result, the chance of some level of visual impairment occurring is higher in deaf and hard-of-hearing children than in children with typical hearing. When a child faces both challenges, the intervention team needs to include specialists in limited vision as well as hearing, and the two specialists need to coordinate closely as they help parents acquire the skills to best support their child's development.

Even when both vision and hearing limits are relatively mild, their co-occurrence presents special challenges for developing social, language, and academic skills. The challenges are said to *multiply* instead of merely add together. This is because some of the avenues for adapting to limited hearing would ordinarily involve greater dependence on vision, while some of the avenues for adapting to limited vision would ordinarily include hearing and listening skills. Instead of using terms like "deaf and blind," it has become common to use the special descriptor *deafblind* to identify these children and acknowledge the unique challenges that result from combining limits in both senses. Deafblind children's activities and environments need to emphasize experiences related to using touch, movement, and order (that is, having expectable routines) through the day. Early, family-focused interventions (medical and educational) have been shown to help children who are deafblind learn, achieve, and develop their potential. In addition, technology that can help increase what the child can actually see (e.g., glasses or surgeries to correct cataracts) and hear (hearing aids or cochlear implants [CIs]), as well as training in looking and listening skills, is very important during the earliest years of life.

One reason that the term "sensitive" is perhaps more accurate than "critical" when talking about the importance of the early months and years for the developing child is, in part, because some gains can actually be made in abilities when development occurs later than at the typical ages. For example, recent research with adolescents in India indicates more plasticity in later visual development than was previously thought possible (Sinha, 2013). Adolescents who had been without functional vision from birth, often the result of being born with cataracts (cloudy, thickened lenses that can prevent seeing more than vague areas of light and darkness), underwent surgery to correct the cataracts or related problems. The resulting improvements were better than anticipated. Although, as expected, the young people typically could not initially make sense of the new visual information the surgery provided, some of them gained significantly better skills after a few months to a year or so of having visual experiences. This does not mean, of course, that their development has been as quick or reached as high a level as it would have if they had been able to see much earlier in life. Some aspects of their visual abilities (such as acuity) remained severely limited, although less so for those who had surgery at relatively younger ages but still beyond the sensitive period for optimal development. This and other emerging research suggests that there is more flexibility in adjusting to information from the eyes than previously believed.

Similarly, evidence related to sensitive age ranges for learning to receive and process information through the ears supports the idea that gaining the ability later than usual challenges but does not necessarily block learning to process sounds. If skills are acquired at later than typical ages, however, they are learned more slowly and will require more effort—more "thinking about" and more conscious practice—than if learned during an earlier, more sensitive period.

Most Sensitive Periods for Learning to Hear and Listen

Compared to vision, hearing is a relatively early-developing sense. This has, in part, led to recognition of the need for very early interventions to support its optimal development. As we discussed in previous chapters, infants with typical hearing can receive sounds even before birth. While in the womb, these babies will blink or move when a sound is played from a microphone placed on their mother's tummy. In response to a sudden or very loud sound, they may produce arm and leg movements which look as though they are trying to grab hold of something to keep from falling; this is called the *Moro reflex*. Newborns with typical hearing recognize their mother's voices and will show this by sucking faster and harder on a pacifier to hear the sound again. They will turn their heads toward a sound, although this turning is an automatic kind of reflex and usually only occurs when the sound continues for a few seconds and is within the somewhat limited pitch range that newborns can hear. To provoke a head turn, the sound must also come from one side or the other of the baby's head, not from a location below or overhead.

By about 3 months of age, babies become more skilled at looking for and finding the location from which a sound is made—in part because they can now control their head movements better. By the time they are 6 months old, they even learn to mimic different vowel sounds (like "ahhh," "ooohh," "eeeeee"). This requires fairly sophisticated listening abilities and shows that although at birth they didn't hear higher pitched sounds, the range of high to low pitches they can hear has expanded. Also, 6-month-olds with typical hearing can hear much softer sounds than they could at birth, although the sounds still need to be louder than they would be for an adult. It remains very difficult for a 6-month-old baby to hear clearly when there is background noise such as from conversations or television, but this ability is also improving.

In fact, when hearing is not limited, there are significant changes during the first 6 months of a baby's life. Not only are the brain cells involved in sending and receiving sounds making more connections, but the axons through which electrical signals pass are being sheathed in thicker layers of a fatty substance called *myelin*. The myelin works like insulation surrounding an electrical wire, preventing small amounts of the energy from escaping along the route. The formation of myelin occurs for axons throughout the brain, not just in the parts involved in sending messages about sounds, but it has been studied in great detail by scientists interested in the hearing system. As the axons become "insulated," their signals are sent along more quickly and efficiently to the waiting cells. The formation of myelin continues throughout childhood in parts of the brain designated for hearing, but its growth is especially rapid during the first 6 months or so of life for a baby who can hear sounds. This is one reason for the early provision of hearing aids, even though it is somewhat difficult to fit and test their effectiveness during the first 3 months of life. (The younger the baby, the more difficult it tends to be to get a hearing aid properly fitted and functioning well. For one thing, babies' ears are physically more pliable than adults', and it is harder to fit the hearing aid mold so that it stays in comfortably.) To the extent that supporting the child's hearing is an important family goal, introducing hearing aids as soon as possible is advised. Increased opportunities for listening during the first 6 months of life, instead of waiting until after 6 months, are associated with better use of and attention to sound in later years (Northern & Downs, 2002).

Despite all the advances in hearing ability by 6 months, one of the most interesting developments is the *loss* of a related ability at about that time by babies with typical hearing. As they have increased experiences hearing, they become more "tuned in" to speech sounds in their parents' language—and lose sensitivity to differences in speech sounds that are not recognized as different by adults. For example, Japanese-speaking adults often do not recognize the difference between the "lah" and "rah" speech sounds because they are not meaningful differences in that language. In contrast, their young babies with typical hearing react differently to the two sounds during their early months of life, showing that they are sensitive to the difference. But by 6 months, Japanese babies no longer seem to hear these as different sounds. Similarly, babies in English-speaking environments initially react to "kee" and "keeee" sounds as though they are different. These latter two sounds can be recognized as different by adult Japanese speakers but not typically by English-speaking adults. Again, although babies exposed only to English initially react to the two sounds as though hearing a difference, they "unlearn" that ability by 6 or so months of age. This loss of sensitivity to speech sound differences not used in the language of their environment is not complete until about 9 months of age. However, it is well under way during the 3–6 month age span as babies listen, often intently, to what is being said to them and around them.

How can this be considered an "advance," and why should such a loss of ability be considered important? In fact, this change indicates that the babies are *learning* what matters in the sounds of the spoken language in which they are immersed. It is an example of the plasticity that we described above: the message pathways through which brain cells communicate with each other are strengthened by what is heard repeatedly, and pathways that would be used to send messages about sounds that are not being used consistently to indicate differences between words are weakened and stop functioning over time. This process of the brain's adaptations as the baby has more and more sensory experiences happens in the hearing system just as it does in the visual and other systems (Fogel, 2009). Researchers (Sininger, Doyle, & Moore, 1999) studying how this occurs in the development of hearing in small animals have actually recorded how the message pathways change after birth in response to the amount of information they receive. When information from sound is cut off, the pathways atrophy—that is, they weaken, stop working, and even disappear. They stay this way if sound is blocked for a long enough time; however, if sounds are again allowed before too much time has passed, the brain cell pathways seem to rebuild and again become functional.

Experiments like those performed by Sininger and her colleagues involved actual surgeries to prevent sounds from reaching specific parts of an animal's brain and would never be done on humans. But there have been "natural" experiments occurring over the past 30–40 years that have given us similar information about how human babies' brain functioning is affected by receiving or not receiving sounds during various ages. Much of this information has resulted from the now widespread identification of hearing levels at or near birth, allowing increasingly earlier use of hearing aids and CIs for many young deaf and hard-of-hearing children. Information from babies using hearing aids during early infancy has supported earlier findings that use by 6 months often (although not always) provides advantages in later hearing skills. It seems, for example, that babies who have at least partial hearing early in life learn to pay attention to sounds. They automatically alert to them. Those who have little or no hearing abilities before about 6 months may need special training or practice to learn that sounds are something to which they should pay attention once more access to sound is provided by hearing aids or CIs. Early experience with hearing also seems to affect babies' and toddlers' abilities to hear differences among speech sounds. For example, babies (as discussed in Chapter 1) who used hearing aids and received intervention services by 6 months are reported to have, on average, close to age-appropriate abilities to understand spoken language by the end of the preschool years—a much better outcome than commonly observed for babies receiving intervention that did not begin until after 6 months. (Interestingly, similarly close to "on time" language development—but for sign instead of or in addition to speech—has also been found for deaf and hard-of-hearing children who began to experience fluent sign language communication at home and in early intervention by 6 months of age. Thus, the idea of a sensitive period for development is not limited to merely language that is heard but also to language that is seen.)

Another natural experiment related to sensitive periods for development of hearing has been the use of CIs in increasingly younger children. For example, investigators in Australia initially found that adults who lost their hearing after it (and spoken language skills) had fully developed were able to interpret the signals from multiple-channel CIs (i.e., implants that had multiple electrodes that were placed in the inner ear) as being sounds. (Review Chapter 2 for more information about how CIs work.) Because these adults had typical hearing for decades before they became deaf, the brain systems that handle hearing during their most-sensitive early years had been fully established. Encouraged by these results, the research team next provided the implants to adolescents. Unlike the older adults who first participated, these young people had very limited hearing experience during their early years. In contrast with the results from the older adults who had been able to hear during their early years, the adolescents' results from using the CIs were discouraging. Although there were some benefits, they were so limited that neither of the adolescents chose to use the devices consistently (also see Dettman & Dowell, 2010).

Since these early trials, CIs have been provided to increasingly younger children, and there is a large amount of evidence suggesting that the devices more successfully promote hearing abilities when they are first used at earlier rather than later years—or when not much time has passed without any sound input. Drs. Johanna Nicholas and Ann Geers (2006), among others, have found that using a CI before the age of about 2 years generally leads to more rapid development of the ability to understand the sounds of speech than is typical when first use is at an older age. More recent research indicates that some babies who receive their first CIs by about 1 year of age can progress in listening skills and even in babbling and early spoken language at ages that are close to those for children with typical hearing. This pattern of results supports the idea that there is a sensitive period during the first year or two of life (if not exactly by 6 months of age) for optimal development of hearing. However, the pattern is neither as simple nor as reliable as this information suggests. These results are usually based on averages, and there is a wide range of achievements across individual children. In addition, it does not mean that children who are older when they first use a CI get no benefits, but their chances of strongly positive results are reduced unless they had already developed significant spoken language skills before receiving a CI. A number of other factors and experiences will affect their outcomes.

In some research we conducted with children who received CIs by 2 years of age, for example, a few children made rapid progress and others made very little after a couple years of use (Spencer, 2004; Spencer, Marschark, & Spencer, 2011). This kind of finding is not unusual for children whose limited hearing is accompanied by neurological disabilities that influence brain function in general, and several of the children in the study were later found to have such difficulties. This is but one example of the way that the development of a specific sensory ability, in this case the ability to hear, can be influenced by multiple factors—other sensory experiences, motor and physical development, and preprogrammed or biologically determined growth of brain and other structures, as well as by the baby's wide array of experiences.

Playing Around with Sounds

Vocalizing is one ability that is most obviously influenced by multiple factors. At birth, this ability is quite limited. Coughing and breathy sounds, as well as the crying that we all know so very well, form most of a newborn's "speech" repertoire. As structures in the mouth grow and change shape (changes that are caused by genes or preprogrammed growth patterns), a baby will become able to make sounds typically called "cooing" or "gooing" that can be produced when the back of the tongue touches the back of the throat. Babies often start to do this by about 3 months. By that age, and even earlier, there are individual differences in the amount of vocalizing one baby does compared to another. These differences are not usually indicators of whether or how much sound a baby can hear. There are "quiet" and there are "chatty" young babies regardless of hearing level. And, although some researchers report that they can identify differences in the quality of even these early vocalizations depending on the babies' hearing status, this is not something that is noticeable to most hearing adults. Parents cannot be expected to know whether their young baby has limited hearing based only on the sounds the baby produces—at least not if they aren't using sophisticated laboratory equipment to analyze sound or haven't been specially trained to listen for such differences.

Between 3 and 6 months of age, a baby's mouth and throat structures grow and begin acquire a shape more like those of older children and adults. Because they gain more control of their head and neck, infants can hold their head upright more of the time, especially when they are sitting supported by pillows or a handy adult lap. The mere act of sitting more vertically gives a baby more flexibility in his mouth and associated movements and changes the shape of the cavity of the mouth/throat area. Structures are also maturing at the brain level, allowing quicker and more varied movements of parts of the body that produce vocal sounds. As a result, and generally for those with limited as well as those with full hearing, babies begin to vary and "play" with sounds. They begin to laugh. Some may shriek, others "trill," change loudness between sounds, or yell playfully. And some babies do it all! They are, in fact, exploring the different sounds they can produce—differences they can hear between these often loud sounds; differences they can feel as their lips, tongue, and mouth/throat contract and move and vibrate; and differences in the reactions they get from people who are listening to the sounds. These sounds are, however, generated more from the baby's attention to her own emerging abilities than to her experiences of listening to others. Although babies love it when someone imitates their noises—and they will tend to produce them more often and in a turn-taking fashion when this happens—the way their vocalizations *sound* at this age does not really seem to depend much on their hearing experience. Instead, the experience of having their vocalizations responded to, vocally, visually, or through some other sense, seems to affect *how often* they vocalize and engage in communicative interactions.

Although hearing experience is not usually reflected in the actual sounds the babies produce up to about 6 months of age, the effects of that experience have been building. As early as 6 months of age, many babies with typical hearing produce vocalizations that sound like a combination of a consonant sound (like /w/ or /b/) and a vowel sound (like "ah" or "ee"). These productions don't really sound like bits of spoken language because they tend to be made very slowly, and parts of the sounds are not quite "right." For example, it might sound like a baby is saying, "buh-wah" instead of "bah." Many babies with limited hearing, especially those who have already had a few months using a hearing aid or those who are hard of hearing (and so can hear many of the speech sounds that others are producing nearby) also make these kinds of sounds at about this age—or a bit later. But from about 6 months of age and onward, stronger effects from hearing experiences become evident in babies' vocalizations. These effects are heard most easily in the production of special types of vocal babbling, called *canonical babbles*, that sound much like speech sounds and will be described in more detail in later chapters. From about 6 months onward, babies with typical hearing (as well as many hard-of-hearing babies) begin to vocalize sounds more and more like those used in the spoken language taking place around them. They reflect more closely their hearing experiences.

Touch and Touching

Up to this point in the chapter, we have mostly discussed the impact of age and age-appropriate experiences on the development of vision and hearing. As we already have mentioned, touch is another very important sense for all babies and perhaps even more so for those who are deaf or hard of hearing. Contact with caring others can both soothe and stimulate a baby. For example, stroking a baby's head, patting her legs, rubbing her back, and even occasionally during the early months swaddling the baby in a soft blanket to help limit the flailing of arms and legs, can help her relax and sleep. Touch can also be used to stimulate a baby and help him reach a state of alertness and readiness to interact. Overall, the touch of others can assure a baby that comfort and company are available. Gentle massage, doubling-up (if you will) on providing tactile stimulation, is known to stimulate growth and help stabilize babies both emotionally and physically, especially when they have been born prematurely or have been born at a lower than average weight. In fact, infant massage is common in many non-Western cultures and is being increasingly appreciated across cultures as beneficial for babies' growth and mental development.

In general, mothers intuitively provide much touch information to their babies: holding, stroking, rubbing them gently. Although we often think of being touched in these kinds of experiences as being rather passive, it involves active mental processing of the information being experienced. Babies learn even in the earliest months of life to associate particular kinds of touches (especially when combined with aromas, sounds, and sights) with different people, different objects, and even special four-legged friends. Think, for example, of a baby feeling the wet touch of doggie Rufus's nose or the rough, scratchy texture of Granddad's sweater. The baby is not likely to confuse the origin of those two very different-feeling objects the next time they are encountered! Noticing differences between the way things feel depends on messages being sent from the skin through nerves, up to parts of the brain where they are "processed" and stored as memories to be later recalled, compared, and even expected when encountered again. Just like the message pathways transmitting visual and auditory information, there are those specialized to transmit and share information from touch. Again, as these pathways become more "practiced" at sending messages, they begin to transmit them more quickly and more efficiently.

For an infant approaching 6 months of age, receiving tactile (touch) information frequently results from his or her own actions—active exploration, moving, stroking, feeling the many shapes and objects, animals, and people in the day-to-day world around her. As she becomes more intrigued by objects, exploration takes on an even more important role. What kinds of objects are soft and cuddly? Which ones are squishy when she grabs them? What about the sides of her crib—so hard that they hurt her when she bumps her head against them? As various objects are encountered, the baby begins to use more varied actions with them—actions that provide the nicest feelings or the most interesting feedback. Over time, the babies' repertoire of different actions becomes more varied based on the feelings as well as on various other kinds of sensory information that those actions cause to happen.

As a baby combines information about the way objects feel with the way they look, taste, smell, and sound, a whole picture of the object, its characteristics, and what actions work best with it is formed. Will, whose exploration of his pacifier at 4 months was recounted at the beginning of this chapter, shows this process in action—looking, sucking, looking from different angles, feeling the smoothness of the pacifier as he turns it in his hands, feeling it squeeze as he again starts to suck on it. This sharing and combining of information across various senses is called *cross-modal perception* (Lamb, Bornstein, & Teti, 2002). Although researchers are now finding that sharing of information across senses happens very early in life, the process becomes more efficient and more able to support learning as the baby ages and grows.

We discussed in earlier chapters that touch is used especially often by mothers who are deaf to alert their babies and signal them to look toward visual communication: tapping on a baby's arm several times means "Look at me, Sweetie, I want to sign to you!" Stroking baby's leg gently means "Hey there, see how I'm smiling and loving you?" Extra opportunities to experience touch may, in fact, be especially helpful to a baby with limited hearing, thus raising the total level of sensory stimulation in a natural way and so compensating for any decrease in the total stimulation that could have occurred due to the lack of auditory information. Of course, the importance of receiving information from touch cannot be overemphasized for babies who have limited vision.

For deafblind babies, whose information from both "distance" senses of vision and hearing is limited, the tactile characteristics of objects can be the primary way that they are identified. Even during the early months, if health issues do not interfere, specific objects with unique textures, softness, or size and shape can be given to or placed on a part of the baby's body to signal that a change in activity is about to occur. Deafblind babies can be encouraged to reach for objects by placing the object in contact with their hand or hands and then slowly moving it away, tempting the baby to reach out and again establish contact with it. This and similar activities will provide a deafblind baby with extra stimulation in general and can, with time, help the baby to become aware of space, distance, locations, and his or her own ability to obtain things and cause things to happen.

Has a "sensitive" period been identified for developing the sense of touch? Remember that this sense is relatively well developed at birth. Over the first year of life, the nerve pathways involved in this sense also become able to transmit messages to the brain more quickly. They become more efficient, and information about touch is combined with information from other senses, helping the baby to learn and remember events and actions that involve touch information. There is some research evidence of an early sensitive period for the development of the tactile sense (touch) in baby mice. Although human babies' recognition and fine discriminations of touch clearly increase with age, we are not aware of reports of a special sensitive period for their development of this sense. However, because we know that touch is important not only for learning about objects but also for early social and emotional development, the quality and the quantity of touch experiences are important input for all babies and perhaps especially for those who are deaf or hard of hearing. Tactile experiences may play even more important roles for those who have multiple disabilities. In addition, tapping and other touches to attract attention to communication have important roles in the development of visual attention (especially in learning to attend to visual communication).

ALL TOGETHER NOW

One of the themes of this chapter has been the benefits of early experiences to feed into and support the infant's brain development—especially the ability to transmit information available to eyes, ears, and skin up to the brain. It should not be forgotten that those messages are sent in two ways: information is combined, organized, and "registered" at higher levels of the brain, and messages are then sent back down through nerves to guide the babies' ongoing actions.

For example, as early as 4 months and increasingly by 5 or 6 months, sighted babies begin more controlled reaching for objects with one hand, modifying the direction and extent of their reach so that their efforts are frequently successful—even when hand and object don't start out close to each other. This quite elaborate set of actions is called *visually-directed reaching*, and it gives a baby much more control over what he or she can explore and investigate. It is truly a great accomplishment! Although visually directed reaching is usually considered to be a motor, or physical, skill, it clearly does not develop in isolation. It requires that brain, hand, arm, balance system, vision, and sometimes hearing (because a noise made by an object can make it more interesting to some babies) work in unison. More than that, what are called "higher level" functions of motivation (the desire to get and manipulate the object), attention, and thinking or problem-solving abilities are put into play. The apparently simple act of reaching accurately requires that messages sent from the brain back to hands and arms and all the other systems that are involved guide the baby's reach: reaching in the right direction, just far enough and not too far, and grasping when the object is touched.

Being able to reach for and grasp objects helps the baby become more aware of and interested in things outside and not attached to his own body, and it forms the basis for part of the motivation to attend more to objects than was the case earlier. Still, the babies' explorations remain limited at this age by an inability to move around very much. Rolling from back to tummy and tummy to back give a bit more range of motion, but crawling or active scooting usually has not yet been achieved. Being able to sit up makes visually-directed reaching easier to accomplish, although most babies even at 6 months of age require some kind of support to sit for more than a few seconds. It also allows the baby to look around more freely, find things that are intriguing, and call out to be handled. For this reason, it is a good idea to hold the baby in your lap, supporting his back and allowing him to sit longer—or to support sitting by arranging pillows or even specially made supports when a baby has difficulties that challenge his learning to sit up. It is also important to remember that sitting first occurs for most babies as they use one hand to hold themselves up—leaving only the other hand to reach or explore objects. The slightest jolt can easily throw off balance and cause the baby to topple over. This is, of course, just a normal learning experience—but the skill and coordination required to simply sit up, look around, and manipulate an object should be not be underestimated!

Are there sensitive periods for optimal development of different motor skills? This is much less clear than for vision or hearing. Instead of focusing on the idea of sensitive periods for development, many researchers have investigated the relative importance of the genetically programmed "unfolding" of abilities as age progresses versus the impact of exercise and experience. That is, the debate has focused on the roles of "nature" versus "nurture" in developing motor skills.

There is clearly a lot of "nature" involved. Development of both large (or *gross*) motor and small (or *fine*) motor skills tends to occur in the same order among children in various cultures. However, there are wide differences in the ages at which each of these skills develop for individual children. Some of the influences on age of development seem to be pre-wired or genetic. For example, babies in some families tend to develop the ability to sit up alone by 6 months. In other families, the pattern may be different, with this ability taking another couple of months on average to develop. These early differences, in the absence of any physical or brain-based disability, seem to have little effect on later development. However, there have been reports of effects from experiences on the rate of motor development in infants and toddlers. For example, there are cultures in Africa in which mothers regularly and routinely stretch and exercise their babies' joints and muscles. On average, their babies develop sitting, standing, and walking skills earlier than do babies in cultures where early motor experiences are more limited (Fogel, 2009). However, this early acceleration in basic motor skills has not been found to predict or influence the level of motor abilities ultimately attained.

SUMMARIZING KEY IDEAS

Development across sensory and other abilities is quite rapid during the first 6 months of a baby's life. In part, this development occurs from biological maturation of the body and brain, but experiences during this time can have both short- and long-term effects on achievements. When experiences of a specific area of development or within a specific sensory system are limited, effects will be seen in the rate of progress.

- Some areas of development have been found to have specifically "sensitive" periods for development so that naturally occurring experiences during special ages can have long-lasting effects on the level of development attained. One such area is that of vision; another is hearing. Experiences during an early sensitive period have also been documented for language development, whether in speech or in sign.
- When experiences related to a specific ability or sensory system are limited during early sensitive periods, advances may still be made at later dates. There is more plasticity in the developing brain than was previously thought; however, learning or refining abilities after the most sensitive period has passed is more difficult and typically requires specific training and practice. The longer a child has to wait for these opportunities, the more difficult it will be for pathways in the brain to re-organize to support learning of new abilities and skills. Optimal levels are best attained when age-appropriate experiences occur during the sensitive period for a particular area of development.
- Although no specific sensitive period has been identified for optimal development of the sense of touch (tactile sense) or for beginning certain motor skills, these abilities become more complex and more refined with maturation.
- Touch, or the tactile sense, is of special importance for infants and toddlers who are deaf or hard of hearing. It can supplement and add to the total stimulation experienced. In addition, parents can begin early on to use touch to signal changes in visual attention and promote turn-taking during interactions. This sense can have an even greater role in supporting the development of babies who have multiple sensory challenges, for example, those who are deafblind.

- Maturation of the brain, increases in and refinement of sensory abilities, advances in motor skills—along with responsive interactions with parents and caregivers and the ability to encounter varied objects, people, and activities—form an exquisitely complex interactive system that supports development. Biological maturation allows more varied experiences that in turn foster the development of more efficient neurological (brain) pathways for supporting learning.
- By the age of 6 months, a baby is no longer primarily reacting to stimulation from others in the environment but is learning to intentionally use motor and sensory skills to contribute to and affect these experiences.

As we discuss in the next chapter, sensitive periods for learning, supported by changes in the brain based on experiences, are evident for abilities beyond development of the senses. The advances of the first 6 months set the stage for rapid growth in communication abilities, for the development of stronger feelings of trust in others, and for a baby's increasing recognition of her own competence and ability to affect the actions of others. As we will see, experiences of receiving supportive input and having comforting interactions with others affect social and personal-emotional development just as strongly as access to and experience with various sensory information (from vision, hearing, etc.) affect the ability to use such information later.

NOTE

1. Cells called *glia*, which provide the structure or framework of other parts of the brain, continue to form throughout life; some additional neurons are also created, but most changes in the brain involve the development of messaging pathways that transfer information from one to another brain cell.

6 Learning, Feeling, and Communicating
3 TO 6 MONTHS

QUESTIONS TO CONSIDER

- What major changes are expected in the baby's physical and motor skills during these ages, and how will they affect her experiences?
- What behaviors are considered to be "play" at these ages? What are the benefits of engaging in early play activities?
- What can we learn about a baby's memory and developing cognitive skills by observing how he responds to different foods, people, toys, or books?
- What types of emotions are typically expressed by 6 months of age? How can parents support positive emotional development through everyday experiences?
- Why is pacing (the timing of adult's interactive behaviors) particularly important when interacting with an infant whose hearing is limited?

Simone, a healthy 5 1/2-month-old girl, is growing up in a large Midwestern city in the United States. She is the first child born to immigrant parents who work full time; in fact, her father has two jobs to help support his family, Simone is already having experiences beyond her home with her extended family and the community. While her mother is at work, Simone spends weekdays and an occasional weekend day with her aunt, who also cares for another infant and a toddler. Simone delights in watching her parents as they prepare the family's morning meal, chattering to each other and to her as she sits in an infant seat on the table. She is equally interested in watching her Auntie as she feeds and plays with her or the other children in her care. There is always plenty to see!

At this age, Simone is still very dependent on others to interpret the meanings of her body language, her facial expressions, the direction in which she gazes, her reaches toward objects and people, and her occasional cries or shrieks of joy. When she is riding in her stroller for a short walk to the corner grocery, Simone especially loves to face Mama and Papa, looking steadily into their eyes as they push her along the bumpy sidewalk. She smiles frequently, and games in which a parent matches or mirrors her facial expressions amuse her easily. Sometimes Simone makes trilling noises or "clicking" sounds, which her mother imitates while leaning down to put her face close to Simone's. During these exchanges, Simone usually waves her arms up and down and kicks her legs with joy. Often, she makes the sound again.

Simone is also increasingly interested in the objects around her. When riding over a bumpy sidewalk in her stroller, she focuses on a colorful rattle hanging from the stroller's handle. It bounces as the stroller bumps, and Simone arches her body and reaches toward it, trying unsuccessfully to grab it as it swings. Noticing her effort, her father takes the rattle off the handle and holds it closer to her. She reaches out and, after a few tries, grasps it with one hand and waves it back and forth across her line of vision before bringing it to her mouth. Simone seems to be intentionally exploring everything about the object: its movements, the vibrations it makes as she waves it, the way it feels against her lips and tongue, and the way it tastes.

Simone is actively participating in social exchanges with her parents; she is also showing more interest in the objects around her. Her increasing motor abilities allow her to actively explore them in varied ways. Simone's movements (for example, reaching and grasping) are less like the reflexes that dominated during her early days and months. They are now more voluntary and are intentional. She is also using all of the sensory channels available to her in increasingly coordinated ways: looking, feeling textures and shapes, sensing her own body movements as the stroller bumps and sways along the sidewalk, smelling odors as she and her parents pass a corner spice market, and tasting as she mouths the rattle.

However, it is not yet clear how much auditory information Simone is receiving as she is strolled down the city sidewalk. Her hearing abilities were affected by an illness her mother had during pregnancy. Follow up after referral from hearing screening in the newborn nursery identified hearing in both ears at the "severe" level. Since a bit before 3 months of age, she has worn hearing aids in both ears, but it is not yet clear exactly how loud different pitches need to be for her to hear them. Her parents have been diligent about her wearing the hearing aids all day, and they are making sure to expose her to a range of sounds in the environment from spoken language, from toys, and from all the noises of a busy and varied life. But experiences in some locations, some environments, will be more useful than others. She can most certainly hear the noise of passing trucks and cars (and even feel the vibrations they make as they roar by), but it is probable that those loud noises drown out the sounds of her parents' voices as they travel along the sidewalk. Can she hear the noise made by the rattle? Probably not in this situation. However, she is attending to and learning about the way that it feels, the vibrations its contents make, and its changing visual patterns as she moves it. Importantly, she is also learning from experience that her own actions can cause these interesting things to happen.

A SYSTEM OF MUTUAL SUPPORT

As at earlier ages, babies' senses and their developing motor skills support each other. Very little, if anything, develops in isolation. For example, in the earliest days and weeks of life, the smell of mother's milk will cause physical "rooting" or moving the head back and forth until the source of the smell is found and the motor movements of nursing begin. We have also seen that visual attention can be attracted very early by sounds. Seeing interesting things can cause a baby to become excited and move in ways that cause actions to happen; over time, this leads to being able to reach more directly for things that are seen. Touches can also attract attention, although this does not seem to be as automatic as vision. Examples could go on and on, but it becomes difficult to think of examples when various senses and motor abilities do *not* act together to support development.

Consider the case of Isabella, a baby with a mild to moderate hearing level. As she reaches 6 months of age, she clearly recognizes her big brother Isaac. When he approaches, smiles, tickles her under her arm, and says "Hi-ya Baby-One!" her initial smile becomes a belly laugh as the tickling starts. By this age, Isabella can mentally connect the visual *and* tactile *and* auditory information she is receiving. She recognizes her big brother by his haircut, his size, how he tickles her, his facial expressions, and his voice. All of these are combined into one coherent and whole picture of who Isaac is and how he's likely to behave.

Some very clever researchers have shown that babies in this age range with typical hearing actually become upset when what they hear does not match what they are seeing. In this research (Golinkoff & Hirsh-Pasek, 1999), the babies were shown a video along with an audio soundtrack in which the voice did not match the visual image—that is, a boy appeared to be talking, but his lips were not synchronized with his voice. The fact that the babies became very distressed in this situation showed that they expected the sound and the visual information to be coordinated. And, although this example shows only that the babies knew that sound and vision "go together," it is clear that they expected information from other senses to match up, too. How do babies learn so quickly to expect this kind of match? How do they know so early in life that the physical world is not random and disjointed—that their environment is made up of many parts that create coherent wholes? This comes about because of the baby's various sensory and motor experiences and because the rapid transmission of "messages" throughout the most complex part of the brain is allowing more and more nerve cells to connect with each other.

Sensory development and motor development are in some ways, however, "simple" in nature. In comparison, learning to solve problems or attain a goal, communicating their needs effectively, and understanding that they are unique individuals and have their own identity are even more complex developments for infants. Not surprisingly, these developing abilities are shaped by sensory and motor activities as well as by early social, emotional, and object-related experiences.

All of a baby's capabilities—sensory, motor, experiential, social— interact as the brain and body grow and develop. The baby is, in fact, a *system* in which various bits of action and experience, as well as pre-programmed growth, influence each other and are, in turn, influenced. When one part of that system is not functioning efficiently—let's (not surprisingly) take hearing as our example—overall developmental patterns may be changed unless steps are taken to either make that part function better or to help the baby learn to use another ability to supplement or substitute for it. As we saw in the previous chapter, both strengthening and substituting can occur most naturally and effectively early in life. During the first months and years of life, the brain is especially capable of laying down message pathways that send information to various parts of the brain (and back to the body) rapidly and efficiently. This is the case not only for sensory information like hearing, vision, and touch, but also for the foundations of complex developmental areas like cognition (thinking and problem-solving), social and emotional growth, and communication.

THINKING WITH ACTION: "WHAT CAN I MAKE THIS THING DO?"

Much of the activity that Simone engaged in during her stroller ride to the store can be called *play*. It may not seem to fit the definition we use when thinking about older children as they pretend or chase each other or make up rules to follow in a game—but playing has its beginnings in infants' early social interactions and their early actions with objects.

At the beginning of this chapter, we saw Simone engage in both kinds of play. She is playing socially as she excitedly exchanges smiles and positive facial expressions with her mother. It is most noticeable that those are actually exchanges. For this play to occur, her mother must be ready, willing, and available to take her turn and to continue the game. The benefits of this kind of play, which are structured much like conversations but without language, are multiple. The positive emotions shown by both partners serve to cement their emotional bonding. The turn-taking structure of the exchanges builds a framework for later language turn-taking. The fact that Simone's own behaviors cause these lovely, happy actions and sights to occur helps build her sense of identity and her sense that she can cause things to happen.

The other type of play we saw from Simone involved her actions with the rattle. At this age, her play with it can be called *simple manipulation*. She focuses on a single toy and uses behaviors she has used with other objects to explore this one. Importantly, notice that her exploration and real enjoyment of the toy was made possible by her father responding to her interest when he put it within her reach. Simone's father noticed her interest in the toy and responded by "upping the ante" and allowing her to experience it more fully. As simple as this may seem, such experiences of parental responsiveness to a baby's interests play a critical role in positive social, emotional, and cognitive growth. They help her to build a sense of trust in her environment, they increase her sense of being able to affect what will happen, and they give her the opportunity to "stay on topic" and have more varied and extended experiences with things she is interested in, thus helping to support learning and attention development.

What might not be apparent from our description of Simone's activities is that her facial expression was quite different when she was playing social games with her mother compared to when she was focusing on the rattle. Babies often look almost "solemn" when they are first manipulating and exploring an object—especially if it is one they have not encountered before. As Simone explores the toy, she uses actions that she has used with other objects and in other situations, repeating those that caused interesting results in the past. As she tries various actions, new ones will emerge. This might occur by accident—perhaps she discovers that hitting the toy against the side of her stroller produces a stronger vibration. Perhaps, because this toy is squishier in the middle than other toys she has, she begins to squeeze it harder than usual. As slightly different actions occur, they become part of her action repertoire, ready for use intentionally with this or another object later.

Parts and Wholes

Simone's actions, like those of most other babies, are accompanied by visual attention to the object as well as by sensations of touch and the feel of her own body moving. And, as her actions give her different views or perspectives of the rattle, she learns to recognize it from different angles. It looks a bit different, but the general characteristics of color and size and shape—its feel, its vibrations—stay the same. This helps to reinforce the idea that objects have permanence about them and that they are "whole" rather than just a series of unrelated parts to be seen and felt one at a time. At Simone's age, most babies with functional vision have learned to see even geometric figures as whole shapes and not just as a group of individual lines. They can actually categorize shapes and figures—if the researcher knows the right way to look for this ability!

One approach researchers use to test what babies recognize is based on the fact that babies (not unlike adults) become bored when they see the same thing again and again. Instead of using the word "bored," however, researchers refer to babies' *habituating* to a particular stimulus. For example, imagine that we want to know whether a baby will recognize that the color blue is different from the color red. We could start with either color, but let's decide to start with red. We repeatedly flash a picture of a circle or some other simple solid red shape to the baby. Typically, the baby will look at that display for quite a few repetitions but will then habituate and stop paying attention to it. Now, imagine that we again flash a picture of the same shape, the same size, but now it is solid blue. The baby who sees the difference between the two colors will start looking at the shape again. It's new and it's different. However, after a number of presentations in this new color, this also becomes "old hat" and the baby's attention will drop off again.

Let's imagine that we want to see whether a baby can recognize a triangle shape and will categorize or group that shape with other, slightly different triangles. After presenting one triangle repeatedly and having the baby show that he is habituated to it and is no longer paying attention, we show a triangle with sides and angles of slightly different lengths and sizes than the first one. If the baby is paying attention only to separate parts of the new triangle, say the length of an individual line or the size of the angle at one corner, the change should attract attention. If, on the other hand, the shape is still seen as another view or example of the same shape—that is, if the baby still sees it as a triangle, he probably won't start looking again. In fact, the latter pattern becomes increasingly common toward 6 months of age: "Oh, it's just another one of those."

A number of other research techniques have been used to test what babies know—or at least what they have learned to recognize and expect—long before they can use any language or answer any question. Sometimes a baby's eye movements are tracked as he or she looks at something. If a shape is drawn with dashed lines, will the baby's eyes track the whole shape smoothly? Or will the eyes stop moving at the end of each dash? (The first pattern is expected by 6 months of age and is assumed to mean that the baby is looking at the shape as a whole.) Babies recognize shapes as categories of shapes. Wow. That seems very smart! How does this happen? Perhaps this ability grows from the very early ability to recognize faces as wholes and to learn to recognize familiar ones quickly. Lines, contrasts, shapes—all seem to be things that baby humans' visual systems are built to recognize quickly.

"I Thought *That Was Going to Happen!*"

Sometimes a baby's expectations can be tested by seeing what she does when the expected *doesn't* happen. For example, babies are learning that moving objects tend to stay on the path they are moving along. When a baby has learned this, he will be startled if he watches an object roll behind a small barrier that hides it briefly, but a different object (or no object at all) rolls out. Not surprisingly, babies are able to remember things longer now, too. If they have learned to perform a new action with a special toy in a special place, they will remember and do that again even after several weeks of no practice. However, the whole situation (location, toy, even sounds and other sights) needs to be the same for the action to be remembered and performed again if more than a few days have passed.

Increasing memory skills can also be seen in a baby's emerging ability to identify various foods, familiar people, and objects from their pictures. But this takes even more than memory. It requires that the baby knows that a still, flat photographic representation of "Mommy" really does mean his mommy. And, perhaps unfortunately, seeing the colorful design on the package of a food he does not like not only lets him identify that food—but he can also remember that he doesn't like it even before it is available to smell or taste. For example, the look on little Will's face when he sees the squeezable package of spinach and not the fruit squeeze that he likes is priceless... unless you are the person responsible for trying to get him to eat something green! It may be helpful to realize that this is just one more indication of how much he is learning and remembering.

Careful observations of babies' behaviors continue to amaze us with how much they seem to know at such very young ages. Babies have even been found to have some concepts about number or quantity earlier than was ever suspected. Those concepts are very limited, of course, but there is evidence that infants have the idea that one of something is different from two or three of something. For example, Dr. Karen Wynn (2000) showed 5-month-old babies one object and then put it behind a screen. Then she showed them a second object and appeared to put it behind the screen also. The screen was pulled away. Sometimes both objects would be seen; sometimes only one would be seen; sometimes three objects appeared! The researcher found that babies looked longer when the incorrect number of objects was shown than when the correct number of objects appeared. They seemed to be puzzled when what should have been two objects was revealed as only one, for example. The babies didn't know the words for "one" or "two" or "three" yet—that learning was far in the future. But it seems that very early in life, they had some basic idea of more, less, and one versus more than one. How can things like this be known so early?

As with many other human thinking skills and abilities, it seems that our brains are genetically built to be prepared to acquire certain ideas, concepts, and skills and to send messages about these. (For example, human brains seem uniquely "ready" to organize in a way to learn language.) In most cases, getting that organization set up and going requires only the kinds of experiences that humans typically have during the first months and years of life.

The specific experiences differ across cultures, but they have core similarities. Consider, for example, a baby looking at a mobile turning above his crib, seeing each object from a slightly different angle as it moves through and around the baby's visual field. Then compare that to a baby being carried by his mother while she walks through the village center—the baby watches people walk by, thus seeing different angles and views of their faces. He sees that the shapes of the small square buildings seem to change as he and his mother pass by them. In both scenes, the visual information is interesting, movement is involved, different perspectives become available to the babies even though the objects (or people) remain the same overall, and the babies are in safe, familiar places where they are comfortable and free to put their energy into watching and remembering and learning. The nice thing is that all these cognitive advances can be built from the interaction between preprogrammed brain and body development with the kinds of easy, everyday experiences that most babies have.

Playing with People, Playing with Objects

It's amazing that so many of a baby's developing perceptual and cognitive or thinking skills can be supported through experiences we call "play," including interacting with people and exploring object characteristics and the actions that can be done with them. In the past, some people considered play to be a waste of time—not an activity leading to any concrete or necessary accomplishments and certainly not one to be encouraged by more serious-minded or goal-oriented adults. Attitudes began to change when a Swiss scientist named Jean Piaget recognized and drew attention to the importance of children's play, even at the very earliest ages (Piaget,

1936/1952). Now Piaget's influence is felt in many early intervention programs, classrooms, and child-care centers around the world; he and others, such as Maria Montessori, helped us to understand that, in fact, *play is a child's work* (Lifter, Foster-Sanda, Arzamarski, Briesch, & McClure, 2011). That is, it is by exploring and simple handling and manipulating objects (and by getting responses from people) even in the earliest months that children build memories, learn how things work, learn that they can cause things to happen—and also learn that other people can cause things to happen, too.

Many researchers have recently concluded that Piaget actually underestimated how quickly mental development occurs for most children, but his basic ideas continue to hold up under close scrutiny (Fogel, 2011; Slater & Lewis, 2007). Piaget outlined several basic principles that help us to understand the role of children's play in their mental or cognitive development (Casby, 2003; Lamb et al., 2002). First, play and mental development are both action-based: at least during infancy, learning is truly based on "doing." Second, the focus of play behaviors, and thus mental development, moves from the self to repetition of actions where the focus is on an object (or another person) and what the actions will cause to happen. Very young infants practice actions that mainly involve their own bodies (e.g., vocalizing repeatedly, rocking or bouncing in their bed, kicking feet in the air, waving hands in front of their faces, etc.). When an object is available, the baby's first reaction will most likely be to put it in her mouth—which is just another way of getting information and sensory input about such things as texture, hardness, taste, and the like. By around 5 or 6 months, this typically changes. Babies become much more interested in the "object world" and explore this with avid curiosity combined with a continued need to repeat actions over and over again as the learning process takes place. Third, unlike some other aspects of mental development, play behaviors are not directed at "practical" goals—that is, they are done for their own sake, not to request food or comfort.

Although most adults, especially parents, are highly attentive to babies' actions, we are sometimes not fully aware of just how important their explorations are. These experiences of the world form the basis of an infant's growing knowledge and help the infant become increasingly less dependent on her own self-centered or *egocentric* view of the world, learn about *causality* (how one thing causes another to happen), and eventually (after the age of about 12 to18 months) learn how one thing can represent or stand for another. Play situations are ideal for learning not only about how things operate and how the child can cause things to happen but also for learning communication and specific language skills.

By observing how children play, we can often tell a great deal about their mental development (Lamb et al., 2002). However, given that play behaviors are still rather limited and repetitive up to about 6 months of age, observations of play may be better used to make decisions about which toys or objects to make available than to try to determine a "mental" level on the basis of play. Measures of play skills in this age range generally include observation of an individual baby's actions with objects. How varied are they? How long does interest last? What kinds of objects—and what kinds of object reactions—attract the most interest? What object characteristics best stimulate a baby's action? Is she repeating the same exploratory behaviors over and over but beginning to modify them to try something slightly different?

Up to the 6-month level, no differences in object-play behaviors have been reported for deaf and hard-of-hearing babies compared to babies with typical hearing. Of course, there are individual variations in what babies like to do. For example, some babies tend to be more sociable from their earliest weeks; they tend to be attracted even more than is typical by people and social play. Others tend toward being more intrigued by objects. There is no indication, however, that the tendency toward initially having more or less social versus object attraction is related to hearing abilities.

It goes without saying, however, that babies with limited hearing will probably be less attracted to (and their behaviors less reinforced by) toys and other objects that produce only sounds when acted on. Objects that reflect or display lights may be more attractive to them, as may objects with varied textures and shapes. These will also be of interest to babies with typical hearing, so selecting toys won't be that difficult to do—although while shopping it will be helpful to approach the toys without attending so much to the sounds they make. On the other hand, toys that primarily give sounds in response to the baby's actions may be tried to determine whether the baby can hear them—and some can have the volume of their sounds increased to make hearing them a bit easier. Not all families with babies have access to standard toys. When that is the case, the visual and textural aspects of objects available for exploration and play, as well as sounds they make, should be noted. In the case of children with special needs who have disabilities in motor skills or generally slowed development, careful observations can help to identify toys and other objects for play that best attract their attention and prompt activity.

All through this process, it should be remembered that social play continues—sharing smiles, giggles, funny faces, sounds, and hand movements. In addition, it is still rare at 6 months for a baby to be able to combine object play with social play. That will happen as time goes on. Finally, parents, other adults, and older children play a critical role in prompting, supporting, and interpreting what babies' play behaviors mean. It is a sophisticated dance when all is working smoothly. The older partner allows the baby time to indicate the object of interest, helps him or her obtain it if necessary, gives more time, and perhaps shows something slightly different that the toy can do—or talks about and names the toy. This is the process that the psychologist Vygotsky (1978) called *scaffolding*. It is as important for deaf and hard-of-hearing babies as for babies with typical hearing, and it is a kind of "natural teaching" on the part of the parent or other adult.

When a baby does not hear spoken language easily, however, this process can present challenges for parents who are used to spoken communication and are having to become especially sensitive to where their baby is looking and to the focus of his attention. It makes the developmental period around 6 months a bit trickier for these parents to scaffold the baby's learning compared to parents whose baby can hear things even when looking away. All of this will become easier as the baby continues to grow and begins to switch visual attention more quickly to include looking at a person (and what that person is trying to communicate) during episodes of paying attention to objects. Meanwhile, this is an activity in which we think it is wise to follow the model that deaf mothers give us: be patient, give the baby time to look back at you, don't push, but if you really want the baby to look at you, move an object he is interested in up near your face. He usually can't resist.

Expecting a Response

Think of the 5-month-old who seems to never grow tired of kicking her feet in the crib so that the musical toy chimes; suddenly, one day she experiments with something new—holding the side bars of the crib and tugging at them so that the same musical toy "answers" her again! What has she learned in the process? First, that her own actions have an effect on the world; second, that different actions can produce the same enjoyable result; and third, that many aspects of her world are predictable and that she can exert some control over them. In other words, she is already learning about cause-and-effect relationships, even in the early months of her life.

It won't be long before she realizes that she can also be instrumental in causing things to happen in her social world as well as in her physical world. What happens when she awakens in her crib and starts cooing or wiggling around? If another person is nearby, they are likely to make an appearance fairly soon to check and see if she's ready to join the family for an evening walk. What happens when she's being held by her mother and starts rooting around, fussing slightly, and searching for the source of her next feeding? Again, most likely her mother will respond by offering breast or bottle, unless she decides the timing is not right or the location is not appropriate. (In many cultures around the world, babies are fed "on demand," are carried almost constantly, and nursing an infant in public is simply considered a normal and accepted aspect of child-rearing.)

Even babies as young as 4 to 6 months of age have developed expectations about social interactions with their close caregivers. Most babies who spend time where they can see their mother's face, for example, have begun to expect their mothers to respond to their smiles, cries, and funny expressions. We saw this in a research situation called the "still face" developed by Dr. Ed Tronick and his colleagues, who studied extensively how babies react when mothers "violate" their baby's expectations by becoming nonresponsive (Tronick, Als, Adamson, Wise, & Brazelton, 1978). Dr. Tronick's team concluded that the babies' responses provide important information about what typically happens when they interact with others—and what they do when the rules they've learned about social interactions suddenly seem to have changed!

We decided to investigate whether babies who are deaf or hard of hearing had different social expectations from those who have typical hearing. In addition, we wondered whether babies with deaf, signing parents would react differently from those whose mothers communicated with them mostly through speech. To set up the investigation, we took an infant seat, like the ones that babies in the United States often sit in (on a table or other high surface), and we bolted it firmly to a strong table. (We didn't want a baby to start squirming around and knock it off the table!) Then the babies' mothers were asked to sit in a chair across from them so that they could easily gaze in each other's eyes.

The mothers were asked to interact and "play" with their babies as they would do if they had some free time at home. They were not given any toys to include in the play because we were interested in looking at what happened socially, without props.

In almost all cases, the first 3 minutes of mother–infant play were happy. They exchanged smiles, mothers stroked and touched their babies, talked to them, signed to them, moved their feet and hands up and down. The babies usually responded with their own indications of enjoyment. (Deaf mothers were most likely to use touching and what we thought to be "exaggeratedly positive" smiles and facial expressions.) A good time was had by all. But then we changed the rules: the mothers were asked to look away from their babies for several seconds and then to look back at the babies but to keep their faces "still" for 2 minutes—no talking, no signing, no smiling, no reaction to what the babies did. Not an easy assignment for the mothers, but equally difficult for the infants! The babies' responses, completely unrelated to their own or their mothers' hearing, showed that they were all—by golly—used to getting a response when they did something cute! Furthermore, at only 6 months of age, they weren't very good at comforting themselves when something strange happened: they expected their mothers to do that for them.

At 6 months, there were very few differences in the kinds of behaviors observed in deaf and hard-of-hearing babies compared to those with typical hearing. When confronted by their mothers' unexpected nonresponsiveness, babies often "upped the ante" by smiling, making faces, reaching toward Mom, and trying things that they had done with their mothers during the play period just ended. But the babies clearly experienced the still-face period of time as mildly stressful. Some of them, after failing in their initial attempts to re-engage their mothers, whined, vocally complained, or gave little cries. (If they began to cry lustily, we quickly ended the still-face time.) Some of them began to move around quickly as though trying to break loose from the straps that kept them from falling out of the infant seat. They often looked away from their mothers, even though they had been "locked in" to eye contact when their mothers were responding to them. We observed that babies with deaf, signing parents tended to make more quick glances back at their mothers—perhaps having learned not to rely on sound but vision to see if their mothers had re-engaged. This group of babies seemed to already have learned to be alert for visual signals. Significantly, this was not true for deaf and hard-of-hearing babies with hearing mothers. This reaction seems to have been based not on the babies' ability to hear but, instead, on the kind of feedback or input they were used to getting from their mothers.

Of course, we always followed the "still-face" period with another several minutes of mothers responding normally to their babies. They could again smile and talk and sign and touch and play however they wished. This was done mostly to get the situation back to normal. But, often, the babies took some time to accept the mothers' again-responsive and stimulating communications. Did they "hold a grudge"? Or did it just take some time for them to realize that their mothers were acting as usual again? We aren't sure, and mothers had differing opinions. It should also be repeated that, in this as in other reports about our research, we almost always are talking about group averages when we refer to "deaf and hard-of-hearing babies," "babies with typical hearing," or any other group description. There are always variations in actions and reactions among the members of a group. We are reporting the general tendencies of each group, and average differences had to be fairly distinctive in order for us to believe they were meaningful.

EMOTIONS AND THE SOCIAL WORLD

Although the foundations for an individual's emotional life are put in place largely over the first 3 years, much of this development actually occurs within the first 6 months. One might think of this initial half-year period as an optimal one for the emergence of the child's primary (or basic) emotions. Most parents as well as researchers have noticed that these basic emotions include surprise, joy, interest, sadness, fear, and disgust (Lewis, 2007). Even very young babies can be seen displaying facial expressions that seem to reflect each of these feelings, although their emotional lives often seem to fluctuate more obviously between "positive" (pleasure, attention, responsivity) or "negative" (distress, irritability, crying) states.

At this age, are any of these emotions likely to be affected by an infant's limited hearing? We assume that the answer is "no" (and our assumption is based on a lack of any reliable reports to the opposite) because it is hard to imagine that access to sound would be a necessary factor in eliciting such reactions. These kinds of reactions depend mostly on receiving information from the senses, but this information is usually received in a "bundle," and the baby's overall experience of an emotional situation doesn't significantly change just because one kind of information (for example, sound) is missing. The startle with which babies with typical hearing react to a loud sound can also occur if the body is moved quickly, and gentle caresses and rocking in mother's arms may have the same effects as the soothing sounds of a lullaby being sung. In short, these early emotions require only very basic mental or cognitive abilities, plus some discrimination of pleasant versus unpleasant events and the beginning of short-term memory.

The emotions that develop somewhat later (but still within the first 3 years) will require more sophisticated thinking and therefore more advanced brain development. Essentially, these more advanced emotions will involve a level of consciousness on the part of the child that will allow her to reflect on or be aware of the fact that she is *experiencing* a particular feeling such as shame or embarrassment. (Some of these more "self-conscious" emotions do seem to involve language comprehension and may therefore be influenced by limited hearing.) Again, it is important to remember that in most child-rearing situations, emotional expressions by a baby do not occur in a vacuum, although there will, of course, be times when no one is available to immediately notice or respond to them. The social environment and the family system surrounding each infant will therefore influence the degree to which emotional expression is permitted, encouraged, discouraged, or even prohibited. Factors such as the child's gender and cultural norms will also play important roles, as will the presence of disabilities that limit the child's awareness of certain responses from others. Consider an infant who is blind, for example, and cannot see the pleasure expressed in her caregiver's face; just as for a young baby with limited hearing, other important sensory experiences can be provided by the caregiver—touch, playful bouncing, gently blowing on the baby's tummy, perhaps rhythmic rocking or spoken language or language signed on the baby's body—that provide comfort, the sense that the baby is not alone, and information about the affective (or emotional) tone of the interaction.

Building Expectations, Building Trust

A psychologist named Erik Erikson (1963) proposed that a baby's most important task during the first 12 months of life is to establish a strong sense of trust in caregivers and the social environment in general. Human babies (unlike, for example, baby ducks or many other animals) are completely dependent on others. And, interestingly, emotional warmth, support, and contact from caregiving adults seem to affect not only the attitudes the baby develops, but his very survival. Of course, the baby from birth to 6 months of age cannot actually think in words or sentences. But, if he could, the following might be important questions: *When I need food or comfort, will it be given? Do my cries and movements get a response?*

Can I get warmth and contact and protection? Will the people in my life be loving, supportive, and trustworthy?

These questions all represent concerns that the child might be experiencing throughout the first year or two (but clearly beginning in the early months), although obviously not in a way that he is aware of yet. The answers to these questions will largely determine the outcome, or whether or not the infant develops a strong sense of trust in others. Erikson felt that if an infant's needs are not being met adequately, the resulting sense of mistrust would have lasting consequences as the child's personality continues to develop. Our own research strongly indicates that deaf and hard-of-hearing infants with either deaf or hearing parents can develop the necessary sense of trust in others when their social partners are nurturing, sensitive to the infant's needs and signals, and use appropriate responses (such as holding, stroking, soothing, etc.) to communicate their affection and appreciation of the child. There is no reason for this process to be disrupted by a child's limited hearing, unless there is a serious absence of effective interactions and nurturing care.

Difficulties in social-emotional as well as in other aspects of development could, of course, be experienced if parent or caregiver experiences a long-term depression (as discussed in Chapter 4). Although there is no evidence of increased incidence of postpartum (after the birth has occurred) depression in mothers of deaf or hard-of-hearing infants, it certainly can occur regardless of infant hearing status. If so, its effects on early interactions and the sensitivity and responsiveness of mother can have long-lasting effects on many areas of the child's development. Medical and early-intervention professionals need to be alert to indications of parents' emotional status and to ensure that needed assistance is provided.

In extreme cases in which early interactive experiences are disrupted, such as when children have been institutionalized in orphanages with little stimulation or responsive care, serious developmental delays have resulted (Fogel, 2009). If positive, responsive experiences were not provided during the first 6 months of life, these difficulties were often long-lasting: many of the children's difficulties continued even after later adoption into loving homes. According to Erikson's theory, these infants were not able to develop a sense of trust that their most basic needs (including emotional) would be met at a time when they were too small, too immature, and too helpless to provide for these themselves. By the time they reached toddlerhood, the foundation of trust was severely lacking so that even after adoption there were likely to be difficulties in establishing secure attachments and developing a sense of autonomy. These achievements are a necessary foundation for developing cognitive and communication abilities, as well as ongoing social and emotional development. Fortunately, such great deprivation is now extremely rare, and most infants' early experiences are both happier and more supportive of development.

COMMUNICATION

> *Six-month-old Shawn is securely propped up into a semi-sitting position in one corner of his family's sofa. He squirms with delight as his older sister entertains him with a game of peek-a-boo. Shawn's gaze of anticipation when she disappears, his facial expression of surprise when she pops up from behind the sofa, and then his delighted laughter all encourage his sister to repeat the routine many times.*

Shawn (who has typical hearing) has communicated his interest very proficiently, he is learning how to take turns with another person, and he and his sister have been engaged in a mutually enjoyable experience. Yet all of this has been accomplished without any real spoken or signed language. In fact, although he can't say any words yet, Shawn already understands a few. For example, he will look at Mama when she is named and Daddy when he is named. He certainly knows who his funny sister is! Shawn's parents are pretty sure that he understands when they tell him it's time for bed and a few other words, but it is difficult to separate what he understands from the sounds of words alone from what he perceives in the whole situation, the people who are around him, how he is being carried, the time of day, or other similar things. He is, of course, also "reading" facial expressions, tone of voice, and the rhythm of the language that is being expressed.

Watching and Listening

This is an age range in which rhythmic games and songs, especially those that include gestures (like "itsy bitsy spider" and "peek-a-boo") become especially fascinating. Because they include interesting sounds and sights (and very often rhythmic touching is also part of the song or game), and they are repeated many times, the baby will begin to recognize the words or signs in them. This is another example of how multimodal "just for fun" activities can provide some of the best possible learning experiences for all babies.

Babies who are hard of hearing or deaf enjoy and benefit from repeated, joyful nursery rhymes just as hearing babies do. Many babies who use hearing aids will be able to hear the tone and rhythm and even the major words in the rhymes. When gestures are added (as they usually are for all children), the rhymes or songs become even more interesting. Signing can also be used. For example, "itsy bitsy spider," "baa baa black sheep," and other nursery rhymes in English can be seen performed in American Sign Language, British Sign Language, and combinations of sign systems with speech on various YouTube sites. Many DVDs and downloadable files are also available. Parents just learning to sign should be assured that when signing nursery rhymes and other "word" games and songs, the rhythm and facial expressions and body language used will be more important than making the signs exactly correctly. Although language learning is a predictable outcome for babies who have repeated experiences with these routines and games, it is the communication of feelings of fun and the dance of hands and body that will be most important in engaging the baby's attention.

Even when parents, adults, and older children are not engaging in nursery rhymes or rhythmic games, it is beneficial to use exaggerated vocal and facial expressions with babies—perhaps most especially for those with limited hearing. But, at least as importantly, caregivers need to be sensitive to the *pacing* of their interactions and communications.

This means allowing the baby time to respond by looking up or giving an excited wave of the arms or some other signal that he or she is ready for the next action or communication. This is one way of "following the baby's lead." And when a baby is using vision as a major way to receive or be aware of communication, a bit of a longer wait between sentences or verses or signs/gestures is often required.

Thus far, we have discussed "communication" mostly as though it is being produced by the older partner in the exchange—that is, the parent or other adult or older child—and we may have inadvertently suggested that the baby him- or herself is relatively passive. Not so! The baby will be making facial expressions, reaching, changing body position, producing movements with hands and arms and feet, and vocalizing, even though these actions are not actually "language." That is, they are usually not "real" words or signs, but they certainly do send messages about how the baby is feeling, what the baby wants, how engaged the baby is, and how the baby is responding to what is happening. Still, it remains up to the communication partner to interpret what the baby is expressing, to make sure the baby is able to see (and perhaps to hear) the language or other communications that are going on, and to give time for the baby to "take a turn" even if it is only with a look or a motor behavior.

Beginning to Gesture

The fact that babies are not yet producing language doesn't mean that they aren't practicing the basic skills and getting ready to do so. As we discussed in Chapter 5, babies seem to play or experiment with vocalizing various sounds as they approach 6 months of age, progressing from earlier cooing and gooing to making a variety of sounds that may or may not occur in their parents' spoken language. Individual babies' repertoires differ but do not seem to be much affected by hearing abilities at this age.

Another area in which babies with and without limited hearing continue to behave similarly at about 6 months of age is in the production of hand and arm movements that seem to be the precursors—or basic skills—that will soon be used to produce gestures and/or signs. Even during the early months of life, babies can be seen making "pointing"-gestures with an index finger extended. This sometimes happens when the baby's attention has been attracted to an object. But although this looks like pointing that will be used later to directly communicate interests, these early gestures do not yet mean that the baby is trying to attract someone else's attention to an object. That is yet to come.

Another gesture commonly seen in deaf, hard-of-hearing, and babies with typical hearing is a repetitive opening and closing of the fists. This usually occurs in both hands simultaneously. Interestingly, there are reports from previous researchers that some deaf babies with signing deaf parents begin producing signs by 6 months of age. However, the signs that are reported often include both "milk" and "want" which are very similar to this hand movement. So, we, among other researchers, remain skeptical about babies intentionally making signs this early. However, just as most babies with typical hearing progress within the next several months from the exploratory vocalization stage into real babbling that sounds like speech, so babies learning sign language progress to a stage of manual, real babbling that uses specific hand movements and shapes found in their parents' language (Petitto & Marentette, 1991). These early reports of signing may well be careful observations of the beginnings of such babbling.

SUMMARIZING KEY IDEAS

Amazing growth happens over the first 6 months after birth. Message centers and systems are developing rapidly in the brain, motor and physical behaviors are becoming more intentional and more controlled, the baby's memory is developing, cause-and-effect relations are learned, and emotions are differentiated and expressed. The following are some additional key ideas from this chapter:

- Sensory systems, including vision, touch, hearing, and balance/motion systems, are not only developing but are increasingly integrated as the baby becomes a more active contributor to interactions with people and with objects.

- Opportunities to engage in social interactions with parents and caregivers continue to be major contributors to a baby's growth and development; however, as the 6-month age approaches, attention to objects and the effects of actions on them grow in importance. Parents of deaf and hard-of-hearing babies face potential challenges in helping them combine attention to objects with attention to communication and social play.
- Regardless of hearing abilities, development appears to proceed well as long as babies are well cared for; adults give them comfort, love, and nurturance; and communications are addressed to them through multiple senses so that limits to one or more senses do not block them from getting to know and trust their caregiver.
- Early intervention with a focus on successful and responsive interactions supports the development of babies who have multiple developmental challenges, including motor, vision, health, or even social disabilities in addition to limited hearing.
- During the time since birth, the baby has been building an increasingly larger store of experiences. Although the effects of individual differences in these experiences are not yet dramatic, they will become more evident over the next few years. It is critical that experiences provided to an individual baby are matched to his or her sensory and other abilities.
- Information about expected rates and patterns of development for deaf and hard-of-hearing babies can help reassure parents as they learn how to give their babies the special supports needed. Confident parents who understand their babies' abilities, as well as their challenges, can be more relaxed and responsive parents—just what a baby with any developmental challenge needs most!

As exciting as the first 6 months have been developmentally, the next half year will be even more eventful as babies continue to learn to be more in control of their own actions and begin to communicate more clearly and specifically what they need and want. The coming months and years will be an exciting but bumpy ride for all families—bumpier for some than for others. But, with support and a good start, it will become smoother with time.

Chart 4: *Advances to Watch For**

By About 9 Months

Physical and Motor Abilities*	• Sits without support
	• Pulls up to sit or stand, may take a few steps
	• May begin to creep or crawl
	• Clasps hands or objects at body's mid-line
	• Reaches for objects with one hand.
	• Picks up small objects with thumb and index finger
Getting Information from the Senses	• Intentionally explores objects with hands
	• Recognizes by sight objects explored manually[V]
	o Increasingly interested in looking at pictures[V]
	o Can judge depth and distance of objects[V]
	• Recognizes and reacts to familiar sounds, songs[H]
	• Looks up when called[H]
Mental Skills (Cognition)	• Recognizes faces from different perspectives, even if expressions are different[V]
	• Recognizes difference between photo of own face and another baby's[V]
	• Understands relative sizes of objects—what will fit in a container and what will not
	o Likes "filling up" and "dumping out" games
	• Can tell "more" from "less": 1, 2, and 3 objects
	• Drops objects and watches them fall[V]
	• Can learn from visual images/pictures[V]
	• Can remember longer visual sequences[V] or sound sequences[H]
	• Remembers locations of hidden objects

(continued)

Chart 4 *Continued*

Communication and Language	• Expresses basic emotions of joy, sadness, disgust, anger, fear, surprise • Acts silly or "clowns" to get a response. • Uses gaze, vocalizing, or gestures to seek help • Begins to follow another person's gaze[V] • Makes "pointing" gestures but doesn't yet look where others are pointing[V] • Vocalizations begin to "sound like" those in home language[H] • Babbles in voice ("ba-ba-ba") or sign • Recognizes and understands a few words or signs
Social-Emotional	• May be fearful of new people or unexpected events • Initiates familiar play routines • Recognizes that other people have intentions • More aware of how own behaviors influence others

*See Chart 1 for partial list of sources for information.

**On all charts, advances in motor abilities assume no physical disabilities.

[H] may be delayed or require different circumstances if hearing is limited; [V] may be delayed or require different circumstances if vision is limited.

Chart 5: *Advances to Watch For**

By About 1 Year of Age

*Physical and Motor Abilities***	• Creeps, crawls, and may take first steps • Goes from standing to sitting without help • May stand without support • Crawls up stairs (and may come down) • Picks up tiny objects with fingers • Left-or-right "handedness" still inconsistent
Getting Information from the Senses	• Uses all available senses to explore objects • Localizes relatively soft sounds from any direction[H]
Mental Skills (Cognition)	• Combines behaviors and uses objects to attain goals • Uses objects "the way they are supposed to be used" • Understands how objects fit together (e.g., stacks blocks) • Imitates novel, interesting actions even after delay • Searches for objects after seeing them hidden in several locations serially[V]
Communication and Language	• Follows another person's gaze or point[V] • Indicates what she wants and enlists help to get it • Understands, responds to many spoken words and/or signs, including "no" • Responds to simple spoken or signed commands like "close your eyes" • If learning signs, may produce single signs, will "sign babble" and use "home signs" • If learning spoken language, may produce a few words, continue babble, proto-words, and gestures

(*continued*)

Chart 5 *Continued*

Social-Emotional	• Uses primary caregiver as "base" from which to explore new situations or people
	• May show distress in unfamiliar situations or with unfamiliar people
	• Expresses "focused" anger, temper tantrums
	• May "tease" and accept teasing from others
	• Shares emotions when seeing something interesting or accomplishing something challenging
	• Begins to be aware of others' intentions
	• Watches adult (or seeks her example) before deciding how to react in uncertain situation
	• "Plays" with peer by imitating actions, giving and receiving toys

*See Chart 1 for partial list of sources for information.

**On all charts, advances in motor abilities assume no physical disabilities; limited vision may also slow advances in locomotion like crawling or walking.

[H] may be delayed or require different circumstances if hearing is limited; [V] may be delayed or require different circumstances if vision is limited.

7 On the Move
6 TO 12 MONTHS

QUESTIONS TO CONSIDER

- Does limited hearing have any effects on a child's large or small motor skills?
- What aspects of visual attention are particularly important for deaf and hard-of-hearing babies, and how can caregivers best support these?
- What is a baby learning as she engages in social play or in play with objects?
- How do advances in physical and motor abilities (like sitting and crawling), in visual attention abilities, and in both social and object-related play support overall development?
- Why is using play to assess a baby's thinking skills especially helpful if the child is deaf or hard of hearing?

Eight-month-old Felix moves himself across the kitchen floor by pulling forward with his arms and elbows while dragging his lower body rather clumsily behind. Noticing this advance with pride but just a touch of panic, his mother quickly removes the last few breakable objects from within his reach in the room, then puts a pan and a couple of plastic plates that he will be allowed to play with just beyond his reach—encouraging him to move forward a bit more. She then calls her mother into the room and excitedly announces that Felix has started to crawl, "commando style." Felix, meanwhile, has spotted a small bit of cereal that had been dropped to the floor earlier. He reaches out, grasps it with his thumb and fingers, and begins to bring it to his mouth just as his grandmother, concerned that this old piece of cereal is probably dirty, races over and takes it from his hand. Dismayed, Felix looks up at her and begins to wail. She immediately picks him up and cuddles him, bouncing him up and down in her arms as his mother comes over and begins to tickle him. Felix quiets and then begins to laugh, looking from grandmother to mother and back.

Felix is lucky to have a mother and grandmother (as well as a big sister who will be home from school soon) to watch over him. Within a few weeks, he will have turned his "commando" creeping movement into more efficient and quicker crawling and will be able to get himself into much more trouble! More than just movement skills will be gained in the process. Most babies, regardless of their hearing status, continue to rapidly increase competence in their physical, thinking, communication, and social-emotional skills during the second half of their first year. In many ways, it becomes more fun to interact with them as they become better able to take turns and play their parts in exchanges. Their "soaking up" of new information becomes more obvious as babies begin to imitate more and express their needs more clearly through gesturing and actions as well as vocalizations. At the same time, increases in development present new challenges as well as opportunities to parents.

MOTOR DEVELOPMENT EXPANDS A BABY'S WORLD

Motor skills are categorized as being "large" or "gross" motor (for example., Felix's creeping and soon-to-emerge crawling) in contrast to "small" or "fine" motor skills (such as reaching, grasping, and picking up small objects). Typically, both types of skills advance greatly during the second half of the first year. These skills interact with increasing visual attention abilities, memory, and representational skills, allowing the infant to engage in more varied activities and increased opportunities for learning.

Between about 6 and 10 months of age, most babies begin to sit up without support. (Supports can be arranged, with consultation from a physical or occupational therapist, to help babies with physical delays sit comfortably.) A more upright position allows more flexible movement of the parts of mouth and throat that produce speech or speech-like sounds. Sitting also allows increased ability to see what is happening around the room, thus widening the babies' potential visual world and increasing the ability to determine on his own what he will watch. The increased opportunities for visual learning are especially important for babies with limited hearing. Also, sitting (after the baby is skilled enough to not require supporting herself with one arm and hand) allows increased use of hands for actions with toys and other objects. In addition, the hands are freed for increasingly frequent gesturing, and even use of baby signing, to communicate needs and interests.

Usually by about 8 or 9 months of age, most babies begin to move around on their own. Some of them, like Felix, begin by "creeping"— moving themselves forward on the tummy—"scooting" on the bottom while pushing legs against the floor, or rocking, rolling, and just finding various ways to get from one spot to another. Sometimes the first across-the-floor moves are actually backward. It doesn't seem to matter that much to the babies; most of them just want to move around. Limited hearing does not seem to affect this. In fact, even babies with physical disabilities often do whatever they can to get around the room (Figure 7.1). One toddler we know, with braces on both legs, was so intent on exploring her world that she managed several times to get herself trapped in

Figure 7.1 Getting around on his own, he discovers new worlds to learn about and explore. (Photo courtesy of Rob Day. Reprinted with permission.)

corners and under objects. This example leads us to another consideration, however, which is that babies who can locomote (or move themselves around) can, in fact, be a challenge. It's even more necessary to keep an eye on them!

This is especially true because of the other abilities that are developing at the same time. For example, between about 8 and 12 months, babies are increasingly able to coordinate their thumb and fingers to efficiently pick up small items—like raisins and cereal but also like tiny pieces of paper or miniature toys left out by an older brother or sister. By a year, just the thumb and index finger can be used efficiently to pick up quite tiny things, and objects explored are still often put into the mouth. The baby, whose vision is now much clearer than in earlier months and who is better at knowing how far away objects are, might for example spot a tiny object in another part of the room, scoot to it, pick it up, look at it while turning it around several times, then pop it in her mouth to suck or chew on it pensively. Because at about the same time babies often begin to reach and pull themselves to a shaky stand-up while holding on to the sofa or coffee table—soon learning to "cruise" or step sideways while still holding on—the number of objects that they can encounter multiplies rapidly. The good news is that this change in how well a baby can explore his or her own world also multiplies her opportunities for learning. It probably also positively affects the baby's sense of her own "self" as someone who can make things happen and go after what she wants. The downside of all this is the increased vigilance required to monitor the baby's activities. Deaf parents may feel a special need to be on guard, as they cannot always be aware when their child is calling them from another room. Although it might seem easier and safer to constrain or control a baby's explorations at this stage by long-term use of play pens or the like, this is not the best situation for learning. Except when the caregiver needs to assure safety while accomplishing some task that requires the baby to be alone for a while, time in such enclosures should be limited.

This need to attend to safety issues, and any restrictions it may require on a baby's freedom to move around, will differ in different environments. We have observed babies who live in small hut-like houses with floors made of packed dirt, a cook-fire on the floor in the same room, and possibly dangerous insects lurking in dark corners. It is fortunate that, in such environments, babies are usually surrounded by a large number of extended family members—including older brothers and sisters—who keep watchful eyes over the wanderings of the youngest in their midst. Nevertheless, concerns about safety inevitably affect the dynamics of how an infant will be encouraged or discouraged to use new-found motor skills to explore and understand the physical world. These concerns may be sufficient reason for babies in such cultures to be carried almost constantly on someone's back—certainly more often than is typically seen in the Westernized world.

Even in difficult situations, however, most babies refine their initial creeps and scoots into at-first-awkward and then smoothly coordinated crawling on all fours. If this happens, it is usually at some time between 9 months and the first birthday. But not all babies crawl, and, despite some suspicions in past years that crawling affects later language and other abilities, there is no evidence to support that idea. Some babies go from the pulling-up-and-cruising stage directly to walking—or sometimes after only a brief spell of crawling. It is not clear why this happens, but there do not seem to be any long-term implications for this individual difference in developmental patterns.

It was thought in the past that motor development depended entirely on a baby's genes; that is, the sequence and speed of motor development were innate and simply "unfolded" with time regardless of experience. It is true that motor development tends to occur in the same sequence for most children—developing first for the head, then for the torso and arms/hands, then for the legs and feet. However, as we mentioned in Chapter 5, there is evidence that experiences and practice have some effects on the rate of motor development (Adolph, Karasik, & Tamis-LeMonda, 2009). In addition to early (but not sustained) advances when babies' limbs are routinely exercised, being carried while supported only by a wrapped cloth or sling also encourages motor development. This is apparently because the movement the babies experience causes them to develop muscle and balance control at an early age. The opposite has been noticed for babies who are carried on rigid backboards (also called cradleboards) much of the time and whose movements are tightly restricted. These babies tend to develop gross motor skills like sitting and walking a bit later than more active babies, although this initial delay disappears with age. Early motor development depends on the mix or integration of naturally occurring brain and muscle development with the type and frequency of motor experiences.

Differences in visual experiences have also been shown to affect motor development. Babies and toddlers who do not see well usually sit up at about the same age as those with vision, but they tend to be late to reach and walk probably due to lack of awareness of objects that are some distance from them. However, closer to on-time development of these skills can be encouraged by use of specific strategies. For example, small toys or objects can be suspended like a "mobile" but within a blind baby's reach, so that simply moving the hands or feet will provide opportunities to experience touching and moving them. If hearing is functional, music, infant-directed speech, and other input from sound can be important to help the baby learn not only that there is an object or person near him but, with time, to learn to understand about how far away it is. Multiple opportunities to grasp and manually explore specific objects, especially those with differing textures and degrees of softness and weight, will help the baby learn to recognize them over time and encourage reaching for them when they are slowly moved beyond his reach. Delays due to a decreased amount of experience with one sense (vision, in this case) can be lessened by increased experiences using other senses—and the coordination of information from those available senses. Although the experiences emphasized are not radically different from those for all babies, to help identify useful strategies most parents need support from professionals who are knowledgeable about the development of babies with limited vision or who are specifically experienced with babies with both vision and hearing limits (deafblind).

Given the effects of visual limitations on motor development, might limits to hearing also have detrimental effects? Researchers have, in fact, reported delayed average motor development in some groups of young deaf and hard-of-hearing children, with as many as half of the children in some studies having delays in sitting and walking. Some researchers have suggested that because sounds tend to elicit hearing babies' attention, the lack of hearing decreases babies' opportunities to alert and physically respond to information from the environment, perhaps even decreasing their "motivation" to move about. Others have suggested that delays occur because of an overall decreased amount of sensory stimulation when hearing is not present (Gheysen, Loots, & Waelvelde, 2008). This is by no means a universal finding, however, and other researchers report no motor delays or deficits in deaf and hard-of-hearing children (when limited hearing is their only developmental challenge) (Nittrouer, 2010). Our own observations have been consistent with this notion: lack of hearing itself does not necessarily result in delayed motor development. This is shown most clearly by studies involving deaf and hard-of-hearing children with deaf parents, whose limited hearing usually results from genetic instead of disease-related or environmental causes. As a group, they have not been found to show early motor delays even though, in our experience, they were less likely to have had early hearing aid use or exposure to the sounds of spoken language than were children with hearing parents.

An explanation for some increased risk for motor delays in deaf and hard-of-hearing children as a group lies in the anatomy of the inner ear (Rine et al., 2000). In addition to the cochlea, the inner ear also contains structures making up what is called the *vestibular system*. The vestibular organs, located near the cochlea (which, of course, is critical for hearing), support balance—a necessary component of walking. A number of causes of hearing loss (for example, meningitis or other infections) can affect both the hearing and the balance systems and so could result in increased balance problems across large groups of children with limited hearing.

But the vestibular organs do not work alone to support balance. Kinesthetic messages sent through nerves to the brain about the position and movement of muscles and joints (like ankle and knee) assist balance, but vision is at least equally important for being able to keep babies' heads and bodies upright and thus to sit or stand. There is an experimental situation, for example, in which babies are carefully supported and held still while they are shown a moving picture on a screen, creating the appearance that the room is swaying. The babies, responding to what they are seeing and not what they are sensing with their bodies, sway along with the movie (Lee & Aronson, 1974).

The implications for babies who have limits to vision as well as hearing are obvious. Given the relatively frequent occurrence of multiple disabilities among deaf and hard-of-hearing children, including damage to the vestibular system, there is good reason to investigate further when motor skills are developing later than expected. An early intervention team should include or have access to specialists in motor or balance development (usually physical or occupational therapists) who can provide targeted exercises and practice activities when a delay occurs. These may involve increased movement experiences, as well as activities to strengthen joints and muscles, thus giving the baby a chance to catch up or learn ways to compensate for problem areas.

Why bother to focus on something that seems as simple as learning to sit up or reach for things or move around a room? Overall, development is supported better when different skills are working together in tandem. Each area affects others and is, in turn, affected. It is important, therefore, to support development that is as "even" or "synchronous" across areas as possible—especially during the early, most sensitive ages. One development that typically occurs during the latter part of the first year of life can illustrate the way in which such abilities operate and support each other to provide a good foundation for learning. That area is attention, specifically *visual* attention.

Advances in visual attention have been shown to support language learning in infants and toddlers with typical hearing (Adamson, 1995/1996). For deaf and hard-of-hearing babies, this ability is even more critical for progressing in language and thinking skills at an age-appropriate rate. But remember that about half-way through the first year of life, babies tend to begin to focus strongly on objects instead of communication partners. Given this phenomenon, how can parents give information and also interact socially, sharing a focus of attention with a baby who does not hear (or at least does not hear well) what is being said?

"DO YOU SEE WHAT I SEE?": SHARING ATTENTION

Ben is looking at a small yellow truck and rolling it back and forth on the floor. His daddy sits beside him and says "Truck. That's a dump truck." Ben continues to look at the truck but stops moving it for a second or two—as if to indicate that he has heard his daddy. Daddy then reaches down and moves the truck bed upward so that it would dump any contents and says "Bam!" Ben reaches out and takes the truck from him, lowers it to floor and—while looking only at the truck—makes it dump repeatedly while saying something that sounds like "Bah!" "Right!" Daddy says delightedly, "Bam!"

Nine-and-a-half-month-old Ben, who used to spend so much time looking directly at Daddy while waving his arms, smiling, and making little sounds, has become more and more interested in objects and events over the past 3 months. Instead of focusing his attention on Daddy, he is now more inclined to look at, manipulate, and explore a toy or something that can serve as a toy. Ben's world is expanding and so are his efforts to "take it all in" and understand it. This is a positive step in development, but it creates a very different and new situation for parents who were once so often the center of their baby's attention.

Ben's father knows, perhaps intuitively, how to participate in Ben's attention to the toy truck—and even how to use this opportunity to teach a little something. Because Ben has typical hearing, his father knows that the words and sentences he speaks can be heard even when Ben is not looking at him. So Daddy begins to talk about the truck. He then leans in and sensitively—without forcing Ben to do anything—shows more about the interesting things the toy can do. Ben shows that he is following along with what Daddy is doing by imitating the behavior—for example, is Ben trying to imitate "bam"? His father seems to think so. This has been an episode of what is called *supported joint attention*. Both baby and parent have focused on the same object, something the baby himself has shown interest in. The parent has given information related to that thing even though the baby was not seemingly giving him attention. "Sharing" has happened, but it has happened only because the parent was sensitive and alert to Ben's interest and found a nonintrusive way to support it. Dr. Vygotsky would be proud! Here indeed was a more knowledgeable adult "scaffolding" learning—giving the baby the opportunity to learn just a bit more than he started out knowing. How much of the sharing in this interaction depended on Ben's being able to hear his father's speech? Is the opportunity for this kind of easy, natural learning activity limited if a baby can't hear—or can't hear clearly enough to relate Daddy's speech to what is happening?

In fact, such opportunities are not necessarily limited for babies who are deaf or hard of hearing, but their accomplishment requires that parents use somewhat different behaviors to establish supported joint attention. We have pointed out before that mothers who are deaf themselves give us many examples of the use of touching and signing on their young babies and moving so that their signs can be seen while the baby looks at an object. So do deaf fathers. These behaviors really begin to pay off for parents and baby during the second half of the baby's first year. Let's look at an interaction between a deaf baby of about Ben's age and his signing, deaf father.

> *Jake is looking at the yellow truck and leans forward to reach out and touch it. Daddy changes position so that the truck is between him and baby Jake. Then Daddy leans over and signs "truck" just behind the truck. Jake looks up at his father when he sees the sign; Daddy quickly fingerspells d-u-m-p and signs "truck," then reaches back down and, leaving the truck on the floor, pushes the back of the truck up so that it would dump out any contents. Then he quickly slaps the floor with his hand. Jake follows Daddy's hand with his eyes; then, looking only down at the truck, repeatedly makes the dumping movement of the bed of the truck, waving his hand up and down in the air. Daddy taps on Jake's arm several times. When Jake looks up, Daddy quickly signs, "Right! D-u-m-p truck!" as Jake looks back down at the truck.*

How did this deaf father join in his son's focus of attention and provide opportunities for both cognitive and language learning? First, he moved his body so that it would be easier for his baby to know that Daddy was involved in the toy play, too. Then the father signed directly next to the toy so that Jake did not have to look away from it to see its label. Interestingly (and we have noticed this many times with deaf and hard-of-hearing babies), although the baby was not looking directly at his parent, he looked up briefly when his father signed. (Remember that, from early in life, vision seems to be drawn to movement?) Daddy took that opportunity to sign a bit more information about the truck—making the signs up near his face while the baby was looking there. But Jake's glance upward was brief. It was still the truck that had captured and was holding his attention, not his father's communication. However, just like the hearing father, Jake's Daddy was able to show him the label for the object ("truck"), give a bit of new information about the truck, and then (by tapping repeatedly to get Jake to look up again) praise and reinforce him.

Both examples represent an episode of *shared attention* between baby and parent. In each case, the burden for making sure the attention focus was shared fell on the fathers. The babies were responsive but did not make any obvious effort to attract their parent's attention to the object of their interest or to even determine whether the parent was looking at the same thing. Now, think about the kinds of abilities that were necessary for the children's participation in these episodes. Balance supported by a well-functioning vestibular system plus vision plus muscle and joint strength were all necessary for the babies to remain upright. Different parts of the body had to be strong and flexible enough for Jake and Ben to change their direction of gaze, turning their heads to look at different things. They needed to use their newly developed grasping abilities to pick up and manipulate the toys. They also needed to be able to see the objects as well as their parents and to know how far away they were. In other words, both babies had to judge distances in three-dimensional space. For these relatively smooth and coordinated movements to occur, their brain and nerve systems had to be able to transmit electrical signals ("messages") quickly and in a coordinated way. In addition, the babies needed to have the social understanding that the person sitting with them was communicating with them. They had to be aware of that communication and, to some extent, the information in the communication. Perhaps they didn't yet understand the words or signs, but they did understand the demonstrations and learned from them. This, plus increasing abilities to remember what they had seen, allowed the babies to imitate: Ben imitated the action with the dump truck itself; Jake seemed to imitate the gesture that his father used to show what the truck could do. Thus, their cognitive (mental or "thinking skills") system was actively involved during the whole episode which, upon reflection, was really quite complex despite taking only a few moments.

Soon, Ben and Jake, like most other typically developing babies, will use these interacting abilities to take another developmental step in visual attention. They will begin to *spontaneously* look from the object that they are interested in to their parent's face, then back to the object—probably several times—while they play or explore. This advance, which may occur by 12 or 13 months but often isn't frequent until about 15 months, makes it easier for parents or other adults to communicate with babies while they play. Events like this, when the baby flexibly switches visual attention to include both the adult and an object, are called *coordinated joint attention* episodes. The major difference between the earlier developing supported joint attention and the newly developing coordinated joint attention is that, in the second type, the baby starts the episodes or at least collaborates in extending them. He or she is no longer merely responding to prompts. Examples of this more advanced state of visual attention are given below. The first is from a hard-of-hearing baby with a hearing parent and the second from a deaf baby with a deaf parent. Both infants are about a year old. In the coordinated joint attention episodes, the baby checks in with the parent repeatedly without being signaled to do so. There is less support demanded from the parent, and these interactions begin to look like truly shared communication and learning "conversations."

> *Reena's mother sits cross-legged on the floor of our laboratory play room. Twelve-month-old Reena crawls to her, sits up, looks at her mother, and holds out her arms to her. Her mother, who is hearing, picks up her daughter, who is hard of hearing, and talks to her about a ring of pop beads that Reena finds interesting. The baby watches quietly but intently as her mother puts the ring of plastic beads around her own neck. Then, looking from the beads to her mother's eyes and back to the beads again, Reena begins to pull on them so that they turn around her mother's neck. She does this repeatedly, continuing to look from the beads to her mother's eyes and back at the beads until they break. Mother has been talking about what Reena is doing, and, when the ring of beads breaks apart, mother says "Aah! Broken!" with an exaggerated "surprised" facial expression. Reena smiles, vocalizes, and waves her arms up and down with excitement.*

> *Jaime is nearing her first birthday. Crawling around her living room, she spies one of her big sister's toys on the coffee table. Jaime begins to crawl in high gear, reaches the table, and pulls herself to standing. Then*

> *she reaches out for the toy—a miniature teenager doll. Holding it in one hand, she looks up at her mother, who has scurried over to the table herself, and then back down at the doll. Looking back up at her mother, Jaime holds the doll out toward her. Mother reaches for the doll and signs, "No, not for you. That's Sister's." But looking back down at the doll, Jaime pulls it to her chest, seeming to be signing "mine" with the doll in her hand; then she looks back up at her mother. "Look," Mom signs, holding up a brightly covered book she has brought with her, "We can read this—you and me." Jaime holds the doll out toward her mother (who takes it), reaches for the book, looks back at her mother, and (holding the book in one hand) holds up her arms to be picked up.*

The earliest episodes of coordinated visual attention are usually much shorter than those just described—perhaps only one look up to the adult and then back down at the toy. By joining in the play and following the baby's lead, parents can extend these episodes, however, and babies soon become fairly adept at intentionally shifting their attention between objects and a communication partner. Important changes have occurred since the newborn period, when attention was usually attracted only by movement, strong contrasting lines, face-like displays, and (for babies with typical hearing) loud sounds from one side or the other. These initially reflexive, nonintentional attention behaviors progressed to periods of extended attention to faces close to them and then to greater attraction to objects and actions.[1]

Even after babies and toddlers become able to engage in coordinated visual joint attention, they don't spend all of their time in that state. All of the other types and levels of visual attention behaviors continue to occur—even the sort of "unfocused" attention episodes that happen occasionally for all of us. In addition, even when episodes of coordinated joint attention are common, babies and toddlers will continue to spend time attending solely to an object or toy. They will also continue face-to-face (or person-to-person) mutual attention, especially if organized around a song (in voice or sign), or a game using gestures (like clapping or peek-a-boo) or funny movements (Spencer, 2000b).

EAVESDROPPING WITH THE EYES

An additional type of visual attention pattern seems to be especially important for babies who depend heavily on vision for communication. This is called *onlooking* and consists of extended periods when a baby sits back and watches what is going on. This happens often if there are boisterous brothers or sisters present—babies will watch their antics avidly for a considerable length of time without actually participating. Onlooking is also especially frequent between 9 and 12 months for children who are deaf or hard of hearing and whose parents use sign language or many gestures. These babies engage in relatively extended "listening with the eyes" to activities or visual communication. Interestingly, babies with typical hearing who have signing deaf parents also spend fairly large amounts of time beginning around 9 or 10 months watching the adults around them sign messages, songs, or the like.[2] Onlooking seems to depend more on having interesting visual communications in the environment than on hearing ability; that is, it seems to increase as a response (or an adaptation) to experiencing communications being signed to and around them. Onlooking seems to be a visual way to "eavesdrop" and learn from conversations occurring around them.

Based on our research, deaf and hard-of-hearing babies who have hearing parents not only spend less time "onlooking" but often take a bit longer to achieve the stage of actively coordinating joint attention than do hearing babies or those with deaf signing parents. When hearing is not available, it seems important for parents to be extra sensitive to babies' needs for tactile and special visual cues to help them learn to switch attention between objects and a communication partner. Even when coordinated joint attention is a bit late to develop, most babies catch up pretty quickly, although the periods of joint attention may remain shorter on average for babies who have limited hearing and whose parents are hearing. It is important to keep in mind, though, that there is great individual variation among babies in this visual behavior, regardless of hearing ability: the tendency of any one baby to look up and include attention to parents and to communication while engaged with an object varies over time and depending on the situation.

Motor disabilities or delays, especially if they interfere with a baby's ability to sit up or to control the muscles of head and neck, will challenge "on-time" development of the more advanced types of visual attention. And babies who have generally slowed development across a number of areas (for example, children with Down syndrome or with delays in cognitive as well as motor development) will be similarly slowed in their progress through the stages of visual attention. In this case, however, their order of development of visual attention behaviors will most likely follow the typical pattern.

For children with limited vision, specialized interventions will be needed in which tactile exploration of objects and physical contact with persons in the environment supplement or substitute for vision; this will help babies learn to combine attention (even if not visual) to communication partners and toys or other objects. (Behaviorally, these babies often become quite still when attending to something.) In addition, technologies that boost the amount of sound the child can hear should be explored; that is, for the child with both auditory and visual difficulties, use of hearing aids or CIs may be particularly important. Of course, glasses or other interventions to support vision are also critical, with the goal of giving the child as much sensory information as he or she can process. As we mentioned earlier, children who also have motor challenges can be helped by specialists in occupational or physical therapy (or by professionals specifically trained to assist parents with children who are deafblind) who can devise supports and positions that will allow more freedom and control of movements. Here again, it is clear that intervention teams working with parents of babies and toddlers need to include or have ready access to professionals with a wide variety of knowledge and experience beyond that of working with children who are solely deaf or hard of hearing. As always, however, it should be remembered that although therapists and teachers from various specialties bring important specific knowledge to families, it remains parents or primary caregivers who are the experts on the individual child.

How Can We Support Coordinated Joint Attention with Baby?

As we have seen, visual attention is attracted by sounds from as early as birth, and there seems to be an inborn—or at least very early developing—connection between sound and sight. Rhythmic, sing-song speech and rhymes accompanied by hand and finger movements play an important part in early interactions between parents and babies with some hearing ability and are very effective at eliciting attention. In addition, even when babies have typical hearing, mothers tend to include touch (stroking, holding) and movement (rocking, gentle bouncing) along with the visual-sound combination. This kind of "bundled" sensory information reinforces the making of connections across senses. It also gives opportunities for a baby who may be less able to process information through one of the senses to receive it through another.

As with other areas of development, there is obviously more than one way to support advances in visual attention skills. One way to support joint attention is to increase the ease with which a baby can hear surrounding sounds and therefore be alerted to look around for a sound source. Providing a hearing aid in the early months of life often enhances the sound part of the message bundles sent by parents and others, thereby assisting in coordination of vision, hearing, and the other senses. By 6 months of age, deaf and hard-of-hearing children in countries where hearing tests are provided soon after birth (and whose parents want to encourage their hearing abilities) typically will have been fitted with hearing aids and may have used them for several months. The aids may be more or less effective depending on the baby's hearing level without the aid, the degree to which parts of the baby's brain-based hearing system can function, and the age at which the aids were first used. It is very important that frequent checks continue to ensure that the aids are functioning well, that they still fit, and that the baby is consistently wearing the aid or aids. Even with careful monitoring, hearing aids are often not very effective for babies with the most limited hearing. (If they were, CIs would not be needed.) However, even less than perfect results from use of a hearing aid may provide enough information to allow visual attention to be elicited by sounds and objects or people making those sounds. Even with effective aids, the addition of touching, moving the baby, and moving objects in or through the baby's field of vision all help to support on-time development of coordinated joint attention, regardless of whether the babies can hear well or not. Although parents of most babies provide them with these kinds of redundant messages through multiple senses or modalities, this is especially important when a baby's hearing is limited.

Expert Models

Parents who are deaf can promote deaf and hard-of-hearing babies' coordinated joint visual attention very effectively. Deaf parents whom we have observed are fluent signers, but deVilliers, Bibeau, Ramos, and Gatty (1993) reported that deaf mothers who use spoken language, not signs, also emphasize visual communications by gesturing more often than is typical of hearing adults. Thus, parents who depend heavily on visual input themselves seem to develop an intuitive sense of the importance of visual attention and how to support it (Koester, 1992).

A number of researchers, some of them deaf themselves, have reported on the behaviors signing deaf mothers use that seem to accommodate their babies' visual needs during the early months of life and, later, help their babies and toddlers learn to manage their own visual attention (Erting, Prezioso, & Hynes, 1994; Maestes y Moores, 1980; Spencer, Swisher, & Waxman, 2004; Waxman & Spencer, 1997).[3] Moving body and hands within the babies' existing focus of visual attention, making signs within the vision focus or on the baby's body, and stroking or touching to help gain visual attention, all occur more often during the early months and tend to drop away as the baby matures. (Touch as a signal is different from sound, of course. Initially, a touch is more likely to draw a baby's attention to the place that was touched than up to the caregiver's face. Looking up is something that must be learned over time. And, indeed, deaf mothers seem to *teach* their babies during the early months that a touch means to look up at mom, not down toward the touch.)

By 6 months, deaf parents are especially likely to move objects into and through their babies' visual field to attract attention, moving the objects up toward their own faces as they produce positive facial expressions and signed language. (Some, but not all, deaf parents combine speech with their signed communications, especially when they know their baby might be hard of hearing.) In addition, these parents increase their tendency to sit, watch the baby carefully, and wait for the baby to spontaneously look at them. Sometimes this requires more than a bit of patience. Not surprisingly, these parents also frequently tap on objects as though pointing at them, and they tap more often directly on the child's arm, leg, or shoulder to prompt attention to the caregiver's face and communications.

Integrated with these attention-getting and attention-prompting behaviors are mothers' signed communications—typically very short messages of one sign repeated several times or only a short signed phrase. Brief repeated communications are perfect for giving the baby language input while not interfering with his or her visual attention focus for long. Signs continue to be bigger, produced more slowly, and are more rhythmical than signs to an adult or older child (Erting et al., 1994; Koester & Lahti-Harper, 2010). Because of the baby's need to switch visual attention to and from the communication partner, as well as deaf mothers' tendency to wait and give a deaf or hard-of-hearing baby time to lead, communicative interactions tend to move at a slower pace than those between hearing mother–baby pairs. Deaf mothers produce less language and take fewer communicative turns with an older infant than a speaking, hearing mother would in the same amount of time.

Signing deaf parents demonstrate highly effective strategies for supporting their deaf and hard-of-hearing baby's visual attention development, and those strategies tend to change over time in reaction to the baby's advances. It is a delicate dance that follows patterns to which hearing adults are not typically sensitive. However, the attention-supporting strategies used by deaf parents are *not* behaviors missing from hearing parents' communicative repertoires. What tends to differ is the frequency with which they are used and, often, the parents' ability to recognize when one of the strategies may be most effective. Interventions that help hearing parents and caregivers develop this sensitivity have been shown to be effective (Mohay, 2000). Many intervention specialists have found it helpful for parents to video record interactions with their babies and then watch that interaction—sometimes with the sound turned off—paying attention to the effects that different strategies have on their babies' attention as well as what effects their babies' actions seem to produce in themselves (Papoušek, 2008). It may be helpful for hearing parents with deaf or hard-of-hearing babies to also to look at video recordings of deaf parents interacting with their babies. It seems universally helpful (regardless of a baby's hearing status) for parents to slow down interactions periodically and to pay careful attention to what a baby is doing—where her attention is directed and what she is interested in at the moment—and then respond to that interest.

Visual attention is only one of the continuously developing abilities that advances rapidly between 9 and 12 months. A baby's various abilities and skills are now so intertwined with each other and with his or her experiences in daily life that it becomes quite difficult—and even artificial—to try to separate them. Advances in one area will affect functioning in another; delays in one area can also impact the whole developmental process. The goal of early intervention for children born with limited hearing is in large part to *prevent* delays in specific areas so that there will not be overall negative effects. Early delays make it harder to catch up developmentally. And, to prevent delays, sometimes special experiences or special emphases in experiences (such as increasing the visual information available) are necessary.

PLAYING TO LEARN, LEARNING TO PLAY

Many intervention experiences for babies and toddlers are designed around episodes of play instead of usually vain attempts to instruct. This is especially important because the experiences are often provided in the home by parents, not teachers. Intervention happens during the family's daily activities, activities with other caregivers, and activities that are simply normal, everyday interactions between babies and parents and even older sisters or brothers. But when a baby or toddler has limited hearing, these normally occurring activities can have special agendas—a special focus—that intervention professionals can help parents integrate. Play is another area of development that requires the integration of varied abilities and skills. It also provides a frequently used context for assessing what the child has achieved and where the next intervention efforts should focus.

When someone is playing, they are doing something that brings them pleasure but doesn't *have* to be done. Young infants "play" when they repeat actions that have produced an interesting movement, sound, or tactile sensation. They also engage in frequent social play with parents and other adults and older children in face-to-face interactions involving smiles, chuckles, and (often) funny faces and limb movements. With age, increasingly efficient communication of messages throughout the brain, and increasing numbers of varied experiences, both object and social play usually follow a standard set of advances in a similar order.

Advances in Object Play

During the early months, babies demonstrate *simple manipulation* play by holding, squeezing, turning, hitting, and dropping objects. Many of these early object explorations involve mouthing and biting. As they encounter and interact with more objects, they begin to develop more flexible actions and start to use different actions depending on the object itself and what it feels like or will do. During the period between about 6 and 10 months of age, babies begin to visually or manually inspect toys and objects and to react to their specific characteristics by modifying their actions; for example, pushing down on a large button causes a light to flash on one toy, but spinning a wheel on another toy results in an interesting display. The baby who can vary actions on objects depending on their characteristics has moved from simple manipulation of toys to more *functional manipulation*.

Modification of actions becomes increasingly possible as abilities to use the hands and fingers become quicker and more coordinated.

In effect, the baby increasingly becomes an explorer focused on "what does this thing do?" Both Jake and Ben, from the examples earlier in this chapter, had discovered that it was pleasurable to roll the toy truck on its wheels. To the boys, *rolling* was what that thing did; a toy drum, in contrast, would probably have been found to give the best feedback when it was patted or thumped, not rolled. This advance in play actions with objects reflects advancing mental or *cognitive* abilities, as well as more finely tuned motor skills.

Trying new actions requires cognitive flexibility, which can grow from having many different experiences with objects. It allows the baby to be an effective explorer of what objects can do, just as he or she is beginning to explore the larger environment by crawling or cruising around in it. The baby continues to gain a stronger sense of cause and effect by seeing what his or her actions produce. This can build a sense of self as being basically competent—someone who can master new skills and obtain desired effects. Increasing memory abilities allow the baby to remember what action worked best with a specific toy, and the ability to recognize categories of objects is also advancing. For example, after spinning the wheels on one toy car, a baby might then immediately do the same action on a second toy car that is a different color and size. In this case, the baby both remembered the action that worked best on the first car and was able to identify the second car as the same kind of object even though it looked somewhat different.

The next advance in object play skills is called *relational* or sometimes *combinatorial play*, and it tends to emerge between about 9 and 12 months of age. At this stage, babies begin to use two objects together, whereas in the past they tended to focus on only one at a time. This play begins very simply, for example, with a baby touching one toy to another or placing one object in another even though they don't have any reason to be associated. But it progresses over time to actual *functional relational* play in which objects that go together are placed together or stacked or used together in the way that they were designed to be used. At this level, the baby might try to put a ring on a stick (usually unsuccessfully) or place a toy cup on a saucer. "In" and "out" also become interesting to the baby, as in the following example from a 12-month-old deaf infant.

> *Becca reaches for and picks up the toy car. Her mother picks up the "driver" (a peg that has a face painted on it), holds it out so Becca can see it and the car at the same time, and inserts the driver into the seat of the car. Becca takes the peg out of the car, then looks up at mother, then back away to inspect the man and the car. Becca tries several times unsuccessfully to put the driver back in the hole where it fits. Mother signs at the edge or periphery of where Becca can see: "Drat! Try, try to put-it-in." Becca then looks up at mother, smiles, and tries again to insert the peg. After several more tries, Becca successfully puts the pegman in its place. As Becca looks at the peg and car, mother leans in so she can be seen without Becca having to look up and, with a big smile, claps her congratulations.*

Clearly, there is more going on in this episode than just play. Becca's mother is indirectly but sensitively involved in her efforts to place the toy driver back in his seat. We will discuss the mother's role in more detail in a bit, but it is clear that she has first modeled the behavior. Then her daughter imitates that behavior—again showing memory for what she has seen and an appreciation for how the two objects (peg and hole) fit together. She also shows persistent goal-directed behaviors, continuing to work at this "in-out" problem even after repeated unsuccessful attempts. Becca gives no evidence, however, that she understands that the peg is representing a person who drives or rides in the car. (In fact, when her mother tried to interest Becca in the face drawn on the toy, Becca ignored her.) The baby's focus is on the way the two items fit together.

But, in the next advance in object play, the objects begin to be recognized functionally by babies. They begin to learn, for example, that a toy plastic teacup is similar to cups that they hold or have had held to their lips for drinking. This new understanding is shown in brief behaviors called *enactive naming* (that is, "naming" through actions). These behaviors don't actually look like play because they are usually performed briefly with a serious or thoughtful facial expression and no attempt to show or share the action with a play partner. It is an important step, however, showing that the baby is learning that one object (or even a picture) can *represent* or "stand for" another.

Not long after enactive naming behaviors are noticed, babies begin to show evidence of simple *representational* or pretend play. When bringing the tiny toy cup to her mouth, the baby will smile or laugh and look at her mother. She recognizes that this is playful behavior—it is pretending. Not all children reach this play level by a year of age, but some do. Their representational play will usually be limited, however, to a single act of pretending about something that the child does herself in real life. She may, for example, suck briefly on a tiny toy baby bottle and laugh—or curl up on the floor and pretend to be asleep. The emerging representational abilities seen in play indicate that a more general ability to represent something by a mental symbol is developing. The baby recognizes that a picture of a shaggy yellow dog is somehow the same as the shaggy brown dog under her high chair begging for dropped food. And she is also learning that the spoken or signed word "dog" can refer to that same shaggy animal—or others that look and act a lot like it. The baby is acquiring new and more efficient ways to think about and remember things.

Object-related play does not develop in a vacuum. The socially focused play that began developing early in life is also changing and advancing. The two types of play often merge as the first birthday approaches, so that play in general includes both social and object- or action-focused components. This merger is facilitated in part by the advances discussed earlier in the development of visual attention and by contributions that parents, other adults, and even older children make to the play episodes.

Playing with Others

Babies and their caregivers have been engaging in face-to-face play since about 3 months of age, when the babies began to smile in response to others' smiles and playful communications or actions. They even took "turns" in these exchanges by vocalizing or moving arms and legs between the actions or vocalizations of the person who was engaged with them. Although adults may employ brightly colored or otherwise inter-esting objects (if available) during these episodes of play, the real focus is on the social aspects—the sharing of positive emotion and the ability to stay engaged over an extended period of time.

Over the next 3 months or so, turn-taking becomes more frequent as the baby actually seems to intentionally wait for the other person to pause before making his or her own contribution by actions, vocaliza-tions, or changes in facial expression. Imitation can play an important role in social play, and it is clearly another two-way street. That is, when either partner imitates the other, it increases the other's interest and posi-tive affect. A good way to get a baby's attention, in fact, is to imitate his actions. Similarly, parents are clearly motivated to continue face-to-face play when it seems that their baby is imitating what they are doing. After about 6–9 months of age, most babies begin to imitate more often and more skillfully, thus giving their interactions with others a more recipro-cal quality.

The second half of the first year is, of course, when attention is often directed solely at an object, and parents frequently must make accommo-dations in order to interact with the baby when he or she is focused on "things" rather than people. But such complex interactions become easier as the first birthday approaches, and the baby begins to show coordinated joint attention and more often spontaneously includes others in the activ-ity. As attention becomes more flexible, a baby who has had positive social experiences and opportunities for guided as well as self-directed actions with objects will begin to combine the two. The result is that both objects and people become integrated into play activities with greater regular-ity. Because rhythm and repetition continue to attract babies' attention and to be reacted to positively, rhymes and turn-taking games become especially good ways to encourage social play. Peek-a-boo, signing or ges-turing songs like "Wheels on the Bus" and the old favorite "Pat-a-Cake" increasingly engage babies who, as their first birthday approaches and their imitation skills improve, can now participate more skillfully.

And, although most playful exchanges have happened so far when an adult or an older brother or sister was the interaction partner, around or just after the first birthday, babies occasionally imitate another baby's actions, especially actions with a toy. Babies in many cultures in which interactions occur routinely during each day with extended family members and neighbors will typically be exposed to communications and interactions with many different people. But, at this point, even babies who spend much of their time with a few close family members will begin to experience an expanded social world and increased opportunities to learn from others.

Hearing and the Beginnings of Pretend Play

We have observed that social play, especially with a parent, develops similarly over the first year of life whether the baby is deaf, hard of hearing, or has typical hearing. We have watched mothers with deaf or hard-of-hearing babies keep them engaged in face-to-face interactions at 3, 6, and 9 months of age even when no objects were present. Whether mothers were using spoken language plus gestures, signing, or signs plus speech, they and their babies matched facial expressions; the babies actively and rhythmically moved arms, legs, and torsos; and at least most of the time the affect (or emotion shown) was highly positive. This was especially the case when mothers used animated and mobile facial expressions, increased amounts of touching and moving of the babies' arms and legs, and exaggerated and interesting rhythmic hand movements (signs or gestures) (Koester, 1988, 1992; Koester, Papoušek, & Papoušek, 1989). Although these kinds of behaviors tended to occur most frequently when mothers were deaf, hearing mothers of babies with limited hearing also increased such behaviors. This was most common, unsurprisingly, in the hearing mothers who were learning and beginning to use signs. Again, behaviors that most effectively support interactions with deaf and hard-of-hearing babies are usually within the repertoire of all mothers, and their use along with increased recognition of the babies' need to rely on visual and tactile information can lead to mutually satisfying parent–infant play.

Where object-related play is concerned, however, we have noticed some effects of hearing abilities at about the 1-year mark in our own studies (Spencer, 1996). We compared play at that age for three groups of babies and mothers: deaf or hard-of-hearing babies with deaf mothers, deaf or hard-of-hearing babies with hearing mothers, and babies with typical hearing with hearing mothers. All the babies and mothers worked with us when the babies were 9 months old; at that age, we found no differences in the play across groups. All the babies were showing manipulative and relational play. At 12 months, however, babies with typical hearing whose mothers were also hearing engaged in measurable amounts of *representational* play, the beginnings of pretend, whereas none of the deaf or hard-of-hearing babies (regardless of their mothers' hearing status) was seen to do so. This observation was puzzling at first—especially because 6 months later (at age 18 months) the same deaf and hard-of-hearing babies with deaf mothers showed as much and as highly advanced play as the babies with typical hearing. What explained the difference in play across the groups at 12 months?

Once again, it is important to remember that many different abilities are developing in the same time frame and that these undoubtedly affect the behaviors of babies and those who are interacting and playing with them. At around 12 months, babies are just beginning to show coordinated joint attention in which they include attention to an object and to a person in the same episode. The slight delay in deaf and hard-of-hearing babies with hearing mothers may reflect, in part, that group's slight delay in developing coordinated joint attention skills. However, this does not explain the lack of representational play observed in the group of deaf babies with deaf mothers. They were as likely as the babies with typical hearing to engage in coordinated joint attention—although it still filled a minority of time for either group. (Most of the babies at this age, regardless of hearing ability, were most often visually focused on the toys without including many spontaneous looks to mother.) Here is a situation in which hearing levels seemed to influence the pattern of babies' behaviors, and we decided that these reflected differences in their mothers' behaviors during interactions. Hearing mothers of babies with typical hearing tended to give many play suggestions by making spoken comments, and such comments were frequent even when babies were looking at a toy and not at their mother. These suggestions might have influenced the babies' play. The situation was different for deaf mothers whose babies were looking away from them; consequently, their behaviors tended to be different. In fact, they were especially likely to watch their babies quietly, without frequent or extended interruptions to make suggestions. Although they signed about and also demonstrated more elaborate play when their babies looked at them, those suggestions were less frequent than those that occurred in pairs of hearing mothers and babies with typical hearing. Babies who heard their mothers' spoken language probably received more frequent guidance from their mothers at this age than did the deaf and hard-of-hearing babies. (Hearing mothers of deaf and hard-of-hearing babies also gave them frequent vocal, spoken language suggestions—but, of course, most of those suggestions went unnoticed.) The fact that the representational play difference between deaf and hard-of-hearing babies and their age-mates with typical hearing at 12 months disappeared over time (as coordinated joint attention episodes increased) suggests that the 12-month difference is not of long-term significance. It might be an age-appropriate pattern when babies' hearing is limited. This pattern should be kept in mind, however, when play is used as a way to assess development at about the 1-year mark.

Play as a Measure of Learning

Play has been said to provide a "window" through which it is possible to view a child's developmental strengths across various domains of functioning: cognition or problem-solving/thinking skills, attention, communication and language, and motor or physical skills (Spencer & Hafer, 1998). Because playing comes naturally to babies and young children, it is an activity that is fairly easy to elicit—given an interesting toy or two and a secure-feeling environment (usually with a parent or caregiver present and perhaps participating in the play), most babies are eager to become engaged and demonstrate their skills both socially and with objects (MacTurk, 2002).

Not surprisingly, play situations can be used effectively to assess a baby's or toddler's skills, both for the purpose of determining developmental levels across domains and to identify profiles of strengths to use as a basis for early intervention programming. This approach is often used to focus on a baby's level of cognitive or thinking skills. Play assessment can be especially helpful for a baby who is deaf or hard of hearing and has a delay in language or communication skills because it is not necessary to use language to accomplish at least the beginning levels of recognizing what can be done with objects. As discussed earlier, slight delays in the beginnings of representational play by babies with limited hearing with either hearing or deaf mothers may not be significant around 12 months of age.

When unexpected differences or delays are observed in a baby's play, situational or temporary factors that may be causing the difference should be investigated. First, assessments should be repeated at regular intervals, making it possible to determine whether any suspected delays are merely temporary. Second, many protocols for play assessments include parts in which play is prompted or even modeled to see whether the baby can perform at a higher level. Third, most assessments include interview-type questions for parents, asking them to describe their observations of the baby's play behaviors in typical situations at home. Sometimes higher levels of play are shown at home than in an assessment situation.

Several instruments and approaches have been used successfully to assess the play of infants and toddlers who are deaf or hard of hearing. For example, the *Transdisciplinary Play-Based Assessment* (Linder, 1993, 2000) provides a comprehensive, functional assessment across many developmental domains, including cognition, communication, social, and motor skills. A second edition, the TPBA2 was published in 2008 and includes month-by-month guidelines for age-level behavior expectations. A play facilitator as well as parent and peer are video recorded with the child. For a child who has limited hearing, the assessment team should include when possible deaf and hard-of-hearing members, and a sign language interpreter as needed. This assessment approach is especially helpful when assessing infants and toddlers and for children who have language or other delays that make the results of many more standardized tests difficult to interpret. The assessment leads directly to setting goals and designing intervention plans. Although there are numerous play scales and checklists available, at least some part of a play-based assessment should include play between parent or caregiver and child due to the influence of parental guidance and how it might help explain the levels of play observed.

How Does Playing Support Learning?

Playing is associated with freedom to explore and to try new actions with objects (after the environment is deemed by adults to be safe) when rules for exactly how things should be done can be relaxed to allow for greater flexibility. Babies and young children can become trial-and-error experts as they figure out how things work and fit together and how they can be used to give pleasant feedback. This is the case whether they are using a specially designed, tested, and marketed toy that makes sounds, vibrations, and light effects, or they are playing with an old set of pots and pans and an assortment of wooden spoons. (Empty cardboard boxes may be among the greatest prompters of creative thinking and joyful play that exist, and they are often available even when more elaborate manufactured toys are not!) An adult watching this kind of exploration may not notice at first the degree to which the baby is using novel behaviors, employing memory for past activities, and classifying this object with others as she tries actions she has used with similar ones. What might be more immediately noticeable is that after the baby has figured out what can be successfully done with the object, she tends to want to communicate with someone about it—smiling, laughing, sharing attention, even gesturing, babbling, or saying or signing a word. Acting alone, the baby has undoubtedly added to her repertoire of behaviors and knowledge, but even more opportunities and encouragement for learning can occur when she is accompanied in play by an older child or adult.

Benefiting from the participation of a more experienced player depends on a number of factors, however. First, there needs to be a positive relationship established between baby and adult (or older child) so that the baby feels comfortable and free to explore. When this is the situation, the second factor is usually in place. That is, the older person should be responsive and follow the interests and play of the baby instead of interfering and trying to change the baby's play focus. A simple example of this kind of responsiveness might be when a parent imitates a baby's behavior: baby raises small cup to mouth (as in enactive naming), and mother then does the same. But it is also possible to be responsive while expanding a baby's behavior. In this case, perhaps mother smiles, rubs her tummy, and says "yum" while "drinking" from the cup. Remember how the fathers of both Jake and Ben, whom we met earlier in this chapter, expanded on their sons' interest in the truck by showing how it could dump out its contents? Furthermore, the fathers both *labeled* the truck, saying or signing/fingerspelling its name. The fathers' language about the truck had a high probability of being meaningful to the boys because both boys had engaged with and focused on the truck by their own choice—and the fathers joined in their attention focus. Play activities shared between parent, caregiver, intervention professional, and baby can support development across a number of areas but most especially cognition, language, and social domains. Maximizing development in these areas is of special importance for children who are deaf or hard of hearing.

SUMMARIZING KEY IDEAS

Babies who are developing at a typical rate, regardless of their hearing abilities, achieve important milestones during the ages of 6 to about 12 months. The first year of life has been quite eventful—and the pace of development seems to actually be speeding up with time! The following key ideas have been discussed in this chapter:

- Motor development increases the kind of experiences a baby can have and the degree to which he can actively explore and learn from the environment. Although hearing does not seem to affect the rate of motor development, slight delays are more frequent among deaf and hard-of-hearing babies than among those with typical hearing. This is thought to be due to a somewhat higher than average incidence of some dysfunction in the balance or vestibular organs in the inner ear.
- Visual input is important for achieving balance and motor skills. Children with limited vision are more likely to be delayed in this

area and benefit from specialized experiences to promote its development.

- The ability to coordinate visual attention between objects or events and another person develops slowly over the first year of life and, when achieved, allows more flexible communication and interactions. When hearing is limited and sounds do not effectively attract attention, sensitive visual communication strategies used by adults to interact with the baby can provide an alternative basis for visual attention development.

- When babies can attend to both communication and other aspects of the environment this allows adults to more effectively scaffold learning and increase the baby's ability to be an active, intentional interactive partner. (Deaf mothers, who are highly sensitive to visual communication needs, are likely to slow the pace of communications and scaffolding behaviors with babies around a year of age to accommodate their still-emerging attention skills.)

- Representation ability—the ability to know that one object can "stand for" another—also emerges at around the first birthday (or just a bit beyond). It is most easily observed in play behaviors, which become more complex and more varied across the first year and are necessary foundation skills for developing language.

- Observation and other measures of play activities can provide useful means of assessing a baby's overall development: cognitive, social, and motor. Because the ability to understand or produce language is not necessary for play at the manipulation, relational, and early representational levels, play-based assessments are especially helpful when babies' language development is delayed or just emerging.

- Both social and object-related play experiences serve as effective laboratories for early learning because babies are free to explore, learn by trial and error, and practice representational, memory, and problem-solving skills. Sensitive, nonintrusive scaffolding of play by parents and caregivers can further promote development.

- Development occurs most efficiently when it is happening synchronously across various domains, without significant delays in one or another area. An ongoing goal of early intervention is to prevent delays from occurring and therefore support across-the-board development currently and with increasing age.

By the end of the first year of life, a baby's initial mostly reflexive, unintentional behaviors have changed dramatically. Behaviors have become more cognitively complex, more intentional, and more varied. Along with the advances in motor and sensory and play that were discussed in this chapter, communication abilities have also become more complex and more functional. These will be the major focus of the next chapter.

NOTES

1. Increased attention to objects is an indicator of typical development at this age. However, striking decreases in attention to the eyes and faces of other people can indicate social-cognitive disabilities, which may be eased by appropriate early intervention. This should not be ignored but instead reported to the intervention team if there is some concern (Jones & Klin, 2013).
2. The majority of babies born to deaf parents have typical hearing. These children usually become bilingual-bimodal language users. That is, they develop sign language as well as spoken language competency.
3. Even when signing is expected to be a baby's first language, many deaf parents choose for their deaf or hard-of-hearing children to use hearing aids (and sometimes even CIs) at early ages in order to support development of any available hearing abilities.

8 Little Communicators

6 TO 12 MONTHS

QUESTIONS TO CONSIDER

- What is the difference between "communication" and "language"?
- What role does "social referencing" serve for babies? Why might this be especially important for those who are deaf or hard of hearing?
- What types of behaviors are expected in a baby's communications by about 1 year of age, regardless of hearing levels?
- What are the similarities between vocal and manual babbling, and what abilities and experiences are required for "canonical babbling" to emerge?
- What characteristics make parents' language to their babies most effective for supporting emerging language? Which, if any, of these characteristics might differ based on the baby's hearing abilities?

Twelve-month-old Reena is sitting on her mother's lap. They are seated at a table and Reena is facing away from her mother, looking at a researcher who is placing a complicated toy in front of her. The

> *researcher demonstrates that pushing down one of the levers on the toy will cause a little plastic bear to fall down a chute. Reena looks at the researcher, then turns around to look at her mother's face. Apparently reassured that this is "all right," Reena turns back and reaches toward the toy. Then, first looking at the researcher and next up toward the ceiling, Reena vocalizes and points with her index finger to the light above, vocalizes again, and looks back at the researcher. When the researcher does not respond to her point, Reena looks back at the toy and plays with it for several minutes, trying to get the bear to slide down the chute. After several tries, she has figured out how to cause the bear to fall not just down the chute but (to the researcher's chagrin) all the way to the floor. But she has now tired of the game. She grabs the rather large toy with both hands and pulls it toward her. When the researcher tries to gently move it back to the middle of the table, Reena looks up at her, pulls it close again, and makes an "angry" face with cheeks puffed out and lips pursed, then shakes her head as if saying "no." She has clearly had enough of this activity!*

Little Reena is neither talking nor signing, but she uses *gestures* (pointing and shaking her head), she engages in *coordinated joint attention* (switching her visual attention between the toy and the researcher), she uses *social referencing* ("checking in" with her mother for reassurance that all is well), and she signals her feelings quite clearly through a physical gesture (pulling the toy toward herself) and her facial expression. She is a very effective *communicator* even though she is not yet producing any language, spoken or signed. In fact, at around the 1-year mark, few babies regardless of hearing status, can express themselves using language. That doesn't keep them from communicating pretty clearly what they want to do and how they feel about a situation.

"I CAN DO THIS!"

This observation of Reena occurred in a situation during which our research team collected information about her *mastery motivation*. This term is used to describe a baby's (or child's or adult's) tendency to independently and persistently attempt tasks that are moderately difficult for them (Morgan, MacTurk, & Hrncir, 1995). Although this is sometimes described as an inherent or in-born psychological characteristic, it is clear that a baby's experiences help to shape his or her tendencies to explore objects and to "master" the environment.

To assess the strength of a baby's mastery motivation, a task administrator (in Reena's case, it was Dr. Koester) sits across from the baby and provides her with an "object problem." The researcher administering the task is not supposed to react to the baby's efforts by smiling or otherwise communicating. Reena sat on her mother's lap—both for physical support and to allow her to feel secure emotionally. However, Reena's mother was asked to react to her baby only minimally and not to encourage or discourage the baby's actions. In the situation presented to Reena, Dr. Koester showed her a fairly complicated toy and demonstrated that pushing particular parts of the toy would cause a pretend animal to slide down a chute. We had found this toy to be interesting for almost all the babies in the study, and we wanted to know whether Reena would be motivated to figure out how to cause the interesting event to happen herself. At other times, for other babies, different toys or situations were used. Regardless of the specific toy, the baby's interest in the toy was noted, along with the frequency and persistence of attempts to activate and explore it. It was also noted whether the baby eventually was successful in solving the object problem presented. Although the focus of this particular situation is on the baby's motivation to interact with and "master" the toy, the baby's social behaviors, especially smiling and attempting to interact with the adults present were also analyzed.

"Well, I Can, but Should I?"

Dr. Robert MacTurk, the research team's specialist in mastery motivation, was especially interested in the mix of object- and socially related behaviors that the babies produced. Sometimes a baby pretty much ignored the researcher and relied only on direct physical attempts to get the object and make it perform. Other babies tried to get the researcher to help them accomplish the task or tried to start a social interaction instead of manipulating the toy. Still others turned to their mothers for some social signal—rather like looking for advice about how to proceed.

Reena tried to engage the researcher in a social interaction—pointing up to the light and babbling, then looking from it to the researcher, who had to work hard not to respond to her! But Reena tried to communicate with the researcher only after she had looked back toward her mother, using a behavior referred to as *social referencing*. This means that the baby "checked in" with mother, looking to see whether mother's facial expression was reassuring and encouraging or fearful or disapproving before turning back around and beginning to interact with the toy and the researcher.

Social referencing becomes common among most babies at somewhat after 9 months of age. Although it seems to be a simple behavior at the surface level, let's consider briefly what it indicates that the baby has achieved. First, looking from an object or event or situation toward the parent and then back again can be thought of as requiring the acquisition of coordinated joint attention, as discussed in Chapter 7. Second, social referencing indicates that the baby has developed a feeling of trust in the parent, "reading" from the parent's facial expression how the parent feels about the situation and therefore how the baby should react. Third, this simple checking of mother's facial expression involves the baby having a memory of what the expressions indicate—and the brain-level coordination of all the sensory, memory, and motor messages that make up this experience. The simple turn and look up at mother's face is actually a very sophisticated transaction, but one that does not rely on use of language. Reena engaged in social referencing along with other socially related behaviors like using gestures and object-related behaviors as she persistently tried to activate the toy as had been demonstrated. Furthermore, she was successful at reaching that goal, enjoyed her accomplishment, and finally grew bored with the task. These behaviors produced by Reena, who was identified as hard of hearing soon after birth, are typical of a baby with strong motivation to understand and "master" her environment, regardless of hearing level.

Is Reena's strong mastery motivation typical of babies with limited hearing? Questions have been raised by researchers and other professionals about whether a relative lack of auditory information—and therefore less than full ability to process the vocal reinforcement given by parents and other adults—might decrease babies' motivation for mastery and exploration. Two major studies have addressed these questions in deaf or hard-of-hearing babies. Dr. Sandra Pipp-Siegel and her colleagues (Pipp-Siegel, Sedey, VanLeeuwen, & Yoshinaga-Itano, 2003) studied a group of 200 young deaf and hard-of-hearing children. About 18% (35) of the children were below the age of 1 year, and the others ranged up to 5 years in age. Approximately half of the children participated in early intervention programming by 12 months of age; almost half had hearing levels in the severe or profound range. Close to 60% of the children's families were using a sign system plus spoken language with their children; the others were using spoken language only. A substantial proportion of the children had a developmental challenge in addition to limited hearing. These statistics show that the group of children represented a wide range of characteristics, much like the larger population of young deaf and hard-of-hearing children in the United States. The researchers used a scale that measured mastery motivation based on mothers' reports of their children's typical behaviors. Unfortunately, there was no comparison group of children with typical hearing in this study; however, the researchers pointed out that the whole range of possible scores, from lowest to highest, was found across individual children in their study on each of the subscales. They found that scales measuring persistence in mastery motivation related to a parent-report measure of children's language skills. Higher object- and socially related mastery motivation scores were associated with higher language skills.

Dr. MacTurk, in his smaller scale but more detailed observational investigation of babies at 9 and 12 months of age (including Reena),was able to directly compare the behaviors of babies with and without limited hearing. (In fact, he included a group of deaf or hard-of-hearing babies with deaf parents as well as a group with hearing parents.) He and his colleagues found that the deaf and hard-of-hearing children were as likely to show strong mastery motivation as were the children with typical hearing (MacTurk & Trimm, 1989). Lack of hearing ability had not depressed the babies' motivation to explore and succeed at mastering the tasks. However, these researchers noted that babies with limited hearing (again, this was on average) tended to "incorporate more 'social' behaviors in their object-related activities" than did the others (MacTurk, Ludwig, & Meadow-Orlans, 2004, p. 99). That is, the deaf and hard-of-hearing babies were doing more social referencing and making more bids for social interaction during the task than were the babies with typical hearing. The researchers further proposed that the frequent socially related behaviors of the deaf and hard-of-hearing children are a positive adaptation or accommodation to decreased ability to hear, by using social behaviors to get feedback about their performance. This was especially frequent at 9 months of age.

MacTurk and his colleagues performed another analysis to compare the tendencies for a generally social- as contrasted with object-focused mastery style. This analysis did not show an effect based on babies' hearing levels alone. Only deaf and hard-of-hearing babies whose mothers were deaf (and used sign language), not those whose mothers were hearing, showed especially high rates of this more socially oriented type of behavior. Babies had begun to show differences in visual attention and communication behaviors before 1 year of age depending on the amount of visual communication in their environment. They had learned "what works" in their own communication environment.

GESTURING: ON THE WAY TO LANGUAGE

Social referencing as well as gesturing are important means for communicating during the early years, regardless of a baby's hearing level. Expressing actual words or signs is quite rare during the last months of the first year of life, but extensive use of gestures for communication is very common. Gestures are usually thought of as being "manual," as the hands and fingers are used for common gestures like reaching and pointing. But gestures can also involve all parts of the body—like turning away from something, or making a "no" head shake. In addition, the mouth and face can be used to produce gestures, like lip smacking to mean "yummy" or like Reena's "angry" facial gesture described earlier. Another common early gesture involves holding out an object to show it to someone. Although this often looks like the baby is asking the other person to take the object, babies (especially around 9 or 10 months of age) frequently pull the object back toward themselves instead of letting the other person take it. It seems this gesture is meant to serve the purpose of getting joint attention to an object, not to give it away! Another common gesture is the raising of arms to ask to be picked up. An even more direct gesture is pulling on mother's skirt or legs to try to get her to go where baby wants her to go.

During this approximate age range, babies also begin to acquire less "direct" gestures. (See Simms, Baker, & Clark, 2013, for a scale including many of these behaviors—with information about ages based on a group of deaf babies who have been experiencing American Sign Language [ASL] communication from birth.) For example, they can learn to wave "bye-bye" in appropriate situations if it is modeled and prompted by an adult or older child. They can even be helped to learn this gesture by having an adult hold their arm gently and wave it for them—as long as the babies "go along" with this manipulation and do not struggle against it. By 1 year of age, babies will turn to look where someone is pointing. Their own pointing expresses communicative functions: making requests ("Can I have that?" "Can we go outside?"),as well as directing another's attention to something specific ("Look at this nifty thing!"). Using gestures along with their direction of eye gaze, their actions with objects, their body postures, and their vocalizations, babies are becoming effective *communicators* even if they do not yet express any actual words or signs.

If a baby, regardless of hearing ability, does not use gestures by about a year of age, some assessment of functioning, including social and cognitive skills, should be performed to see whether anything is interfering with communication development. Deaf and hard-of-hearing babies without other developmental challenges should not be delayed in using gestures no matter which language approach—oral (spoken only), oral plus signs, or signing only—is being used by their parents.

BABBLING: PRACTICING THE BASIC SOUNDS AND MOVEMENTS OF LANGUAGE

Unlike gestures, the pre-language behavior of *babbling* is not often used to serve a communicative purpose—although when it is imitated and responded to it can do so. The term "babbling" is sometimes used informally to mean any kind of vocal sound that a baby makes. But we use a slightly different definition here. In this discussion, "babbling" refers to specialized movements of the hands of babies learning sign language as well as to the sounds produced by the mouth.

Babbling Sounds

You may recall that by about 3 months of age most babies produce "cooing and gooing" sounds. Then, by about 4–6 months or so, many babies become vocal "experimenters," producing shrieks, trills, and other nonspeech-like but very interesting sounds along with those coos and vowel sounds. All of these kinds of early vocalizations tend to occur at similar ages regardless of babies' hearing levels. Furthermore, *volubility* (how often vocalizations are made) generally does not differ between babies with different hearing levels (Ertmer & Iyer, 2010).

For babies with typical hearing, new kinds of vocal sounds begin to be produced by about 8–10 months of age (sometimes a bit later). The new type of sound consists of consonant-vowel combinations that sound like real syllables used in spoken language, syllables like "bah" and "gah." Sometimes these syllables are repeated in strings like "da-da-da" and "ga-ga-ga-ga." These syllable-like vocalizations are called *canonical babbling* or *syllabic babbling* and typically include a fairly small number of consonants, including the sounds of /p/, /b/, /c/, /d/, /n/, /k/, and /g/, as well as a variety of vowel sounds. (Many babies also use a breathy /h/ sound as in "huh-huh-huh," but combinations of vowels with this consonant are not usually considered to be canonical babbles.) This set of consonant sounds occurs in the babbling of babies in a number of different spoken language environments, including but not limited to those whose parents speak English, French, Swedish, and Japanese (Vihman, 1993).

As babies produce these kinds of babbles repeatedly, the neurological (brain and nerve) circuits as well as the muscle movements they control are practiced and become more automatic. Canonical vocal babbling serves as a sort of training period for producing speech-like sounds. Over time, the syllables become specialized to match those in the specific spoken language the baby is hearing. The babies have keyed into and show they are paying special attention to differences in sounds that matter in the spoken language they are expected to learn.

Although canonical babbling consists of combinations of those sounds that are used in adult language, the babbling baby is still just making sounds and not words. In addition, the baby isn't really trying to communicate any specific word or message beyond generally inviting interaction. (In this regard, gesturing may be considered more advanced communication than babbling.) However, even though the baby isn't trying to say a word, the babbling sounds so much like the syllables in spoken language that many parents interpret babbles as being real words. Perhaps baby is happily playing with sounds while looking around and produces "da-da-da-da-da." Her mother excitedly concludes: "Oh, listen, she said 'da-da.' . . . She must want her Daddy!" This is a positive adult response to babbling. Although the baby has not yet actually matched this sound with a specific meaning, a parent reacting to it with pleasure and providing it with a meaning will encourage the baby to say it again . . . and again. Over time, and especially if Daddy is present when this happens, the baby will learn to actually match these sounds with that guy called "Daddy." (Again, notice the importance of social feedback, not only in terms of shaping early sounds into words but also in terms of the impact it has on the baby's desire to communicate with others and to use language to influence others.)

What allows a baby to reach the canonical babbling stage of vocal development? It is obvious that this kind of babbling requires quick, coordinated movements of all parts of the speech system: the mouth, tongue, lips, palate and throat, the larynx (voice box), even the lungs. The ability to do all this is based on the maturing nerves and brain structures that allow coordinated movements and on the muscles involved in producing them. This is one reason that canonical babbling doesn't occur before the first half-year of life and usually not until months after that. But more seems to be required than physical development. Dr. Lorraine McCune (2008) suggests that canonical vocal babbling is a result of babies' overall cognitive development, representing advancing coordination of thinking skills, attention development, hearing experiences, and motor abilities used to produce speech sounds. Unlike earlier developing vocalizations, canonical babbling also *depends on experience hearing.*

Babies who are hard of hearing may begin to produce vocal canonical babbles at about the same age as those with typical hearing, although they are often a bit delayed in doing so; however, babies who are deaf and have little to no hearing are almost always quite late to develop this ability. There are reports of babies with severe or profound hearing levels beginning to babble vocally—but not until 6, 9, or even 12 months later than is typical for a baby with typical hearing, if at all (Oller, 2006). Even after vocal babbling begins, there tend to be differences between children with typical hearing and those who are deaf or hard of hearing in the proportion of total vocal utterances that contain canonical babbling syllables and the consistency with which the syllables occur (Moeller et al., 2007a; Nathani, Oller, & Neal, 2007). In general, researchers and speech/language specialists consider a baby to have reached the canonical babbling stage if 15–20% or more of their vocal utterances have one or more canonical syllables in them. Over time, the proportion of vocalizations that are from earlier stages (cooing, yelling or trilling, vowels only) decreases, and the more advanced babbling increases.

Of course, it is always important to keep in mind the differences that occur among individual children. For example, some babies with typical hearing will have a "favorite" consonant sound that they use a lot when babbling; others may, for unknown reasons, produce another sound more often. Usually a variety of different sounds are produced. Children with limited hearing usually show a limited number of different consonant sounds and have slower growth in the proportion of their vocalizations that are canonical babbles. Deaf and hard-of-hearing babies and toddlers may also tend to specialize in producing consonants that are more "visible" when produced by others. These include consonant sounds like /b/, in which both lips are brought together and then released, and /d/, in which the tip of the tongue contacts the top of the mouth.

One way to know whether a hearing aid is giving a baby access to the sounds of speech is to listen for the development and frequency of canonical babbling (Bass-Ringdahl, 2010). The emergence of canonical babbling can also be evidence of whether a cochlear implant is providing effective input (Ertmer & Iyer, 2010). When neuromuscular and other developmental abilities are already in place, a fairly brief time of quality hearing experience is sometimes sufficient to support babbling. However, the variation among children is again quite striking.

Thus far, we have discussed babbling that is produced vocally—but is canonical babbling a "speech" phenomenon that occurs only in babies learning a spoken language? Fascinating observations of deaf babies who are exposed to sign language from birth suggest that this is not the case. Instead, babbling at the level of syllables may be a universal step in getting ready to produce language whether it is spoken or signed.

Babbling with the Hands

In the early 1990s, Drs. Laura Petitto and Paula Marentette (1991) published a report of their study of the manual behaviors of two deaf babies with signing deaf parents and three babies with typical hearing who had hearing parents and had never seen sign language. The researchers recorded the babies at about 10, 12, and 14 months of age and used a detailed coding system to identify specific hand shapes, their locations, and the direction of arm/hand movements that the babies produced. They then compared across children the productions that were neither standard ASL signs nor gestures. Looking only at the manual behaviors that contained hand shapes and other characteristics that could be used in ASL, the researchers found that the deaf babies produced far more possible "manual syllables" (or manual babbling) than did the babies with typical hearing. This was the case despite the fact that the groups produced similar numbers of regular communicative gestures. Manual babbling increased in the deaf babies at about the same ages that vocal babbling accelerates in most hearing babies (see also Simms et al., 2013).

Some have suggested that what has been called "manual babbling" in deaf babies is simply a different interpretation by adults of the hand movements common to all babies—for example, the repeated closing and opening of both fists mentioned in an earlier chapter. But Petitto and Marentette made a strong case that the frequencies of specific hand movements were different for the deaf and hearing babies. Babies with typical hearing produced fewer types of what might be called manual babbles, and they produced such movements less often. And, just as individual babies can have favorite sound combinations in their vocal babbles, the two deaf babies showed individual preferences in the locations of their manual babbles and the kinds of movements used. Thus, vocal canonical babbling seems to have a counterpart in the production of "manual babbling" or babbling with the hands by babies whose parents fluently use a sign language in the home environment. Just as vocal canonical babbling grows from a combination of social and physical experiences plus the experience of listening to the sounds of spoken language, manual canonical babbling emerges from social, physical, and visual experiences with signed language. This is one bit of evidence that "language is language" and that human babies are equally prepared to learn language whether it is heard and expressed through speech or seen and expressed through sign.

Babbling seems to serve similar functions and to be responded to similarly whether it is vocal or manual. Deaf mothers who sign are as quick to notice babbling with the hands as hearing mothers are to notice vocal babbling. Just as a vocally babbled "dah-dah-dah" may be interpreted as "Daddy" by a hearing mother, the opening and closing of hands we described earlier may be interpreted as meaning "milk" or "want" by an American deaf mother. If she interprets this as a request for food and responds to it as such, the initially nonmeaningful hand movements will acquire that meaning over time. Does a baby initially know that "dah" means Daddy or that closing the hand repeatedly means "milk"? Almost surely not. Will the baby *learn* to use that sound or movement over time to express those meanings if the movements are reinforced by the parent? Almost certainly!

As adults interpret and reinforce meanings that they think the babbles express, they are shaping the babies' emerging "real" language skills and helping them make the transition from babbles to words or signs. Therefore, the overinterpreting that many mothers do is a positive not a negative thing. This is part of parents' intuitive, helpful responses to their baby's naturally occurring developmental advances. The reactions of deaf mothers to their baby's manual babbling suggest that hearing mothers who are learning and using signed language with their babies should also be alert for potential manual babbles that could be interpreted and responded to as though they were signs.

Babbling seems to be an important step just preceding the expression of actual, specific meanings in language—whether that language will be signed or spoken—providing practice of the movements (of either hands or the vocal articulators) that will soon be used to express language. This undoubtedly helps strengthen the nerve and brain message pathways that will allow quick and automatic (without effort or thinking) movements to produce either the sounds or the signs of language. *Automaticity* is an important step in the learning of many motor skills, whether of hands or mouth and vocal apparatus to produce language; trunk, legs, and feet for walking or running; or the magnificent twisting, leaning, and balancing required to ski down a steep slope. It's only after the basic movements are so practiced as to happen without conscious thought that special challenges (thinking about which word to use, figuring out how to manage a mogul that wasn't on the slope yesterday) can be effectively handled.

In some of our own research (Meadow-Orlans, Spencer, & Koester, 2004), we have observed babies progressing from vocal canonical babbling to production of actual words. We unfortunately did not measure manual babbling. Petitto and Marentette looked at the manual babbling to sign transition, however, and discovered that syllable shapes and movements in manual babbling formed the core of those used in the first signs that the deaf babies learned and used. These observations suggest that babbling is a signal that language is about to emerge—whether in spoken words or signs. It is not yet known, however, exactly how much auditory input from spoken language or how much fluent sign language is required for canonical babbling to emerge. Nor is it clear to what extent babbling is a necessary step in language emergence.

UNDERSTANDING LANGUAGE

Thus far, we have said quite a bit about things that are *not* language. Communication of feelings, basic needs, and desires can occur through gestures like reaching and pointing, postures, vocalizations like crying or grunting, changes in direction of eye gaze, or pulling or pushing on someone's hand or leg. As Drs. James McLean and Lee Snyder-McLean put it, "children's demonstration of intentions to communicate does not mean that they begin to use language. It simply means that they have discovered that they can have effects on people through their own actions" (1999, p. 50).

Hopefully, it has become clear that deaf and hard-of-hearing babies develop abilities to communicate when they are cared for by adults who are sensitive to their needs, are responsive both physically and emotionally, and when the babies have no significant organically based developmental challenges beyond limited hearing. Abilities such as gestures may be delayed when babies have vision or motor/physical difficulties or have an overall slowed rate of development. However, even if delayed, they should appear—especially when prompted by interventions, modeling, and encouragement. When a baby's skills in social and motor areas are developing on time, but communication is either rare or does not occur, a more intensive investigation of overall development is necessary. However, it is entirely possible for communication skills to develop, but if language is not seen or heard well by a baby then language itself is likely to be significantly delayed.

So, What *Is* Language? (Some Technical Definitions)

What makes an expression "language" and not just "communication"? Notice that although gestures and even vocal and manual babbling seem to be mostly universal—that is, they look and sound similar across a number of cultures—this is not the case for language. A pointing gesture is used across the world by babies, but, in contrast, languages use specific sounds (or, in the case of a sign language, specific hand movements) that have culturally defined meanings. The sounds in the word "good" have a specific meaning to speakers of English, for example, while the sounds in the word "bueno" have a similar meaning for speakers of Spanish. There is no direct connection between the sounds of the words in either language and the meanings they represent. This characteristic of language is called *arbitrariness*. A word (or a sign, for that matter) means what it means because the people using that language have historically agreed on its meaning. Some signs, more often than spoken words, bear resemblance to the meaning they represent. For example, in ASL, "want" is made with a grasping movement; "BIRD" is made with finger and thumb placed and moved like a beak. However, although these relationships may be clear to older children and adults, they are usually not so apparent to babies learning sign language. From a baby's perspective, most signs are just as arbitrary as are spoken words.

In addition to being specific to a culture, language is *symbolic*. A symbol represents or stands for a thing or a meaning, and, unlike a pointing gesture, for example, it "brings to mind" that meaning even when the thing it represents is not present. A symbol can be spoken, signed, or written. However, the symbols used in language are not limited to single words for objects, events, and ideas. There are also symbols for grammatical terms (as in spoken English "the" or "is"; in Spanish "el" or "es") or for parts of words that represent or modify the meaning of a root word. For example, the English word "softness" is made up of two morphemes "soft" and "-ness" (which means something like "having the characteristic of"); "boys" is made of two morphemes, the base word "boy" and the "–s" that means "more than one." Morphemes can be combined to represent a wide variety of meanings in each language. (Natural sign languages also have specific, but different, ways to express such meaning combinations.)

The units of language cannot be strung together in just any old way because languages are also *rule-governed*. There are rules about the way sounds and meaning units (morphemes), words, and even phrases can be combined and the order in which a particular language allows them to be combined. The same is true for hand shapes and movements in sign languages. Again, the rules and the strictness with which they must be followed can differ across languages, but there are always rules.

Although a desire to communicate provides much of the motivation for learning language, language is a much more complicated mental achievement than communication through gestures or even using pictures. Babies who have had a year's worth of experience with fluent visual, signed language as well as those who have experienced sound-based, spoken language from their parents and other family members will understand significant amounts of their family's language by the end of that first year. They are typically "on the cusp" of producing single words or signs themselves. However, for the majority of 1-year-olds who are deaf or hard of hearing, this is not a reality, even with early identification of limited hearing. Even with early use of hearing aids—and quick-as-possible learning of sign language by new parents—babies with limited hearing will have had fewer months of exposure to language by age 1 than will babies with typical hearing. Keep in mind that babies with typical hearing, who begin to hear some sounds even before birth, actually have had 14 months or so of hearing experience by their first birthday. This makes it amazing that, as we will see, deaf and hard-of-hearing babies with signing deaf parents actually keep up with age expectations in the early stages of language development despite not having had any experience with signed language in the womb! This attests to the "value added" of having parents who can intuitively respond to visual communication needs because of personal experiences.

How Do We Know What Babies Understand?

By about 1 year of age, most babies with "typical" language experiences (those who have heard spoken language or have seen fluent and consistent sign language)—and who have responsive parents who provide them with rich and varied language models—seem to understand some words, phrases, and sentences. It is notoriously difficult, however, to determine what exact language babies understand separate from the totality of activities happening around them. For example, suppose a mother says or signs "Time for lunch!" as she carries her baby into the kitchen. The baby begins to raise and lower his arms in a motion like that he uses to beat on the tray of his highchair when being fed. "Oh!" mom might exclaim, "You know what the word 'lunch' means!" Well, maybe. They probably eat lunch about the same time every day…and they are heading into the kitchen where baby always has meals…and mom might even have unconsciously pointed to the highchair or smacked her lips when saying it was lunchtime. Does baby understand that it is lunchtime? Yes. But if the word "lunch" had been spoken in a different context, outside the usual time and place, would he have recognized that word? Furthermore, if the baby actually recognized that word out of context, would he have done anything to show that he recognized it? Maybe or maybe not. As you can see, getting a firm grip on what a 10- or 11-month-old actually understands from language alone is not an easy task.

Despite the complexity of measuring what words or signs a baby really knows, parents remain the most reliable and trustworthy sources of this information. They will know if a child reacts to a word or sign in varied situations and when it is produced by various people. Parents' decisions about what words or signs their babies understand become more trustworthy and consistent if they are given a list of specific words and asked to remember circumstances when babies understood them rather than if, for example, parents are simply asked to list words their baby understands. The former approach is used in the MacArthur-Bates Communicative Inventories (CDI; Fenson, Marchman, Thal, Dale, Reznick, & Bates, 2007a, 2007b), which has one form for babies from about 8–16 months of age and another form for those who are older (16–30 months). The form for younger babies (Words and Gestures) specifically asks about words that are understood. Parents report those words and separately report words that are spoken and gestures that are produced. Most of the words on the infant-level CDI have sign equivalents. However, not all of the items on the instrument designed for babies learning American English are appropriate for babies who are deaf or hard of hearing. For example, a deaf baby may not have heard animal sounds the test asks about (although these items may be appropriate for many hard-of-hearing babies), and there are no signs to represent those sounds. But when the necessary changes are made appropriate for a specific baby's level of hearing, the CDI can provide a helpful guide for parents and professionals. Although the English-based CDI has been widely used with deaf and hard-of-hearing babies, a separate form has been developed for babies who are learning ASL. There have also been adaptations for many different languages around the world, including Italian, Japanese, Spanish, and British English. Dr. Laureen Simms and her colleagues (Simms et al., 2013) have developed an additional scale that consists of a checklist of developmental steps for babies who have been exposed to ASL from birth. This scale does not directly address specific vocabulary items but can provide an overall check on whether development in sign language is meeting age expectations.

Results from use of research and language assessment instruments across many cultures confirm what parents already know. By a year of age, babies recognize many words (or signs) for often-used objects (for example "ball" and "cup") and people they know ("Mama" and "Papa"). They usually clearly understand only about 10–50 or so words. However, some babies are actually not simply understanding but are expressing several words or signs consistently by that age (although usually only about 3 to about 10), while many others in equally supportive environments may not do this until about 15 months. And this wide age range is "normal" even when there are no special challenges to language development.

Promoting Language Understanding

Although babies between 6 months and about 1 year of age produce little if any expressive language, the developmental stage marked by gesturing and use of facial expressions for communication—as well as babbling in sound or sign—is a period during which language models can have significant impact. Babies are "taking in" much more language than they are giving back. However, this presupposes that the language being presented to and modeled for the child has a couple of important characteristics. First, language input is more effective if it is about an object or topic in which the baby is currently interested. Second, the language needs to be easily accessible or available for the child to perceive—to receive—to hear, see, or feel.

Staying on the Baby's Topic

Throughout this volume, the idea of *responsiveness* has been brought up and discussed. It has been used to describe nurturing parenting behaviors in response to a baby's physical and emotional needs. It has also been mentioned regarding ways to encourage visual attention and emerging play behaviors. But here, we want to focus on one form of responsiveness that specifically relates to promoting language understanding: *topic responsiveness*. Parents are usually quite good at topic responsiveness. It merely means talking (or signing) about something the baby is playing with, looking at, or showing interest in. For instance, if a baby is holding and paying attention to a ball, and his mother says, "That's a ball," she is being topic responsive. On the other hand, if the baby is holding a doll but mother picks up a ball and bounces it in front of the baby, saying "This is a ball. Look at the ball," she is changing the topic—not being responsive. It has been shown in a number of studies, and recognized by many professionals and parents themselves, that babies are more likely to learn to recognize words that are topic-responsive than those that are about a new topic not introduced by the baby him- or herself. This might be for social reasons—few of us like to have our focus of attention ignored or disrupted. But it certainly is due at least in part to cognitive or thinking processes. When a baby is already focused on something, and someone provides the word or sign for that thing, learning it is essentially a one-step process. The baby is already thinking about that particular object and attending to it, so the only real additional requirement is that the label given be matched with that current focus of attention. In contrast, when something new is introduced, the baby must first change the focus of his or her attention. That is one step. Even if that happens, matching the label with the focus of attention is a second, additional step. It's simply more complicated. Of course, adults can't go around always responding with language to a baby's current interests any more than they can encourage every action that the baby decides to try to perform. (And there will, in fact, be some instances when distracting the child from something such as an electrical outlet by changing the "topic" is an appropriate parenting strategy!) But when promoting language is an expectation of an activity (and that can include things like getting ready for bed, eating, going outside, as well as playing together), a greater proportion of topic-responsive language is beneficial. Although this is the case at many ages and developmental stages, it seems most important as language understanding and first productions are emerging (Figure 8.1).

Intake Versus Uptake

No matter how responsive an adult's language is to the baby's topic, nothing is gained unless the baby can actually receive it through sound, sight, touch, or a combination of senses. Even when parents are speaking to a baby with typical hearing, the baby may not be attending to what they are saying (although the baby is more likely to "tune in" when the adult is being topic responsive). But these parents can be reasonably confident

Figure 8.1 Listening and looking and learning. (Photo courtesy of MICHA—Society for Deaf Children, National Council. Reprinted with permission.)

in this situation that the baby is getting at least some of the message. This is not the case when a baby has significantly limited hearing, of course. Dr. Margaret Harris (1992) made a point of differentiating language being modeled for a deaf or hard-of-hearing baby, called "input," which she described as the language produced by the adult, from the baby's "uptake," that is, the language of which the baby is actually aware. Others have referred to this distinction as language that is "available" versus that which is "accessible" (Sass-Lehrer, 2015). Limited hearing interferes with the accessibility of spoken language that is produced around and even directly to a baby. In addition to technologies that can increase the strength and clarity of the sounds of spoken language, making language more accessible visually can also support early "on-time" language development.

Because babies' coordination of visual attention between communication and the object world is still emerging as their first birthday approaches, we have noticed many deaf mothers making even more use of visual strategies now than with younger babies (Waxman & Spencer, 1997). Some of these strategies are easily adopted by hearing mothers, although others seem to take more effort to implement. Hearing mothers who are learning and using sign language have, in our observations, been more likely to be alert to visual attention needs than are those who are depending on spoken language only. But, just as older people who are losing some hearing tend to focus on a speaker's face to help them understand what is being said, the same is true for babies and toddlers whose limited hearing allows only partial uptake of spoken language through listening alone. Interestingly, both signing and oral-only toddlers tend to look at their mothers' faces, not their hands, during communicative interactions, so these strategies can be useful regardless of the language method being used by the mother. Let's review some of the visually sensitive strategies commonly used by signing deaf mothers with deaf and hard-of-hearing babies who are beginning to understand (and perhaps even produce) language:

- Mothers "pace" their interactions to meet their babies' visual attention patterns. When mothers wait longer for their babies to look up, communication turns occur more slowly. The number of signed utterances produced by the mother over a specific amount of time will be lower than the number of spoken utterances typically spoken by a hearing mother in the same amount of time. But the signed utterances seem to be quite powerful. Babies experiencing fluent sign language environments develop understanding and expression of their first language at least as early as do babies with typical hearing who are in supportive spoken language environments.

- Mothers use the tapping "look at me" signal more consistently, giving the baby time to look up before signing. They now rarely move themselves to make signs where their baby is already looking. Instead, they expect the baby to respond to the "look at me" signal—unless the baby, as some do, has already learned to look up frequently enough to assure easy communication without signaling. The practice of moving an object to attract a baby's attention up to mother's face, then signing about it, continues.

- Mothers tend to make their sign movements fairly large, slow, and rhythmic. They don't use many signs in one utterance, though. In fact, many signed expressions are only one or two signs long plus some pointing or similar gestures. This makes it easier for the baby to get the message with a fairly quick look.

- Mothers use a lot of repetition—even more, it seems, than at earlier ages—to give the baby multiple chances to see and receive the signed message.

- Some mothers, but not all, make signs in the periphery of their babies' visual fields—that is, on the edge of where the baby can see without turning the head—instead of signaling the babies to look up at them directly. Babies (like adults) tend to be sensitive to movements in their peripheral vision and so may look in that direction when seeing movement. Mothers will then often repeat the signed message.

These visual communication strategies will be just as useful when a combination of signs and speech (or a system like cued speech; see Chapter 1) is being used by the adult. Similarly, if speechreading (lipreading) is a tool that the baby is expected to learn to use, these visual strategies will also be helpful. Hearing mothers (and intervention professionals, for that matter) can and do learn to use these strategies when they find out how helpful they are in supporting language development in deaf and hard-of-hearing babies. The hardest adaptation for many hearing people who learn sign language as adults (and we are speaking from personal experience) is to slow the pace and wait for visual attention. Yes, it sounds easy enough, but it is quite a challenge for many of us. As in other things, however, practice results in improvement. As mentioned in an earlier chapter, hearing people have found it helpful in increasing their effective use of visual strategies to video-record themselves interacting with their babies, then watch the recording with the sound turned off. How much of their language did the baby have the opportunity to "uptake"? This activity will also help new signers see what they are actually signing because many hearing people (again, as we have personally experienced) can be misled when using speech plus signs—thinking that they are signing more (and more clearly) than is actually the case.

It is important to recognize that babies are taking in and beginning to understand language before they can produce it. This period of "absorbing" language is critical. The rate of learning depends upon the modeled language being easy to process. This means that the best "input" is language that occurs in real-life, everyday situations; that is easily accessible to the baby; and that relates directly to the baby's current interests. These input characteristics allow the best chances for "uptake"—the taking in and using of language experiences to build increasingly sophisticated knowledge. The results of this input will be increasingly evident over the coming 12 months.

SUMMARIZING KEY IDEAS

Over the first year of life, babies typically acquire skills and abilities at an incredibly fast rate. By the time they reach about 1 year of age, most babies (regardless of hearing levels) are effective communicators. They intersperse visual attention to people and communications with their efforts to explore and master objects and situations. They use gestures and facial expressions as well as vocalizations to express interests and needs. They understand how to look where someone is pointing, and they begin to understand some words or signs if they are given access to visual or spoken language on a regular basis. The following are some key ideas discussed in this chapter:

- By 1 year of age, the effects of a baby's experiences with objects, people, and especially with communication and language are increasingly reflected in their own behaviors: Vocal babbling requires hearing experience; manual babbling requires experience in seeing sign language. Babies who have been immersed in fluent sign language environments are especially likely to incorporate social referencing and flexible visual attention in interactions.

- Other aspects of development seem not to be influenced by hearing status or type of communication input: similar gestures are used in communications by all babies who are developing at a typical rate; the strength of motivation to explore and master objects and situations does not seem to be affected by hearing abilities.

- Hearing ability itself should not affect a baby's ability to communicate. Effective communication is a necessary base for language learning, although it does not assure language will be acquired. That requires, among other things, sufficient exposure to meaningful and accessible models of language.

- If language input has been both accessible (in a modality a baby can receive) and responsive (often related to the baby's interests or focus of attention), and if interactive experiences have been warm and supportive, an understanding of simple language should emerge by the end of the first year. Using visually sensitive communicative strategies in interactions with deaf and hard-of-hearing babies promotes development regardless of the modality (spoken or visual) of language to be learned.

- As they reach 1 year of age, the majority of deaf and hard-of-hearing babies will have some delay in development of language. The delay is usually due to less-than-typical experience with accessible, fluent language models. Language learning is usually more delayed, when a baby has multiple developmental challenges; however, progress should be evident.

Individual differences resulting from varied opportunities for experiencing language, opportunities for exploration and problem-solving, and opportunities for social interaction with others will become more evident in the next 2 years. A solid foundation built during the first year or so of life can provide optimal support for the development of each child's capabilities, regardless of the level of hearing abilities.

Chart 6: *Advances to Watch For**

By About 18 months

*Physical and Motor Abilities***	• Walks without support
	• Walks up and down steps with help
	• Walks backwards, runs, climbs
	• Holds small objects with fingers
	• Feeds self using fingers, perhaps spoon
	• Scribbles with large crayons/pencils
	• May begin to show "handedness" by 18 months
Getting Information from the Senses	• Improved hearing of higher pitches; sounds still must be somewhat louder than for adult to hear[H]
	• Sees almost as well as an adult[V]
	• Balance improves
	• Responses to touch become more rapid:
	○ Better able to localize touch on body
Mental Abilities ("Cognition")	• Imitates novel sequences of actions
	• Uses trial and error to make things fit, work right
	• May remember new sequences of actions for a month
	• Imitates short "real-life" sequences with toys
	• Tracks and finds objects hidden in different places sequentially
	• Imitates peers' actions with objects
	• Play can be other-directed (e.g., "feeding" bottle to mother or doll)

(continued)

Chart 6 *Continued*

Communication and Language	• Can express about 50 words or signs • Recognizes, knows own name • Combines signed/spoken words with gestures • May produce 2-word or 2-sign phrases • Imitates new words or signs • Makes repeated attempts to communicate, even if first attempts fail

Social-Emotional	• Shows happiness after successful accomplishment
	• May be distressed by new person or novel situation:
	  o Calmed by primary caregiver's presence
	• Jokingly exaggerates facial expressions and actions
	• Smiles and waves to initiate contact
	• Gestures and/or vocalizes to request help
	• Plays alongside same-age toddlers:
	  o Play focuses on actions, not language
	• May not yet understand rules, limits:
	  o Tantrums, negative behaviors often result

*See Chart 1 for partial list of sources for information.

**On all charts, advances in motor abilities assume no physical disabilities; limited vision may also slow advances in locomotion like crawling and walking.

H may be delayed or require different circumstances if hearing is limited; V may be delayed or require different circumstances if vision is limited.

9 The Symbol Users
REPRESENTING, REMEMBERING, RECREATING
12 TO 18 MONTHS

QUESTIONS TO CONSIDER

- How does the ability to use symbols relate to the development of language, play, and the developing sense of "self" as a unique individual?
- What roles can gestures and signs play in the language development of deaf and hard-of-hearing toddlers, as well as in those with typical hearing?
- What kinds of adult responses to babies' early expressive language best promote further growth?
- Does being deaf or hard of hearing have a predictable impact on the development of secure attachments to caregivers?

As Kiki (at 18 months of age) and her mother sit on the floor with some toys, Kiki picks up a small plastic cup, then takes one of the blocks her mother has been stacking. She places it in the cup, brings the cup to her mouth, and pretends to take an exaggerated drink from it. Mother looks puzzled and says/signs "Drink the block? Oh... coffee? Where's the coffee?" then picks up the coffee pot and hands it to Kiki. Kiki drops the block from the cup, then pretends to pour coffee into her cup and drinks again. Mother says and signs "pour"; Kiki repeats the sign "pour." Mother places the lid on the coffee cup, but Kiki removes it and pretends to take a long drink from the coffee pot itself. She signs "hot" and mother asks "Is that hot?" (signing "hot"). Kiki then engages in a sequence of pouring from the cup into the coffee pot and drinking from the pot. She does this a number of times and seems to think it's funny. Mother then picks up a doll, lays it down, and says and signs "Baby wants a drink. She's thirsty." Kiki pours from the coffee pot into the cup, then holds the cup to the doll's mouth. She pretends to drink again herself, and then repeats the sequence. Throughout this time, Kiki has been looking from the toys up to her mother and back frequently, being sure to keep Mom in the loop!

Mother is sitting in a chair, with Kiki on her lap. Mother reaches around Kiki to sign in front of her as she looks toward the toys on the floor. Mother points to the floor and says/signs "Wanna play?" Kiki turns, looks up, and signs "sleep." Then she climbs down, goes over to the toys, picks up the boy doll, and lays him down (as if to sleep) in the bedroom of the toy house.

Kiki, who has just turned 18 months old, was identified with profound bilateral hearing levels soon after birth. By the time she was 6 months old, she was wearing two hearing aids, and her hearing parents were focused on learning and using a sign system with her. Since then, Kiki's parents had become competent users of Signed English (although with fairly limited vocabularies) and consistently signed when communicating directly with her. Kiki's 18-month play behaviors, recounted here, were quite advanced. But let us begin by looking back at her play when she was 12 months old.

On an earlier visit to our lab, at 12 months of age, Kiki was less than impressed with the toys and the activities we offered. Kiki was focused on learning to walk, and practicing this new skill was her main goal.

Confronted with a room of attractive toys spread across the floor, Kiki for a long time refused to play with any of them. Instead, she demanded (through facial expressions, tugging and looking up at her mother, complaining vocalizations, and "pick me up" gestures) that her mother hold her hands so she could stand upright. She toddled slowly but intentionally toward each toy, then stepped on it—hard—before repeating this with the next toy. Her mother seemed both bemused and a bit embarrassed at this display of the "stronger" side of her lovely daughter's personality, but Kiki's assertiveness and ability to communicate her needs will most likely serve her well in the long run.

Kiki finally did participate in our activities, but never seemed to fully approve of the toys or tasks we had planned for her. At this 12-month session, she did, somewhat grudgingly, manipulate toys by banging and placing two together, as in the relational/combinatorial play discussed in Chapter 8. She also briefly showed some *enactive naming*–level play, briefly bringing a toy cup to her mouth and a hairbrush to her (barely visible) hair. As Dr. Lorraine McCune (2008) explained, this type of behavior involves a brief, realistic but not functional enactment—using a familiar object in a way that shows recognition of how it is used. Enactive naming behavior is usually accompanied by a quiet, even solemn, facial expression. Babies who engage in play at this level (but not higher) are usually not yet using either real words or signs, but their actions give evidence of emerging representational or symbolic abilities. Kiki was at just about the typical age to display this level of behavior in play.

Kiki's communication behaviors at 12 months were also within the typical range for toddlers, regardless of hearing abilities. She communicated nonverbally frequently and effectively by using gestures. She also engaged in coordinated joint visual attention—looking in directions her mother pointed toward and shifting her gaze between toys and her mother's face. This gaze-shifting usually occurred after a prompt of some kind from her mother, such as a tap on the arm or the movement of a toy. Except for the quality of her vocalizations (she did not yet produce any canonical or syllabic vocal babbling), Kiki showed developmental skills in the motor, social, and cognitive areas that were all highly appropriate for her age. Appropriately for a 12-month-old toddler, Kiki's actions and her communications were still focused on the "here and now": *I want this thing I'm looking at now!* Although Kiki's parents confirmed that she was not using any signs at 12 months of age, her mother later reported that she started producing the sign "more" at 13 months. She seemed on the verge of using symbols (mental images and representation) in her play and language behaviors, but that ability was not yet fully evident.

USING SYMBOLS IN PLAY

By the age of 18 months, Kiki had blossomed in a number of areas. Most noticeably, her head was now covered in blonde ringlets that framed her hearing aids beautifully. She walked alone competently, although she occasionally swayed a bit to keep her balance. Her good fine motor skills were evident as she manipulated and explored objects; for example, at one point, she demonstrated highly competent eye and fine motor coordination by inserting her index finger into a tiny hole in a door on the toy house, then skillfully pulling to open the door. Most importantly, Kiki had become a *symbol user*: she was now using signs to express her needs and thoughts and to organize those thoughts into memories about where things were, what they could do, and what they were called.

By 18 months, the "almost pretend" enactive naming with toys (displayed by Kiki at 12 months) had changed into actions that clearly showed she was pretending. This transition often occurs by about 13 months of age, when enactive naming actions become more complete or extended—but still replicate activities the toddler has experienced in real life like eating, drinking, sleeping. Unlike enactive naming, *pretend* behaviors are often accompanied by sound effects like slurping and by smiling or other "play" facial expressions. The toddler shows that she knows what she is doing, she knows it is fun, and she has a fairly stable mental representation of the activity prompted by seeing the object. At the 18-month session, Kiki clearly showed that she had achieved this and even higher levels of play, although she did not use sound effects. Instead, she showed that she was pretending by exaggerating the manner of her actions—for example, sometimes she used an overly extended, head-thrown-back posture during a "drinking" episode. Not surprisingly, this substitution of physical and visual evidence of pretend in the absence of sound-based pretend is somewhat common among babies with limited hearing. When analyzing their levels of play, therefore, these additional indicators must be considered.

Kiki's action of giving the doll a drink (prompted by her mother but continued on her own) is a more advanced play behavior than simply pretending to drink herself. This level of play is more advanced because it involves behaviors the baby has only observed; she has not actually performed them yet herself. Even though Kiki has probably never given a baby a drink from a cup, she performs this act quite proficiently with the doll after mother informs her that the doll is thirsty. (We can also see evidence here of beginning to appreciate another person's—or doll's—feelings, needs, and state of mind. This ability is referred to as *theory of mind* and will be discussed in a later chapter.) Other play actions that would show a similarly *decentered* or "other-focused" level of symbolic thinking could include imitating mother's texting, using a toy tool as if to fix something, or performing an action an older brother or sister has performed.

Interestingly, Kiki was following a route shared by children with typical hearing when she began to demonstrate her first sign at about the same age that pretend play emerged. In fact, Dr. McCune and others (Folven & Bonvillian, 1991; Kelly & Dale, 1989) have repeatedly found that a child's first single-word or single-sign expressions occur at about the same time as self-pretend and other-pretend types of play. Both the play behaviors and the language indicate an ability to think in *symbols* (to have a mental representation of something or someone), even though it is being expressed in different ways.

Kiki's play at 18 months demonstrates two important things. The first is that lower level play behaviors do not disappear when higher level ones emerge. In fact, she also continued to engage in many play behaviors that were in her repertoire before 1 year of age. For Kiki, as for all typically developing babies and toddlers, beginning-level behaviors continue but are gradually supplemented by or combined with higher level behaviors. This should not be cause for concern. (Compare this to your own behaviors: as an adult, you can obviously think in highly theoretical and abstract ways, but do you always do that? Or do pragmatic, functional, or occasionally superstitious thoughts sometimes guide your actions?) Kiki's play also demonstrated that a deaf child with hearing, newly signing parents need not experience a delay in play development. She uses play behaviors equal to those expected for children her age with typical hearing and for deaf or hard-of-hearing toddlers with deaf parents. Given a supportive environment and age-appropriate physical and brain development, therefore, limited hearing need not interfere with the emergence of appropriate symbolic behaviors at this age.

Did you also notice some higher level play in Kiki's example? If you read back over our description, you will see that she has shown the ability to produce a *sequence* of pretend behaviors—not just one at a time. Although the sequences don't always seem to be in the correct order (for example, she pours from the cup into the coffee pot and then drinks from the pot!), she shows the correct order at other times (as when she pours from the pot to the cup so that the doll can drink). We can't be sure, of course, but it appears that her incorrect sequences are intentional "jokes" on her part. She certainly indicated that she thought she was being funny at times during this session! The ability not only to combine a self-pretend (she drinks from the cup) and then involve another (doll drinks from the cup) shows that Kiki is not just imitating an actually seen sequence but is manipulating symbols for each of those actions mentally and even combining them. Sequenced play like this typically occurs at about the same time that typically developing toddlers advance to producing two-word or two-sign expressions ("allgone cookie"). With this in mind, look at 18-month-old Kiki during a juice-and-cookies break with her mother:

> *Kiki picks up her cup and intentionally pours juice onto the table. Mother responds "No, no. Eat your cookie." Kiki looks at her and signs, "Cookie finish." Mother picks up an animal-shaped cookie, points to it, says and signs "Cat. Cat cookie." Kiki looks, points to it and signs "cat." (Her sign movement is made in the wrong direction—like the "baby" production of "cat" we have seen from other signing toddlers.) Mother says/signs "Yeah, it's a cat cookie." Kiki signs "cat" again, points to her cup, and signs "more more." She then points to a picture on the*

cup. Mother says and signs "What's that? It's a duck." Kiki responds, "Duck," then points to it again and again signs "duck." Grinning, she then points at mother's cup (with no picture) and signs "duck." Mother laughs and says and signs, "No, that's not a duck." Kiki grins, points playfully several times at the table, then at mother's cup, and again signs "duck."

When she signs "cookie finish," Kiki is producing a two-sign (like a two-word) expression just as is expected from a child who is beginning to engage in sequences of play. Of course, we wouldn't see this from a deaf or hard-of-hearing child who had almost no opportunity to see or hear language. Kiki's experiences with language, in fact, began later than those of most babies with typical hearing or most deaf or hard-of-hearing babies with deaf parents. Furthermore, because Kiki's parents aren't really fluent signers yet, the language they can model for her remains rather limited. To their credit, however, they are clearly giving her enough sensitive, responsive, and clear models to promote emerging language skills. It also appears that her language abilities are keeping up with the cognitive and symbolic skills she is demonstrating in play and nonlanguage areas. In fact, Kiki is more than just "keeping up." She is demonstrating several symbolic behaviors that don't usually emerge until at least 18 months of age—an age range she is just entering.

One of these higher level behaviors was shown in the example when Kiki signed "sleep" before toddling over to put the doll to bed. Clearly, she had planned this action before she performed it. This means that she was able to think using symbols, remember what she wanted the doll to do, and keep that in mind while getting down from her mom's lap and making her way over to the toys. This is referred to as *hierarchical representational* (or pretend) play in that it involves a number of nested steps. This kind of play is not usually seen until toddlers are 18 months or older: Kiki's age at the time of this observation.

Another example of high-level play is shown in the very first excerpt from Kiki's play, also described at the beginning of this chapter. Kiki seems to be intentionally substituting the block (which she puts in the cup before "drinking" it) for the liquid that she clearly knows is what one usually drinks from a cup. *Substituting* one object for another, especially when they do not even look similar, requires a lot of symbolic thinking. To do this, Kiki needs to recognize that the block can "stand in" for the liquid, even though they are very different. She then incorporates this substitute object into a play sequence: *"What do I do with the cup? Hmm. Empty...no water. Let's use this block to "stand in" for it. Ah, now a big pretend drink!"* Again, this level of planning and thinking is almost never seen before a child approaches 18 months of age. Within a few months of the appearance of this level of play, children with typical hearing and rates of language development usually begin to learn vocabulary more rapidly and to produce increasing numbers of different two-word expressions.

Toddlers, like Kiki, who are beginning to use language, give us clues through their language (for example, announcing they are putting the doll to sleep) that they are planning their play activities in advance. But it is important to remember that there are also nonlanguage ways through which toddlers can demonstrate their planning abilities. For example, a toddler who has not yet begun to express language through either words or signs may be observed working his way carefully through a set of toys, selecting some and rejecting others, then using the selected toys to engage in an activity such as "fixing" a toy car or "cooking" with a pot. The fact that the child was looking for just the right toy or toys shows that he had something in mind already. He knew what he wanted to do. He kept the symbolic representation of that activity in mind as he found the toys or other objects needed to accomplish it. This kind of behavior indicates planning just as much as does the use of a word or two to announce upcoming play activities. We often saw this nonverbal kind of planning used by deaf and hard-of-hearing toddlers in our own studies.

How "Typical" Is Kiki?

Kiki showed us that a child with limited hearing whose parents are hearing will not necessarily have slower than usual development of early play behaviors or delays in cognitive advances such as being able to use mental symbols. However, Kiki had some real advantages compared to many other young deaf and hard-of-hearing children—and even compared to many children with typical hearing. She apparently had no significant challenges cognitively (mentally), socially, or in terms of her motor skills. Despite a comparatively late start, her parents learned to produce language that could be seen and processed by her, and they provided frequent language input while taking into account her current interests and her visual attention focus, allowing her to "uptake" their language. Kiki also had a close, positive, and secure relationship with her parents (the implications of which will be discussed in more detail later). We were able to see that in our laboratory as she went through a procedure that measures and classifies the relationship between child and mother. Secure mother–toddler relationships promote more sophisticated play by deaf or hard-of-hearing toddlers as well as by those with typical hearing—encouraging them to engage in more exploration and more pretend activities (Slade, 1987a, 1987b). Kiki also showed high levels of mastery motivation that led her to focus intently on achieving goals. We saw this at 18 months when, left to play without a partner for a few minutes, Kiki investigated and figured out how to open, close, and effectively operate the parts on every available toy while staying focused by herself for quite a long time. Finally, Kiki also seems to be a child with a generally high level of interest in social interactions. She showed this during her "alone play" time by continually visually scanning the adults in the room—always on the lookout for the possibility that they wanted to play again. Her use of eye gaze to monitor and invite interaction from her mother and researchers was so flexible and appropriate that her mother rarely had to use any attention-getting signals at all. All of these characteristics came together to help Kiki achieve age-level expectations, despite having had the challenges of being ill as a newborn and not being able to hear the language being spoken around her.

Not all babies with limited hearing who participated in our study had these advantages. It was not surprising that, *on average*, the deaf and hard-of-hearing babies with hearing parents were somewhat delayed in higher level pretend play at 18 months compared to the *average* baby with typical hearing—or the *average* deaf or hard-of-hearing baby with deaf parents (Spencer, 1996; Spencer & Meadow-Orlans, 1996). We emphasize the term "average" because in play (just as in many other areas of development) there is a wide range of abilities within each group. There were babies with typical hearing in our study who had highly responsive parents and no disabilities, yet who, just because of the way they were genetically "programmed," were developing some abilities very slowly. Following up these babies, measuring their language development at 3 years of age, some of them were at age level in their developmental progress by then. They just got off to a slower start. The same is true for the deaf and hard-of-hearing babies with deaf parents: some seemed to leap into language and symbol use, while others took their time. Nevertheless, all of these babies were functioning at age level when we last saw them.

In a recent review of the available research (Spencer, 2010), we concluded that play levels are a product of a highly integrated web of abilities and experiences. This is true during infant and toddler years—and beyond. Kiki provides us with a picture in which the strands of that web are strong and integrated. For many deaf and hard-of-hearing children (and occasionally for those with typical hearing), these strands may be weaker. The overall structure of the developmental web can be weakened by difficulties in receiving language input, less responsiveness from adults (who may try to "lead" too much, fearing that the baby will fall behind), interference from illness or additional developmental challenges, lowered ability of adults to appreciate the baby's visual needs, and even personality variables such as a baby who avoids taking risks. By 18 months, many deaf and hard-of-hearing toddlers with hearing parents are experiencing delays due to limited language uptake and a lack of accessible language models. The result may include less rich play experiences and decreased ability to use language for communication on a routine, daily basis.

USING SYMBOLS IN LANGUAGE

None of the deaf and hard-of-hearing babies with hearing parents in our study was using words or signs at 12 months (not even Kiki). However, half of the babies with deaf parents were signing, and half of the babies with typical hearing were producing some spoken words at that age.

A few of the deaf and hard-of-hearing babies with hearing parents (those whose mothers signed with about 40% or more of their spoken utterances) began to produce some signs at about 13 months (Spencer & Lederberg, 1997). At 18 months, more than half of the toddlers with deaf parents or with typical hearing were producing utterances including two or more words or signs. This is consistent with data reported by Simms and her colleagues (Simms, Baker, & Clark, 2013) for children learning American Sign Language (ASL). However, only three of the deaf and hard-of-hearing toddlers with hearing parents in our study were keeping up with those in the other groups. These three included Kiki and two for whom hearing aids had been quite effective and who were beginning to produce spoken language. Although Kiki demonstrated that on-time development of symbols in play and early language is possible for deaf or hard-of-hearing toddlers with hearing parents, the majority of those in her group were showing delays by 18 months.

When development is proceeding in a typical fashion, play and language advances continue to emerge fairly closely in time. For example, substitution play or more elaborate *preplanned* play that looks like a short "script" for related activities often emerges as the rate of word or sign learning increases and vocabulary size blossoms. What happens when the child cannot receive sufficient language input to allow this expected on-time development? Play behaviors can continue to advance, although they don't look as rich and are not as elaborated as when language is keeping up with thinking skills. Advances in play such as substitutions, preplanning, and longer sequences, however, can provide important evidence that the symbolic ability necessary to support advancing language is in place. When language is not occurring in step with play, it is time to engage in a more in-depth assessment of the child's language learning environment. Changes in intensity or in the approach to supporting language development should be considered.

Does Signing Develop Earlier than Spoken Language?

There have long been reports of infants with deaf parents producing signs much earlier than 13 months of age—the "average" age for hearing children's first spoken words (for example, Anderson & Reilly, 2002; Orlansky & Bonvillian, 1985). Some of these reports of earlier signing seem to reflect the naturally occurring differences in ages at which individual babies produce first words, regardless of hearing status. An "average" is always just a statistical calculation—in fact, each baby proceeds a bit differently—and there are babies with typical hearing who talk before 13 months just as there are signers before that age. Drs. Diane Anderson and Judy Reilly reported that one of the deaf children (with deaf parents) who participated in their study of early vocabulary development was producing signs by 8 months of age. Interestingly, these signs were limited to "milk" and "bath"—both of which are much like gestures also used by children with typical hearing. Another early sign, observed by 11 months, was the verb "clap." However, this "sign" is produced by simply clapping—another common action gesture that is produced at about that age by most children regardless of hearing ability. More recently, Simms and her colleagues (Simms et al., 2013) obtained teacher reports of language development of more than 80 young deaf children learning ASL. They developed a scale, the *Standardized Visual Communication and Sign Language Checklist for Signing Children* (VCSL) and have provided information about the ages at which different language attainments were reported. Most of the children in their study did not produce expressive signs until after their first birthday.

The general conclusion held by most language specialists is that first signs may occur earlier on average for deaf children with deaf parents compared to first spoken words for most children with typical hearing, but that any potential advantage disappears by the end of the second year of life. It is important to recognize, however, that there are absolutely *no reports* that signing emerges *later* on average for deaf children with fluently signing parents than does speaking for children with typical hearing. (The information from Simms and her colleagues suggests that the deaf and hard-of-hearing children with deaf parents in our own studies were, in fact, using signs a bit earlier than those in their research. However, our information is based on observations with mothers and on parent reports; behavior observations for the VCSL checklist are taken from teachers' reports. These two methods may explain the differences, which are not large.)

It does appear that signing begins at about the same age as hearing babies' first spoken words, if signing is the usual mode of communication experienced. In addition, use of sign-like gestures may actually promote the development of spoken language for babies who have sufficient hearing to be able to uptake the language spoken around them. Drs. Linda Acredolo and Susan Goodwyn (1988; 2002) found that encouraging babies with typical hearing (and with hearing parents) to practice a fairly small number of gestures allowed them to communicate needs earlier than first words are usually produced. Importantly, it also seemed to support the development of better understanding and expression of spoken language compared to babies whose gesturing had not been encouraged. Because the researchers and others referred to these gestures as "baby signs," there has been some argument about whether the babies were really signing or just using more gestures. However, even if "baby signing" by those with typical hearing is thought of as simply enhanced use of gestures, the fact that gesturing seemed to help instead of hurt the babies' spoken language development is important. This is a strong argument against those who say that allowing a baby to use visual language (signs and gestures) will interfere with learning to talk. When babies can hear spoken language, using specialized gestures ("baby signs") seems to give practice in using symbols to communicate and get ready to talk. Toddlers with typical hearing gradually dropped the "baby signs" when they began to use spoken language. This may also be the case for many babies whose limited hearing is sufficiently enhanced with hearing aids, early intervention, and sometimes cochlear implants. But early use of gestures and signs can give them an important introduction to effective communication that will then help them make the transition to language, whether spoken or not.

Proto-Words and Home Signs

Intervention specialists, caregivers, and researchers often have problems distinguishing the first "real" words or signs produced by a child from the babbled sounds or gestures that precede them. Some babies with typical hearing, in fact, have been reported to develop "proto-words," which are intermediate between babbling and actual words. These are sounds that an individual baby uses consistently to stand for something unique to that baby; it seems as though he has invented it instead of its being an attempt to produce a word from the family's language. An example from a baby we are familiar with was "loy-loy" to mean water. Little Mikey persisted for months using this proto-word even though his parents couldn't connect these sounds with any word they had used, and the only language he had ever heard was English. Nevertheless, his early attempts to "invent" words didn't stand in his way later because Mikey (who had typical hearing) grew up to be quite a gifted linguist.

A proto-word shares one characteristic with the first real spoken words: it is used consistently to stand for a meaning that is identifiable by family and others who know the baby well. But to be a "real" word, the production also needs to sound like the word used by family and community for whatever it represents. Some researchers have been more specific and have said that, in addition, at least two of the sounds in the production must match those in the word it is thought to be (Huttenlocker, Haight, Bryk, Seltzer, & Lyons, 1991). "Loy-loy" (to mean "water") clearly does not meet this criterion. In contrast, a production such as "ah-puh" ("apple") would be close enough. But there is yet another requirement for a "real" spoken word: it must be used in more than a single setting or context. For example, if "ah-puh" is used only to indicate a red apple-shaped toy and nothing else, it is still functioning as a proto-word. A "real" word will be used in various contexts and for different examples of the object—for a nice juicy eatable apple, for the large red apple toy that rocks back and forth, or for the small plastic apple in a toy kitchen set. By about 15–18 months of age (or soon after), toddlers with typical hearing are usually expressing spoken words using many of the sounds heard in the family's language. Although their development is typically slower, toddlers with mild to moderate or even severe hearing levels should soon, with effective use of hearing aids and supportive input, also become able to produce many of those sounds and some spoken words. The rate of development varies widely and depends on a number of factors both within the child (such as the types of sounds her ear can actually receive and her developing attention abilities) and within the family and other support systems. Assessment of the spoken language progress of these toddlers is critical to determine how much they are benefitting from their hearing aids and whether the language intervention they are being provided is effective. Therefore, careful checks on the speech sounds and the number of spoken words a baby produces are necessary when speech is expected to be an important modality for language development. It is far more effective to prevent than to try to remediate delays.

It is similarly important to be able to assess the level and rate of development of infants who are learning signs and sign language. Rather like proto-words, many deaf and hard-of-hearing babies develop what can be called "home signs." These are gestures that become accepted by the family as having a specific meaning. Especially when fluent "real" signs are not available to the child and family, a number of home signs will be developed and can be used in fairly effective communication exchanges. For many deaf or hard-of-hearing children around the world, home signs are their only means of communication. Dr. Susan Goldin-Meadow and her colleagues (for example, Goldin-Meadow & Mylander, 1990) studied the home signs of several young children in the United States. They concluded that when hearing does not function and no other kind of language input can be received, children will use gestures to communicate in systematic ways if cognitive and social foundations are in place. Although these naturally developed gestures can be helpful for communication, they cannot facilitate the child's learning or social interactions in the same way that learning a language shared by the wider community does.

To assess sign language acquisition, it is necessary to have some guidelines to distinguish between gestures and "real" signs. In our own studies (Meadow-Orlans et al., 2004; Spencer & Meadow-Orlans, 1996), we modified the guidelines that had been set up and used to identify a "word" spoken by a toddler with typical hearing. To be considered a "sign," the toddler's hand production had to be used more than once to indicate the same meaning. It also had to include two characteristics matching the sign that the parent (and other adult observers) *thought* it represented—hand shape, location, the orientation of the palm, or the movement involved. For example, Kiki signed "cat" on her cheeks, which is the correct location; she moved the sign across her cheeks, which is the correct motion even though she used a downward instead of upward movement; but she used a "5" handshape (all five fingers extended on both hands) instead of the "F" handshape used in adult ASL. This met our "two characteristics" requirement. In addition, her mother immediately recognized the sign as "cat." Finally, Kiki produced it more than once for slightly different pictures of a cat.

Getting the Movements and the Sounds "Right"

Phonology is the set of sounds and the system for combining them in any particular spoken language. The term has also been used to describe the set of features making up signs—for example, locations, hand shapes, movements—and the system or rules for how to combine them. We usually use the term "articulation" to refer to how closely a child's word or sign production matches an adult's. Just as hearing babies learning to speak make certain fairly predictable articulation errors (like saying "gog-gie" instead of "doggie"), sign language researchers have catalogued common articulation errors of toddlers learning signs. At around 12 months, babies learning ASL seem to prefer to use the following hand shapes: extended index finger, all five fingers extended, and a closed-fist hand shape like a fingerspelled "s." By about 18–20 months, the hand shapes for fingerspelled "C," "O," and "A" are used often. Babies will substitute one of these simpler-to-produce hand shapes when the "real" sign requires a more complex hand shape. Interestingly, deaf young adults who helped us analyze our tapes often didn't immediately recognize a sign when one of these "baby shape" substitutions was made. They required training to do so. In contrast, deaf mothers or adults who had worked with a number of deaf babies were much quicker to identify these as signs. They had developed an almost intuitive understanding of these substitutions after repeated exposure to them.

Similarly, our young adult research assistants who were hearing but had not worked extensively with infants and toddlers with typical hearing had to be trained to understand simplified substitutions produced in the babies' vocal utterances. Babies with typical hearing often use the sounds /p/, /b/, and /d/ to substitute for more difficult-to-produce speech sounds, typically adding /m/, /n/, and /w/ by about 18 months. Hence "wahk" is a common pronunciation in English-speaking toddlers for the word "rock." It should be obvious that, whether learning sign or speech, toddlers don't start right out producing words or signs exactly like adults do. It takes time to get their hands, fingers, lips, or tongues to move in a smooth and coordinated fashion. It also takes time and repeated interaction with babies and toddlers for adults to develop the ability to understand many of their early words or signs. And, because babies don't all show exactly the same patterns or characteristics in their early productions, parents and others with intimate, everyday knowledge of the child are usually the best sources of information about what they say or sign.

Hearing level usually influences the rate and pattern of babies' production of speech sounds, which in turn affects production of spoken words. At about 12 months of age, most babies with even mildly limited hearing will vocalize differently from most babies with typical hearing. Babies with limited hearing show a stronger tendency to produce consonant sounds like /p/ and /b/ that can be seen on the lips, rather than those that require more movements farther back in the mouth (McGowan, Nittrouer, & Chenausky, 2008). This pattern was not found, however, in a group of toddlers who received cochlear implants by about 18 months of age. The consonant and vowel sounds they made were more like those of children with typical hearing (Schauwers, Govaerts, & Gillis, 2008). When differences in articulation (or early pronunciations) occur, however, they can have ongoing effects. For example, Dr. Mary Pat Moeller and her colleagues (Moeller et al., 2007a, 2007b) suggested that differences or delays in perceiving and producing speech sounds can affect the rate of vocabulary growth. Because vocabulary is a fundamental aspect of language skill, this is an area in which frequent assessment is critical.

What Do Toddlers Talk—and Sign—About?

Toddlers' first signs or spoken words tend to communicate the same meanings and ideas that they were expressing using gestures or proto-words.

The first words and signs are used to refer to objects, events, and people and to express meanings that are already familiar to the toddler. At this point in development, toddlers still need to "know about things" through experiences and communication activities before they learn the related words or signs.

Regardless of the language used, the first words typically include names or nicknames for people in the family (Mommy/Daddy, Auntie, sister/brother, pets) and names of favorite foods ("milk," "cookie"). The specific words will differ across families and cultures, of course. Despite a general emphasis on nouns, there are also some commonly used verbs ("go"), some expressions for requests ("more," "all-gone," "no," "stop"), and often some words that have a primarily social function ("please," "thank-you"). Dr. Diane Anderson (2006) compared reports of the early vocabulary productions of toddlers learning spoken English, forms of Signed English, and ASL. She identified many similarities. A majority of the first productions could best be classified as nouns, although Dr. Anderson reports that toddlers learning signs may produce a somewhat larger proportion of action verbs than is typical for English-speaking babies. Dr. Nini Hoiting (2006) similarly reported that children learning Sign Language of the Netherlands (SLN) focused on verbs to a greater degree than is common in many spoken languages.[1]

If signing is being used by the family, whether it is a natural sign language like ASL or SLN or a sign system like Signed French, the everyday, routine, functional signs will be demonstrated earliest by the parents and learned most readily by toddlers. Although it isn't possible for most adults to fully learn a new language (like a sign language) as quickly as their baby will reach "languaging" age, signs that will be used every day for important events and people should be targeted for a family's early lessons. Most of these "everyday" people and events have some emotional meanings, too: comfort, getting one's needs met, social connections. Signs (or words) that can be used often and have an emotional "layer" to their meaning will be especially interesting for the language-learning toddler.

Early words or signs usually don't occur in isolation, of course, as the toddler continues to combine them with facial expressions, gestures, and actions. This helps communication partners understand the intent of the utterance. Is the toddler signing or saying "apple" just to label the fruit? Or is he requesting a piece of it to eat? The sign or word alone won't clarify the toddler's purpose, but the context in which this occurs (Are others eating? Is it lunch time?) and the child's nonlanguage expressions often help us figure out the intent.

The functions or purposes for which language is used are referred to as language *pragmatics* (Dore, 1974; McLean & Snyder-McLean, 1999). The first words or signs can be used to request actions, to get someone to respond, to get attention, to greet and say good-bye, to be polite ("please" and "thank-you"), or to protest. The first words/signs are also used just for the joy of labeling things now that labeling is possible. A toddler who recently visited us pointed out every boat that went up and down a nearby canal, each time pointing and yelling "boat!" He didn't want to have the boat or get on it, he was merely delighting in using his new ability to call things by their name!

Enjoying this new power to name is one reason that toddlers (and their parents) find looking through picture books to be so much fun; it offers a good way to practice existing words and signs, even more than to learn new ones. Many parents (Weir, 1962) have noticed that toddlers learning spoken language will talk to themselves, especially when winding down for a nap or sitting alone with toys—seeming to practice labeling the things they are playing with or have just put away. This same phenomenon has been noted for toddlers learning signs—repeating and practicing signs during relaxed time alone (Petitto, 2000).

Most reports of the pragmatic aspects of emerging language during the toddler stage show little difference based on hearing abilities or even level of language development. However, differences will become evident by preschool and later ages for deaf and hard-of-hearing children, especially if their language is delayed (Lederberg & Everhart, 2000; Nicholas & Geers, 1997; Spencer Day, 1986). Although children with typically developing language use it often to request information (for example, "Why?") as they reach about 3 years of age, children with delayed language development do not do so as often. Dr. Diane Goberis and her colleagues (Goberis et al., 2012) reported delays in pragmatics for many deaf and hard-of-hearing children at about 7 years of age even when some other aspects of language were appropriate for age. However, the basic functions expressed during the first 18 months or so can usually be communicated effectively by deaf and hard-of-hearing toddlers, as well as by those with typical hearing. Being able to infer the purpose of a toddler's early one-word or one-sign expressions not only helps adults (and older siblings) to respond with appropriate actions, but it also allows them to give feedback related to the language itself.

What's a Parent to Do?

It is during the 12- to 18-month age range that significant differences become obvious between toddlers who have had full access to language and those whose experiences have been limited due to being unable to hear or to see the language occurring around them. Developing cognitive abilities such as understanding cause and effect, knowing that objects continue to exist when they have been hidden, remembering the activities of daily routines and the way objects are used can all provide the foundation upon which language is built. However, only frequent, meaningful experiences with language itself can ensure that language is acquired. Needless to say, babies who have received hearing aids late in infancy or whose aids do not provide enough benefit to allow them to hear spoken language clearly will not learn spoken language "on time." Those who are in environments where sign language is expressed by only a few adults or adults who are themselves still learning that language can be expected to develop sign language at a slower than usual pace. In most cases, unlike the example of Kiki, deaf and hard-of-hearing toddlers will be later than usual in producing their first words or signs.

So, what should a parent or other caregiving adult do to help build the toddler's storehouse of language experiences? Mostly just keep talking and/or signing to the toddler; keep referring to things that are familiar; keep providing models of language that relate to the toddler's current interest and, usually, to things in the surrounding area. At the same time, the adult needs to continue to "read" the toddler's nonlanguage communications (gestures, vocalizations, eye gaze, etc.), try to determine what the toddler is communicating about, and then model that meaning in language (Nicholas, Geers, & Kozak, 1994). This might mean modeling only a single sign or word—or it might mean saying/signing a whole phrase or sentence that the adult believes represents what the toddler is trying to communicate. The number of words or signs accessible to a toddler—if they are responsive to his interest and match his sensory abilities—has a strong influence on the size of vocabulary he will develop. (And vocabulary, as simple as it might seem, is key to many language and academic accomplishments to come.) In fact, researchers have found that the number of words heard in their early years by children with typical hearing is reflected in vocabulary size years later (Hart & Risley, 1995). We found in our own research that the number of different signs deaf mothers produced with their deaf babies at 12 months of age was a good predictor of the amount of language the babies themselves produced at 18 months. Because all the mothers were very responsive to their babies' communicative attempts and visual attention, it seemed to be the quantity of different signs that affected the babies' language development most. Of course, this can also be overdone. We know that "talk, talk, talk" is sometimes the advice given to hearing mothers of deaf and hard-of-hearing children learning spoken and not signed language. However, it is important to remember that following the baby's lead and giving the baby time to attend to objects and events being talked about are also necessary. Babies need to be given time to process what was said and, importantly, to take a turn in the communication exchange. *It is not just the quantity of language others produce that is important but, instead, the amount of meaningful uptake and participation that occurs.* In other words, timing, pacing, and responding to the child's cues are also important.

Parents' reactions to communication efforts change as the toddler's skills increase. In some cases, parents will focus on labeling things that their babies seem to be trying to express. Many times, they may repeat the labels while adding indicators like pointing to ensure that whatever is referred to is clear. At other times, parents will both correct and expand on what they *think* toddlers have said or signed, but most often corrections refer to the content of the toddler's language, not its form. To illustrate, we return to Kiki: her mother tried to correct her when it appeared that Kiki was signing "duck" where there was no picture of a duck. What we did not mention was that Kiki had not made the sign correctly. (She turned her hand so that it was pointing toward rather than away from her own mouth.) Interestingly, Kiki's mother signed back "That's not a duck," reacting to the content of the message. She did not sign "You made that sign wrong. Here's how to do it." The latter correction might well have been given a few months later—but at this time and this developmental level, Kiki's mother was reacting to the information, not its exact production. Many times "corrections" of form (either pronunciation in voice or handshapes and movements in sign) are not made explicitly; instead, the parent will repeat what was signed or said but will sign/say it correctly and with emphasis on the correct form. *Frequent direct corrections can inhibit instead of encourage communication attempts.*

Another common parent behavior that is both communicative and instructive occurs when the parent *expands* on what the toddler has said or signed. An example from a deaf toddler in our study involved the father (who had been in the room with mother and baby) leaving the room. The little boy, Sean, looked puzzled, tilted his head, and gazed directly at his mother, signing "Daddy" by touching his index finger to his forehead. ("Daddy" should be signed in ASL with the hand open in a "5" shape and the thumb touching the forehead.) Mother correctly understood this to be a question and signed in reply, "Where's Daddy? Daddy went to work. Daddy went to work. We'll see Daddy later." In this case, the deaf mother first signed the correct form of the sentence "Where's Daddy?" which she assumed captured Sean's meaning. Then she answered, signing "Daddy" several times and adding more information in her response. The mother had re-signed the question correctly, giving just a slightly more complicated model than Sean himself had signed. She then expanded the information, using signs that were generally slower, larger, and with more emphasis than they would be if conversing with an adult. This kind of signing tends to make the sign easier to process and remember (Spencer & Harris, 2006). Finally, she gave new information (about seeing Daddy later) that could also serve as reassurance. All this was based on and expanded from Sean's own interest and communication effort. He was looking directly at his mother and could see her signing, so this experience was particularly supportive of Sean's language learning. Again, the mother did *not* mention that Sean had signed "Daddy" using an incorrect hand shape.

Drawing from a number of sources, especially the McLean and Snyder-McLean book (1999), the following are modifications we suggest as helpful for parents of deaf and hard-of-hearing toddlers who are at the stage of producing one-word or one-sign expressions: (1) respond to what you think is the child's intent and meaning; (2) talk and/or sign about things happening "here and now"; (3) use short sentences with much repetition; (4) frequently use vocabulary you think the child can already understand; (5) talk and/or sign more clearly and slowly than usual, emphasizing the important words or signs; (6) exaggerate stress and tone of voice and/or facial expressions; (7) model a simple but correct way to say or sign what the child produced and expand on what the child has said or signed, but do *not* try to correct every mistake; and (8) use language that is just a bit more complicated than the child's current level.

Again, it is important to give the child enough time to take another communication turn, understanding that he may need some time to adjust eye gaze and attention to you and to what you are communicating. Try your best to make your language *visible* to the child who may be learning signs and/or using lipreading (speechreading) to add information to what he or she is hearing. Remember that tapping signals, movement of objects through the child's visual field, or even waving a hand to attract the child's attention can help to direct the child's attention to communication.

Finally, it is important to remember that deaf mothers made relatively few language-based comments and expressions with their deaf babies at 12 months. This was obviously a response to the babies' still-emerging abilities for coordinated joint attention. Mothers did a lot of waiting and carefully watching the child. They appeared to think it best not to produce too much language input until their babies showed that their attentional abilities were advanced enough to allow for easy uptake. At 18 months, when the children's visual attention was more flexible and the children themselves were using more language, the deaf mothers increased the amount and even the complexity of their signed expressions. Hearing mothers of deaf and hard-of-hearing babies might do well to follow these deaf mothers' lead in this regard by matching the quantity of language produced to their babies' attention development.

Most of these suggestions by now should be "old hat" to our readers. Many if not most parents will make these modifications almost automatically, especially if they have had the benefit of early intervention support, and they will not need more specific training. However, when a child's language is developing more slowly than expected, or when parents believe they have reason to worry about the levels being achieved, intuitive responses can be disrupted and parents may need to be reminded (and given more demonstrations) of these beneficial communication behaviors. (See Koester & Lahti-Harper, 2010, for a summary.) It may also be important for professionals (with the family's help, of course) to assess the child's language progress in order to describe the current level of skills and to give reminders of what can be expected next. Assessment should take place in both meaningful (daily routines) and play contexts, should include parent participation and information, and should take into consideration other developmental areas and skills. It is approximately during this 12- to 18-month age range that the effects of toddlers' earlier experiences, any latent (or previously not obvious) disabilities, and the effects of language-supportive technologies and approaches begin to be evident. There is still much time for modification and increased intensity of support if needed, but parents and professionals should be especially alert as the baby approaches 18 months of age.

EFFECTS OF THINKING WITH SYMBOLS ON SOCIAL-EMOTIONAL DEVELOPMENT

Children's symbolic or representational skills contribute to their understanding of themselves and of others who are significant in their lives and may have both social and cognitive implications that persist into adulthood. By 12 to 18 months, most children will have formed close bonds with at least one important caregiver (Bowlby, 1958, 1969). This process is often referred to as *attachment,* and its meaning is more significant than that word might at first imply. If an infant forms a healthy, secure attachment to a caregiver, this bond will serve her well in later stages of development. Because exploring and understanding the world involves certain risks, the attachment figure provides reassurance and a "secure base" for the child during times of anxiety or uncertainty. We saw examples of this in our own research, when infants were reunited after a brief separation from Mom: the securely attached babies actively sought comfort and closeness to her and were then able to get back to their play knowing that this trusted caregiver was available nearby.

In contrast, an infant or toddler who has not developed a secure attachment with caregivers may be less likely to be socially competent, less able to cope when on his or her own, and less able to learn as quickly and to take appropriate risks. Secure attachment has been found to relate to better learning of symbolic and play behaviors and to language development—especially important for deaf and hard-of-hearing children. As we noted in an earlier chapter, the majority of infants will develop positive attachments, regardless of their hearing status or that of their parents.

Nonetheless, a not insignificant percentage (roughly 20% of North American infants with typical hearing) appear to be "avoidant" of their caregivers; for example, they seek very little contact with the mother, they show no distress when she leaves, and they generally appear somewhat indifferent to people around them. Even when the mother returns after a separation, these infants may not greet or acknowledge her, or they may overtly turn away and show little joy that she is back. A somewhat smaller percentage (around 15%) actively resist contact when the caregiver returns, perhaps by pushing away or kicking if picked up, and the signals they send are ambiguous: "*Yes, I want you to hold me!*" "*No, put me down!*" It can be hard for parents to interpret such behaviors, and they might need additional support to find ways of turning these patterns around before they become too entrenched and difficult for all involved. These patterns can be expected to occur occasionally in young deaf and hard-of-hearing children as well as in those with typical hearing. It is important that these behaviors be identified when they occur so that specific assistance can be provided, given their importance across various areas of development.

In describing attachment, we tend to refer to the relationship between baby and mother. The mother is most often an infant's primary source of comfort, confidence, trust, and reassurance. However, fathers, grandparents, other relatives, childcare providers, and even siblings may also be attachment figures, and these individuals should not be overlooked when emotional bonds are considered. Their roles and styles of interacting may be somewhat different from those of the mother, but, in many families, several people may be equally influential and important for the child's social and emotional well-being. Cultures that place a high value on interdependence have traditions that teach these social expectations even to infants. For example, one group in the Congo believes that the mother should not be the first one to hold her newborn—instead, the infant is introduced to other community members first, and other women may even nurse an unrelated baby. Others are expected to protect the youngest in their midst from commonplace dangers, and infants, in turn, naturally develop attachments to more than just biological parents (Gardiner & Kosmitzki, 2008). Although this pattern is different from that typically seen in European and North American cultures, it illustrates that there is more than one way to develop and show positive emotional attachments. The ways of demonstrating attachments, and the differences such as the specific people with whom they are developed, can differ across cultures; nevertheless, the need for attachments is universal.

Behaviors indicating attachment change over time as an individual develops. For example, as a baby becomes more mobile, she is able to actively seek proximity or stay close to caregivers by following them around, crawling, or walking closer to them. At the same time, her communication skills should also be improving so that she cans use voice or signs to indicate pleasure, fear, or the need for comfort.

Her "calls" to caregivers become more specific and easier to interpret, and these are another way of establishing and keeping contact with important people in the social environment. Although it does *not* appear that language itself is needed to develop initial emotional bonds with caregivers—rather, responsive, sensitive, and nurturing behaviors seem to form the basis of these early attachments—language will begin to play an increasingly greater role with age (Figure 9.1).

Figure 9.1 Big brothers and sisters can be attachment figures, too. (Photo courtesy of Lynne Koester. Reprinted with permission.)

How Secure Is this Child?

How can we tell whether a child (who may still be communicating without any real spoken or signed language at this age) is securely attached or not? An often-used method for assessing this is a laboratory observation called the Strange Situation Procedure, which we also used in our study of deaf and hard-of-hearing children at 12 and 18 months (Ainsworth, Blehar, Waters, & Wall, 1978; Meadow-Orlans et al., 2004). For most toddlers, this is indeed a strange experience. This procedure involves bringing the child and parent into an unfamiliar setting (a play room with toys prearranged on the floor) and then guiding them through a series of separations and reunions lasting a total of 20–30 minutes.

First, parent and child are familiarized with the room, and the procedure is explained. Next, an unfamiliar adult "stranger" arrives and stays with the toddler while the parent leaves the room, giving observers an opportunity to see how the child reacts to strangers and how she reacts when her primary caregiver departs. The separation only lasts for 3 minutes, at which time the parent returns. Next comes perhaps the most challenging part of the procedure: first the stranger and then, a few minutes later, the mother leaves and the child is alone. (The mother leaves a reminder of her presence as an indication that she will return—often a purse or diaper bag that the child associates with her.) Remember that these episodes only last up to 3 minutes each (about the time a parent might typically take to send a text message). But, judging by some children's reactions, we might think this was an eternity! (We want to stress, however, that if a child becomes really upset, the practice is to stop the "alone time" and immediately send someone in to comfort her. The child's comfort is more important than any data that might be collected.) However, even at this young age, children often have strategies for self-comfort, such as clutching Mom's handbag, calling to her, or climbing into Mom's chair to wait. Following the only episode in which the child is alone, the stranger reappears and offers comfort before the parent is sent back for the final reunion. What major toddler behaviors are we looking for in these episodes? And what might they tell us about the relationship between mother and child? Although the child's reactions to each episode during this procedure are considered, it is particularly interesting to see how the child behaves when both mother and stranger have left the room—and when mother returns. Here was Kiki's reaction:

> *Kiki is alone in a play room with toys. During these few minutes, she toddles over to her mother's purse and pulls out a sealed plastic bag containing some crackers; she tries unsuccessfully to rip open the bag with both her fingers and her teeth. Her mother re-enters the room and says/signs "hi" to which Kiki responds by waving "hi." Mother sits in the chair again; Kiki jumps up, runs back to mother's purse, pulls out the plastic bag, and points to the crackers while looking back and forth between the bag and her mother's face. Mother says and signs, while pointing to the crackers, "You want a cracker?" "What is that?"*

> *Kiki responds by signing "cracker" and handing the bag to mother.*
> *Mother says and signs "They're broken," but Kiki signs "Eat!" She then*
> *gestures "pick me up" (with great feeling!) and climbs onto her moth-*
> *er's lap. Finally munching on a cracker, Kiki signs rapidly "more more*
> *more" "cracker cracker cracker."*

What have we learned from this brief observation? Kiki has clearly remembered that this is her mother's purse, and she seems to understand that Mom will come back for it. Meanwhile, Kiki has also remembered those crackers in the purse and perhaps takes the opportunity to reassure herself with them—or, maybe she just wants to get to them before her mother returns. In any case, the important part of this process is often how the child behaves when the mother reappears. In Kiki's case, she handled the separation quite well. Apparently, remembering and tackling the bag of crackers in Mom's purse helped her cope. Even if a toddler has been distressed by this situation, it is helpful if she is able to communicate this by seeking and accepting comfort upon the return of her mother—the *attachment figure*—the one who provides security and a soothing presence. In another example we saw in our research, a deaf child walked around the room signing to herself—seeming to comment (using only one-sign and two-sign expressions) that *"Mommy was sitting there. She left. Where is she? When is she coming back? We were playing—I want to play again—but where's Mommy?"* This little girl had good use of "private language" (similar to talking to oneself, like many of us do while cooking, driving, etc.) and was able to rely on this strategy to help regulate her emotions in a stressful situation—quite an accomplishment for someone so young! In her case, however, both parents and older siblings were also deaf, so her home environment was rich in language input, and her signing skills were already quite advanced for an 18-month-old.

Does Limited Hearing Increase the Risk of Insecure Attachment?

It is important to distinguish between two ideas here. The first is whether deaf and hard-of-hearing children are likely to be as securely bonded with their parents, deaf or hearing, as are children with typical hearing (and hearing parents). The second is whether the Strange Situation Procedure we just described, and which has been used for decades across numerous cultures, adequately measures the security of attachment of infants and toddlers with limited hearing.

Let's first address the potential impact of hearing ability on the development of secure attachments. Is this often affected by (hearing) parents' surprise, grief, or lack of confidence in their ability to adapt to the infant's hearing level? Or might the baby's lack of contact with sound and spoken language have a direct effect on whether she develops a secure or insecure attachment? These concerns have been raised in the past by some professionals working with families of deaf and hard-of-hearing children (e.g., Luterman & Kurtzer-White, 1999). To date, however, researchers have not found that a child's hearing level has a direct effect on the security of attachment (Lederberg & Mobley, 1990; Meadow-Orlans et al., 2004). As mentioned earlier, in our own studies, we have found that the overwhelming proportion of all participating babies and toddlers showed a positive attachment pattern. Other researchers (Thomson, Kennedy, & Kuebli, 2011) have agreed with this observation, finding that having limited hearing in infancy may slightly raise the risk of attachment problems but only when other risk factors are also present.

It appears that secure attachments can be established by deaf and hard-of-hearing infants and toddlers to the same degree and as often as by children with typical hearing—regardless of parents' hearing level. But what happens as the children grow to adulthood? Although interview procedures have been established to examine adults' own attachment histories, few studies have used these in signed versions with deaf adults. An exception to this is the research of McKinnon, Moran, and Pederson (2004), who found no support for the idea that deaf adults are less likely than hearing adults to be rated as having a healthy attachment history. According to van IJzendoorn and colleagues (van IJzendoorn, Goldberg, Kroonenberg, & Frenkel, 1992), the important factor influencing these outcomes seems to go back to the deaf adult's earlier childhood experiences. In particular, were their parents able to view the child's limited hearing as just another aspect of their child's uniqueness, thus allowing them to interact with their infant in a sensitive and responsive manner? The sensitivity displayed during parent–infant interactions seems to play a vital role in determining both the child's early attachment security and the further development of those important relationships.

Now for the second issue. Is the Strange Situation Procedure valid—that is, does it measure what we think it is measuring—when used with young children who are deaf or hard of hearing? There are legitimate concerns about the value of the procedure, despite the fact that it has been used widely throughout the world for many years to study parent–child attachment. Some of these concerns go beyond the questions raised by hearing ability. One might wonder, for example, whether a one-time snapshot of a child's behavior truly reflects the typical patterns within the family. What if the child is teething that day, or hungry, or didn't sleep well the night before? What if the mother is preoccupied about getting to another appointment on time and is therefore not as responsive as usual? Does her toddler sense this and respond with greater clinginess? Other possible factors should also be considered when assessing attachment, such as medical conditions, the sensitivity of caregivers, whether there is a history of positive interactions, and the broader social environment.

There are additional specific questions about whether this procedure works well with children whose hearing is limited and so fail to hear Mom opening the door to return to the room and therefore may appear to be avoiding or ignoring her. Dr. Marta Montanini-Manfredi (1993) commented on a deaf child's need to rely on direct contact and vision in order to be assured of another person's presence. Following a separation, such a child cannot anticipate the arrival or return of her mother by hearing the sound of her footsteps approaching or by hearing her reassuring voice from another room. The result may be emotional discomfort and feelings of uncertainty or isolation rather than security. In addition, Dr. Marc Marschark (1993) has suggested that the Strange Situation Procedure may not be the best measure to use with deaf and hard-of-hearing infants because deaf and hearing *parents* may differ in their behavioral standards and expectations regarding mother–child attachment.

Clearly, how secure Kiki and others in her age group feel in relation to their primary caregivers will be influenced by multiple factors. Having limited hearing is only one consideration and is undoubtedly less important than the quality of her relationship with the significant adults in her life. The process of becoming attached to significant others has important implications for much later in life as well because it involves developing internal models (or representations—symbolic images) of both the self and others. Does the child perceive others as being trustworthy, helpful, protective, and comforting? Does the child perceive herself as being worthy of care, nurturance, and attention from others? Attachment theorists believe that early sensitive, responsive caregiving provides the foundation upon which these personal beliefs will develop. There is nothing inherent in limited hearing that interferes with this process.

Who IS that Baby in the Mirror?

One of the wonders of early development is the child's emerging recognition of herself as being unique and having the power to cause things to happen. This coincides with an understanding that others are separate from oneself, they are also causes of actions, and they have different perspectives or ways of seeing things. Have you ever wondered what it might be like to look in a mirror and not realize that the person looking back is, in fact, *you*? Although it is true that a very small percentage of people do have chronic difficulties recognizing faces, including their own (Sacks, 2010), most infants begin to recognize themselves in a mirror during the second year and can indicate this without fail by the end of toddlerhood. Some researchers, such as Dr. Robert Emde (1983), have noted that this timing is similar to the onset of a child's ability to use a personal pronoun (*"That's ME!"*) when shown a picture of himself—another indication of increasing self-recognition as an individual.

Is this process even more difficult if the baby has limited hearing, but other members of the family do not? In our own study, we found most infants whose parents shared their same hearing status demonstrated recognition of themselves in a mirror somewhat earlier than the deaf and hard-of-hearing babies whose parents were hearing. This recognition is usually shown by most children at around 18 months (Eliot, 1999), and it was in place for the majority of our participating toddlers with typical hearing and for deaf and hard-of-hearing toddlers with deaf parents (Koester & Forest, 1998). Performance of the deaf and hard-of-hearing toddlers with hearing parents was not as consistent at this age, although Kiki gave us the following nice example of her own self-awareness: At the 18-month observation, we quickly put a spot of red (rouge) coloring on her nose while she was looking away from the mirror and then directed her gaze toward her reflection. It took only a few seconds before she had solved the *"who's that in the mirror"* problem, reaching up to rub the spot and turning to her mother, then pointing to herself as if to say *"Hey, what's that funny mark on my nose?"* It is probably relevant when considering this that Kiki was developing both language and pretend play skills "on time" for her age. In addition, she appeared to have a positive and secure attachment with her mother. It seems that all of these symbolic functions were developing together and at expected ages.

Some have proposed that vocalizations by a baby and imitations of those vocalizations by others may play a role in helping an infant with typical hearing develop a sense of self. According to our own observations, similar experiences of signed communication also facilitate this process in deaf or hard-of-hearing babies. Being able to see or hear informal conversations that aren't necessarily directed at oneself often allows exposure to labels and references that identify objects and events, but also people and their relationships to each other. However, a child who is unable to access these opportunities will usually lag behind in his or her overall language comprehension and experiences with taking turns in communication episodes. This may have effects on their social and emotional development. The effects, although certainly not inevitable, may be seen in the quality of toddlers' relationships as well as in their understanding of who they are and even the seemingly simple ability to recognize themselves in a mirror.

The period between 12 and 18 months is one during which the infant is becoming increasingly aware of himself as someone who can cause things and people around him to respond in predictable ways. When caregivers respond sensitively and contingently to an infant's unique signals and communication efforts, such as by imitating or "mirroring" their baby's actions (including vocal or manual babbling), they are inadvertently helping the child to develop an awareness of how his own behaviors can affect others. The interrelationships found in a child's early social development are complex, involving not only knowledge about the self and others, but also knowledge about the self *in relation* to others: "*Who am I? Am I still the same little person today that I was yesterday? Who are all these other people—of all sizes, shapes, and personalities—whom I see around me all the time? And how do I fit in with them—am I the same or different?*" What an exhausting—but exhilarating—process it must be, growing from an infant to a toddler and then becoming a preschooler, and having to sort out all of these things!

SUMMARIZING KEY IDEAS

The ability to represent objects, events, people—and even the self—becomes increasingly evident with typical development during this 12- to 18-month age range. As language and thinking become more flexible and complex, these representational skills will also continue to develop and become more sophisticated over time. At this early stage, however, learning remains tied closely to experiences—both social and those related primarily to objects and actions. Learning will be easier, more efficient, and more thorough when direct actions are involved, but it will also be enriched as language emerges and becomes increasingly integrated with activities and interactive experiences.

The following are some of the key ideas in this chapter:

- The ability to represent, remember, and recreate can be seen as the child's play behaviors develop; these begin with simple enactive naming, followed by single and then sequenced pretend activities, and are finally expressed through preplanned and substitution play.
- The ability to represent something symbolically emerges in communication and language behaviors at ages that parallel certain advances in play; however, similar progress in language occurs only if meaningful models of language have been provided.

- Without sufficiently accessible language experiences, language itself will be delayed. Such a delay can have noticeable effects after the first birthday when toddlers typically begin to understand simple language and to express themselves in words or signs.
- During the same age range, as trust in others develops, toddlers also become increasingly aware of themselves as unique individuals with the power to influence others and cause things to happen.
- Parents of deaf and hard-of-hearing toddlers who are in the early stages of language development, whether in sign or speech, can support development by responding to the content that the child seems to be trying to express. Responses are most effective when they use much repetition and short sentences; involve expressive face, voice, and hands; use words or signs that the child can understand but also model new words and signs when appropriate; and use expansion to provide a slightly more advanced model of what the child can already say or sign. It remains important to allow time for the toddler to process what is being communicated and to participate as a turn-taking partner in these interactions.

The next chapter focuses on developments expected as a toddler nears his or her second birthday. Cultural and individual influences on social-emotional, as well as communication/language and cognitive, development will be even more influential with age.

NOTE

1. There are spoken languages in which verbs are emphasized in sentences more than they are in spoken English or French. In languages where verbs are more emphasized, toddlers' first vocabularies tend to include a larger proportion of verbs than is the case in languages that tend to have a stronger noun focus. However, even in these cases, toddlers' vocabularies contain more noun-like words than verbs—and toddlers (as well as preschoolers) appear to learn new nouns more quickly than they learn new verbs.

Chart 7: *Advances to Watch For**

By About 2 years

Physical and Motor Abilities*	• Walks independently; may run
	• Feeds self with spoon or fork; drinks from cup
	• Assists with dressing
	• May begin to participate in toilet training
	• Releases objects from grasp smoothly, intentionally
	• Stays on paper when scribbling
	• Begins drawing circles and lines
	• Brushes teeth with help
	• Stacks several blocks
Mental Abilities ("Cognition")	• Plans, thinks about ways to accomplish a goal
	• Creates groupings of similar objects
	• Remembers sequences of actions
	• Play includes related actions, simple real-life scripts
	• Can pretend one object represents different one
	• Increased interest in books, visual media[v]
Communication/ Language	• Produces at least 50 words or signs; may produce over 300
	• Produces "telegraphic" phrases, 2–3 words/ signs
	• Learns new names for objects rapidly, if attending to object and the language modeled
	• Names, identifies several body parts
	• Names or identifies pictures in books[v]
	• Responds to simple "what?" or "where?" questions
	• Asks for names/labels of things

(continued)

Chart 7 *Continued*

Social-Emotional	• Initiates laughter, smiles frequently
	• May show fears indicating imagination at work:
	○ Comforted by others, or may use blanket, etc. for self-comfort
	• May show preferences for "friends" among peers
	• Imitates, takes turns with peers:
	○ Play is still "parallel." not cooperative
	• Recognizes self in mirror[V]
	• Shows pride in accomplishments, shame at mistakes or bad behavior
	• Intentionally communicates anger
	• Displays pretend emotions in play:
	○ Cries or acts sad
	○ Talks, signs about imagined feelings

*See Chart 1 for partial list of sources for information.

**On all charts, advances in motor abilities assume no physical disabilities; limited vision may also slow motor advances. Family and cultural expectations also influence physical and motor achievements at this age and beyond.

[H] may be delayed or require different circumstances if hearing is limited; [V] may be delayed or require different circumstances if vision is limited.

10 Almost Two and Look What's New!
18 TO 24 MONTHS

QUESTIONS TO CONSIDER

- How does the role of play vary in different cultures, and how might child-rearing beliefs influence these differences?
- What are the major changes expected in a child's patterns of play during the second year, and are these different for a child with limited hearing?
- What changes in typical language development reflect increasing cognitive and symbolic abilities?
- Why are opportunities to "overhear" or "oversee" language important for language-learning toddlers? How can we enhance opportunities for such incidental learning by deaf and hard-of-hearing toddlers?
- How can adults modify their communications with deaf and hard-of-hearing toddlers in order to share books successfully?

BECOMING A MEMBER OF THE FAMILY'S CULTURE

A child's play, communication, and interactions with others are all intertwined in ways that reflect the norms and expectations of the surrounding culture. Our first example occurs in a small farming village in the highlands of East Africa. Toddler Mesfin has a few plastic toys, some discarded kitchen implements, and one tattered board book to keep him entertained while his Grandpa helps older sister Tesfaye with her homework. Mesfin has a moderate-to-severe hearing level but no opportunity for hearing aids. His parents have been given advice by medical specialists at the clinic a day's distance away and are committed to creating "home signs," many developed from gestures that Mesfin himself has first used. Mesfin is beginning to communicate with members of his close-knit, extended family. Grandparents live nearby and frequently join the family for meals, outings to the market, and child care in general. Aunts, uncles, and, of course, cousins live nearby in the community. The family is working hard to communicate with him and use gestures, home signs, and speech made loudly and slowly near his ear or where they are close enough for him to see them.

> *Mesfin sits on the floor in the same room as Tesfaye and Grandpa. Grandma carries in a plate of flatbread and sliced bananas, gesturing to Mesfin and telling him that he can pass them around to the other family members. Mesfin hops up eagerly, takes the plate, and, walking to each person in the room, offers a snack. At 23 months of age, he has learned that he should approach the eldest first: Grandpa accepts the food and smiles, thanking Mesfin by using their home sign. Mesfin proceeds to Grandma, and then to his sister. Following this daily ritual, Mesfin returns to his mat, looks up at his Grandma and waits expectantly. Grandma motions to Mesfin, pointing out some wood scraps to indicate that he can create a pretend serving plate. She demonstrates, using a piece of newsprint to serve as "flatbread"—like those that he has just served to his family. Although Grandma has already put away the real snack, Mesfin recreates the previous activity*

> *by using various objects to represent the actual food, and he elaborates on this by pretending to set the communal platter for dinner for the entire extended family. Surveying his work silently, Mesfin looks at Grandma and points over toward Grandpa and Tesfaye, who are reading together. Looking in a corner, Mesfin pulls out a small book. When he holds it out toward her, Grandma sits with him and they look at the book—seemingly imitating Grandpa and Tesfaye. Mesfin points to pictures in his book; Grandma gestures and speaks labels. Mesfin looks back and forth from the book to his Grandma's face. He is excited to have someone "help him with his homework," just like Tesfaye.*

With a supportive and attentive adult nearby to offer suggestions and encouragement, Mesfin has taken his level of play several steps beyond where it began 5 or so months ago as "simple pretend." As he offers pretend food and sets up a pretend dinner platter, he has engaged in play that is both realistically sequenced and includes using substitute objects as symbols for the real objects. This play is so elaborate that it can be considered an emerging "script." *Play scripts* (which do not emerge until about 18 months) are detailed sequences with symbols used in realistic order, learned from social experiences. Despite limited experience with formal language, Mesfin's family encourages his use of family-devised symbols to represent, remember, and recreate situations from his real life. In daily communication and play, Mesfin is learning lessons about his culture, where being part of the wider social group is of utmost importance. This involves politeness routines and awareness of the hierarchical system in his family's culture, where elders hold the highest ranks, as well as learning appropriate social rituals and greetings.

Our second example is from rural South Dakota in the United States. Kaitlyn is the same age as Mesfin, but has worn two hearing aids since age 6 months. Her parents mostly use spoken English to communicate with her and her brothers, but they have taken a few sign language classes. They meet with other parents of deaf and hard-of-hearing children once a month; this group includes several deaf, fluently signing parents who often demonstrate new signs and how to be sensitive to deaf and hard-of-hearing children's visual attention. A caregiver is provided to watch the children during meetings while the parents take some time to themselves to share experiences and suggestions.

Kaitlyn's parents have difficulty getting to the meetings, however, because both work full time. In addition, Kaitlyn's older brothers, both with typical hearing, need attention in the evenings just as she does. Her grandparents, aunts, and uncles all live in other states, so family social interactions are mostly limited to parents and brothers. Kaitlyn stays with a child care provider who keeps two other small children—both of whom have typical hearing—and she has opportunities for play and interaction with other toddlers there. The child care provider knows a few basic signs but depends mostly on spoken language and gestures to communicate with Kaitlyn. Kaitlyn's mother takes a half day off work weekly to meet with the early intervention specialists who provide information and support about Kaitlyn's development in a number of areas. Her mother shares this information, plus the "new signs of the week" with the family at dinnertime. Kaitlyn's mother also takes time off from work for periodic visits to an audiologist who checks how well the hearing aids are working.

Kaitlyn arrives home from day care in the arms of her father, who picks her up on his way from work. They greet her mother, who is already in the kitchen putting together dinner. After hugs and hellos, Kaitlyn and her father go to her "toy corner," just across the room from where mother is working. Daddy sits down with Kaitlyn as she looks around, then reaches for her little kitchen toys, including a couple of plastic pots, lids, some large spoons, and plates. She looks up at Daddy, who picks up one of the pots and a spoon, stirs, and while holding it out to Kaitlyn, signs and says "You cook. Like Mommy." As Kaitlyn takes the spoon and begins to stir, Daddy taps on her shoulder. When she looks up, he says/signs "You play. I'll help Mommy cook." Then he walks over to help his wife fix dinner. They look at Kaitlyn when she looks up at them, smile at her, but tell her to stay and play.

Just then, older brothers Seth and Toby burst through the door, throwing their backpacks down and yelling "hello" to all. They have been dropped off by their soccer carpool driver. Seth runs over to

Kaitlyn, kisses her on the forehead, and says, "How ya do'in, short stuff?" She grins as he runs off with Toby toward their room, yelling "okay!" when their mother asks how their day went.

Kaitlyn's parents continue to talk about their day as they cook. Kaitlyn, occasionally looking up to see what they are doing, puts a toy plate in front of one of her plastic figures. She stirs the pretend substance in her pot and spoons it onto the plate. Then she picks up the plastic figure carefully and tips it over on the plate—eating. She then picks up the figure, holds it toward her parents, toddles toward them, and vocalizes something loudly. "Yes," her mom says and signs, "He is eating, right?" and goes back to her own task. Daddy gently guides Kaitlyn back to her play area, and picks up one of her books. She eagerly sits down and looks as Daddy points toward a picture of a puppy. "Dah-ee!" Kaitlyn exclaims, points to the picture herself and pats her leg to sign "dog." Her Daddy, even her Mom from across the room, clap their hands vigorously to reward her, and Daddy signs "dog" as he says, "Yes, that's a doggie! Good girl!" Mom calls out that dinner is ready, and the family collects at the table. Kaitlyn is lifted to her high chair, the tray lowered to keep her in, and her plastic bib is secured. "Eeee!" Kaitlyn says with excitement. "Yep," her brother Tobey says, smiling, "Let's eee-T!" emphasizing the "t" sound at the end of the word as he signs it.

Like Mesfin, Kaitlyn has many advantages. Both are lucky to have families that, despite limitations in resources (and Kaitlyn's family's most limited resource appears to be time), provide them with warm, secure environments in which to grow and learn. Both families are working hard to communicate with their children. Like Mesfin, Kaitlyn shows her ability to engage in script-like play, combining actions and objects in realistic, ordered sequences. Mesfin has also shown substitution play (using wood chips and other objects to represent food, for example); Kaitlyn has substituted *nothing* for something—a blank space of "spooned out food" has been placed in the plastic figure's plate and then "eaten." Mesfin has included others in his play, and Kaitlyn has pretended that the plastic figure is "acting" in the play sequence. Finally, both children have shown that they understand something about books and that pictures represent real objects. These behaviors all give evidence that both children are developing cognitive skills appropriate for their age. They are both eager to engage socially in ways acceptable to their families and use their visual attention effectively in communication. Both, however, have some delay in language. Kaitlyn is just beginning to use single signs and word-like vocalizations. Mesfin is using the home- and self-developed gesture symbol system available to him, but his communication system will not be useful beyond the extended family and perhaps close community. Both children are benefiting from the guidance and knowledge of adults and older children, gaining skills from more knowledgeable models, as Dr. Vygotsky (1967) would have us expect. Their families are even making sure that they have literacy experiences, engaging with books.

Despite these similarities and shared advantages, it is also apparent that Mesfin and Kaitlyn are experiencing important differences in their environments. One noticeable difference is in Kaitlyn's access to hearing technology and to frequent intervention sessions designed to maximize her development—especially in the language area. It seems that Kaitlyn's hearing aids and language activities are helping her to hear more of the sounds of spoken language around her. Furthermore, she is getting an introduction to a formal system of signing that can eventually be used in interactions with other signers beyond family and close friends; this will also support her vocabulary development and other language skills—including literacy or reading and writing. Unless and until Mesfin can obtain specialized schooling within a few years, his ability to learn a language to communicate effectively beyond his family and close community will undoubtedly remain limited.

Although opportunities to acquire a formal language are greater for Kaitlyn than for Mesfin, there are experiences in other areas in which Mesfin and his family may be considered more advantaged. Perhaps the most striking difference is in the levels of extended family support available to the families. Mesfin's extended family—grandparents, aunts, and uncles, undoubtedly a large collection of cousins, and other family members—provide more people ready and able to interact with him and to assist and support his parents on a daily if not hourly basis. Kaitlyn's family does not have that advantage. Although grandparents and other extended family members are almost certainly loving and generally supportive, they are not located close enough to provide daily support for her parents or extra attention to her and her brothers. Even if they lived closer, it is probable that her grandparents continue to have daily work obligations, just as her parents do. As her parents face extra demands on their time to ensure that Kaitlyn gets the developmental support she needs, they must juggle schedules and divide their own attention across daily activities without anyone else in the home to provide back-up.

In addition, there is a difference between the two children in the relative emphasis in their family's cultures on the degree to which they are expected to focus on exploration of the object world as opposed to the social world. The African example represents a more collective culture than that found in much of North America, so play activities tend to occur during spontaneous gatherings with other children (often siblings), interactions with a variety of adults, or even while being carried on an older sibling's back. Cooperation, respect, communication with each other, and learning to work out problems with peers are all essential aspects of Mesfin's family environment.

In South Dakota, Kaitlyn's family—although clearly very interested in engaging socially and emotionally with her—is more likely to foster and reinforce independence and autonomy rather than interdependence with others. They will encourage her to learn to use the many toys and books in their home for learning and entertainment independently and to investigate the physical properties of those objects and how her own actions affect them. Emphasis is placed on mastering the physical environment, becoming increasingly independent, and incorporating pretend into her use of objects in ways that may or may not involve other people. Her brothers are usually off doing their own things, her parents are nearby and watchful but often not very directly involved in Kaitlyn's current activities, and she is learning that self-sufficiency and competence are valued in her family. To be sure, children in both cultures are expected to be respectful of each other and of their elders, to manage any conflicts with civility, and to show interest in the welfare of others. Nevertheless, compared to the scene in an East African village, the American family in this case places somewhat less emphasis on these primarily social lessons at this early stage in Kaitlyn's life.

Patterns of politeness and expressions of respect vary not only across large cultural boundaries but within smaller groups. This is seen clearly when traveling across wide sections of the United States, for example. Deaf and hearing communities even within a fairly small geographic area can also differ in social and behavioral expectations. This is evident in ways of greeting others, signals for turn-taking in conversations, and other social rituals and practices (Holcomb, 2013). Even the amount of autonomy toddlers are permitted to have and the kinds of interactions they are allowed with persons beyond the family can vary across cultural settings. Culturally influenced differences like these should be expected, acknowledged, and respected in intervention and education practices. Children's hearing levels themselves will not define or override the cultural expectations and experiences of families. Indeed, intervention specialists should be knowledgeable and comfortable with cultural patterns so that they may draw on the strengths in each. The specific ways in which symbol use (in play and in language), social skills, and various developmental steps are displayed in behavior will differ according to the culture in which the child and family are embedded (Bronfenbrenner, 1979), but development in all these areas tends to "unfold" in similar sequences across cultures.

STILL ON THE MOVE, BUT FASTER NOW

When we think of a toddler's day, the complexity of what is being achieved and demonstrated behaviorally may escape our notice. The examples of Mesfin and Kaitlyn show rich, multifaceted, interdependent sets of behaviors: social and emotional abilities, cognitive or thinking skills, communication and language skills, and even developing knowledge of family and community cultural norms. Yet another aspect of development, motor skills, also plays a critical role in the toddler's experiences and learning.

During the second year, "expert crawling," walking, climbing, running, even jumping typically emerge and are refined to some extent once the child's muscle strength, coordination, and balance have all matured a bit. We mentioned in Chapter 9 how Kiki (at 18 months) was able to use carefully aimed fine motor skills to fit her finger into a small opening in a play house and then coordinate larger muscles to pull the door open. Mesfin, just a bit older, is able to handle small objects easily and place them carefully on his "tray" for handing out to others at his pretend dinner. This requires that fine motor skills be coordinated with vision and smoothly operating balance and gross motor skills as he sits, stands, and walks without any obvious difficulty through the room to distribute the goodies. Like Mesfin, Kaitlyn easily manipulates her toys; she walks to get to her toys and her parents; best of all, she almost breaks into a run to get to that dinner table! Still, she is not yet completely steady on her feet—and her father finds it easier to carry her from the car into the house instead of waiting for to make slower progress on her own.

Although Mesfin and Kaitlyn are developing motor skills at about the same rate, there are going to be differences in the ways those skills are expressed depending on the expectations of the adults around them—that is, on their culture. Methods and expected ages for toilet training will differ, as may expectations for skills such as using utensils for eating and other daily activities like brushing teeth. In many Western families, children will be expected by 2 years of age to use utensils for self-feeding, to help get themselves undressed, and perhaps to begin learning how to use a toilet rather than needing diapers. For many other families around the world, such skills are considered neither necessary nor even desired, or modifications are made according to local customs. These are situations in which intervention specialists and other adults supporting a family need to be sensitive to cultural norms and beliefs, as well as knowledgeable about typical rates of development.

Both fine and gross motor skills enable expression of advancing play abilities, abilities to approach and interact socially with others, and the production of language through either manual movements of hands and body (signs, cued speech, gestures) or movements of the muscles and organs involved in speech production (tongue, lips, etc.). Furthermore, motor experiences enable the child to express cognitive, social, emotional, and linguistic knowledge, building on existing skills. Practice may not make perfect—at least not right away—but it strengthens and increases opportunities for varying experiences.

Some deaf and hard-of-hearing children experience delays or difficulties with balance (due to the nearness of the hearing and balance parts of the inner ear), with slowed initial abilities in standing and walking. However, this is a minority of the group; in general, hearing level does not have much effect on developing motor skills. Dr. Lise Eliot (1999) pointed out that although the *sequence* in which motor skills develop is highly predictable across children and across cultures (unless there is interference due to some physical or neurological disability), the *rate* of motor development varies to a considerable degree "so that a more advanced child may lead a slower one by several months in the emergence of each basic skill" (p. 261).

There were few differences between the motor skills that Mesfin and Kaitlyn displayed, and their abilities to play, communicate, and learn did not appear to be limited by motor skills. If a child has motor disabilities that interfere with age-appropriate experiences, however, it becomes necessary to find alternative ways to support this area of learning. A specialist in motor abilities—gross motor, like balance and locomotion, as well as fine motor required for handling and exploring objects—is an important member of an early intervention team. Specialists in occupational or sensory-integration therapy can be especially helpful if a child has problems learning to perform activities of daily life or needs special practice and activities to increase balance. When a baby or toddler with limited hearing seems to be developing motor skills at a noticeably slower rate than other children of the same age, further assessment should be performed. Usually, the child will just be on the later end of the typical developmental age range. However, in motor areas, just as other developmental areas, it is easier to prevent an increasing delay than to correct or remediate one later. Furthermore, overall development is most efficient when various areas are developing in synchrony.

ADVANCES IN SOCIAL AND THINKING SKILLS

Both Mesfin and Kaitlyn showed advances in social and thinking skills in their play as well as in their interactions with others in their homes. Although it is not uncommon for adults in some contexts and situations to not give much encouragement to play—especially understandable in situations in which resources are scarce and children have to contribute to family duties at early ages—a lack of time for free play can mean a loss for overall development. According to many researchers, theorists, and educators, there is a lot more going on inside a child's brain during play than is obvious: "Babies who are figuring out what people think play imitation games; babies who are figuring out how we see objects play hide-and-seek; babies who are figuring out the sounds of language babble. It's all very serious fun" (Gopnik, Meltzoff, & Kuhl, 1999, p. 153). Similarly, babies who are figuring out the *sights* of language babble with their hands! In other words, a child's explorations, which we often think of as "merely play," actually incorporate and provide practice in mental or cognitive functions, developing social skills, and increasingly sophisticated communicative behaviors.

Mesfin and Kaitlyn both have families that encourage play, and both toddlers showed play behaviors illustrating cognitive advances typical of about 18–24 months of age. Their play showed symbolic representation of events that happen in their daily lives. That is, they used mental symbols to remember and organize their actions. This was shown in their ability to imagine that one thing is another—to make substitutions in play and to imagine objects that weren't even present.

Both children created short but accurate sequences as they combined play actions around a particular "theme." (In most cultures, early themes will represent daily routines like mealtime and bed time.) Practicing theme-based sequences may be especially important for children with limited hearing because one area in which older deaf and hard-of-hearing children often experience difficulties is that of sequential memory (Hamilton, 2011; see Marschark & Hauser, 2012, for more about memory and learning in deaf and hard-of-hearing children). Although no direct link has been proved, it is possible that play-based practice with sequencing activities will help to strengthen this type of thinking in the long run.

Mesfin and Kaitlyn both gave evidence of beginning *decentered* play (Fenson & Ramsay, 1980), in which they took the perspectives of others: Mesfin adjusted the tray he held as he offered snacks, and Kaitlyn oriented toy cups so a doll or a play partner could pretend to drink at the correct angle. These actions give evidence that the children were overcoming their initial *egocentric* understanding of the world. ("Egocentric" does not mean that the child is self-centered in a "selfish" way, but simply that he or she cannot yet fully comprehend that others have different perspectives or ways of understanding the world [Piaget, 1936/1952, 1962].)

In more advanced decentered play, the child enacts and represents activities from the perspective of another. This is seen when he or she doesn't merely involve others as recipients of play behaviors (like the sips of pretend tea offered to play partners) but actually has others (whether a real person or a doll, etc.) enact a play behavior. For example, a 2-year-old may use a plastic hammer to "fix" a car, then hand the hammer to mother and indicate that she is to do it, then place it in a doll's hand and move it so the doll is hammering on the bench. A single play theme begins to be repeated to involve different actors, not just recipients of action. We saw this demonstrated by Kaitlyn, who helped her plastic doll "eat."

Engaging in play also supports increasing understanding of *cause and effect*—in the physical and also the social realm. The basics of this understanding are usually evident by about a year, when infants begin to repeat activities like dropping objects, apparently for the purpose of getting a response from another person. The baby is learning the laws of physics and of psychology! Thus, during the first year, babies learn something about how their own behaviors, events beyond their control (such as caregivers' sometimes unpredictable responses), or objects themselves can cause certain reactions or can influence each other. But by the end of the second year, with advances in thinking skills, most toddlers will be able to mentally anticipate such consequences, rather than needing to go through the whole routine engaged in earlier. They still have a long way to go before becoming truly skilled social partners and before they can understand the innumerable complexities of the physical world. However, these abilities grow dramatically during the second year.

Plays Well with Others?

Opportunities to experience and explore social play, with peers as well as older children and adults, contribute to the child's understanding of cause-and-effect relationships. In addition, negotiating turn-taking, sharing, and imitating, as well as simply running around and actively playing with others, helps develop a strong sense of "self" as well as a beginning awareness of the feelings and goals of others (Figure 10.1).

More play with other children—or at least play in the presence of other children—is typical of the toddler approaching the 2-year mark. As motor skills increase, children begin to run together, one child climbing on an object will provoke another to do so, one dropping to her hands and knees to begin a "fast crawl" may soon be joined by another in a bit of a race. This early play with a same-age peer often occurs in a *parallel* fashion, with both children playing at the same thing but without

Figure 10.1 Learning language with mother and teacher and friends. (Photo courtesy of MICHA—Society for Deaf Children, National Council. Reprinted with permission.)

coordinating their activities. For example, one may lie down and curl up with a playtime blanket to pretend to sleep, and the other child will do the same with his own blanket. Another way to look at this is that a lot of (inexact) imitation or "action contagion" begins to happen.

This reflects awareness and interest in the other's behaviors, and the toddler begins to identify him- or herself as being like the same-aged child in various ways. Another child may actually be preferred as a play partner over the parent who brought the child to the play group (especially if large or gross motor play is possible). Toddlers start learning the names of their playmates and refer to a "friend" or playmates' names when they are not around. It can be particularly helpful for a toddler who is deaf or hard of hearing to have another child around, especially one who is using the same general approach to learning language (signs, cues, speech), although play with age-mates at this point usually does not involve much language use among the children.

The value of play sessions and play groups will also be increased if the adults present are careful to communicate so that what they say or sign is accessible to the children. In a study of slightly older children in a day care center (Spencer, Koester, & Meadow-Orlans, 1993), we found that pairs of children interacted on more advanced levels when there was an aide nearby who could communicate effectively with both of them. Toddlers with typical hearing and those who were deaf and hard of hearing attended this center; spoken as well as signed language (or a combination of the two) was used. Teachers and aides also varied in their hearing levels—although all used signs fluently—so communication differences among the children could be accommodated.

Learning about cause-and-effect contingencies, other perspectives, feelings, and attitudes can occur whether the child is sighted or blind, tall or short, American or Chinese—and regardless of hearing level. Individual differences play a role in determining the speed at which a given child learns about and comprehends the world around him or her, but, in the absence of severe physical or cognitive difficulties, this process is likely to follow similar patterns across children. Much research on play by children with disabilities has focused on those with behaviors on the autism spectrum and has often indicated that these children are less likely than their peers to incorporate a wide variety of behaviors into their play. Thus, the child's use of pretend play can be seen as an important indicator of later social skills (Sigman & Ruskin, 1999). Therefore, not only is observing play activity useful for the purposes of assessing a child's mental abilities, but it can also be used to identify delays in social and communicative skills. Play experiences can then provide a context to effectively teach social and communicative skills to young children for whom these are areas of difficulty.

Of course, play is only one avenue for developing social and emotional understandings and abilities. The activities of daily life, routine and expectable events of each day, and excursions beyond home and family are major sources of experiences that support and encourage development. Children's minds along with their bodies—and their feelings and emotions—are engaged during their everyday activities (Figure 10.2).

Figure 10.2 Playing actively with other children helps build thinking and social and communication skills. (Photo courtesy of MICHA—Society for Deaf Children, National Council. Reprinted with permission.)

Feelings and Emotions

Participation in play, as well as in daily routines and activities of family and community life, can also have positive emotional consequences (as well as cognitive and communicative consequences) as a child experiences the pleasure of being the cause of certain effects—of making things happen in the physical world, such as seeing the stack of blocks remain standing—or not. Similarly, when children join in with family and community activities, pretending or not, they are equally likely to see themselves as causal *agents*. A child is (hopefully) receiving not only the self-satisfaction of that physical accomplishment but also the reinforcement that comes in the form of parents' delight, praise, laughter, and so forth. As with all communications with a toddler with limited hearing, caregivers or social partners need to be aware of the child's attention needs, ensuring that she is able to detect the caregiver's positive emotional expressions in order to appreciate that feedback. This may be as simple as an affectionate pat on the shoulder or a broad grin and animated facial expression that is easily visible to the child. Along with positive facial and vocal expressions, clapping can often be detected fairly easily because it involves sharp changes in sound energy (Fletcher, 2013). It is often used by both deaf and hearing parents to praise a toddler's accomplishments. It is also usually easy for an adult to move hands (and even body and face) into the child's visual field to make the clapping motion and associated positive feedback visible.

"I Know You're Upset, but . . ."

Toddlers nearing 2 years of age are notorious for communicating their anger quite effectively and intentionally (often without using language)—not just crying in frustration, but also at times becoming adamant about their desires, their disappointments and dislikes, and even their jealousies. It is also not uncommon for toddlers to try using aggressive behaviors such as kicking and biting when they are upset with another child or an adult. Usually, these behaviors subside fairly soon, especially if they are treated in a firm but matter-of-fact way and efforts are made to understand what has provoked this behavior. This can be followed in most cases with communication about limits, acceptable and unacceptable behaviors, and consequences of aggression. The key concept here is *communicating*. It is difficult when parents are struggling to use a new language or language system to communicate ideas like this. How do they use the child's communicative strengths to "get through" to him or her about behavioral expectations?

Dr. Paula Pittman and her co-authors (Pittman, Benedict, Olson, & Sass-Lehrer (2015) report that hearing parents participating in "deaf mentor" programs (in which a deaf adult meets regularly with the family and shares both language and cultural expertise with them) benefit significantly from what the mentors share—and sometimes demonstrate—with the child. Parents often say that they have learned from the mentors how to use touch, eye gaze, signs, and/or gestures to help their child calm down and to figure out what is wrong. Neither words nor signs (nor cued speech nor any other language method we can imagine) will quickly resolve a 2-year-old's classic episodes of being "adamant"; however, as the child begins to be able to label and understand other peoples' emotions better, and to communicate her own frustrations more effectively through language, physical acting out is less likely to be her first reaction. Similarly, being able to use at least a bit of language can be helpful for a child who becomes afraid of the dark or is frightened after having seen part of a too-scary movie or a violent video game (often a possibility when there are older children in the home). In some environments, it will help to define and even begin to explain why some areas are dangerous and not to be explored.

Drs. Rosemary Calderon and Mark Greenberg (2011) pointed out that the following social-emotional competencies should be achieved by toddlers who have experienced a predictable and responsive environment: (1) having self-confidence and a trusting attitude toward those they know; (2) having inquisitiveness, curiosity, and eagerness to investigate things; (3) having the ability to relate well to other people; and (4) beginning to understand the feelings of others. For these outcomes to be accomplished, it becomes increasingly important over time that parents model healthy and effective ways to interact with others and handle disagreements, model social behaviors that are appropriate to place and time, help the child develop social and personal routines, and demonstrate ways to manage impulses (see also Schlesinger & Meadow, 1972). But here is the catch, and it is a concern for hearing families with a deaf or hard-of-hearing toddler: it is usually helpful (and often necessary) to use language to communicate these ideas and explain these behaviors. Such language will not be very sophisticated regardless of a toddler's hearing levels because 2-year-olds don't yet understand the nuances and finer details of language meanings. However, it is important to begin to be able to label feelings of self and others, to use words or signs to help remember behavior rules and safety warnings ("Hot! Will burn you!"), and to use words or signs as "mediators" that the toddler can internalize and use to help regulate his sometimes impulsive behaviors. It is easier to remember, and even to think about and to plan things, if you have a symbol like a word or sign to represent it mentally.

ADVANCES IN LANGUAGE

If a good foundation for communication using gestures and some signs or spoken words is in place—along with rich interactive and social-emotional experiences—a toddler will have gained increasing understanding of language and will begin producing it by this age. However, if a deaf or hard-of-hearing child is to "keep up" with age-level expectations, language experiences must continue to be rich, responsive, frequent, and to occur in meaningful situations.

Building a Vocabulary

A major advance typical of the 18- to 24-month age span is increasingly efficient learning of new words or signs. Although different children advance at different rates, most hearing children will begin to increase their vocabularies rapidly after a rather slow start in which each new word seems a great accomplishment. By 24 months, spoken vocabularies of more than 100 words are common. An early version of the Communicative Development Inventory for Spoken English (CDI; Fenson et al., 1993) indicates that the child who performs in the middle (or 50th percentile) compared to age-mates with typical hearing will produce between about 75 and 110 words at 18 months and about 200 to 300 at 24 months. (This test shows an advantage for girls over boys, and it warns that these findings may not hold true for children in resource-impoverished environments.)

Assuming that a toddler has had regular access to a model of signs, how does vocabulary development typically proceed? Deaf and hard-of-hearing children learning sign language from fluently signing deaf parents also show rapid increases in their receptive (understanding) and expressive (production) vocabularies during this period. Drs. Diana Anderson and Judy Reilly (2002) used an American Sign Language (ASL) version of the CDI to study the acquisition of vocabulary by deaf children with deaf parents in the United States. They found that vocabulary size up to 18 months was actually a bit larger for the deaf infants in their study who were learning ASL than is usually reported for children with typical hearing who are learning spoken language. (By 18 months, 150 or more different signs were produced.) However, this difference had disappeared by 2 years, and the deaf children with deaf parents produced about the same number of signs as words from the hearing children.

In a study of sign vocabulary development in deaf children of deaf parents in the United Kingdom, Woolfe and colleagues (Woolfe, Herman, Roy, & Woll, 2010) found a similar (although somewhat slower) rate of vocabulary development between 8 and 36 months as in the study from the United States. These findings confirmed that *understanding* of signs develops earlier than using them for *expression* and that there is much variation across children in the pattern of development. Some showed slower and fairly steady development, while others showed more rapid growth—sometimes in "spurts."

These patterns and their variations suggest that development of sign language in sign-rich environments proceeds much like development of spoken language by children with typical hearing in a speech-rich environment. Included among the similarities is the acquisition of specific words for asking questions *(Where? What? Who?* and *Which?)* after about 2 years of age—but only after a vocabulary of about 200 signs has already been learned. Signs for feelings *(sad, happy, scared)* are used by about the same age and when a similar vocabulary size has been reached. As readers will no doubt attest, "no" is also used by this age by most toddlers, with those who sign also often signing "none" or "don't-want." (See Anderson, 2006, for further discussion; see also the Visual Communication and Sign Language (VCSL) scale [Simms, Baker, & Clark, 2013] for an instrument to assess language development in children from birth to age 5 years who experience a natural sign language [ASL] environment at home.)

What about deaf and hard-of-hearing toddlers with hearing parents? Those whose parents use signs fairly consistently have usually begun to produce signs themselves by this age. Typically, however, their vocabulary size doesn't keep up with that of the other two groups. We saw this pattern in our own research. At 18 months, the *average* vocabulary size of the group of deaf and hard-of-hearing children with hearing parents was below that of the children with typical hearing and the deaf children with deaf parents. However, the "top" children with limited hearing who had hearing parents were using about as many words or signs as the "average" children in the other two groups. (The children with limited hearing who produced spoken words had either moderate-to-severe or severe hearing levels and had used hearing aids since no later than 6 months of age.) When we followed up with a vocabulary check of many of these children at 24 months, however, none of the deaf and hard-of-hearing children with hearing parents was keeping up with the "average" for children in the other groups.

Dr. Anderson (2006) compared several available studies in which children's actual early vocabularies were listed sign by sign. She found that there is much overlap across the signs used by children learning ASL and those learning a signed English system after the latter group had 6 months of experience with signing. In addition, both lists overlap significantly with early words reported for children with typical hearing who are learning spoken English. Although the pattern of word learning for the three groups of children is similar, there are other characteristics that are specific to the deaf and hard-of-hearing children with hearing parents: (1) on average, they show delays in language development, with some delay apparent even with identification of hearing levels in infancy; (2) these delays are lessened when identification and intervention begin by 6 months of age compared to later; (3) a minority of children show the ability to keep pace with age-level expectations for children with typical hearing; (4) for signing children, the amount of signing they have seen relates to their speed of language development; and (5) with early identification and individualized early intervention programming, average rates of development are similar for those whose hearing families have chosen "oral" approaches (spoken language only) and those who have chosen a signed English approach (signing plus speech).

To understand this final point, it is important to understand that many programs actively encourage families to choose the approach that seems to best fit their own and their child's characteristics; therefore, the lack of a difference in development based on the language approach used seems to indicate that good decisions are being made. It is also the case that families change their approaches over time. This can be seen when a toddler begins to actually respond to and even produce spoken language (perhaps through use of effective hearing aids, perhaps with use of a CI) and the family members spontaneously reduce signs and increase speech. We have seen this occur with several families. The opposite is also true. Parents tend to increase signs (and gestures), especially if they have support available from fluently signing adults, when a child is not responding to their spoken language. We observed a process similar to this in a family that wanted to use a combination of cued speech (and spoken English) along with ASL. When the child consistently responded to and produced signs more reliably than cued language (Spencer, 2000), they moved more strongly to use of signs. After the child received a CI at about age 3 and began to speak and respond to spoken language, the family began to rely increasingly on spoken language; however, they also continued to communicate at times using ASL.

"Wha-zat?"

Many children start learning new words rapidly just as they begin to repeatedly request the names of things. They are learning an important language rule: Everything has a name! A toddler using spoken language will often point to an object or event (or even person), give a quizzical facial expression, and ask with a rising intonation: "dat?" or "wha-zat?" The adult being addressed is expected to supply a name or label for "that." This sometimes seems to become a game structured not unlike the earlier repeated dropping of objects from high-chair trays and the like: "I do something (in this case it is something involving language) and I learn that the other person will reply (in this case, with language)." In addition to being a language-learning mechanism, this bolsters a growing feeling of power to obtain a response. What parent can resist (for more than a few minutes) an adorable toddler actually *asking* to be taught something?

Do toddlers learning signs also begin to ask for the names of things? Yes. In this case, the "what?" or "well?" gesture, with one hand turned up and held to the side while the other hand either holds or points to or otherwise indicates an object or event, often serves the same function as a spoken "dat?" For some deaf and hard-of-hearing toddlers, this request is made simply by pointing and making a quizzical facial expression. Fortunately for adults who are new to signing, toddlers usually ask for the names of familiar objects for which signs are taught and learned early in sign language classes. It is also useful to have a sign "app" available on whatever electronic device is handy (or, in other circumstances, an actual print copy of a sign dictionary) to be able to respond to the toddler.

For parents new to signing, the ability to fingerspell, which is fairly easily learned, can be useful when the sign is not known. Deaf parents often use fingerspelling with their infants and toddlers, so this need not be saved for older children. In fact, sometimes there really is no accepted sign for an object, event, or idea, and, in those cases, fingerspelling is particularly helpful.

Requesting the names of things, although it can push adults to their patience limits at times, is a powerful learning mechanism. Only a few exposures to a new word or sign may be required before it is remembered—sometimes only a single time is necessary. For such quick learning, it is usually necessary for the child to be attending to what the new word or sign refers to—and for the label to be provided in a way that is easily accessible through hearing and/or vision. At earlier ages, parents were primarily responsible for setting up situations in which they shared attention to something with the baby and then provided its label.

The toddler is now setting up a similar situation himself, and this accelerates learning when parents are responsive.

Of course, learning words or signs does not depend on the toddler's requesting a response. Parents and other adults continue to provide language models in conversation form, taking turns and often waiting for the toddler to respond—even if he or she does not yet use language. Just as during the previous 6 months, parents will continue to correct toddlers' productions, usually by accepting and interpreting them, perhaps repeating them in a correct form, and responding to them. Short but grammatically correct sentences, use of words the toddler understands—or is in a position to learn now—and frequent repetition of statements in the same or slightly varied form are common. Expansions of things the toddler says, signs, or gestures serve to increase effective language input while keeping his or her attention. And although parents will now begin to talk or sign about what happened recently (especially if looking at pictures or an object associated with the events) and what will happen later in the day or tomorrow, most parental language continues to relate to the "here and now." Strong facial expressions as well as vocal intonations and slightly exaggerated stress on important words or signs will also keep attention and promote language learning.

It is important to keep in mind that language is *learned*, but it is *not usually taught*. Specific teaching strategies are required when language becomes significantly delayed or when some extra challenges are presented. However, when language is accessible (can be heard or seen as needed) and occurs in meaningful interactions during the first 2 years of life, structured teaching is not necessary. In fact, we have probably all experienced situations when toddlers saw or heard language that we did not anticipate they would understand or repeat—but, to our embarrassment, they did.

Learning Incidentally

Language is also often processed and remembered when it is merely "overheard." Thus, a toddler with typical hearing who is nearby and attending to others who are conversing can learn simply from this exposure.

This process of *incidental learning* is obviously available for children with typical hearing, who can hear language while looking away from conversation participants. It also occurs for deaf and hard-of-hearing children in environments where there are multiple signers who converse in their presence. "Onlooking" allows them to see more of the conversation. Of course, a child with limited hearing may have decreased access if he or she looks away to engage in play or some other activity. Still, what is "over-seen" can be powerful language input and result in efficient language uptake. However, access to incidental language learning is often greatly decreased for deaf or hard-of-hearing children with parents who rarely sign.

We were embarrassed to see examples of this in our own laboratory when we recently reviewed recordings made with 18-month-olds in the presence of adults with typical hearing. In one situation, although both the researcher and mother were able to sign, neither did so while they sat in the laboratory and conversed. The deaf child, sitting on the floor at the adults' feet and playing quietly, looked up repeatedly as though wondering what was going on. At one point, she held a toy out toward her mother with a quizzical expression—seeming to ask for attention more than to actually invite shared play. But this prompted only a brief signed reply from her mother, who was providing spoken information to the researcher instead.

Unfortunately, many hearing people, including some of us who spend our professional lives working to promote deaf and hard-of-hearing children's learning, typically revert to our most comfortable communication mode (in this case, spoken English) unless there is a specific reminder to sign. A similar thing happened at Kaitlyn's house as her parents conversed in spoken language while cooking together. We do not bring this up to chastise or criticize. That's one reason why we used our own project as an example. Instead, we mention it as an example of the challenges faced by deaf and hard-of-hearing language learners even in advantaged situations. Most simply lack exposure to as many words or signs and to as much information presented in language compared to hearing children of the same age. This includes language for expressing emotions, attitudes, feelings, and fears, as well as for learning and remembering culturally approved rules for behavior and self-regulation.

Stringing Together Words or Signs

About the same time toddlers begin learning new words or signs more rapidly, another important advance occurs. They begin a transition from mostly one-word or one-sign expressions to longer ones. They may begin by producing two one-word/sign expressions closely together in time: "Cookie." "More." These still look and sound like one-word expressions. Signers' hands pause or drop between making each sign; speakers' intonation might drop, and there is a distinct but brief pause between the two spoken words or signs. At about the same time, toddlers start combining a gesture (like pointing) with a sign or spoken word. For example, a point to the cookie may be accompanied by the word or sign "more." We and others have noted that this kind of two-part expression is often observed just before actual two-word or two-sign expressions emerge (Spencer & Harris, 2006).

The move to expressions of longer than one word or sign is gradual, but usually happens only after a child has learned to produce between at least 50 to 100 individual words or signs (Anderson, 2006). The move to combinations (sequences of words or signs) in part reflects children's growing cognitive abilities, which are being demonstrated in sequences of play behaviors at about the same age. But there is also a very practical payoff for a toddler who produces multiple signs and/or words in a single expression. Giving more information at once helps the communication partner better understand the toddler's meaning—his intent. Less guesswork is involved when the "listener" is trying to interpret and respond appropriately to the toddler's message. This means that communication becomes (in the words of James McLean) "more effective, efficient, and less ambiguous" (McLean & Snyder-McLean, 1999, p. 157). The toddler's feelings of competence are reinforced. He is more likely to get what he wants!

When two-word or two-sign expressions are emerging, they typically have several characteristics. (1) They often, but not always, follow a "topic-comment" order (McLean & Snyder-McLean, 1999). If the message is "I want more cookie," the expression is likely to be "cookie (the topic) + more." Noticing a big truck roar by may be expressed "truck (topic) + big." This order is common for deaf or hard-of-hearing toddlers and for those with typical hearing; for those learning sign as well as those learning spoken language. (2) Early expressions usually consist of nouns, adjectives, and perhaps a verb (action word or sign). It will be some time (usually well into the third year) before children learning speech will start adding words like articles (a, the); prepositions (of, with); or word endings signifying plurals (-s), tenses (-ed), and the other niceties of spoken language grammar. Similarly, toddlers learning natural sign languages tend to omit the complicated grammatical features of those languages and produce the same kinds of "telegraphic" expressions as their hearing age-mates. At this stage, signing deaf mothers continue to simplify the grammar of their own productions, at least as their children begin the transition to two-sign expressions. For example, in ASL, "I'm looking at the truck" might be signed to an adult with the sign for "looking at" originating at the eye of the signer and smoothly moving toward the truck. That is, the actor or subject and the object are shown as an integral part of the verb—they are merged. However, a deaf mother of a toddler might instead first actually point to herself to indicate "I," then make the "looking at" verb in its classic form, then indicate the truck and actually sign "truck." This has broken the meanings into more easily understood units.

As two-word and two-sign expressions become more frequent, toddlers begin to use the word/sign orders that occur most often in the adult language of their own culture. This order differs in some respects for ASL and spoken English, for example. The main ideas, or *semantic structures* expressed across languages remain similar, however. Two-word or two-sign expressions often indicate a noun plus an action, an action plus its object or recipient ("read book"), "that" to indicate an object plus a label or name, a possessor plus the possession ("my truck"), or the recurrence of something ("more cookie"), as well as characteristics of things ("big boy"), objects' locations, and the nonexistence or disappearance of things ("all-gone milk").

Although reports of the progress of deaf and hard-of-hearing toddlers with hearing parents into the two-word stage are scarce, all indications are that they follow the same sequence, produce the same meanings or intents, combine gestures and signs or words in the beginning, and then move to two-word or two-sign expressions just like children with typical hearing or deaf children with deaf parents. The major difference is that these steps are often delayed, or at least begin at a later age and require major "catch-up" efforts when access to language is increased. Access to language may increase during the second year if intervention services are started later than usual, perhaps due to a late identification of need, or if the language approach being used changes to include signs. Increased opportunities to interact with fluent signers, either due to enhanced parent or caregiver learning, changes in sign skills of intervention providers, and attending play groups or intervention groups with fluent signers, can all provide more effective sign models and experiences. Improved hearing aids, use of technology like FM systems or CIs, can increase access to the sounds of spoken language—and the latter two technologies are often not used until the second year of life. If increased opportunities occur, an upswing in language acquisition can also be expected. Nevertheless, it should be remembered that the child is starting out with less language experience than most of his or her age-mates, so that the hoped-for catching up will require time.

It is appropriate for the level of language being used with a toddler—and the goals of any speech or sign or cued language therapy—to be based on the *order of acquisition* of typical development. If a toddler's language is developing at a slower than typical rate, it will only be frustrating to try to skip developmental steps usually seen at earlier ages. When setting goals and developing strategies for language learning, it is critical to start by determining what the toddler is currently capable of doing with language. It is helpful to provide language input and experiences that are not only accessible but are "just a bit" beyond what he or she currently knows and is using. The fact that skills are advancing is more important than the absolute level of skills at any specific age. Language, like other aspects of development, is like a ladder—it's easier to get to the top by taking one rung at a time than trying to stretch upward over several with one step.

Reading Books Together

The benefits of sharing books between caregivers and infants or toddlers are widely recognized. Early experiences with book "reading" often
involve sitting on someone's lap or snuggling up to the adult reader while
the pair looks at pictures. These warm, enjoyable experiences help associate literacy with comfort and pleasure from an early age. In addition to
obvious social-emotional benefits, literacy skills seem to be supported by
early experiences with pictures, print, and words or signs used to interpret or talk about what is being seen. As fruitful as these experiences are
for children with typical hearing, they may be even more critical for those
who are deaf or hard of hearing. A picture book provides an easily established point of joint visual attention, and it gives the adult something
on which to base language input that is directly related to the baby's or
toddler's interest. Books with repeated phrases that can be read almost
like rhythmic refrains are especially interesting to most toddlers, who
often enjoy joining in with the repetitions. Sitting together means that the
adult's spoken language will be produced fairly close to a listening child's
ear, and if the adult is sensitive to the child's visual attention—waiting
and allowing the child to look up to see the language being spoken—then
facial expressions and speechreading (lipreading) can help the child process and even learn the spoken words and their meanings. A parent who
is using signs can sit the baby on his or her lap and reach around to sign
in the child's visual space—perhaps while speaking the word near the
child's ear—or can sit side by side and give the child time to look from
picture to sign and even up at the parent's face.

Because babies and toddlers usually like to "read" the same book again
and again, a parent new to signing can learn the set of signs required
for a specific book and not have to worry about figuring them out each
time reading occurs. Similarly, parents who are reading in their second
language (if, for example, their native language is Spanish but they have
decided to use their second language, English, with their deaf or hard-of-
hearing baby) also have the advantage of being able to practice and really
learn the words required by a specific book. This allows comfortable,
easy reading. There is a danger, of course, that such experiences can be

negative if the adult tries for too much structure, too early. Insisting on reading all the words just as they are printed, for example, can result in an inattentive and even escape-prone toddler. Refusal to allow the toddler to hold the book and turn more than a page at a time—or even look back at earlier pages—can result in an unpleasant experience for both participants. (Thick-paged board books are a good way to prevent the ripping and chewing of thin paper pages that toddlers are inclined to indulge in.)

Shared book reading, like shared play with objects, is a bit more complicated with a deaf or hard-of-hearing child. The need to be sensitive to visual attention, to use gentle attention-getting behaviors like tapping on the child's body, and to allow time for the child to take a turn that might involve looking back and forth between the book and the reader are all especially important. The Clerc Center at Gallaudet University has developed and tested procedures for effective book-sharing with deaf and hard-of-hearing children (Delk & Weidekamp, 2001). Fifteen principles, drawn from observation of and consultation with deaf parents, have been found to be useful guides for hearing as well as deaf families. The principles include being sensitive to visual needs; using role-playing, pantomime, and facial expressions to communicate about the book; allowing the child to lead; and not being afraid to stray from the printed words themselves to communicate about the book and its story.

SUMMARIZING KEY IDEAS

The second half of the second year of life is typically one of rapid development of motor skills; of the ability to represent objects, events, and feelings using symbols; and (if language experiences have been accessible and meaningful to the child up until this time) of language itself. These developments are seen in more complex, sequenced pretend play as well as in language. They are also reflected in the toddler's abilities (and desires) to play and interact with people beyond the immediate family. The following key ideas have also been addressed in this chapter:

- As symbol use becomes more flexible and language skills grow, toddlers' behaviors and even attitudes begin to be influenced more strongly by the culture of their families and communities. Differences in cultural practices and expectations for behavior will be reflected across areas of development, but the foundation of developmental processes for symbolization, combination and sequencing of behaviors, and ability to express oneself using language will be the same.

- At this age, toddlers very often have strong emotions, definite desires, and little patience when their demands are not met. The result can be frustrating for both child and parents, particularly when the toddler's attempts to communicate are still quite limited. This is therefore an age during which it is especially important to help the toddler to understand and use language (either spoken or signed) for expressing emotions.

- Opportunities increase for incidental learning if toddlers are in an environment where they can observe and learn from conversations going on around them and not only from those directed toward them. Learning incidentally from observing conversations requires, however, that the persons conversing use a type of language (sign/speech/cued) that is accessible to the child.

- Sharing books with simple, well-known stories is another way in which experiences and ideas unique to a family's culture can be transmitted while language, literacy, and positive emotional interactions are also being supported. This kind of experience is possible because of the interactions that have occurred during the first year or so of life and the child's steadily growing abilities to use symbols to represent and remember names, events, and feelings. It provides a wonderfully integrative experience—not unlike that possible during shared play—that supports continuing development during the next year of life.

With these developments, the ability to share a language and therefore to communicate easily with adults and other children in the family and beyond becomes increasingly important. It is during this second year of life when differences and—when conditions are not optimal—delays due to limited hearing will become evident. Such delays can still be remediated, but clear assessment of an individual child's functioning, patterns, and rates of progress becomes critical if appropriate support is to be provided to ensure optimal development into the coming years. In the next chapter, we discuss the exciting developments that typically occur between about ages 2 and 3 years—and ways in which to nurture and support those developments in deaf and hard-of-hearing children.

Chart 8: *Advances to Watch For**

In 2- to 3-Year-Olds

*Physical and Motor Abilities***	• Uses spoon competently
	• Opens jars, turns large bolts/screws, etc.
	• Scribbles circles and lines
	• Puts small objects together (e.g., stacking toys)
	• Walks rather than crawling down steps
	• Climbs on and off furniture
	• Kicks ball, throws objects (not catching yet)
	• Jumps, both feet leaving floor together
	• Uses feet to propel self in large-wheeled toys; may use pedals by age 3
	• Enjoys tumbling, dancing, hopping, balancing
	• Toilet training begins or proceeds
Mental Abilities ("Cognition")	• Understands "categories," including gender labels
	• Aware of rules, but cannot follow consistently
	• Make-believe play becomes more complex, involves others, imagination
	• Enjoys picture books[v], turning pages
	• Can think and talk/sign about things that aren't physically present
	• Follows instructions to carry out sequences of actions
	• Can attend longer to activities, books, media
Communication/ Language	• Can describe own capabilities, preferred activities
	• Talks more about self and others' emotions
	• Understands more than produces; may produce 1,000+ words or signs by 3 years
	• Begins to add grammatical units to longer expressions: tenses, plurals, articles, prepositions in English; location, classifiers, direction in ASL
	• Asks "when?" "where?" and "why?" questions
	• Uses language to inform and obtain information as well as to direct and make requests; learning family's rules for polite social expressions

(continued)

Chart 8 *Continued*

Social-Emotional	• Experiences sense of pride, shame, sadness, or guilt
	• Self-confidence increases as motor skills improve
	• Develops awareness of own characteristics, likes/dislikes, emotional reactions
	• Enjoys helping with simple chores
	• Shows concern for others, some awareness of their feelings
	• Asserts own will, tests how far limits can be pushed
	• Frustration level escalates easily; physical aggression not uncommon
	• Associates with other children in play, choosing same activities, toy sets

*See Chart 1 for partial list of sources for information.

**On all charts, advances in motor abilities assume no physical disabilities; limited vision may also slow motor advances. Family and cultural expectations also influence physical and motor achievements at this age and beyond.

H may be delayed or require different circumstances if hearing is limited; V may be delayed or require different circumstances if vision is limited.

11 Little Psychologists and Budding Linguists
FROM 2 TO 3 YEARS OLD

QUESTIONS TO CONSIDER

- What can observations of play tell us about a toddler's cognitive, language, and emotional experiences and developing abilities?
- What can toddlers learn from interacting with age-mates or brothers and sisters?
- When a toddler has experienced responsive and accessible communication and language during infancy, what language advances are expected as the third birthday nears?
- Why might learning some aspects of grammar (or syntax) prove to be especially challenging for deaf and hard-of-hearing children?
- What effects can the early language experiences and attainments of deaf and hard-of-hearing infants and toddlers have on later-developing skills and abilities?
- What has been the impact of early identification and intervention, along with access to more complete visual and/or auditory language experiences, on the developmental achievements of deaf and hard-of-hearing toddlers? What challenges often persist?

Bridgette and her mother are busy with a set of toys. While mother pretends to wash a set of small plastic dishes, Bridgette picks up a baby doll, and makes noises as though it is crying. "Baby hungry," she signs. "Need milk." Cradling the doll in one arm, Bridgette holds her other hand toward mother, palm up. Mother signs "Wait, I need to wash this" and pretends to wash out a toy baby bottle, then carefully fill it with imagined milk. When she hands it to her little girl, Bridgette shakes the bottle as though to drop milk on her arm. "Not hot," she confirms and proceeds to feed the doll. After feeding, mother suggests that she "burp" the baby, and Bridgette places the doll on her shoulder and pats its back rhythmically. "Good!" she exclaims after some extended patting, smiles at the doll and then wipes her mouth with a small cloth. Bridgette then feels the doll's diaper and signs "diaper wet." Mother helps her find a small cloth triangle and comments on what Bridgette is doing as she pretends to clean, powder, and rediaper the doll. Bridgette then announces "baby sleepy" and carries the doll over to a small cradle, putting her down for a nap.

Twenty-eight-month-old Bridgette and her mother have just collaborated on an episode of extended scripted play. To accomplish this, Bridgette had to use her memory for a logically ordered sequence of activities common in her culture. She used receptive language skills to understand and respond to her mother's suggestions and contributions to the play. She used expressive language to communicate with her mother, but also as important parts of the play itself by announcing the doll's imaginary feelings and needs and the steps she was pre-planning in response. She showed emotional understanding as she announced the doll's feelings such as discomfort, hunger, and fatigue. Bridgette's large motor skills allowed her to move around the room freely, just as her fine motor skills allowed her to manipulate the small toys strewn on the floor.

Sometimes known as the "terrible twos" due to toddlers' increasing sense of autonomy—and their demands for it—this stage could just as well be known as the "terrific twos." By the age of 3, important transitions and maturation in almost all realms of development have usually occurred. During their second and third year, toddlers are well on their way to becoming preschoolers. As in Bridgette's case, both large and small motor skills are becoming much more refined. Children of this age are increasingly aware not only of themselves as individuals with personalities, distinctive physical features, and certain skills, but they can also better appreciate others' feelings and thoughts. (This is related to a developing ability that has been referred to as "theory of mind," which we will discuss in more detail later in this chapter.) In most cases, communication abilities are accelerating, and abilities in memory, recognizing categories, problem solving, and other mental skills are blooming as well. Although some of these advances will not be directly affected by a child's ability to communicate with others (think of learning to hop on one foot or scribble with crayons), others will be. During this period, effects of earlier opportunities to learn language and participate in reciprocal interactions become increasingly evident.

BY LEAPS AND BOUNDS...

In the absence of any specific motor disabilities, many basic skills (like walking and climbing) are mastered by about age 2. Stamina, speed, and agility increase as large motor activity becomes more vigorous, more "exercise-like." By the third birthday, most children can jump, run, walk on tiptoes, throw a fairly large ball a considerable distance, and even alternate feet when walking up stairs. Much learning occurs through movement as young children explore what happens on different surfaces, anticipate where different routes will take them, and notice how different objects react when they're squeezed or moved or run into. Memories are stored and problems are solved, all while having fun. By supporting safe, appropriate times and places for large motor practice, parents can easily encourage activities that will build strong bones and muscles, physical coordination, balance, and self-confidence. Although extra safety precautions may be necessary if a child has some balance difficulties, when this is the case, opportunities to practice motor skills are even more important than they otherwise might be. (In this case, safe spaces and equipment should be made accessible with help from professionals on the intervention team who are specialists in this area.)

Along with advances in large or gross motor skills, small (fine) motor skills are also increasing as the third birthday nears. There are individual differences, of course, in the timing of children's learning to use a cup and a spoon for self-feeding; drawing circles, lines, or dots with chunky crayons or chalk; placing large pieces in simple puzzles; stringing large beads or stacking rings or cups; and even beginning to make cuts on paper with blunt-ended scissors. To some extent, these skills appear earlier when they have been practiced or guided by parents and older children with specially designed toys. Where such toys are not available, however, similar skills will be learned from everyday activities: *Where does this object fit? Will this cardboard box fit into this other one? How do I turn this to get it loose?* It serves no purpose to try to accelerate the development of these skills unless a specific delay is evident. Otherwise, opportunities should be provided, but development will depend on a mix of motivation (some toddlers simply prefer to focus on the larger motor activities for a while) and on individual differences in the rate at which eye and hand coordination emerges.

There have been some reports of delays in fine motor development in children with limited hearing, and, as mentioned in an earlier chapter, there have also been reports of increased risk for balance and gross motor delays. However, we failed to find evidence of delays of this kind in the infants and toddlers who participated in our studies. Dr. Susan Nittrouer (2010), who studied early development in more than 100 deaf and hard-of-hearing children from 12 to 48 months of age, similarly found no evidence of effects of hearing on either fine or gross motor abilities. In general, hearing level in and of itself seems to have no effect on motor development unless the vestibular (inner ear balance) system has been affected by whatever caused the limit to hearing. Similarly, no effects from hearing levels have been seen on right- or left-hand preference, which is developing during this age range. Dr. John Bonvillian and his colleagues (Bonvillian, Richards, & Dooley, 1997) reported that hand preferences tend to arise during early production of signs. Old attitudes about the advantages (for learning) of being right-handed have been disproved; it seems to be more important for the child to proceed at her own pace in establishing this preference.

Not even motor skills develop in isolation from other abilities, of course. When development is occurring in a synchronous manner—with communication, social, and mental abilities advancing along with physical abilities—the interactions and mutual influences are impressive. The complexity of the system can be illustrated by an advance that often occurs around this time, one that is usually of great importance to parents: the child's mastery of "toilet training" or, in some cultures, simply learning where and when elimination is acceptable. There are many parenting advice books that provide details about strategies for training a toddler to control his or her bladder and bowels. We do not intend to offer more of these instructions; however, we want to make the point that successful training requires muscle control as well as awareness of neural and physical signals that elimination is imminent. This is, to some extent, based in general brain maturation. Given this maturation, which occurs at different individual rates and is often achieved earlier by little girls than little boys, mental abilities to understand what is being expected, communication skills, and even social experiences will affect progress. This developmental milestone involves virtually all of the different areas of the child's growth, and the ability to communicate will certainly be of importance.

COGNITIVE AND THINKING SKILLS, 2–3 YEARS

Cognition, as we have considered it, includes attention, memory, making categories, solving problems, and using symbols in play as well as in language. During this year, the child also develops an ability to think about—to imagine—things that aren't physically present. This means that he can now "manipulate" ideas and images about objects or people without having any direct feedback (that is, without actually feeling, seeing, hearing, smelling them, etc.). Impressive changes are occurring as he begins to use his memory more effectively, to understand that signs and symbols represent real people or things, that much of the physical and social world can be organized into logical categories and complex sequences, and that he can *pretend* to be involved with these in a marvelous variety of ways!

During the first years of life, few differences in these cognitive skills seem to be based on hearing levels. However, differences have been reported for older children, and they may stem at least in part from differences in early communication and social experiences. One important role of language is to provide a framework for mentally structuring and organizing experiences and sensory input. In cases when deaf and hard-of-hearing children have had less opportunity for language "uptake," delays begin to be seen in the second and third years of life in reproducing sequences in play and in coordinating attention to communication partners and objects. Although these differences are minor, it may be relevant that, in later childhood, deaf and hard-of-hearing children are more likely to be diagnosed with attention disorders, and sequential memory strategies for learning may be used less efficiently than by hearing children (Hamilton, 2011; Marschark, Machmer, & Convertino, 2016). Delays during the infant and toddler years might be early indications of these differences. At the same time, deaf and hard-of-hearing children who experience rich visual environments are more sensitive to movements in their peripheral visual field than are hearing children (a potential safety advantage), and memory for visual displays can be advantageous for future learning.

Researchers looking for the bases of these differences during the early years believe they are influenced in part by auditory experience. Dr. Alexandra Quittner and her colleagues (2007), for example, compared attention and inattention to a puppet display in deaf children awaiting a CI with that of children with typical hearing. Before getting the CI and increased access to sound-like information, deaf children engaged in slightly more inattentive episodes than the other group, and their episodes of inattention lasted longer. Tested again 1 year after getting a CI, when they were still 3 years or younger, differences had disappeared. This suggests that access to sound-like information during the first 3 years, while brain pathways continue to form and be strengthened rapidly, can result in visual attention patterns more like those of children with typical hearing as the need to visually scan the environment decreases.

Another cognitive area developing rapidly during the third year of life is that of categorizing—making groupings based on common attributes or uses. One way the infant makes sense of a world with all its constantly changing sensations is by finding similarities, then grouping or clustering things, people, and events together in logical ways. Thinking about categories makes the world more comprehensible and helps to store and retrieve information from memory. In experimental procedures, it has been noticed that even young infants make associations between images of objects that share perceptual characteristics. In testing situations, most 2-year-olds can separate objects into two categories based on perceptual attributes such as color or even functions. Gopnik and Melzoff (1987) reported that when two-category grouping appears, a burst in learning of new words often co-occurs.

By 3 years of age, classifying is based on more than perceptual characteristics. For example, grouping by second-order characteristics like "fruits" versus "animals" can be observed in experimental situations. Within several months after the third birthday, "scripted" groupings such as "foods for breakfast" can be seen, not surprisingly at about the same time that complicated scripts such as Bridgette's begin to be acted out in play. Both of these behaviors involve increasing numbers of items associated together (such as in categories) so they can be retrieved from memory. When we observe toddlers playing with an array of toys, it is informative to notice how organized they are in their approach. Do they flit randomly from one object to the next, with little effort to combine or to determine how each one works? Or do they first explore the tea set, the sandbox toys, and then the race cars as if already aware that certain things "belong together"? The latter is an example of categorization in action.

Tendencies to categorize, which will be an important foundation for later learning, can be enhanced if games using this skill are played with toddlers and preschoolers. It will be both fun and beneficial to include games with objects that can be categorized by how they are used so that action (as well as words or signs) can be used while deciding where to put the hammer as opposed to the truck or the car that rolls. With time, play in which the same objects are grouped and regrouped various ways—by color, by action, perhaps by size—will be helpful, each time emphasizing with language the reason they belong together. At older ages, deaf and hard-of-hearing children have been noted to be less flexible in using multiple ways to group or categorize (Marschark & Hauser, 2012), so these kinds of activities may be especially helpful.

In general, the process of categorizing seems to become progressively more conceptual with age. Not surprisingly, this develops best when language is being learned and can be used to label and symbolize meanings and relationships. But even if language development is proceeding "on time," using arbitrary rules to guide groupings is still too difficult for most children at age 3. Even when a rule is actively taught (for example, all blue things go with the picture of the blue rabbit), switching to a new rule (now change and put all blue things with the picture of the blue boat) is difficult and will not be consistently followed. Progress has been made, but understanding and using rules remains to develop in the next years.

Categorizing involves more than just objects, actions, and rules, of course. Children will begin to think about people in categories, too: boys, girls, grown-ups, friends, and non-friends. In addition, feelings and emotions will be categorized, labeled, and, perhaps in the process, become not only more clearly expressed but a bit better controlled.

"HOW DO I TELL YOU WHAT I'M FEELING?"

One major advantage of being able to communicate and to think using language more effectively at this age is that it helps the child recognize and talk about emotions. Children need to learn to identify their feelings as well as their internal, physical states such as hunger, fatigue, discomfort, and the like. This is true across most cultures, although the ways in which emotions are allowed to be expressed may vary tremendously from one family or culture to the next.

Cultural experiences and expectations continue to play a major role in this process. Members of different cultures learn to respond to and express their internal feelings of anger, embarrassment, shame, and so forth in different ways. This is a learning process, though, as children are gradually reinforced for displays of emotion that are deemed appropriate in a given family or community: *Is it permissible to laugh at someone who looks "funny" to me? Is it okay if I stare at or make fun of a child who rides in a wheelchair? Do children in my culture stand up and bow when an elder enters the room? And am I allowed to make eye contact with that person, or must I look away and keep a very straight face when I'm in the presence of adults?* On a more emotional level, children in some cultures must learn to contain their disappointment and their pain, whether it is from falling down and being embarrassed, scraping an elbow, or having their feelings hurt by someone else. Learning the rules of when, how, and to whom one can express emotions is all part of the socialization process for young children. Even when language is significantly delayed, however, social interactions are a medium through which a child is introduced to the attitudes and the rules of his or her culture (Dammeyer, 2009). Similar to some of the other developmental processes we have already covered, many of these behaviors (ways of expressing emotional reactions by crying, hiding in shame, laughing, etc.) are already present for the child but will be refined and come under more conscious control during the third year.

Expressing Emotions: Actions and Emerging Language

Physical aggression (hitting, kicking, biting, pinching, etc.) seems to occur more often during this time than at any other age, perhaps as a result of the widening social network many children experience. Although some children rarely show any aggressive behaviors, others may develop habits that persist for several years. Adult responses to these bouts of aggression play an important role in determining whether this will be a passing phase or become one of the child's primary means of communicating displeasure to others. Recall from Chapter 10, for example, that many toddlers try out their new teeth on playmates, without realizing the pain this may cause. It should be very apparent that social interactions, emotional regulation, and communication competence are all so intertwined that it becomes difficult to determine which one causes or influences the other. Nevertheless, children who can express their emotions easily with language rather than with fists are likely to be more effective at resolving conflicts with their peers without resorting to aggression.

For adults working with or parenting children during the 2- to 3-year age range, it is important to acknowledge the child's happy as well as angry emotions, to give permission for both to occur, and to normalize these emotional experiences but still to require that the child adheres to reasonable limits. Modeling and attaching language to those emotions not only helps a child learn to control them but also leads to better understanding of other people's feelings. Explaining that "*it's okay to be mad at your baby sister, but it's not okay for you to push her down*" validates the child's feelings while also requiring a level of civility and acceptable behavior. Developmental tasks at this age include improving the child's ability to control or regulate his own emotional responses, as well as expanding his use of various ways to express his frustration, anger, or disappointment to others.

This is also the classic time for a child to assert her own will, to shout "no!" many times during the day, and in general to test just how far she can go before there are serious consequences. Remember, she's increasingly aware of being (or becoming) an autonomous little being with a mind of her own, and she wants to practice using it and making everyone else aware of it too. But, of course, this is also a time when she is being frequently told what to do and what not to do: "*Eat your beans.*" "*Ask politely.*" "*Don't step in the puddle.*" "*Be nice to the kitty.*" "*Don't take your jacket off.*" And the list goes on. Two-and-a-half-year-old Sheri is a hard-of-hearing child (using hearing aids to supplement her access to speech sounds) growing up in a large American city. Many times a day, she is faced with choices of either resisting or complying. Sometimes resistance becomes overt, angry defiance both at home and at her baby-sitter's house. For example, rather than simply *not* putting the toys away when asked to, Sheri sometimes throws them across the room and stomps out. This kind of "oppositional behavior," although not unusual for a child Sheri's age, can be exacerbated in an overly controlling family or child care situation, in which case a bit more flexibility may need to be arranged. In other cases, it may simply reflect a child's more "impetuous" temperament or perhaps just fatigue and hunger at the end of a tiring day. Although it is important for parents to be firm, protective, and to enforce certain limits, they should also show respect (and warmth) for the child.

Once again, we must ask how a child's hearing level and its effects on language development might affect this process. Rules, restrictions, and disapproval can be communicated in many ways by adults. Spoken or signed communication is not always required. Stern facial expressions, physically removing an object or the child from a situation that is prohibited, and commonly understood gestures are usually part of the repertoire of anyone working with children—and can be highly effective. Nevertheless, using language in such situations becomes increasingly important with development. If a deaf or hard-of-hearing child does not understand the expectations or does not have access to explanations about these, then she will be at a distinct disadvantage when it comes to learning to control her own behavior. Although Sheri is beginning to use spoken language, her vocabulary is limited for age, and expressions are limited to one or two words at a time. In addition, her articulation (pronunciation of words) is not yet typical for age, making her difficult to understand. This results in her child care provider having difficulty understanding her. In an environment that includes several other toddlers, communication difficulties seem to occur quite frequently. As Sheri's language skills develop, she will be better able to let the adults and other children around her know what she likes and dislikes, what she's feeling and experiencing, and how she's responding to their requests or demands. Gradually, her use of language will replace her tendency to express her emotions physically.

It may be tempting to give in to the noncompliant child in an effort to avoid confrontations and maintain some semblance of calmness in the house. The risk, however, is that caregivers who repeatedly give in may make fewer demands for mature behavior: the result is that the child actually has fewer opportunities to develop self-regulation skills and to become more socially competent. This may also lead to increased nagging by the parents or other caregivers, so that a cycle of regular and repeated adult–child conflict develops. It is important to break this cycle before it becomes too entrenched, and sometimes interventions may be needed to assist families who are struggling with these dynamics. Otherwise, behavior problems and poor adult–child interactions can become an unfortunate and repetitive pattern that becomes increasing difficult to change.

In Sheri's case, her parents can work with her child care provider and her early intervention team to devise approaches to help Sheri learn new ways to express herself more positively. For example, it is important that expectations for behaviors be consistent at home and in the child care setting and that adults' responses to her behaviors recognize them as fairly typical for age but in need of sensitive correction. It is also important that the child care provider understand Sheri's current level of understanding spoken language and how it will be more difficult for her in a noisy situation. Finally, it is important that parents help the child care provider better understand the spoken language that Sheri is producing. It might also be helpful to introduce some simple signs for Sheri and the adults to use (or, perhaps increased use of specific gestures) in situations where communicating with speech is difficult.

The good news is that this phase usually doesn't last long! Typically, defiant or disobedient behavior gets worked out over the course of the child's third year as she becomes more able to use language to negotiate and to compromise with others. This will be especially true if Sheri's parents and child care provider are willing to see her perspective, to model negotiation strategies, and to communicate about reasonable compromises. For example, can they accept an agreement for Sheri to play five more minutes, but then she must clean up without a fuss? Or if she eats three more pieces of lettuce can she then have dessert? Of course, parents must also remember that they are the adults in any situation, that they are wiser and more experienced, and that, ultimately, they know what is in the child's best interest—and they must be willing to stick to that line when necessary.

Brothers and Sisters, Friends and Relations

The kinds of emotional attachments formed with parents and other family members have been repeatedly shown to influence social behaviors beyond the family. For example, if Elisha is secure in his relationship with his mother and also uses his father as a positive source of trust and protection, he is likely to have better self-control and to interact more easily with his peers in the sandbox. Older siblings can also serve as attachment figures, so younger ones will sometimes venture further away from and explore a new environment more readily when a brother or sister is nearby. This means that a younger child has the advantage of observing and following an older "guide" in terms of exploration, discovering physical activities and the social environment, and numerous opportunities to imitate. (Parents find that although this is often an advantage, it may also expose the younger child to behaviors their parents would prefer they not see quite so soon!) One positive outcome of this situation is that the older sibling may be more in tune with others' feelings, having already developed the ability to empathize, so that the younger child can be effectively comforted by him or her. This assumes, of course, that the siblings are able to communicate with each other. Although warmth and physical comfort may be offered regardless of language, a child's ability to learn from an older sibling will depend on being able to share information as well as feelings. Of course, brothers and sisters are quite capable of competing as well as cooperating, so the relationship is bound to have its ups and downs even in the easiest of family situations—fluctuating daily or perhaps even within a single day.

Dr. Kathryn Meadow-Orlans and her colleagues (Meadow-Orlans, Mertens, & Sass-Lehrer, 2003) conducted a survey of the experiences and attitudes of families with deaf or hard-of-hearing children in the United States and received mixed messages about sibling relationships when the children's hearing levels differed. [Only about 13% of deaf or hard-of-hearing children in the United States who qualify for special education services have a brother or sister with similar hearing status (Gallaudet Research Institute, 2008).] They described families in which responses from a brother or sister with typical hearing to a deaf or hard-of-hearing child ranged from being highly supportive to being embarrassed. Some siblings were proud of their abilities to communicate with the brother or sister who had limited hearing. Many simply accepted it as not important. But others refused to use sign language outside of the home and expressed a wish that others would not notice the hearing aids their brother or sister wore. In this study, less-than-positive reactions seemed to be more common when the brother or sister with typical hearing was older than the child with limited hearing. Later-born siblings tended to accept the communication system being used in the home—whether sign or spoken language. This pattern suggests that it is more difficult to change a family's interaction and communication system once it has developed. In fact, stress may occur particularly for older siblings when the new arrival seems to require extra time and attention even beyond what is usual when a baby is born.

In contrast with some less positive reports, we are familiar with a family in which sibling reactions were highly positive, with both older sisters (who, as well as the parents, had typical hearing) beginning to learn signs as soon as their sister's profound hearing level was identified. It may be significant that the parents were both quite active in adopting communication and other strategies to match their deaf child's visual strengths and that their expectations for their child (who had multiple disabilities) were realistic but positive. This is a family in which parents and children are used to supporting and accepting each other and in which the siblings of the deaf child were included in group activities and learning experiences focused on families of children with special needs.

Having a younger brother or sister also provides opportunities for older siblings to learn about caregiving, nurturance, and increased understanding of another child's perspective. (This may be particularly true if one of the siblings has limited sight, hearing, or mobility.) The actual situation and relationship among siblings in any given family will depend greatly on individual differences and the characteristics of each child. It will also depend on the family—the degree to which family members accept each other and the child with limited hearing, the family's own approach to problem solving and resolution of competition between the various members, and the degree of comfort with which they communicate and share feelings with each other. While having a shared language is important for all of this, it is not the only factor; it is merely one more that will interact with existing family dynamics (Figure 11.1).

Figure 11.1 Sharing language and experiences with Dad. (Photo courtesy of Texas School for the Deaf. Reprinted with permission.)

"Are You Thinking What I'm Thinking?" Maybe Not

As children develop ways of talking about and expressing their own emotions, they will also be learning to interpret more accurately how other people are feeling: *"When my big sister looks stern and serious, is it because I did something wrong or because she's concentrating on her work from school?" "If Daddy looks sad, should I bring him the newspaper or tickle his feet?"* Those who show good understanding of others' emotions tend to be in families where there is frequent conversation about feelings and what causes them. This occurs not only when a conflict or difficulty has arisen, but also during everyday dinner table or car trip conversations about what each person has done during the day, how they're feeling, and the like. When this kind of informal communication cannot be overheard or seen, as is the case for many deaf and hard-of-hearing children, opportunities to learn about emotional expression and interpersonal relationships may be missed. Parents need to be particularly aware of this and to make special efforts to include the deaf or hard-of-hearing child by using a language method that he or she can process, staying within the child's visual space when possible, and holding these discussions at a place and time so that all family members are included. The degree to which parents use language to label feelings, thoughts, and emotions has effects on a child's later understanding that other people's feelings and perspectives differ from their own (Moeller & Schick, 2006; Spencer, 2010).

A short time after the age of 3 years is reached, typically developing children are often observed to act in ways showing that they understand that other people have feelings, wants, and ideas just as they do but that these mental states may be different for the other person. This understanding is referred to as *theory of mind*. Researchers have found that during the preschool and early school years, deaf and hard-of-hearing children whose language is developing at a typical rate (in most studies, these have often been children with deaf parents) generally match children with typical hearing in demonstrating this kind of understanding. Deaf and hard-of-hearing children with delayed language skills (most often but not always with hearing parents), in contrast, usually show delayed development of theory-of-mind understandings, even when the assessment tasks used do not directly involve language. (See Spencer, 2010, for a summary of research about deaf and hard-of-hearing children's theory-of-mind development.) These understandings are tested by a variety of clever tasks in which a child has to differentiate between what she knows to have happened and what another person would expect to have happened. For example, in one task, a child being tested watches as a second person (or sometimes a doll being controlled by the researcher) hides an object and then leaves the room. While the second person is gone, the child being tested watches as the object is moved to a new hiding place. The child is then asked where the person who originally hid the object will look for it when returning to the room. The purpose of this task (and other variations) is to find out whether the child can differentiate what *he* knows from what the person who has left the room will think has happened.

The ability to understand others' perspectives and feelings, as in the theory of mind tasks, relates not only to language development but also to cognitive and general developmental advances. It is also reported to be influenced by children's early communication experiences: exposure to vocabulary used by parents to represent feelings, emotions, and mental states (Moeller & Schick, 2006); being in a communication environment in which language is often used to explain things (Al-Hilawani, Easterbrooks, & Marchant, 2002); and being a full participant in conversations with other children as well as adults (Remmel & Peters, 2008). Although theory of mind (understanding others' feelings, perspectives, and what they know) is not expected to develop until after at least the third birthday, we (Spencer, 2010) have proposed that these abilities can be seen in emerging form in play behaviors during the second year of life. For example, when toys are "animated" and made to perform actions, when a toddler pretends that a doll or stuffed animal is feeling an emotion, and when she recognizes that a playmate is sad or hurt, these are all indications of the beginnings of a theory of mind.

Remember Sheri? As her language skills progress, she will increasingly be able to communicate "to herself" (maybe when she is upset or when she's trying to figure something out), but she might also begin to tell others "about herself," such as announcing to a neighbor that she's now a Big Sister or to an uncle that she has curly brown hair. Within this year, she may also begin communicating more clearly about her own emotions, such as telling someone that she doesn't feel well or that she's happy about seeing her friend. These will all be indications that Sheri is developing a sense of who she is, of what her personal characteristics are, of what she likes and does not like, and of how she reacts emotionally to certain situations. However, unless her delay in language is overcome, her ability to express these kinds of meanings with language may continue to be limited. Understanding Sheri will require that the listener be familiar with her experiences and her speech patterns. This will not only affect what others learn about what is happening or what she is feeling; it will also affect what others say and/or sign to her. That is, when language expression is limited, it affects not only a child's language understanding but even the potential language experiences that will be provided. Furthermore, beyond language itself, opportunities for social and cognitive experiences begin to differ significantly when language is delayed, compared to those experiences available for toddlers who are showing typical rates of development.

PLAY: INTEGRATING MOTOR, COGNITIVE, LANGUAGE, AND SOCIAL-EMOTIONAL GROWTH

Play is another activity that is highly integrative, involving many aspects of learning, including social, emotional, cognitive, communicative, and even motor skills. During the early months of life, "play" can be described as making an interesting object move repeatedly, or simply exchanging smiles and facial expressions with a parent. The changes over the course of 3 years are incredible, and they are not necessarily limited by hearing levels. However, play is greatly enriched when language exchanges are included. In the absence of well-functioning communication, play may be less effective as a setting or activity that fosters further learning.

Both Bridgette and her mother, in the story that began this chapter, are deaf and use American Sign Language (ASL). Bridgette's play sequence in no way differed in complexity, level, or integration of language and cognitive-thinking skills from that expected for a child with typical hearing and rate of development. This kind of progress assumes, of course, that cognitive, social, and communicative skills have been developing in a supportive environment and that there is no great disparity in the levels of development across those areas. We would be remiss if we did not mention that reports of play by some deaf and hard-of-hearing children between 2 and 3 years do not match those of Bridgette and many of her age-mates.

As one example, Dr. P. Margaret Brown and her colleagues (Brown & Remine, 2004; Brown, Rickards, & Bartoli, 2001) have reported studies of play during the third year that focused on profoundly deaf children with hearing parents. These children, who were expected to learn spoken language without sign support, experienced significantly delayed language development. Although the children's actions gave evidence of early stages of representational play, the variety of different play behaviors and the highest levels the children demonstrated between 2 and 3 years of age did not match age expectations. Unlike their age-mates with typical hearing, few of the deaf children showed sequenced, script-like play, pre-planned play, or imaginary substitution play. Although this entire group of deaf children with hearing parents showed delays in cognitive and social aspects of play, those whose play was more advanced were also the ones who were making the most progress in language.

The children in Dr. Brown's studies seemed to be delayed in achieving coordinated joint attention as well as language, and the researchers reported that the mothers had to "work hard to maintain the interaction" (p. 147). In order to get and maintain their children's visual attention, the mothers spent a lot of time modeling play behaviors. Due to the children's delayed language and limited hearing, however, the mothers were unable to encourage their children's play by making comments and suggestions using language. Dr. Brown noted that these mothers were less likely than most to simply relax and watch their children's play—therefore missing some opportunities to build on what their children were already doing. These observations are not unlike many from earlier times, when disruptions in interactions between hearing mothers and their deaf and hard-of-hearing children were often reported. Such observations clearly indicate that the children's development is not proceeding well and that significant changes are needed to promote language and attention abilities and even basic communication exchanges. It is not surprising that play interactions were easier and more positive for mother–child pairs in which child language and communication development was relatively good.

When considering mother–child interactions, we should always keep in mind the two-way nature of communication. In the absence of functional hearing and without increased use of visual communication, reciprocal turn-taking patterns seemed not to have developed for the mothers and children in Dr. Brown's study. This put increased pressure on mothers to "work" not "play" during toy time with their children, thus decreasing the apparent pleasure in interactions for both mother and child.

Our studies of deaf and hard-of-hearing 2- and 2 ½-year olds, many of whom were acquiring language at typical or near-typical rates (Spencer, 1996; Spencer & Deyo, 1993), presented a very different picture. Deaf and hard-of-hearing children with hearing parents were delayed in only one aspect of play—that of the sequenced "script-like" play shown by Bridgette at the beginning of this chapter. Delays in this area were most noticeable for those children with the greatest language delays. The greater range of child language achievement in our studies, due at least in part to signs being used by a number of the hearing as well as deaf parents, seemed to allow increased maternal comfort as well as child play and attention levels. Although not always, the mother–child play in our studies usually looked like fun!

Many other studies have been conducted of the play of deaf and hard-of-hearing children between 2 and 3 years of age, and the results of these studies vary depending on the characteristics of the children and the families who participated. During the first and second year of life, the degree to which mothers' play and communication behaviors are responsive to their baby's interests and actions relate to the level of play shown. However, the child's communication progress also consistently relates to the sophistication of their play, and language becomes an increasingly important factor with age. This relation continues well into the third year of life (Snyder & Yoshinaga-Itano, 1999) and undoubtedly beyond.

Playing and Interacting: Beyond the Family

Increasing abilities in motor, communication, thinking, and social skills affect toddlers' interactions with parents, other adults, and older children. Advances in these abilities also allow more opportunities to interact and play with children of similar ages. With increasing numbers of dual-earner families and out-of-home infant care in the industrialized world, young children are more likely than in the past to be in group situations outside the family unit.

Between the ages of 2 and 3 years, children typically learn to respond positively to others and to adapt their communication to some degree to take account of another person's feelings and understanding. As a result, social interactions involving similarly aged children are likely to increase along with more effective communication exchanges. Previously common *parallel play* (in the sandbox together, but Stephanie is pushing a dump truck, Fiona is digging with a shovel, and Elisha is pretending a piece of wood is a train) is being replaced by more *associative play*. At this level, the children actually engage in similar activities—if one begins to put on clothes from the "dress-up" play box, others might join in and do the same. This often involves communication, mutual visual attention, sharing of toys (in this case, clothes), and even some turn-taking. Although language exchanges are sometimes important parts of this kind of play, much of it can occur even without language. Truly *cooperative* or *social play* that involves not only more communication, but agreements about joint goals *("Let's all dig a tunnel for the train and the dump truck")* usually does not occur until about 4 or 5 years of age. However, opportunities during the third year to play near each other and with toys and objects around a similar theme provide the foundation for that next step.

As we mentioned previously, we (Spencer, Koester, & Meadow-Orlans, 1993) had the opportunity to observe children who were between 2 and 3 years old in a child care center for deaf and hard of hearing as well as children with typical hearing, including some whose parents were deaf. The deaf and hearing teachers and aides in this center were all fluent in sign language, and many used both spoken and sign language effectively. This allowed a perhaps unique situation in which children's varied communication modes and abilities could be accommodated, with teachers facilitating child-to-child communications.

The children in this program communicated and played with each other in ways typical for their age—regardless of their hearing level. Children with typical hearing not infrequently adapted communications, often using gestures, to communicate with the deaf and hard-of-hearing children. This was especially the case when a teacher or aide was involved and helped to structure peer interactions. Despite this, however, children were most likely to interact with age-mates from families in which parent hearing status was like that in their own. This probably occurred because they tended to share language modes (sign or speech), and it is not unlike what has been observed with older children. We suspect that, in some cases, children also knew each other from family interactions beyond the center and may have therefore tended to associate with children they had already seen or played with.

Dr. Amatzia Weisel and his colleagues (Weisel, Most, & Efron, 2005) studied four children, aged 33–36 months with hearing levels from moderate to profound (measured unaided; one used a CI), who attended preschool classes with either deaf and hard-of-hearing children or children with typical hearing. Although the hard-of-hearing and deaf children were primarily learning spoken language, two of them had some facility with signs. Even at this young age, the children seemed to adapt their communication patterns according to the hearing levels of their playmates. With children with typical hearing, those who were hard of hearing or deaf tried more vocalizing, object sharing, moving closer, and touching; with other deaf and hard-of-hearing children they used signs, eye gaze to locate potential play partners, and entering directly into play situations. Despite these social and cognitive modifications, interactions remained easier with other children with limited hearing, and there were many failed attempts to initiate interactions with the children with typical hearing.

Friendships do not inevitably evolve from peer interactions at this age, but they often start during the second year and can offer an important source of comfort and security. Spotting a friend can ease transitions to new programs, new environments, and new situations. It is important, therefore, to consider the significant role that other children of similar ages play in the lives of many very young children in today's world. Sharing a language makes social interactions easier even as abilities to modify communications continue to develop.

GROWTH IN LANGUAGE: UNDERSTANDING AND EXPRESSING

As we have discussed throughout this book, one advantage of advancing language skills is the increased ability to make one's messages clear and therefore prompt appropriate responses from others. Toddlers with typical rates of language development will have an easier time accomplishing this as they approach 24 months. Their vocabularies, both for understanding and for expressing meanings, will have generally increased in size, from 1 to perhaps 10 words or signs at 12 months, to as many as 300 or more at 2 years. As we discussed in Chapter 10, after a vocabulary size of about 50 to 100 words or signs is reached, children usually begin to combine these with gestures to make two-unit expressions ("cookie" + flat-palm-up gesture = I want cookie), and soon afterward begin to combine two signs or words in a single expression ("want cookie"). Even though these expressions are "telegraphic" (short and without grammatical endings or modifiers), they result in communications becoming clearer and more specific.

Between the ages of 2 and 3 years, if the basics of language are in place, children show more rapid vocabulary growth. Children may begin to learn words or signs more quickly, especially after their expressive vocabularies contain about 200 or more items (Lederberg, Prezbindowski, & Spencer, 2000). After they can sign or say about this many words, learning new ones becomes easier and faster. Sometimes only one or two exposures in meaningful situations are needed to learn new words/signs, and the number of different words or signs also increases rapidly, although there is much variation in reports of "typical" rates. We were amazed and amused to find in a recent review of Internet sites devoted to language development that various sites reported the "average" expressive vocabulary of 3-year-olds with typical hearing to be as low as 450 or as high as 1,500 words! Although there are clearly great differences among children at this age, these different estimates probably reflect the different ways in which researchers collected information and the different characteristics of the groups studied. However, effects of both individual learning patterns and the kinds of language learning environments experienced begin to be obvious by this age. Children who are exposed to more words or signs in meaningful and sensitive communication exchanges over time usually develop their own language more rapidly (Figure 11.2).

Before about 30 months of age, even when language development is progressing typically, transcriptions of children's expressive language would look much the same whether spoken or sign language was being used. Expressions generally contain only one or a few words or signs, and no special grammatical features like tenses or plurals are included. As the grammar or structure of the language begins to be expressed, however, children's productions will begin to reflect those of the actual language they are learning and the specific grammatical rules or syntax of that language. Obviously, for these grammatical rules to be learned, children must hear or see them modeled frequently and consistently. Although the *meanings* behind spoken or signed messages have been more crucial up to this point, it now becomes increasingly important to have a

Figure 11.2 She is playing with glasses, she watches "*glasses*" signed: a new word is learned! (Photo courtesy of Texas School for the Deaf. Reprinted with permission.)

more complex language model if the rules are to be learned and language is to advance. If English is to be learned, for example, the grammatical structures of English must be seen or heard (or both). Similarly, if a sign language like ASL or a signed system like Signed English is to be learned, children need opportunities to interact with persons who are fluent signers. Seeing occasional signs or groups of signs is not the same as observing a full model of a language. This does not mean that simplification of language by adults should stop; it does mean that adults should gradually expand the complexity of the sentences and language they are producing to allow their children to have experience with the "next steps."

Adding the Little Bits: Beginning to Use English Morphemes[1]

After children with typical hearing who are learning spoken English progress from two- to three-, and four -word expressions, they begin to add what McLean and Snyder-McLean (1999) call the "little bits" of English grammar. These "bits" are the grammatical morphemes used in English to add meanings, like "-ing," or the plural "-s" sound at the end of words. They include prepositions like "on" and "in," which begin to be used where needed, and possession comes to be marked by a final "-s," as in "Mommy's purse." A little later articles ("a," "the"), irregular past tenses (like "ran" and "went"), and, even later in the year, forms indicating the regular past tense of verbs ("-ed") emerge. Of course, this process is neither simple nor consistent. Children often go through periods of overusing some forms, generalizing their use inappropriately ("she goed to the store"). However, these changes emerge naturally as the children engage in lengthier conversations, sharing turns with more knowledgeable communication partners who model correct forms and use them to expand on what the child has said. As these bits are being added, question forms now may include "where…?" and "when…?" Questions using "who?" often appear by about 3 years, but yes–no questions (like "Is…?", "Do…?") and "why" questions may take another year to emerge (www.zerotothree.org). A similar timeframe is needed before actual grammatically correct "sentences" are produced, and even more complex sentence structures continue to emerge into adolescence.

The "little bits" of spoken language grammar rarely cause extended problems for children with typical hearing and are usually learned through naturally occurring interactions, but children who are deaf or hard of hearing often have problems learning these English language subtleties. This is easily explained when only spoken language is used because many aspects are difficult to hear (not produced with a lot of sound energy) and difficult to see (not very visible on the lips). Even using hearing aids, many deaf and hard-of-hearing children receive little evidence that these grammatical morphemes exist.

In systems like Signed English or Signed French, etc. (see Chapter 1 for more information), special signs have been created to represent the "little bits" of grammatical morphemes. The idea is for these small grammatical meanings to become perceptually accessible through vision and therefore to be more likely to be learned and used. Drs. Brenda Schick and Mary Pat Moeller (1992) reported that even in adolescence, however, when experience with signed English has resulted in children's being able to produce complex sentences, many of those little grammatical "bits" are missing or misused. This is a commonly noted problem, and it may be due to inconsistent models of the English system having been provided for the children. Numerous studies of the signing of hearing parents (and other hearing adults like teachers) have shown that the grammatical morphemes, such as tenses and articles, plurals or possessives, are often not actually signed by adults. One reason may be that including signs for such things as past tense or "first person singular" (as in "he eats") slows down signing and makes it difficult to produce at the same pace as accompanying spoken language. Hands just don't move as quickly as do the parts of mouth and throat that produce speech sounds. (We want to acknowledge, however, that several reports from Dr. Barbara Luetke and her colleagues [e.g., Nielsen, Luetke, & Stryker, 2011] indicate that, with training and feedback, both teachers and parents have been able to increase their productions of these signed English grammatical markers and provide more consistent input.) Whether due to inconsistent models or because expressing these grammatical meanings in a visual language requires a different approach (see Chapter 1), deaf and hard-of-hearing children in environments using forms of signed English very often have difficulties learning these "little bits" even after having built up a sizeable vocabulary of signs. Differences and delays in expressing these grammatical meanings are often seen by about 3 years even if other aspects of language skills are developing well.

Adding the "Bits" of Sign Language Grammar

Children learning ASL add grammatical units to their previously "telegraphic" expressions at about the same age as do children with typical hearing who are acquiring spoken language. Although grammar development in natural sign languages is still being investigated, there are some interesting findings about the progress of children with fluently signing deaf parents. Dr. Brenda Schick (2006; Lederberg, Schick, & Spencer, 2013) has summarized much of this research. One grammatical form that has been the focus of research is that of the developing ability to indicate the location where something happened as a verb is being signed—one of the grammatical markers evident in adult sign language. Its use can emerge around age 2 (particularly for deaf children with deaf parents), and it becomes routine by about age 3 (Meier, 1982). (For example, the verb "spill" may be produced to include a movement toward the location where it happened.)

Use of grammatical forms called "classifiers" is common among natural sign languages, such as when a specific handshape is used to indicate the size and shape of a container or the movement of a person or animal. These grammatical forms have also been noted to emerge between 2 and 3 years of age in children learning ASL (Simms, Baker, & Clark, 2013) and other natural sign languages, including Sign Language of the Netherlands (Lillo-Martin, Bellugi, Struxness, & O'Grady, 1985). Their use emerges after children produce "telegraphic" expressions of two or more signs fairly routinely, but they are not frequently seen until about 3 years of age. (The system for using classifiers is quite complex, however, and is not used in complete adult form until around 8 years of age.)

Other grammatical advances are seen as deaf and hard-of-hearing children learning ASL approach 3 years of age. These include use of some of the special facial expressions that have grammatical meaning (for instance, indicating a "wh-" instead of "yes/no" question) in the adult form of the language as opposed to simply producing emotion-based facial expression with language. Three- and four-sign expressions, as well as question forms ("Who?" "Which?" "For-for?"—which is a way to sign the meaning often expressed as "Why?" in English), and pronouns/possessives ("my," "your") all emerge. (See Simms et al., 2013, for a more complete list.)

Even though the ways grammatical modifications and "little bits" of language are expressed differ in significant ways between natural sign languages and spoken languages, they emerge at similar ages and stages after a sizeable vocabulary has been built, when words or signs are combined in expressions, and when children have had access over time to the language being learned. Thus, the underlying process of development is similar, and the requirements of cognitive, social, and language experience needed to reach this stage appear to be the same regardless of the language or type of language being used. It should be noted, however, that deaf and hard-of-hearing children with hearing parents who are new learners of ASL do not usually keep pace with their age-mates whose parents are deaf. Whether the model is spoken language, a signed system, or a natural sign language, daily communicative experiences with fluent and consistent users of a language are necessary to support "on-time" development. Input from multiple persons who can interact with the child and fluently model the grammar of the language being learned becomes even more important as language skills and age progress. As always, of course, it is crucial that the child actually be able to receive and process the language being modeled if it is to be acquired sufficiently to allow its natural use in communication situations.

Making Use of Language: Pragmatics

In an early study (Spencer Day, 1986), we found that deaf and hard-of-hearing 3-year-olds learning a system for signing English made functional use of their still-limited language, along with gestures and vocalization, to establish a shared focus of attention and to express a wide variety of needs. However, they were delayed in use of what is called the "informative-heuristic" function—using language to give information and to ask for it. It seemed that this function required more vocabulary and more complicated grammar skills than these children had acquired at that age. Dr. Christine Yoshinaga-Itano (1992) later noted that emerging use of language for this function was a significant predictor of later language. Dr. Johanna Nicholas (2000) found language level, not chronological age, predicted use of the informative-heuristic function for deaf and hard-of-hearing children aged 12–54 months who were in spoken language (without sign) environments. At 3 years, children with typical hearing made more information-based statements, asked more questions, and gave more answers than did deaf or hard-of-hearing age-mates who had delayed language development. The deaf and hard-of-hearing children made more directive expressions and imitated more often. However, as their sentence length and vocabulary increased, so did their expression of more advanced functions.

The importance of being able to use language to exchange and to acquire information is obvious. To the extent that this is delayed, opportunities to learn from others are limited. Older deaf and hard-of-hearing children have repeatedly been reported to know less in general about the world—to have limited access to general information—than those with typical hearing. This lack of information interferes with later language, academic, and even social learning. As we discussed in the previous chapter, Goberis and her colleagues (2012) found that even when the vocabulary of deaf and hard-of-hearing school-aged children was developing at a typical rate, but complex grammar skills were delayed, pragmatic use of language was also delayed. Small differences based on language skills in the first few years seemed to persist and even grow larger with age.

IS EARLY INTERVENTION ENOUGH?

The purpose of identifying hearing levels in early infancy is to begin intervention as early as possible and to prevent delays that might otherwise be resistant to remediation. After all, if a child starts out delayed by 6 or 12 months in a particular area, he or she must develop even faster than other children to make up for that delay. We know that early intervention, use of sign language, and use of advanced hearing technologies are helping to prevent or at least decrease delays and, perhaps, to make up for some gaps. But have the effects of hearing limits been nullified—done away with—because of early intervention?

We noted earlier that on a checklist of children's expressive vocabulary, participants in our studies made progress from 2 to 3 years, but the deaf and hard-of-hearing children with hearing parents failed to keep pace with either children with typical hearing or those with deaf parents (Meadow-Orlans, Spencer, & Koester, 2004). The gap was larger at age 3 than it had been at age 2, despite the fact that the deaf and hard-of-hearing children with hearing parents had begun intervention by the age of 9 months at the latest. The Colorado study of children identified by 6 months of age as deaf or hard of hearing indicated that language development "averages" hovered in the range considered "low average" for children with typical hearing (Mayne, Yoshinaga-Itano, & Sedey, 1999; Mayne, Yoshinaga-Itano, Sedey, & Carey, 2000). A more recent study of deaf and hard-of-hearing children in the state of Ohio in the United States (Meinzen-Derr, Wiley, & Choo, 2011) gave similar results, but with early intervention services by 6 months of age predicting more rapid development than when intervention began later. (Note, however, that even those enrolled in programs after 6 months of age also showed significant progress.) This represents a highly significant improvement compared to that experienced by the majority of deaf and hard-of-hearing children with hearing parents in previous decades. However, the message is a mixed one in that the gap has not been completely closed despite great strides forward.

Dr. Susan Nittrouer (2010) studied language development of 118 children with moderate-to-profound hearing levels whose hearing parents wanted to specifically encourage spoken language development. Seventy-seven of these families used some signs to support spoken language, but sign use was never extensive and had essentially stopped by the time the children reached 4 years of age. Assessing the children's language from 12 to 48 months of age using a variety of instruments, Dr. Nittrouer found that the average expressive spoken vocabulary of deaf and hard-of-hearing children at age 2 was just below what is considered the "average" range for children with typical hearing. She noted that the variability within the group with limited hearing—that is, the range of individual differences—was quite large. Performance of deaf and hard-of-hearing children varied depending on time in intervention and hearing level. Although their average score was somewhat below that of children with typical hearing, approximately half of deaf and hard-of-hearing students were scoring within "normal limits" on the tests. Furthermore, when words that the children knew only in sign were added to those they knew in speech, this increased the measured vocabulary size significantly for those who used signs and had early identification and intervention by 6 months. They had larger vocabularies than children whose limited hearing was identified later.[2]

The deaf and hard-of-hearing children in Nittrouer's study also performed well on a measure of understanding language that did not rely heavily on knowledge of grammar or syntax. However, on a test with more emphasis on grammar (Auditory Comprehension, Preschool Language Scales; Zimmerman, Steiner, & Pond, 2011), their performance was below that of children with typical hearing—and the difference increased rather than decreased with age. Even children who began intervention by 6 months of age had difficulties understanding and using grammatical structures—the English grammatical "bits" that seem to be so difficult for deaf and hard-of-hearing children regardless of the language approach used.

Finally, Dr. Nittrouer found that clearness and accuracy of the speech production of the deaf and hard-of-hearing participants was generally poor despite use of hearing aids and, for some, CIs. In her study, intelligibility was judged by listening only, without being able to see the face of the child who was speaking or what was happening in the environment. This may have led to lower ratings than would have been the case in real-life, face-to-face situations. However, her results suggest that early intervention may not sufficiently resolve the problem of speech intelligibility for many young children with limited hearing. The degree to which children's speech can be understood by others will affect their opportunities for social interaction and even the degree to which their learning might be effectively guided. It remains an important issue for children who are expected to communicate using spoken language. There is some evidence, however, that speech skills continue to develop at later-than-typical ages for deaf and hard-of-hearing children with early identification and intervention (Yoshinaga-Itano, 2006)—perhaps as late as 5 years of age. This suggests that continued experiences with spoken language may prove beneficial.

Early Intervention and Hard-of-Hearing Children

Most toddlers and young children with mild-to-moderate or even moderately-severe hearing levels experience spoken language-only environments more often than those including signs. Meinzen-Derr and her colleagues found that hard-of-hearing children (as well as those with hearing limited in only one ear) who received intervention before 6 months, on average, achieved language skills appropriate for age by 3 years (Meinzen-Derr et al., 2011). In general, with high-quality early intervention, most hard-of-hearing children's spoken language performance is closer to age expectations than that of children with severe-to-profound or profound hearing levels. The amount of hearing ability predicts the rate at which children learn to produce consonants and vowel sounds, and speech intelligibility tends to be related to hearing levels. However, delays in speech intelligibility and phonology (understanding the set of sounds and the rules for combining them in a language) are more common with even slight decreases in access to speech sounds than in children with typical hearing (Moeller, Hoover et al., 2007a, 2007b; Moeller, Tomblin, et al., 2007). Speech sounds called *fricatives*, that include /s/, /z/, /j/, /sh/, and /v/ (along with a few others) seem to be the hardest for most hard-of-hearing children to hear and produce correctly. It is easier to learn to say something that has been heard clearly; otherwise, much of the mental energy that could be used to learn to say the word must be used to try to hear and figure out its sounds (Jerger et al., 2006). Therefore, difficulties in recognizing sounds or the differences between sounds can make it harder to learn new words.

Overall, vocabulary size tends to be lower for children with limited hearing than for children of the same age who have typical hearing (Mayne et al., 1999, 2000), and this seems to hold true for many (although not all) children with mild-to-severe hearing levels as well as those with profound level. Reports differ about this and other aspects of language learning. The fact that hard-of-hearing children are at greater risk than are hearing children for language delays does not mean that all of them will experience delay. For example, many school-aged children with mild-to-moderate hearing levels have vocabulary sizes similar to those of their classmates with typical hearing (e.g., Gilbertson & Kahmi, 1995).

However, even what are thought to be "minimal" restrictions of hearing should not be ignored. For example, up to 35% of children with hearing limited in only one ear are at risk for language delays—and later academic delays. These children, as well as others classified as hard of hearing, have sometimes been assumed to be developing on time because they are able to learn to speak and can participate in spoken language conversations. However, this ability can sometimes mask problems in areas such as the depth of understanding of vocabulary and, especially, understanding and use of grammar and advanced syntax (or sentence structure). It is important that assessment of these children's language abilities be performed periodically during their infant and toddler years. Because so much language is typically learned and used by the age of 3 years, it is especially important that any delays be addressed without more time passing.

Like reports of hard-of-hearing children's vocabulary development, those regarding their development of grammar also vary. Again, there are more reports of delays or differences in learning grammatical morphemes and complex sentence structures than reports showing no differences. The quality of programming the children experience seems to make a significant difference, however, just as the quality of language they experience at home (for example, the variety of words and sentence structures used, the amount of reciprocal turn-taking in conversations, the responsiveness of the language model provided) makes more difference than the quantity itself (VanDam, Ambrose, & Moeller, 2012). Studying older hard-of-hearing children (aged about 7 years), McGuckian and Henry (2007) reported that their use of grammatical morphemes (those "little bits" of grammar) developed not only more slowly but also in a different order from that reported for children with typical hearing. The children with limited hearing had the most problems with the "-ed" (past tense), the "-s" (possession), and the third person singular "-s" (as in, "he walks"). It may be important to give extra attention to these forms earlier in life if they are to develop at typical rates. Adding a visual accompaniment (such as a signed English grammatical marker or cued speech) to the not-easily heard speech sound for these grammatical meanings might aid learning, at least during instructional sessions focusing on them.

Early Outcomes for Children Using CIs

For children with little or no ability to hear speech sounds, CIs are often of great benefit. The outcomes of CI use, however, vary greatly across children depending on a multitude of differences in the child, the technology used, and the quality of intervention provided. There has been general agreement for decades, however, that CIs provide most children who have profound or even severe-profound hearing levels with significantly better access to the sounds of spoken language than is possible with hearing aids. Children whose hearing is restricted to these levels are a minority of the population of children with limited hearing, but they have traditionally been the ones whose access to language and learning has been most problematic.

CIs are wonderful—but they are not magic. Their effectiveness depends in part on the age at which they are first used, on the cognitive ability of the child, on the place and type of damage that caused the limited hearing, on parent/family involvement in the child's programming and support for development in general, on the quality and consistency of intervention services, and, not least, on the "generation" of technology being used in the CI (see Spencer, Marschark, & Spencer, 2011, for a summary). CI technologies are, in fact, like all others of our time, constantly evolving and improving, and innovations continue to emerge. Dr. Nittrouer (2010) captured some of the complexity of determining how well cochlear implants work when she related the array of CI use patterns in her study of children between 12 and 48 months of age—the age range during which CIs are commonly obtained. She discovered that some children in her study received one CI and stopped using a hearing aid in the other ear, some continued using the hearing aid after getting their single CI, some received two CIs—either at the same time or in sequence, one at a time. Of course, the CIs were obtained at different ages by different children. This obviously makes it difficult to draw sweeping conclusions about effectiveness, even when individual differences in other abilities and experiences are ignored. Interestingly, Dr. Nittrouer reported that changing from the input provided by a hearing aid to the different kind of input from a CI (electrical signals) seemed to require a period of adaptation. In other words, language growth might slow or cease temporarily after implantation before speeding up. She noted that children in her study who continued use of a hearing aid in one ear when getting a CI in the other tended to have less interruption in their language progress.

When all other things are equal, a general pattern has been noted: earlier CI use seems to predict later development more in keeping with age expectations. A number of researchers have found that using a CI by about 2 years of age predicts vocabulary growth close to that of children with typical hearing. Barker and her colleagues (Barker, et al., 2000) similarly found that, 4 years after getting a CI, children who received them before 2 years of age had better speech production than those who first used CIs after age 2. Others have found, but with only small groups, that getting a CI by 12 or 18 months of age allows the children to catch up with age-mates who have typical hearing. These age-of-first-use findings are in keeping with the idea that there are sensitive periods for brain development during the first years of life, as described earlier. Brain pathways for processing and transmitting information about sound are developed most efficiently and effectively during the earliest years of life (Dettman & Dowell, 2010). But age of first use has certainly not been the only factor found to affect language and speech development at 3 years and later.

Tait, Lutman, and Robinson (2000) found that, regardless of age, a child's contributions to communicative interactions—even at a pre-linguistic or pre-language level—predicted progress after getting the implant. It didn't matter whether the child was using gestural or vocal communication before the implant, only that they were full communicative participants who would introduce communicative topics on their own. In other words, little ones who were good communicators in general before the CI made the best progress with spoken language after getting a CI. This, of course, again reminds us of the importance of early, responsive, supportive communication experiences—even before the child can use language.

The potential of a CI to support language development when communicative experiences are positive is evident in a report by Ruggirello and Mayer (2010) about the development of twins, one with typical hearing and one profoundly deaf, when they were between 1 and 3 years of age. The deaf twin received CIs for both ears at 1 year. Her language was delayed compared to that of her hearing sister before the CIs and continued to be so for about 7 months afterward. However, after a year of experience with the CIs, the deaf girl's spoken language skills were assessed to be at age level, and, by 33 months of age, they were even better than average for age. The researchers pointed out that the twins were in a family environment that was highly supportive of language development and concluded that, given such an environment, early age of first use of CI, and typical development in other areas, it is possible for spoken language progress to catch up with that of children with typical hearing.

Of course, this is only one case, and the most frequent comment we have seen in reports of groups of children with CIs is the by-now-familiar refrain that there is great variation in achievement from child to child. It is the case, in addition, that some time is usually required for the child to adjust to the input from the CI, so that gains may accelerate over time. A child who receives a CI at age 2 may not yet have reached a peak rate of growth until beyond the age of 3. However, Tobey and her colleagues (Tobey et al., 2013) report that great variability (ranging from above-average achievement compared to age-mates with typical hearing to far below expected performance for age) continues to exist among children even 6 years after they begin using CIs. As is typical in development, the range of differences tends to increase rather than decrease throughout childhood.

Based on the conversational language of 76 children who received CIs by their third birthday, Drs. Johanna Nicholas and Ann Geers (2008) compared their growth rates in language skills from 3 ½ to 4 ½ years of age. Performance on language measures, including the number of words used, length of utterances, and use of grammatical morphemes increased as the length of time using the CI increased, but these improvements were greater if the CI was first used by 18 months of age. In their study, children who received CIs by about 18 months of age showed a period of accelerated growth in the months after the CI is activated, but this "burst" of growth was less common when the CI was received later. These researchers predicted that children receiving a CI before 24 months of age can be expected to catch up with their hearing peers by the time they enter kindergarten; however, those who are age 3 or older when first using a CI most likely will not.

Over the past decade, reports have become available about the effects of CI use by deaf children with deaf, signing parents (see Gale, 2010, regarding attitudes of deaf adults toward CIs). This information is especially important because it could show whether being in an environment with frequent use of sign language supports or interferes with (or perhaps has no effect on) developing spoken language. Recent research (Cramer-Wolrath, 2012; Davidson, Lillo-Martin, & Pichler, 2013; Hassanzadeh, 2012) indicates that these children's early sign language skills and usually supportive communication environments actually increase their rate of spoken language development after getting a CI. Somewhat surprisingly, even when early language development is based on vision more than hearing—and when it develops on time and in naturally occurring communicative interactions—it seems to offer an advantage when access to sound is then attained. The children's development in their first language, a natural sign language like ASL or Swedish Sign Language, can provide not only an ongoing means of communicating with family and friends but also a foundation for learning a second language (see also Knoors, 2016).

Progress for Young Children with Multiple Disabilities

Not surprisingly, multiple disabilities are generally associated with slower growth in communication and language skills. The term "multiple disabilities" covers a wide variety of challenges, however, not all of which are as formidable as might have been the case before early intervention during infancy was possible. Some recent reports indicate that mild to moderate cognitive delays or disabilities do not necessarily lead to poorer listening, speech, or language skills for children using a CI or hearing aids compared to those with typical cognitive abilities.

Children who are deafblind have traditionally been reported to experience highly significant delays in basic communication abilities as well as in language, cognitive, and social areas. This may be because children who are deafblind often have a constellation of disabilities, not all of which are easy to identify. Dammeyer (2009) reported on the progress of five children in Scandinavia who were deafblind from birth and who were receiving intervention services. These children were provided with CIs and began using them between the ages of 2 and 4 years. When observed and assessed between 5 and 8 years of age, the children had improved behaviors despite no obvious changes in language development itself. Using the CI, the children produced more vocalizations, were rated as having a higher quality of interactions with parents, engaged in less self-stimulation and gave more attention to what was going on around them, and gave generally more positive emotional responses. The children's cognitive abilities were associated with their degree of benefit from the CI. Those roughly within the low-average range cognitively made more gains than those who functioned less effectively on cognitive tasks. Along with other reports of decreased aggression and even increased perception of rhythm and voices, this report suggests that increasing access to information from sound can be of value to the quality of life of deafblind children.

A major analysis has recently been conducted of the language development of 119 deaf and hard-of-hearing 3-year-olds with additional disabilities in three states in Australia (Cupples et al., 2014). Using several formal tests as well as parent report measures, the goal was not to compare the performance of these children with multiple disabilities with either typically hearing or deaf/hard-of-hearing children without such disabilities; instead, the aim was to identify relationships with a number of background and experiential factors. Children participating in the study, all of whom had limited hearing, were classified as having autism spectrum disorder (ASD), cerebral palsy (motor disabilities), developmental (cognitive development) delays, vision impairment, speech output disorders, specific syndromes, or medical disabilities. These seven groups were then combined into two clusters. The first cluster included children with ASD, cerebral palsy, or developmental/cognitive delays; the other groups were in a second cluster. The most striking finding was that children in the second cluster tended to have higher levels of language skills than those in the first cluster. Although in general children in homes using spoken language without signs outperformed those in homes where a mix of speech and signs was used, this turned out to reflect the fact that oral or spoken approaches were most often used in the homes of children in cluster two. Speech intelligibility overall was poor, but vowels were produced more accurately than consonants.

All of the children had been fitted with hearing aids during infancy, and some had started using CIs, although this did not have much influence on outcomes. For children in cluster one (ASD, cerebral palsy, developmental/cognitive delay), the disability seemed to influence language development more than the hearing level. Cluster two was different, and milder hearing levels were positively associated with better language development. It was in this group that use of oral or spoken-only communication at home was associated with better language development; however, it is not clear whether communication mode was a cause of development or was chosen based on progress being made. Regardless of disability type or severity, access to resources for supporting development had a strong effect. Overall, this study leads to cautions against assumptions that any and all disabilities in combination with limited hearing will have significant effects on the development of language. Other factors are important for these children, as well as for those with limited hearing as their only developmental challenge. Once again, we are reminded that early, high-quality intervention with a focus on family functioning and with frequent assessments of progress can support more positive development at earlier ages than was expected in the past. Nevertheless, children with multiple disabilities will often need significantly more time to reach specific levels of skill in language and related areas than will those with similar hearing levels but without multiple developmental challenges.

SUMMARIZING KEY IDEAS

When children have had opportunities to actively participate in meaningful and accessible communicative interactions, and when overall development is occurring at a typical rate, amazing growth in language occurs between ages 2 and 3 years. Vocabulary increases rapidly, language expressions become longer, and these expressions begin to sound and/or look more like those used by significant adults and children in the social environment. Children are beginning to learn the grammar rules of their language, to engage in longer conversations with more people, and to use language to express a variety of meanings. Importantly, this includes the more effective use of language to communicate emotions, needs, and desires without needing to resort to physical behaviors for this purpose. Language, if it is developing at typical rates, will increasingly become a critical avenue for learning across all areas of development. These language skills have not bloomed without careful tending, however. Early identification of hearing levels accompanied by early intervention services can support effective, naturally occurring experiences that build positive social-emotional, cognitive, and communicative development.

The following are some key ideas in this chapter:

- It is crucial that deaf and hard-of-hearing children be provided supportive and accessible communication and language experiences as early as possible. By the age of 3 years, children with typical development (regardless of the language or language system they are using) should be acquiring language skills that increasingly influence social as well as thinking skills. The foundation is thus created for the ability to learn throughout childhood and beyond.

- Early identification of hearing levels, plus family participation in early intervention, can decrease language and related delays and allow a greater proportion of deaf and hard-of-hearing children to keep pace with the advances of children with typical hearing during the toddler and even preschool years. When access to a responsive language model has been limited, delays in development will become increasingly evident by 30 months to 3 years. Additional, focused activities will be necessary to prevent additional delay; after about 3 years, simply participating in naturally occurring interactions may not be sufficient to help the child remediate or make up those delays.

- Early identification plus early intervention also benefit children with multiple disabilities who have limited hearing. Their speed and patterns of development will depend on a number of individual and family characteristics, including the specific types of disabilities that are complicating development. However, progress *can* be made, at a faster rate and reaching higher levels than was previously thought possible.

- Cognitive development becomes increasingly influenced by communication and language skills by 3 years and beyond. Concepts related to categories, the ability to understand the perspectives (and feelings) of other persons, and effective memory for events and even sequences of events are all promoted through emerging language abilities, which are influenced in turn by communicative experiences with adults and other children.

- The child's ability to express and regulate emotional reactions is changing rapidly throughout and beyond the third year as well. Positive and consistent communications and positive social interactions can help children modify behaviors through which they express their natural desires for autonomy.

In three short years, the tiny baby has grown physically, mentally, socially, emotionally—navigating the toddler years with nurturing guidance from others—and should be ready now for more expanded experiences as the preschool years approach. Family-focused early intervention and the provision of an accessible language model in the home and beyond will in many cases have promoted now rapidly developing language skills, whether in a primarily visual or primarily auditory-based language or language system. Providing such models for a baby or toddler who is deaf or hard of hearing usually presents challenges, and those challenges can be expected to continue. However, a solid base in sensitive and mutual interactions and communication experiences during the early months and years will help the child to successfully reach this point. This nurturing environment can continue to support the child's development over the coming years, regardless of hearing levels or developmental challenges. There are exciting experiences awaiting as the young child exits the worlds of infancy and toddlerhood—with so many changes and so much growth still to come!

NOTES

1. We are focusing on English, signed English systems, and ASL in our discussion of language in this chapter because it is these with which we are most familiar. The general steps outlined, with differences reflecting the order of difficulty of acquiring grammatical rules of another language, are similar across languages.
2. In fact, the group with later identification and use of signs lagged behind the other groups fairly consistently, including those with early identification and those with late identification not using signs. Dr. Nittrouer interpreted this to mean that signs interfere with learning to speak if language development is delayed beyond an early, critical period before intervention (and the signing) begins. We suspect, alternatively, that this is because parents chose to use signs with children who were experiencing more of a lag in spoken language at the time they were identified. That is, these children may have started out behind.

12 Where We Are...And Where We Are Going

Let us now take a few minutes to review the impressive progress most deaf and hard-of-hearing children and their families have made during the first 3 years, as well as to explore what challenges they may still face in the future. The child is no longer an infant, no longer a toddler, but well on the way to being a preschooler. Periods in which brain mechanisms and organization are most sensitive to inputs for development are beginning to close, at least for some abilities: from now on, learning in these areas will tend to be slower and require more focused effort. Delays in specific areas, whether they involve motor, language, or social and behavioral development will require extra "catching up" efforts if they have persisted to this point. Of course, opportunities for learning are certainly not over, but it would be difficult to accomplish as many advances in any subsequent 3 years as typically occur in these first three.

In the United States, early intervention services often come to an end at age 3, and the transition to preschool is expected. In some cases, special supports are continued for children with limited hearing, but in other cases they are not. We have been shocked to find that children who test high enough to be in the "average" range on various language measures not infrequently have all special services withdrawn after age 3. Our concern is that the supports that were necessary to allow development to proceed on time until this age may well continue to be needed if these children are to stay on track over the next few years as well. Should it be necessary for a child to start falling behind in order to continue receiving services? Frankly, this doesn't sound very practical, nor beneficial for the child's long-term achievements—and actually not cost-effective for schools that may have to provide more intensive supports when older ages are reached.

INCREASING THE POTENTIAL FOR AGE-TYPICAL DEVELOPMENT

The good news is that, increasingly, deaf and hard-of-hearing children are achieving language levels near those expected for their age at 3 years and beyond. This is largely due to the benefits of early identification and intervention, recognition of multiple ways to model and support language development, and use by parents and other adults of communication strategies that build on deaf and hard-of-hearing children's visual and tactile sensitivities, as well as auditory abilities. As has been shown over the years, when early interactions are responsive and reciprocal, and when families develop shared language abilities, social and emotional growth is also positively encouraged. Some of the difficulties that were seen in the past in those areas are becoming rare. Of course, this positive perspective grows from experiences in parts of the world where early services and technologies are readily available and effectively employed. It also assumes that disabilities in motor, cognitive, social-emotional, or medical areas are not complicating a child's developmental progress. Even in the case of multiple disabilities, however, where sufficient resources are available, deaf and hard-of-hearing children are learning and developing more quickly than was the case in the past.

Attending and Responding to Multiple Developmental Challenges

This improved development is, however, dependent on all challenges to development being identified early so that appropriate changes in experiences and additional supports can be wisely applied. The following is an example in which an important challenge was missed when a child's disabilities were being identified. It happened in the United States before hearing screening at birth was widely available. Nonetheless, this is a child for whom screening in various areas would have been expected due to complications at birth. We know that, in many parts of the world, her story may still be happening, and we relate it not only as a cautionary tale but as an example of the strength and the resourcefulness of the human spirit—in this case both of the child and her family—when sufficient information and resources are available.

Ellie's birth was complicated by a diagnosis of severe cerebral palsy (CP), and she needed immediate medical care. Despite her special needs and challenges, her family made positive adaptations and very quickly grew to recognize the special qualities she brought to their lives. The effects of CP are usually visible and apparent to all, but other more subtle limitations may not be so obvious. During her pre-school years, Ellie fooled her parents and her siblings (all of whom had typical hearing) and other caregivers by developing a charming and astute sense of "visual humor" and by being so sensitive to vibrations that she predictably looked at them, alerted, and smiled when someone entered the room. Her social skills were engaging and helped tremendously in the development of her strong attachments to family members, but they were perhaps also to her detriment in that this caused a delay in recognizing her limited hearing.

In fact, to the initial dismay of those close to Ellie, she was not identified as having limited hearing until she was almost 5 years old. (It is not clear whether this was present at birth, but that is suspected to be the case.) It wasn't until Ellie and her parents attended a regional assistive technology conference—and a hearing test was recommended—that the full extent of her developmental challenges was revealed. Ellie's hearing level was in the profound range. Ellie's parents felt that this late identification of limited hearing had unacceptably delayed their making informed decisions about amplification or other technological assistance, other communication strategies, and early intervention approaches related to hearing and language. In Ellie's case, her "invisible" limits to hearing were overshadowed for far too long by the more noticeable effects of CP on her motor control and physical development. Even her cognitive and communicative delays were blamed on CP.

After her identification as deaf, Ellie's family went into high gear to determine how they could best meet the needs of this little girl who was not only wheelchair-bound but also needed to have visually based language input. Her parents had been aware that she had not shown as much progress as expected in mastering "cause-and-effect" and other cognitive tasks, but they were also impressed at how quickly gains were made as soon as Ellie began to have consistent and systematic access to visual language. It soon became evident that she had considerably greater cognitive abilities than had previously been assumed. For Ellie's family and caregivers, these were watershed moments: painfully, they realized just how easy it is to overlook a child's being deaf when the focus is on more obvious and visible challenges like CP.

Following the delayed identification of her profound hearing level, Ellie's family had to insist on the appropriate educational services, school placement, and opportunities for their deaf child whose academic skills were lagging behind so unnecessarily. But things had to change at home as well, so that the entire family could begin to communicate with Ellie more effectively. Attending "Family Learning Weekends" at their state's School for the Deaf and Blind provided the entire family with social, emotional, psychological, and communication support. There were engaging and wonderful activities for them all, including times when the children could simply be with others their age who were also growing up in unique circumstances.

> *Ellie's sisters benefitted from learning more about deaf and hard-of-hearing people, they made friends and found support there, and they quickly began to look forward to attending future events. In addition to advancing the participants' skills in sign language, these "Family Learning Weekends" provided guidance about alternatives to signing that still relied on vision. Since Ellie's motor difficulties made it hard for her to sign (even though she understood what others were signing), this was a particularly valuable component of the experience for her family.*
>
> *Just as siblings are inevitably affected by each other's temperament, intellectual abilities, social and communication skills, and all the other factors that make us each unique, so are mothers, fathers, and other family members touched and influenced by the presence of a child with special needs. Although there are, of course, extra, perhaps unexpected demands and stressors that accompany this, it is important to emphasize the potential for growth, empathy, and expanded horizons as well—as exemplified by Ellie's supportive family.*

Although Ellie's family had to initially seek out resources on their own, most families in industrialized countries will, in this century, have intervention teams available that include professionals with a range of specialties. Although a cluster of disabilities including cerebral palsy, autism spectrum disorder, and cognitive delays have particularly significant effects on the development of deaf and hard-of-hearing children, even these children will make progress—just perhaps more slowly and along slightly varying paths. It is important going forward, however, for professionals as well as families to avoid making assumptions about the limits to development that children with multiple disabilities will experience. They vary as much from individual to individual as do children in the rest of the population. It is also important to recognize that potential disabilities like mild cognitive delays do not necessarily result in great disruptions in the course and rate of development. We must insist that each individual's potential and strengths be recognized.

SENSITIVE, INFORMED, AND INTUITIVE PARENTING MAXIMIZES POTENTIAL DEVELOPMENT

Throughout this book, we have emphasized the critical role of sensitive early interactions with parents and other family members in the development of deaf and hard-of-hearing infants and toddlers. In this way, they are no different from children with typical hearing—but the adaptations that can best fit their needs differ in some ways from those often automatically made in communications to infants. They are not wildly divergent differences, however. The increased touch, slowed and rhythmic language, and enhanced responsiveness to an infant or toddler's attention and interests are beneficial regardless of hearing level. They may be even more important, however, when a baby or toddler has limited hearing. Also, if the child is developing at a slightly different rate than expected for age, parents and other adults must adapt their input to that particular child's developmental level across different areas of skills. One of the most pervasive difficulties is for a deaf or hard-of-hearing child to be developing "out of step," with language abilities trailing those in other areas. This requires sensitive adaptations on the parents' part. We have seen that adaptations to limited hearing come rather naturally to parents who are deaf themselves and are used to visual communication. They can provide not only models of visual and tactile communicative behaviors but also sources of social support for hearing parents who are just figuring out what being deaf or hard of hearing may mean for their infant or toddler. However, we have also seen that hearing parents can themselves learn to modify communications to best support their child's limited hearing. It is "natural" to repeat the kinds of behaviors that draw a positive response from an infant. When hearing parents are able to identify these responses (with assistance from intervention professionals when needed), their communicative behaviors are usually modified in ways that increase them. A major benefit of early intervention, therefore, is often to increase parents' confidence in their abilities to successfully support their deaf or hard-of-hearing infant or toddler's development—and feeling more confident almost always leads to increased competence because parents can relax and enjoy shared time with their baby.

THERE IS NO "ONE BEST WAY"

How easy it would be if we could say "Here it is! This is the one best approach for building language skills!" We'd probably even feel more comfortable if we mistakenly thought that one way could best build the language skills and support the development of all deaf and hard-of-hearing children. But, looking at all the reports available, remembering all the different deaf and hard-of-hearing children we have known, we find it impossible to become true believers in any one approach. Individual babies and their families will have their own strengths and their own often culturally based ways to respond to the realities of limited hearing and the options available. We believe that there is no convincing research indicating that early signing creates problems with learning to speak if that is otherwise possible—but there *is* a long history of problems when children have been denied access to sign in hopes of developing spoken language (see Spencer & Marschark, 2010, for a longer justification of this view). Signing during the early months can provide a bit of a safety net and can be increased or decreased over time depending on child and family responses. Certainly, incorporating visually sensitive strategies into communications with a deaf or hard-of-hearing infant or toddler has only positive implications. At the same time, we are fans of a family's choosing to use whatever available technologies will best support their child's and family's needs. Whatever is chosen, however, it needs to be remembered that the technology alone does not "fix" everything. Positive social-emotional experiences and language models are at least as necessary for deaf and hard-of-hearing infants and toddlers as for those who have typical hearing. Active physical experiences as well as opportunities to see new places, people, and things are critical for building a foundation for later social, cognitive, and academic learning.

THE ADVENTURE CONTINUES

At this point, we want to revisit the young adults whose stories opened this book. Amy, Stan, and Rob are beginning their adult lives with any number of advantages despite the challenges that they and their families have faced. When they were babies, resources for families were not as readily available as is now the case, but their families did their best for them. Each of the young adults is drawing on his or her strengths to continue to make progress educationally and at work. Undoubtedly, they will achieve different degrees of financial and other kinds of success—just like their peers with typical hearing. Perhaps most importantly, they have each developed self-confidence and social abilities that allow supportive interactions and relationships beyond as well as within their own families.

School years, especially for Rob, were not easy. And it remains the case that those years tend to be difficult ones for deaf and hard-of-hearing students. Language and literacy and "a fund of information about the world" still tend to be delayed to varying degrees for students with limited hearing. Special educational accommodations and supports are not always but are usually necessary, especially when early language development has been delayed or there are even mild challenges in other areas. Investigations are currently under way, however, to identify ways of teaching and supporting literacy development using approaches that draw on the strengths of students with limited hearing, as well as specific support for areas of special difficulty (Marschark et al., 2016). Additional major studies are under way to provide more information about the special needs of young children and students who are hard of hearing and whose needs have not been fully recognized in past years. We have confidence that progress will be made and that improved approaches to teaching and learning will become available in the years ahead as today's babies and toddlers become elementary and secondary school students.

Children born in still-developing parts of the world face challenges far beyond what we could consider in this book. We have personally seen success stories, however, across several continents. Even in what seem to be dire situations, it is possible for deaf and hard-of-hearing people to achieve productive and satisfying lives. It was particularly impressive to see in one Middle Eastern country, for example, young adults who had achieved impressive goals despite limited hearing or other developmental challenges; these young people were forming organizations and agencies focused on supporting families and helping improve the lives of younger children who faced difficulties like their own.

Despite recognizing that limited hearing adds significant challenges to the development of infants and toddlers—and despite acknowledging that their families will almost universally experience increased stress (even if only in scheduling and logistics)—we continue to look at that proverbial glass and think it is not only half full, but that the level is beginning to rise above the midpoint. No, the glass isn't full. No, the playing field is not yet level. But there have been enormous steps forward over the past several decades that are increasing the probability that deaf and hard-of-hearing children can reach their individual developmental potential. Continuing research, clinical, and educational practice and empowerment, and increased confidence in families, all justify the ever-greater expectations we share for all our children.

APPENDIX

RESOURCES AND WEBSITES FOR PARENTS AND PROFESSIONALS

The following are just a few of the organizations (and their websites) that can provide materials and support for parents and professionals working with deaf and hard-of-hearing infants and toddlers. We have listed them because we are familiar with them and the quality of their work and services.

Alexander Graham Bell Association for the Deaf and Hard of Hearing, Inc.
www.agbell.org

American Academy of Audiology
www.cdc.gov/ncbddd/hearingloss/recommendations.html

American Society for Deaf Children
www.deafchildren.org

American Speech, Language, and Hearing Association
www.asha.org

Beginnings: For Parents of Children Who Are Deaf or Hard of Hearing
www.ncbegin.org

Boys Town National Research Hospital
/www.boystownhospital.org
www.babyhearing.org

Center for Early Intervention on Deafness
www.ceid.org

The Children's Institute
www.amazingkids.org

Deafblind International
www.deafblindinternational.org

Educational Resource Center on Deafness, Texas School for the Deaf
www.texasdhhresources.org (multiple resources including online support for sign language learning and shared reading)
www.familysigns.org

Families for Hands and Voices
www.handsandvoices.org

("Guide by Your Side" programs provides parent mentors)
Foundation for the Care of Persons with Deafblindness (Spanish)
www.foaps.es

Hesperian Foundation
www.hesperian.org (books in various languages, such as: *Helping Children Who Are Deaf; Disabled Village Children*)

John Tracy Clinic
www.jtc.org

Laurent Clerc National Deaf Education Center at Gallaudet University:
www.gallaudet.edu/clerc_center/information_and_resources/info_to_go.html (includes information about Shared Reading and Cochlear Implant programs)

MICHA, (Israel) Society for Deaf Children
www.micha-israel.org.il/micha/

National Association of the Deaf
www.nad.org

National Center for Hearing Assessment and Management
www.infanthearing.org

National Cued Speech Association
http://www.cuedspeech.org

Our-Kids
http://www.our-kids.org

Postpartum Support International
www.postpartum.net

Self-Help for Hard of Hearing People (SHHH)
http://www.shhh.org

Ski-HI Institute at Utah State University
http://www.skihi.org/
(includes access to information, Ski Hi Curriculum and assessment
  instruments)

Zero to Three
http://www.zerotothree.org (also link to their Center for Training
  Services website)
www.zerotothree.org/littlekids-bigquestions (free podcasts)

REFERENCES

Ackley, R. S., & Decker, T. N. (2006). Audiological advancement and the acquisition of spoken language in deaf children. In P. Spencer & M. Marschark (Eds.), *Advances in the spoken language development of deaf and hard-of-hearing children* (pp. 64–84). New York: Oxford University Press.

Acredolo, L., & Goodwyn, S. (1988). Symbolic gesturing in normal infants. *Child Development, 59*, 450–466.

Acredolo, L., & Goodwyn, S. (2002). *Baby signs: How to talk with your baby before your baby can talk.* New York: McGraw-Hill.

Adamson, L. (1995/1996). *Communication development during infancy.* Boulder, CO: Westview Press.

Adesope, O., Lavin, T., Thompson, T., & Ungerleider, C. (2010). A systematic review and meta-analysis of cognitive correlates of bilingualism. *Review of Educational Research, 80*(2), 207–245.

Adolph, K., Karasik, L., &Tamis-LeMonda, C. (2009). Moving between cultures. Cross-cultural research on motor development. In M. Bornstein (Ed.), *Handbook of cultural developmental science, Vol. 1, Domains of development across cultures.* Mahwah, NJ: Lawrence Erlbaum.

Ainsworth, M. D. S., Blehar, M. C., Waters, E., & Wall, S. (1978). *Patterns of attachment: A psychological study of the strange situation.* Hillsdale, NJ: Erlbaum.

Al-Hilawani, Y., Easterbrooks, S., & Marchant, G. (2002). Metacognitive ability from a theory-of-mind perspective: A cross-cultural study of students with and without hearing loss. *American Annals of the Deaf, 147*(4), 38–47.

American Academy of Audiology. (2011). Childhood Hearing Screening Guidelines, 2011, http://www.cdc.gov/ncbddd/hearingloss/recommendations.html.

American Speech, Language, and Hearing Association. (2008a). *Service provision to children who are deaf and hard of hearing, birth to 36 months* (technical report). Joint Committee of the American Speech, Language, and Hearing Association and the Council on Education of the Deaf. www.asha.org/policy.

American Speech, Language, and Hearing Association. (2008b). *Loss to follow-up in early hearing detection and intervention* (technical report). www.asha.org/policy.

Anderson, D. (2006). Lexical development of deaf children acquiring signed languages. In B. Schick, M. Marschark, & P. Spencer (Eds.), *Advances in the sign language development of deaf children* (pp. 135–160). New York: Oxford University Press.

Anderson, D., & Reilly, J. (2002). The MacArthur Communicative Development Inventory: Normative data for American Sign Language. *Journal of Deaf Studies and Deaf Education, 7*, 83–106.

Anderson, X. (2002). *Early listening functions: Discovery tool for parents and caregivers of infants and toddlers.* www.phonak.com.

Antia, S. D., & Kreimeyer, K. H. (2015). *Social competence of deaf and hard-of-hearing children.* New York: Oxford University Press.

Bailes, C. (2001). Integrative ASL-English language arts: Bridging paths to literacy. *SignLanguage Studies, 1*, 147–174.

Barker, E., Daniels, T., Dowell, R., Dettman, S., Brown, P., Remine, M., … Cowan, R. (June 2000). Long term speech production outcomes in children who received cochlear implants before and after two years of age. Proceedings of 5th European Symposium on Paediatric Cochlear Implantation, Antwerp, Belgium.

Bass-Ringdahl, S. (2010). The relationship of audibility and the development of canonical babbling in young children with hearing impairment. *Journal of Deaf Studies and Deaf Education, 15*(3), 287–310. doi:10.1093/deafed/enq013.

Beattie, R. (2006). The oral methods and spoken language acquisition. In P. Spencer & M. Marschark (Eds.), *Advances in the spoken language development of deaf and hard-of-hearing children* (pp. 103–135). New York: Oxford University Press.

Bernard-Bonnin, A.-C., & Canadian Paediatric Society (2004). Maternal depression and child development. *Paediatric Child Health, 9*(8), 975–983. Online update 2015: http://www.cps.ca/documents/position/maternal-depression-child-development]

Biringen, Z. (2000). Emotional availability: Conceptualization and research findings. *American Journal of Orthopsychiatry, 70*, 104–114. doi: 10.1037/h0087711.

Biringen, Z., & Robinson, J. (1991). Emotional availability in mother-child interactions: A reconceptualization for research. *American Journal of Orthopsychiatry, 61*, 258–271. doi: 10.1037/h0079238.

Biringen, Z., Robinson, J., & Emde, R. N. (1998). *Emotional Availability Scales* (3rd ed.). Ft. Collins: Department of Human Development and Family Studies, Colorado State University.

Bodner-Johnson, B., & Sass-Lehrer, M. (Eds.). (2003). *The young deaf or hard of hearing child: A family-centered approach to early education.* Baltimore, MD: Paul Brookes.

Bonvillian, J., Richards, H., & Dooley, T. (1997). Early sign language acquisition and the development of hand preference in young children. *Brain and Language, 58*(1), 1–22.

Boons, T., Brokx, J., Dhooge, I., Frijins, J., Peeraer, L., Vermeulen, A., Wouters, J., & van Wieringen, A. (2012). Predictors of spoken language development following pediatric cochlear implantation. *Ear & Hearing, 33*(5), 627–639.

Bornstein, M. (Ed.). (1990). *Manual communication: Implications for education.* Washington DC: Gallaudet University Press.

Bornstein, M. H. (1995). Parenting infants. In M. H. Bornstein (Ed.), *Handbook of parenting* (Vol. 1, pp. 3–39). Mahwah, NJ: Erlbaum.

Bowlby, J. (1958). The nature of the child's tie to his mother. *International Journal of Psychoanalysis, 39*, 350–373.

Bowlby, J. (1969). *Attachment and Loss, Vol. I. Attachment.* New York: Basic Books.

Brazelton, T. B. (1982). Joint regulation of neonate-parent behavior. In E. Z. Tronick (Ed.), *Social interchange in infancy: Affect, cognition, and communication* (pp. 7–22). Baltimore, MD: University Park Press.

Brazelton, T. B. (1984). *To listen to a child: Understanding the normal problems of growing up.* Reading, MA: Addison-Wesley.

Brazelton, T. B., Koslowski, B., & Main, M. (1974). The origins of reciprocity: The early mother-infant interaction. In M. Lewis & L. Rosenblum (Eds.), *The effect of the infant on its caregiver* (pp. 49–77). New York: Wiley.

Bronfenbrenner, U. (1979). *The ecology of human development: Experiments by nature and design.* Cambridge, MA: Harvard University Press.

Brown, P. M., & Remine, M. (2004). Building pretend play skills in toddlers with and without hearing loss: Maternal scaffolding styles. *Deafness and Education International, 6*(3), 129–153.

Brown, P. M., Rickards, F., & Bartoli, A. (2001). Structures underpinning pretend play and word production in young hearing children and children with hearing loss. *Journal of Deaf Studies and Deaf Education, 6*(1), 15–31.

Calderon, R., & Greenberg, M. (2011). Social-emotional development of deaf children: Family, school, and program effects. In M. Marschark & P. Spencer (Eds.), *The Oxford handbook of deaf studies, language, and education,* Vol. 1 (2nd edition) (pp. 188–199). New York: Oxford University Press.

Calderon, R., & Naidu, S. (2000). Further support for the benefits of early identification and intervention for children with hearing loss. *Volta Review, 100*(5), 53–84.

Carpenter, M., Uebel, J., & Tomasello, M. (2013). Being mimicked increases prosocial behavior in 18-month-olds. *Child Development, 84*(5), 1511–1518.

Casby, M. (2003). The development of play in infants, toddlers, and young children. *Communication Disorders Quarterly, 24*(4), 163–174.

Centers for Disease Control and Prevention (CDC). (2010). *Identifying infants with hearing loss: United States 1999–2007.* http://www.cdc.gov/ncbddd/hearingloss/documents/ehdi_mmwr_2010.pdf.

Chess, S., & Thomas, A. (1996). *Temperament: Theory and practice.* New York: Brunner/Mazel.

Cole, E, & Flexer, C. (2011). *Children with hearing loss: Developing listening and talking. Birth to six: 2nd Edition.* San Diego CA: Plural.

Cone, B. (2011). Screening and assessment of hearing loss in infants. In M. Marschark & P. Spencer (Eds.), *The Oxford handbook of deaf studies, language, and education, Vol. 1,* 2nd ed. (pp. 439–452). New York: Oxford University Press.

Connor, C., Heiber, S., Arts, H., & Zwolen, T. (2000). Speech, vocabulary, and the education of deaf children using cochlear implants: Oral or total communication? *Journal of Speech, Language, & Hearing Research, 43,* 1105–1204.

Cramer-Wolrath, E. (2012). Attention interchanges at story-time: A case study from a deaf and hearing twin pair acquiring Swedish sign language in their deaf family. *Journal of Deaf Studies and Deaf Education, 17*(2), 141–162.

Cupples, L., Ching, T. Y., Crowe, K., Seeto, M., Leigh, G., Street, L., Day, J., Marnane, V., & Thompson, J. (2014). Outcomes of 3-year-old children with hearing loss and different types of additional disabilities. *Journal of Deaf Studies and Deaf Education, 19*(1), 20–39.

Dammeyer, J. (2009). Congenitally deafblind children and cochlear implants: Effects on communication. *Journal of Deaf Studies and Deaf Education, 14*(2), 278–288.

Davidow, M., Zahn-Waxler, C., Roth-Hanania, R., & Knafo, A. (2013). Concern for others in the first year of life: Theory, evidence, and avenues for research. *Child Development Perspectives, 7*(2), 126–131.

Davidson, K., Lillo-Martin, D., & Pichler, D. C. (2013). Spoken English language development in native signing children with cochlear implants. *Journal of Deaf Studies and Deaf Education, 19*(2), 238–250.

DeCasper, A. J., & Fifer, W. P. (1980). Of human bonding: Newborns prefer their mothers' voices. *Science, 208*, 1174–1176.

Delk, L., & Weidekamp, L. (2001). *Shared Reading Project: Evaluating implementation processes and family outcomes.* Washington, DC: Gallaudet University, Laurent Clerc National Deaf Education Center.

Dettman, S., & Dowell, R. (2010). Language acquisition and critical periods for children using cochlear implants. In M. Marschark & P. Spencer (Eds.), *The Oxford handbook of deaf studies, language, and education* (pp. 331–342). New York: Oxford University Press.

Dettman, S., Pinder, D., Briggs, R., Dowell R., & Leigh, J. (2007). Communication development in children who receive the cochlear implant younger than 12 months: Risks versus benefits. *Ear & Hearing, 28*, 11–18.

deVilliers, J., Bibeau, L., Ramos, E., & Gatty, J. (1993). Gestural communication in oral deaf mother-child pairs: Language with a helping hand? *Applied Psycholinguistics, 14*, 319–347.

Dore, J. (1974). A pragmatic description of early language development. *Journal of Psycholinguistic Research, 3*, 343–350.

Dowell, R., Dettman, S., Blamey, P., Barker, E., & Clark, G. (2002). Speech perception outcomes in children using cochlear implants: Predictions of long-term outcomes. *Cochlear Implant International, 3*, 1–18.

Drebohl, K. F., & Fuhr, M. G. (2000). *Pediatric massage for the child with special needs (revised).* The Psychological Corporation, Harcourt Health Sciences.

Easterbrooks, M., & Biringen, Z. (2000). Guest editors' introduction to the special issue: Mapping the terrain of emotional availability and attachment. *Attachment & Human Development, 2*, 123–129.

Edwards, L. (2010). Learning disabilities in deaf and hard-of-hearing children. In M. Marschark & P. Spencer (Eds.), *The Oxford Handbook of deaf studies, language, and education* (Vol. 2, 425–438). New York: Oxford University Press.

Eliot, L. (1999). *What's going on in there? How the brain and mind develop in the first five years of life.* New York: Bantam.

Emde, R. (1983). The prerepresentational self and its affective core. *Psychoanalytic Study of the Child, 38*, 165–192.

Erikson, E. H. (1963). *Childhood and society*. New York: Norton.

Erting, C. J., Prezioso, C., & Hynes, M. O. (1994). The interactional context of deaf mother-infant communication. In V. Volterra & C. J. Erting (Eds.), *From gesture to language in deaf and hearing children* (pp. 97–106). Washington, DC: Gallaudet University Press.

Ertmer, D., & Iyer, S. (2010). Prelinguistic vocalizations in infants and toddlers with hearing loss: Identifying and stimulating auditory-guided speech development. In M. Marschark & P. Spencer (Eds.), *The Oxford handbook of deaf studies, language, and education* (Vol. 2, pp. 360–375). New York: Oxford University Press.

Evans, C. (2004). Literacy development in deaf students: Case studies in bilingual teaching and learning. *American Annals of the Deaf, 149*, 17–26.

Fenson, L., & Ramsay, D. (1980). Decentration and integration of the child's play in the second year. *Child Development, 51*, 171–178.

Fenson, L., Dale, P., Reznick, S., Thal, D., Bates, E., Hartung, J., ... Reilly, J. (1993). *MacArthur Communicative Development Inventories: User's guide and technical manual*. San Diego, CA: Singular.

Fenson, L., Marchman, V., Thal, D., Dale, P., Reznick, J., & Bates, E. (2007a). *MacArthur-Bates Communicative Inventories (CDI): Words and Gestures; Words and Sentences*. Baltimore, MD: Paul Brookes.

Fenson, L., Marchman, V., Thal, D., Dale, P., Reznick, J., & Bates, E. (2007b). *MacArthur-Bates Communicative Development Inventories: User's guide and technical manual—Second edition*. Baltimore, MD: Paul Brookes.

Field, T. (1995). *Touch in early development*. Mahwah, NJ: Lawrence Erlbaum.

Field, T. M. (1978). The three R's of infant-adult interaction: Rhythms, repertoires, and responsivity. *Journal of Pediatric Psychology, 3*, 131–136.

Fletcher, N. (2013). Shock waves and the sound of a hand clap—A simple model. *Acoustics Australia, 41*(2), 165–168.

Fogel, A. (2009). *Infancy: Infant, family, and society (5th edition)*. Cornwall-on-Hudson, NY: Sloan.

Fogel, A. (2011). *Infant development: A topical approach*. Cornwall-on-Hudson, NY: Sloan.

Folven, R. J., & Bonvillian, J. D. (1991). The transition from nonreferential to referential language in children acquiring American Sign Language. *Developmental Psychology, 27*(5), 806–816.

Fortnum, H., Stacey, P., Barton, G., & Summerfield, A. Quentin (2007). National evaluation of support options for deaf and hearing-impaired children: Relevance to education services. *Deafness & Education International, 9,* 120–130.

Fortnum, H., Summerfield, A. Q., Marshall, D., Davis, A., & Bamford, J. (2001). Prevalence of permanent childhood hearing impairment in the United Kingdom and implications for universal neonatal hearing screening: Questionnaire-based ascertainment study. *British Medical Journal, 323,* 536–539.

Gale, E. (2010). Exploring perspectives on cochlear implants and language acquisition within the deaf community. *Journal of Deaf Studies and Deaf Education, 16*(1), 122–139.

Gallaudet Research Institute (November 2008). *Regional and national summary report of data from the 2007-08 annual survey of deaf and hard of hearing children and youth.* Washington, DC: GRI, Gallaudet University.

Gardiner, H. W., & Kosmitzki, C. (2008). *Lives across cultures: Cross-cultural human development.* Boston, MA: Pearson.

Geers, A., Brenner, C., & Davidson, L. (2003). Factors associated with development of speech perception skills in children implanted by age five. *Ear & Hearing, 24*(1 Suppl.), 24S–25S.

Gheysen, F., Loots, G., & Waelvelde, H. (2008). Motor development in deaf children with and without cochlear implants. *Journal of Deaf Studies and Deaf Education, 13*(2), 215–224. doi:10.1093/deafed/enm053.

Gilbertson, M., & Kahmi, A. (1995). Novel word learning in children with hearing impairment. *Journal of Speech and Hearing Impairment, 38,* 630–642.

Goberis, D., Beams, D. Dalpas, M., Abrisch, A., Baca, R., & Yoshinaga-Itano, C. (2012). The missing link in language development of deaf and hard of hearing children: Pragmatic language development. *Seminars in Speech and Language, 33*(4), 297–309.

Goldin-Meadow, S., & Mylander, C. (1990). Beyond the input given. The child's role in the acquisition of language. *Language, 66*(2), 323–355.

Golinkoff, R. M., & Hirsh-Pasek, K. (1999). *How babies talk: The magic and mystery of language in the first three years of life.* New York: Penguin Group (PLUME).

Gopnik, A., & Melzoff, A. (1987). The development of categorization in the second year and its relation to other cognitive and linguistic developments. *Child Development, 58,* 1523–1531.

Gopnik, A., Meltzoff, A. N., & Kuhl, P. K. (1999). *The scientist in the crib: Minds, brains, and how children learn.* New York: Wm. Morrow.

Greenberg, M. (1983). Family stress and child competence: The effects of early intervention for families with deaf infants. *American Annals of the Deaf, 128,* 407–417.

Gustason, G., Pfetzing, D., & Zawolkow, E. (1980). *Signing exact English*. Los Alamitos CA: Modern Sign Press.

Hamilton, H. (2011). Memory skills of deaf learners: Implications and applications. *American Annals of the Deaf, 156*(4), 402–423.

Harkins, J., & Bakke, M. (2010). Technologies for communication: Status and trends. In M. Marschark & P. Spencer (Eds.), *The Oxford handbook of deaf studies, language, and education* (Vol. 2, pp. 425–438). New York: Oxford University Press.

Harris, M. (1992). *Language experience and early language development: From input to uptake*. Hillsdale, NJ: Erlbaum.

Hart, B., & Risley, T. (1995). *Meaningful differences in the everyday experience of young American children*. Baltimore, MD: Paul Brookes.

Hawley, T., & Gunnar, M. (2000). *Starting smart: How early experiences affect brain development*. Washington, DC: Zero to Three.

Hassanzadeh, S. (2012). Outcomes of cochlear implantation in deaf children of deaf parents: Comparative study. *Journal of Laryngology and Otology, 126*(10), 989.

Hepper, P. G. (2007). Prenatal development. In A. Slater & M. Lewis (Eds.), *Introduction to infant development* (pp. 39–60). New York: Oxford University Press.

Hintermair, M. (2000). Hearing impairment, social networks, and coping: The need for families with hearing-impaired children to relate to other parents and to hearing-impaired adults. *American Annals of the Deaf, 145*, 41–51.

Hintermair, M. (2006). Parental stress, parental resources and socioemotional development of deaf and hard of hearing children. *Journal of Deaf Studies and Deaf Education, 11*(4), 493–513.

Holden-Pitt, L., & Diaz, J. (1998). Thirty years of the Annual Survey of deaf and hard-of-hearing children & youth: A glance over the decades. *American Annals of the Deaf, 143*(2), 72–76.

Hoiting, N. (2006). Deaf children are verb attenders: Early sign vocabulary development in Dutch toddlers. In B. Schick, M. Marschark, & P. Spencer (Eds.), *Advances in the sign language development of deaf children* (pp. 161–188). New York: Oxford University Press.

Holcomb, T. (2013). *Introduction to American Deaf culture*. New York: Oxford University Press.

Holt, R. F., & Svirsky, M. A. (2008). An exploratory look at pediatric cochlear implantation: Is earliest always best? *Ear and Hearing, 29*(4), 492–511. doi:10.1097/AUD.0b013e31816c409f

Hubel, D. H., & Wiesel, T. N. (1959). Receptive fields of single neurons in the cat's striate cortex. *Journal of Physiology, 148*, 574–591.

Huttenlocher, J., Haight, W., Bryk, A., Seltzer, M., & Lyons, T. (1991). Early vocabulary growth: Relation to input and gender. *Developmental Psychology*, *27*, 236–248.

Jerger, S., Damian, M., Tye-Murray, N., Dougherty, M., Mehta, J., & Spence, M. (2006). Effects of childhood hearing loss on organization of semantic memory: Typicality and relatedness. *Ear & Hearing*, *27*(6), 686–702.

Johnson, R., Liddell, S., & Erting, C. (1989). *Unlocking the curriculum: Principles for achieving access in deaf education*. Gallaudet Research Institute Working Paper 89-3. Washington DC: Gallaudet University.

Joint Committee on Infant Hearing. (2007). Year 2007 position statement: Principles and guidelines for early hearing detection and intervention programs. *American Academy of Pediatrics*, *120*(4), 898–921.

Jones, T., & Jones, J. (2003). Educating young deaf children with multiple disabilities. In B. Bodner-Johnson & M. Sass-Lehrer (Eds.), *The young deaf or hard of hearing child* (pp. 297–332). Baltimore, MD: Paul Brookes.

Jones, W., & Klin, A. (2013). Attention to eyes is present but in decline in 2-to-6-month-old infants later diagnosed with autism. *Nature*, *504*, 427–431. doi:10.1038/nature12715.

Kagan, J., & Snidman, N. (2004). *The long shadow of temperament*. Cambridge, MA: Harvard University Press.

Kelly, C., & Dale, P. (1989). Cognitive skills associated with the onset of multiword utterances. *Journal of Speech and Hearing Research*, *32*, 645–656.

Knoors, H. (2016). Foundations for language development in deaf children and the consequences for communication choice. In M. Marschark & P. Spencer (Eds.), *The Oxford handbook of deaf studies in language: Research, policy, and practice* (pp. 19–31). New York: Oxford University Press.

Knoors, H., & Marschark, M. (2012). Language planning for the 21st century: Revisiting bilingual language policy for deaf children. *Journal of Deaf Studies and Deaf Education*, *17*(3), 291–305.

Knoors, H., & Vervloed, M. (2011). Educational programming for deaf children with multiple disabilities: Accommodating special needs. In M. Marschark & P. Spencer (Eds.), *The Oxford handbook of deaf studies, language, and education, Vol. 1*, 2nd ed. (pp. 82–96). New York: Oxford University Press.

Koester, L. S. (1988). Rhythmicity in parental stimulation of infants. In P. G. Fedor-Freybergh (Ed.), *Prenatal and perinatal psychology and medicine* (pp. 143–152). Lancashiere, UK: Parthenon.

Koester, L. S. (1992). Intuitive parenting as a model for understanding parent-infant interactions when one partner is deaf. *American Annals of the Deaf*, *137*(4), 362–369.

Koester, L. S., & Forest, D. S. (1998, April). Self-recognition responses among deaf and hearing 18-month-old infants. Poster presented at the International Conference on Infant Studies, Atlanta, GA.

Koester, L. S., & Lahti-Harper, E. (2010). Mother-infant hearing status and intuitive parenting behaviors during the first 18 months. *American Annals of the Deaf*, 155(1), 5–18.

Koester, L. S., & McCray, N. (2011). Deaf parents as sources of positive development and resilience for deaf infants. In D. H. Zand & K. J. Pierce (Eds.), *Resilience in deaf children: Adaptations through emerging adulthood* (pp. 65–86). New York: Springer.

Koester, L. S., Papoušek, H., & Papoušek, M. (1989). Patterns of rhythmic stimulation by mothers with three-month-olds: A cross-modal comparison. *International Journal of Behavioral Development*, 12(2), 143–154.

Koester, L. S., Papoušek, H., & Smith-Gray, S. (2000). Intuitive parenting, communication, and interaction with deaf infants. In P. E. Spencer, C. J. Erting, & M. Marschark (Eds.), *The deaf child in the family and at school* (pp. 55–71). Mahwah, NJ: Lawrence Erlbaum.

Korner, A. F., & Thoman, E. B. (1970). Visual alertness in neonates as evoked by maternal care. *Journal of Experimental Child Psychology*, 10, 67–78.

Korner, A. F., & Thoman, E. B. (1972). The relative efficacy of contact and vestibular-proprioceptive stimulation in soothing neonates. *Child Development*, 43, 443–453.

Lamb, M. E., Bornstein, M. H., & Teti, D. M. (2002). *Development in infancy: An introduction*, 4th ed. Mahwah, NJ: Lawrence Erlbaum Associates.

Langhorst, B., & Fogel, A. (1982). *Cross validation of microanalytic approaches to face-to-face play*. Paper presented at the International Conference on Infant Studies, Austin, TX.

LaSasso, C., Crain, K., & Leybaert, J. (Eds.). (2010). *Cued speech and cued language for deaf and hard of hearing children*. San Diego, CA: Plural.

Lederberg, A., & Everhart, E. (2000). Conversations between deaf children and their hearing mothers: Pragmatic and dialogic characteristics. *Journal of Deaf Studies and Deaf Education*, 5(4), 303–322.

Lederberg, A., & Golbach, T. (2002). Parenting stress and social support in hearing mothers of deaf and hearing children: A longitudinal study. *Journal of Deaf Studies and Deaf Education*, 7(4), 330–345.

Lederberg, A. R., & Mobley, C. E. (1990). The effect of hearing impairment on the quality of attachment and mother-toddler interaction. *Child Development*, 61, 1596–1604.

Lederberg, A. & Prezbindowski, A. (2000). Impact of child deafness on mother-toddler interaction: Strengths and weaknesses. In P. E. Spencer,

C. J. Erting, & M. Marschark (Eds.), *The deaf child in the family and at school: Essays in honor of Kathryn P. Meadow-Orlans* (pp. 73–92). Mahwah, NJ: Lawrence Erlbaum.

Lederberg, A., Prezbindowski, A., & Spencer, P. (2000). Word-learning skills of deaf preschoolers: The development of novel mapping and rapid word-learning strategies. *Child Development, 71*(6), 1571–1585.

Lederberg, A., Schick, B., & Spencer, P. (2013). Language and literacy development of deaf and hard-of-hearing children: Successes and challenges. *Developmental Psychology, 49*(1), 15–30. doi:10.1037/a0029558

Lederberg, A., & Spencer, P. (2005). Critical periods in the acquisition of lexical skills: Evidence from deaf individuals. In P. Fletcher & J. Miller (Eds.), *Developmental theory and language disorders* (pp. 121–145). Philadelphia, PA: John Benjamin.

Lee, D., & Aronson, E. (1974). Visual proprioceptive control of standing in human infants. *Perception and Psychophysics, 15*, 529–532.

Leigh, G., Newall, J., & Newall, A. (2010). Newborn screening and earlier intervention with deaf children: Issues for the developing world. In M. Marschark & P. Spencer (Eds.), *The Oxford handbook of deaf studies, language, and education* (Vol. 2, pp. 345–359). New York: Oxford University Press.

Leigh, J., Dettman, S., Dowell, R., & Sarant, J. (2011). Evidence-based approach for making cochlear implant recommendations for infants with residual hearing. *Ear and Hearing, 32*(3), 313–322.

Lewis, M. (2007). Early emotional development. In A. Slater & M. Lewis (Eds.) *Introduction to infant development* (pp. 216–232). New York: Oxford University Press.

Leybaert, J., Bayard, C., Colin, C., & and LaSasso, C. (2016). Cued speech and cochlear implants: A powerful combination for natural spoken language acquisition and the development of reading. In M. Marschark & P. Spencer (Eds.), *The Oxford handbook of deaf studies in language: Research, policy, and practice* (pp. 359–376). New York: Oxford University Press.

Lifter, K. Foster-Sanda, S., Arzamarski, C., Briesch, J., & McClure, E. (2011). Overview of play: Its uses and importance in early intervention/early childhood special education. *Infants & Young Children, 24*(3), 225–245.

Lillo-Martin, D., Bellugi, U., Struxness, L., & O'Grady, M. (1985). The acquisition of spatially organized syntax. *Papers and Reports on Child Language Development, 24*, 70–80.

Linder, T. W. (1993). *Transdisciplinary play-based assessment: A functional approach to working with young children* (Rev. ed.). Baltimore, MD: Paul Brookes.

Linder, T. W. (2000). Transdisciplinary play-based assessment. In K. Gitlin-Weiner, A. Sandgrund, & C. Schaefer (Eds.), *Play diagnosis and assessment, 2nd edition* (pp. 139–166). New York: John Wiley.

Luetke-Stahlman, B., & Nielsen, D. (2003). The contribution of phonological awareness and receptive and expressive English to the reading ability of deaf students with varying degrees of exposure to accurate English. *Journal of Deaf Studies and Deaf Education, 8*, 464–484.

Luterman, D., & Kurtzer-White, E. (1999). Identifying hearing loss: Parents' needs. *American Journal of Audiology, 8*, 13–18. doi: 10.1044.1059-0089 (1999/006).

MacTurk, R. H. (2002). Social and motivational development in deaf and hearing infants. In D. Messer (Ed.), *Mastery motivation: Children's investigation, persistence, and development* (pp. 149–167). New York: Taylor & Francis.

MacTurk, R. H., Ludwig, J. L., & Meadow-Orlans, K. P. (2004). Mastery motivation at 9 and 12 months: Traditional and nontraditional approaches. In K. P. Meadow-Orlans, P. E. Spencer, & L. S. Koester, *The world of deaf infants: A longitudinal study* (pp. 92–114). New York: Oxford University Press.

MacTurk, R., & Trimm, V. (1989). Mastery motivation in deaf and hearing infants. *Early Education and Development, 1*, 19–34.

Maestes y Moores, J. (1980). Early linguisitic environment: Interactions of deaf parents with their infants. *Sign Language Studies, 26*, 1–13.

Mann, W., & Haug, T. (2016). New directions in sign language assessment. In M. Marschark & P. Spencer (Eds.). *The Oxford handbook of deaf studies in language: Research, policy, and practice* (pp. 299–310). New York: Oxford University Press.

Marschark, M. (1993). Origins and interactions in social, cognitive, and language development of deaf children. In M. Marschark & M. D. Clark (Eds.), *Psychological perspectives on deafness* (pp. 7–26). Hillsdale, NJ: Lawrence Erlbaum.

Marschark, M. (2007). *Raising and educating a deaf child*, 2nd ed. New York: Oxford University Press.

Marschark, M., & Hauser, P. (2012). *How deaf children learn*. New York: Oxford University Press.

Marschark, M., Machmer, E., & Convertino, C. (2016). Understanding language in the real world. In M. Marschark & P. Spencer (Eds.), *The Oxford handbook of deaf studies in language: Research, policy, and practice* (pp. 431–452). New York: Oxford University Press.

Marschark, M., & Spencer, P. E. (Eds.). (2016). *The Oxford handbook of deaf studies in language: Research, policy, and practice*. New York: Oxford University Press.

Mayne, A., Yoshinaga-Itano, C., & Sedey, A. (1999). Receptive vocabulary development of infants and toddlers who are deaf or hard of hearing. *Volta Review, 100*(5), 29–52.

Mayne, A., Yoshinaga-Itano, C., Sedey, A., & Carey, A. (2000). Expressive vocabulary development of infants and toddlers who are deaf or hard of hearing. *Volta Review, 100*(5), 1–28.

McCune, L. (2008). *How children learn to learn language.* New York: Oxford University Press.

McGowan, R., Nittrouer, S., & Chenausky, K.(2008). Speech production in 12-month-old children with and without hearing loss. *Journal of Speech, Language, and Hearing Research, 51,* 879–888.

McGuckian, M., & Henry, A. (2007). The grammatical morpheme deficit in moderate hearing impairment. *International Journal of Language and Communication Disorders, 42,* 17–36. doi: 10.1111/jlcd.2007.42.issue-S1/issuetoc

McKinnon, C. C., Moran, G., & Pederson, D. (2004). Attachment representations of deaf adults. *Journal of Deaf Studies and Deaf Education, 9*(4), 366–386. doi:10:1093/deafed/enh043.

McLean, J., & Snyder-McLean, L. (1999). *How children learn language.* San Diego CA: Singular.

Meadow-Orlans, K. (1994). Stress, support, and deafness: Perceptions of infants' mothers and fathers. *Journal of Early Intervention, 18,* 91–102.

Meadow-Orlans, K., Mertens, D. M., & Sass-Lehrer, M. A. (2003). *Parents and their deaf children: The early years.* Washington, DC: Gallaudet University Press.

Meadow-Orlans, K., Spencer P., & Koester, L. (Eds.). (2004). *The world of deaf infants: A longitudinal study.* New York: Oxford University Press.

Meadow-Orlans, K., & Steinberg, A. (2004). Mother-infant interactions at 12 and 18 months: Parenting stress and support. In K. Meadow-Orlans, P. E. Spencer, & L. S. Koester, *The world of deaf infants: A longitudinal study* (pp. 115–131). New York: Oxford University Press.

Meier, R. (1982). Icons, analogues, and morphemes: The acquisition of verb agreement in American Sign Language. Unpublished doctoral dissertation, University of California, San Diego.

Meinzen-Derr, J., Wiley, S., & Choo, D. (2011). Impact of early intervention on expressive and receptive language development among young children with permanent hearing loss. *American Annals of the Deaf, 155*(5), 580–591.

Mitchell, R., & Karchmer, M. (2004). Chasing the mythical ten percent: Parental hearing status of deaf and hard of hearing students in the United States. *Sign Language Studies, 4,* 138–163.

Moeller, M. P. (2000). Intervention and language development in children who are deaf or hard of hearing. *Pediatrics, 106,* E43.

Moeller, M. P. (2002). *Mothers' mental state input and theory of mind understanding in deaf and hearing children.* The University of Nebraska–Lincoln, ProQuest, UMI Dissertations Publishing, 3059958.

Moeller, M. P., Hoover, B., Putman, C., Arbataitis, K., Bohnenkamp, G., Peterson, B., ... Stelmachowicz, P. (2007*a*). Vocalizations of infants with hearing loss compared to infants with normal hearing: Part I—Phonetic development. *Ear & Hearing, 28,* 605–627.

Moeller, M. P., Hoover, B., Putman, C., Arbataitis, K., Bohnenkamp, G., Peterson, B., ... Stelmachowicz, P. (2007*b*). Vocalizations of infants with hearing loss compared with infants with normal hearing: Part II—Transition to words. *Ear & Hearing, 28*(5), 628–642.

Moeller, M. P., & Schick, B. (2006). Relations between maternal input and theory of mind understanding in deaf children. *Child Development, 77,* 751–766.

Moeller, M. P., Tomblin, B., Yoshinaga-Itano, C., Connor, C., McDonald, C., & Jerger, S. (2007). Current state of knowledge: Language and literacy of children with hearing impairment. *Ear & Hearing, 28*(6), 740–753.

Mohay, H. (2000). Language in sight: Mothers' strategies for making language visually accessible to children. In P. E. Spencer, C. J. Erting, & M. Marschark (Eds.), *The deaf child in the family and at school: Essays in honor of Kathryn P. Meadow-Orlans* (pp. 151–166). Mahwah, NJ: Lawrence Erlbaum.

Montanini-Manfredi, M. (1993). The emotional development of deaf children. In M. Marschark & M. Diane Clark (Eds.), *Psychological perspectives on deafness* (pp. 49–63). Hillsdale, NJ: Lawrence Erlbaum Associates.

Moores, D. (2010). The history of language and communication issues in deaf education. In M. Marschark & P. Spencer (Eds.), *The Oxford handbook of deaf studies, language, and education, vol. 2* (pp. 17–30). New York: Oxford University Press.

Morgan, G. A., MacTurk, R. H., & Hrncir, E. J. (1995). Mastery motivation: Overview, definitions, and conceptual issues. In R. H. MacTurk & G. A. Morgan (Eds.), *Mastery motivation: Origins, conceptualizations, and applications* (pp. 1–18). Norwood, NJ: Ablex.

Nathani, S., Ertmer, D. J., & Start, R. E. (July 2006). Assessing vocal development in infants and toddlers. *Clinical Linguistics & Phonetics, 20,* 351–369.

Nathani, S., Oller, D. K., & Neal, A. R. (2007). On the robustness of vocal development: An examination of infants with moderate-to-severe hearing loss and additional risk factors. *Journal of Speech, Language, and Hearing Research, 50,* 1425–1444. doi: 10.1044/1092-4388(2007/099)

Nicholas, J. (2000). Age differences in the use of informative/heuristic communicative functions in young children with and without hearing loss who are learning spoken language. *Journal of Speech Language and Hearing Research, 43*, 380–394.

Nicholas, J., & Geers, A. (1997). Communication of oral deaf and normally hearing children at 36 months. *Journal of Speech, Language, and Hearing Research, 40*, 1314–1327.

Nicholas, J., & Geers, A. (2006). The process and early outcomes of cochlear implantation by three years of age. In P. E. Spencer & M. Marschark (Eds.), *Advances in the spoken language development of deaf and hard-of-hearing children* (pp. 271–297). New York: Oxford University Press.

Nicholas, J., & Geers, A. (2008). Expected test scores for preschoolers with a cochlear implant who use spoken language. *American Journal of Speech and Language Pathology, 17*, 121–138.

Nicholas, J., Geers, A., & Kozak, V. (1994). Development of communicative function in young hearing-impaired and normally hearing children. *Volta Review, 96*(2), 113–135.

Nielsen, D., Luetke, B., & Stryker, D. (2011). The importance of morphemic awareness to reading achievement and the potential of signing morphemes in supporting reading development. *Journal of Deaf Studies and Deaf Education, 16*(3), 275–288. doi: 10.1093/deafed/enq063

Nittrouer, S. (2010). *Early development of children with hearing loss.* San Diego CA: Singular.

Northern, J., & Downs, M. (2002). *Hearing in children,* 5th ed. New York: Lippincott Williams & Wilkins.

Norton, S., Gorga, M., Widen, J., Folsom, R., Sininger, Y., Cone-Wesson, B., & Fletcher, K. (2000). Identification of neonatal hearing impairment: A multicenter investigation. *Ear and Hearing, 21*, 348–356.

Nugent, K. (2011). *Your baby is speaking to you: A visual guide to the amazing behaviors of your newborn and growing baby.* Boston, MA: Houghton Mifflin Harcourt.

Oller, K. (2006). Vocal language development in deaf infants: New challenges. In P. Spencer & M. Marschark (Eds.), *Advances in the spoken language development of deaf and hard-of-hearing children* (pp. 22–41). New York: Oxford University Press.

Olusanya, B. (2006). Early hearing detection and intervention in developing countries: Current status and prospects. *Volta Review, 106*(3), 381–418.

Orlansky, M., & Bonvillian, J. (1985). Sign language acquisition: Language development in children of deaf parents and implications for other populations. *Merrill-Palmer Quarterly, 32*, 127–143.

Padden, C. (2006). Learning to fingerspell twice: Young children's acquisition of fingerspelling. In B. Schick, M. Marschark, & P. Spencer (Eds.), *Advances in the sign language development of deaf children* (pp. 189–201). New York: Oxford University Press.

Palmieri, M., Berrettini, S., Forli, F., Trevisi, P., Genovese, E., Chilosi, A. M., ... Martini, A. (2012). Evaluating benefits of cochlear implantation in deaf children with additional disabilities. *Ear & Hearing. 33*(6), 721–730.

Papoušek, M. (2008). Disorders of behavior and emotional regulation: Clinical evidence for a new diagnostic concept. In M. Papoušek, M. Schieche, & H. Wurmser (Eds.), *Disorders of behavioral and emotional regulation in the first years of life* (pp. 53–84). Washington, DC: Zero to Three.

Papoušek, H., & Papoušek, M. (1987). Intuitive parenting: A dialectic counterpart of the infant's integrative competence. In J. D. Osofsky (Ed.), *Handbook of infant development* (2nd ed., pp. 302–331). New York: Wiley.

Paradis, G., & Koester, L. (2015). Emotional availability and touch among deaf and hearing mother-infant dyads. *American Annals of the Deaf, 160*(3), 303–315.

Petitto, L. A. (2000). On the biological foundations of human language. In K. Emmorey & H. Lane (Eds.), *The signs of language revisited: An anthology in honor of Ursula Bellugi and Edward Klima* (pp. 449–473). Mahwah, NJ: Lawrence Erlbaum.

Petitto, L, & Marentette, P. (1991, March 22). Babbling in the manual mode: Evidence for the ontogeny of language. *Science, New Series, 251*(5000), 1493–1496. http://links.jstor.org

Piaget, J. (1936/1952). *The origins of intelligence in children* (M.Cook, trans.). NewYork: International Universities Press.

Piaget, J. (1962). *Play, dreams, and imitation in childhood.* New York: Norton.

Pipp-Siegel, S., & Biringen, Z. (1998). Assessing the quality of relationships between parents and children: The emotional availability scales. *Volta Review, 100,* 237–249.

Pipp-Siegel, S., Blair, N. L., Deas, A. M., Pressman, L., & Yoshinaga-Itano, C. (1998). Touch and emotional availability in hearing and deaf or hard of hearing toddlers and their hearing mothers. *Volta Review, 100,* 279–298.

Pipp-Siegel, S., Sedey, A., VanLeeuwen, A., & Yoshinaga-Itano, C. (2003). Mastery motivation and expressive language in young children with hearing loss. *Journal of Deaf Studies and Deaf Education, 8*(2), 133–145. doi:10.1093/deafed/eng008

Pipp-Siegel, S., Sedey, A., & Yoshinaga-Itano, C. (2002). Predictors of parental stress in mothers of young children with hearing loss. *Journal of Deaf Studies and Deaf Education, 7,* 1–17.

Pittman, P., Benedict, B., Olson, S., & Sass-Lehrer, M. (2015). Collaboration with deaf and hard-of-hearing communities. In M. Sass-Lehrer (Ed.), *Early intervention for deaf and hard-of-hearing infants, toddlers and their families: An interdisciplinary perspective.* New York: Oxford University Press.

Prendergast, S. G., & McCollum, J. A. (1996). Let's talk: The effect of maternal hearing status on interactions with toddlers who are deaf. *American Annals of the Deaf, 141*, 11–18.

Pressman, L., Pipp-Siegel, S., Yoshinaga-Itano, C., & Deas, A. M. (1999). Maternal sensitivity predicts language gain in preschool children who are deaf and hard of hearing. *Journal of Deaf Studies and Deaf Education, 4*, 294–304.

Pressman, L., Pipp-Siegel, S., Yoshinaga-Itano, C., Kubicek, L., & Emde, R. N. (1998). A comparison of the links between emotional availability and language gain in young children with and without hearing loss. *Volta Review, 100*, 251–277. doi:10.1093/deafed/4.4.294

Qi, S., & Mitchell, R. E. (2012). Large-scale academic achievement testing of deaf and hard-of-hearing students: Past, present, and future. *Journal of Deaf Studies and Deaf Education, 17*, 1–18.

Quittner, A., Barker, D., Snell, C., Cruz, I., McDonald, L-G., Grimley, M., ... CDACI Investigative Team (2007). Improvements in visual attention in deaf infants and toddlers after cochlear implantation. *Audiological Medicine, 5*, 242–429.

Remmel & Peters (2009). Theory of mind and language in children with cochlear implants. *Journal of Deaf Studies and Deaf Education, 14*, 218–236.

Rhoades, E., & Duncan, J. (2010). (Eds.). *Auditory-verbal practice: Toward a family-centered approach.* Springfield, IL: C. C. Thomas.

Rine, R., Cornwall, G., Gan, K., Locascio, C., O'Hare, E., Robinson, E., & Rice, M. (2000). Evidence of progressive delay in children with hearing loss and concurrent vestibular dysfunction. *Perceptual and Motor Skills, 90*, 1101–1112.

Robbins, A., Koch, D., Osberger, M., Zimmerman-Philips, S., & Kishon-Rabin, L. (2004). Effect of age at cochlear implantation on auditory skill development in infants and toddlers. *Archives of Otolaryngology-Head and Neck Surgery, 130*(5), 570–574.

Robbins, A., Renshaw, J., & Berry, S. (1991). Evaluating meaningful auditory integration in profoundly hearing-impaired children. *American Journal of Otolaryngology, 12*, 144–150.

Rosenblum, L. D. (Jan. 2013). A confederacy of senses. *Scientific American, 308*, 73–75.

Rubin, R. J. (1997). A time frame of critical/sensitive periods of language development. *Acta Otolaryngology, 117*, 202–205.

Ruggirello, C., & Mayer, C. (2010). Language development in a hearing and a deaf twin with simultaneous bilateral cochlear implants. *Journal of Deaf Studies and Deaf Education, 15*, 274–286.

Sacks, O. (2010). *The mind's eye.* New York: Alfred A. Knopf.

Sass-Lehrer, M. (2011). Early intervention: Birth to three. In M. Marschark & P. Spencer (Eds.), *The Oxford handbook of deaf studies, language, and education, Vol. 1,* 2nd ed. (pp. 63–81). New York: Oxford University Press.

Sass-Lehrer, M. (Ed.). (2015). *Early intervention for deaf and hard-of-hearing infants, toddlers and their families: An interdisciplinary perspective.* New York: Oxford University Press.

Schauwers, K., Govaerts, P. J., & Gillis, S. (2008). Co-occurrence patterns in the babbling of children with a cochlear implant. In B. L. Davis & K. Zajdó (Eds.), *The syllable in speech production* (pp. 187–204). New York: Taylor & Francis Group.

Schick, B. (2006). Acquiring a visually motivated language: Evidence from diverse learners. In B. Schick, M. Marschark, & P. Spencer (Eds.), *Advances in the sign language development of deaf children* (pp. 102–134). New York: Oxford University Press.

Schick, B., & Moeller, M. P. (1992). What is learnable in manually-coded English sign systems? *Applied Psycholinguistics, 13*, 313–340.

Schlesinger, H., & Meadow, K. (1972). *Sound and sign: Childhood deafness and mental health.* Berkeley: University of California Press.

Sheldon, M., & Roush, D. (2010). A primary-coach approach to teaming and supporting families in early childhood intervention. In R. McWilliam (Ed.), *Working with families of young children with special needs* (pp. 175–202). New York: Guilford.

Sigman, M., & Ruskin, E. (1999). *Change and continuity in the social competence of children with autism, Down syndrome, and developmental delays.* London: Blackwell.

Simms, L., Baker, S., & Clark, M. D. (2013). The Standardized Visual Communication and Sign Language Checklist for Signing Children. *Sign Language Studies, 14*(1), 101–124.

Sinha, P. (2013, July). Once blind and now they see. *Scientific American, 308*(7), 48–55.

Sininger, Y., Doyle, K., & Moore, J. (1999). The case for early identification of hearing loss in children. *Pediatric Clinics of North America, 46*, 1–14.

Slade, A. (1987a). A longitudinal study of maternal involvement and symbolic play during the toddler period. *Child Development, 58*, 367–375.

Slade, A. (1987b). Quality of attachment and early symbolic play. *Developmental Psychology, 23*, 78–85.

Slater, A., Field, T., & Hernandez-Reif, M. (2007). The development of the senses. In A. Slater & M. Lewis (Eds.), *Introduction to infant development* (pp. 83–98). New York: Oxford University Press.

Slater, A., & Lewis, M. (Eds.). (2007). *Introduction to infant development (2nd Edition)*. New York: Oxford University Press.

Snyder, L., & Yoshinaga-Itano, C. (1999). Specific play behaviors and the development of communication in children with hearing loss. *Volta Review*, 100(3), 165–185.

Spencer, L., Tye-Murray, N., & Tomblin, J. B. (1998). The production of English inflectional morphology, speech production and listening performance in children with cochlear implants. *Ear & Hearing*, 19, 310–318.

Spencer, P. E. (1996). The association between language and symbolic play at two years: Evidence from deaf toddlers. *Child Development*, 67(3), 867–876.

Spencer, P. (2000a). Every opportunity: A case study of hearing parents and their deaf child. In P. Spencer, C. Erting, & M. Marschark (Eds.), *The deaf child in the family and at school* (pp. 111–132). Mahwah, NJ: Lawrence Erlbaum.

Spencer, P. (2000b). Looking without listening: Is audition a prerequisite for normal development of visual attention during infancy? *Journal of Deaf Studies and Deaf Education*, 5, 291–302.

Spencer, P. (2001). A good start: Suggestions for visual conversations with deaf and hard of hearing babies and toddlers. In *Kids World DeafNet*. Washington, DC: Gallaudet University Press.

Spencer, P. (2004a). Individual differences in language development after cochlear implantation at one to three years of age: Child, family, and linguistic factors. *Journal of Deaf Studies and Deaf Education*, 9, 395–412.

Spencer, P. (2004b). Language at 12 and 18 months: Characteristics and accessibility of linguistic models. In K. P. Meadow-Orlans, P. E. Spencer, & L. S. Koester, *The world of deaf infants: A longitudinal study* (pp. 147–167). New York: Oxford University Press.

Spencer, P. (2010). Play and theory of mind: Indicators and engines of cognitive growth. In M. Marschark & P. Spencer (Eds.) *The Oxford Handbook of Deaf Studies, Language, and Education* (Vol. 2, pp. 407–424). New York: Oxford University Press.

Spencer, P., Bodner-Johnson, B. A., & Gutfreund, M. K. (1992). Interacting with infants with a hearing loss: What can we learn from mothers who are deaf? *Journal of Early Intervention*, 16, 64–78.

Spencer, P., & Deyo, D. A. (1993). Cognitive and social aspects of deaf children's play. In M. Marschark & M. D. Clark (Eds.), *Psychological perspectives on deafness* (pp. 65–91). Hillsdale, NJ: Lawrence Erlbaum Associates.

Spencer, P. & Hafer, J. (1998). Play as "window" and "room": Assessing and supporting the cognitive and linguistic development of deaf infants and young children. In M. Marschark & D. Clark (Eds.), *Psychological Perspectives on Deafness, Vol. 2* (pp. 131–152). Hillsdale NJ: L. Erlbaum Associates, Inc.

Spencer, P., & Harris, M. (2006). Patterns and effects of language input to deaf infants and toddlers from deaf and hearing mothers. In B. Schick, M. Marschark, & P. Spencer (Eds.), *Advances in the sign language development of deaf children* (pp. 71–101). New York: Oxford University Press.

Spencer, P., Koester, L., & Meadow-Orlans, K. (1993). Communicative interactions of deaf and hearing children in a day care center: An exploratory study. *American Annals of the Deaf, 139*, 512–518.

Spencer, P., & Lederberg, A. (1997). Different modes, different models: Communication and language of young deaf children and their mothers. In L. Adamson & M. Romski (Eds.), *Communication and language acquisition: Discoveries from atypical development* (pp. 203–230). Baltimore MD: Brookes.

Spencer, P., & Marschark, M. (2010). *Evidence-based practice in educating deaf and hard-of-hearing students.* New York: Oxford University Press.

Spencer, P., Marschark, M., & Spencer, L. (2011). Cochlear implants: Advances, issues, and implications. In M. Marschark & P. Spencer (Eds.), *The Oxford handbook of deaf studies, language, and education, Vol. 1*, 2nd ed. (pp. 452–472). New York: Oxford University Press.

Spencer, P., & Meadow-Orlans, K. (1996). Play, language, and maternal responsiveness: A longitudinal study of deaf and hearing infants. *Child Development, 67*, 3076–3101.

Spencer, P., Swisher, M. V., & Waxman, R. P. (2004). Visual attention: Maturation and specialization. In K. P. Meadow-Orlans, P. E. Spencer, & L. S. Koester, *The world of deaf infants: A longitudinal study* (pp. 168–187). New York: Oxford University Press.

Spencer Day, P. (1986). Deaf children's expression of communicative intentions. *Journal of Communication Disorders, 19*(5), 367–385.

Sternberg, M. (1987). *American Sign Language dictionary.* New York: Harper & Row.

Stredler-Brown, A., & Johnson, D. (2003). *Functional Auditory Performance Indicators: An Integrated Approach to Auditory Development.* http://www.cdc.state.co.us/cdesped/SpecificDisabilty-Hearing.htm.

Tait, M., Luterman, M., & Robinson, K. (2000). Preimplant measures of preverbal communicative behavior as predictors of cochlear implant outcomes in children. *Ear & Hearing, 21*(1), 18–24.

Tang, G., & Yiu, C. (2016). Developing sign bilingualism in a co-enrollment school environment: A Hong Kong case study. In M. Marschark & P. Spencer (Eds.). *The Oxford handbook of deaf studies in language: Research, policy, and practice* (pp. 197–217). New York: Oxford University Press.

Thomas, A., & Chess, S. (1963). *Behavioral individuality in early childhood.* New York: New York University Press.

Thomson, N. R., Kennedy, E. A., & Kuebli, J. E. (2011). Attachment formation between deaf infants and their primary caregivers: Is being deaf a risk factor for insecure attachment? In D. H. Zand & K. J. Pierce (Eds.), *Resilience in deaf children* (pp. 27–64). New York: Springer.

Tobey, E., Weissner, N., Lane, J., Sundarrajan, M., Buckley, K., & Sullivan, J. (2007). Phoneme accuracy as a function of mode of communication in pediatric cochlear implantation. *Audiological Medicine, 5*(4), 283–292.

Tobey, E., Thal, D., Niparko, J., Eisenberg, L., Quittner, A., & Wang, N. (2013). Influence of implantation age on school-age language performance in pediatric cochlear implant users. *International Journal of Audiology, 52,* 219–229.

Tomasello, M. (1999). *The cultural origins of human cognition.* Cambridge MA: Harvard University Press.

Tronick, E., Als, H., Adamson, L., Wise, S., & Brazelton, T. (1978). The infant's response to entrapment between contradictory messages in face-to-face interaction. *Journal of the American Academy of Child Psychiatry, 17,* 1–13.

Tronick, E. Z. (1989). Emotions and emotional communication in infants. *American Psychologist, 44,* 112–119.

Tronick, E. Z., & Field, T. (Eds.) (1986). *Maternal depression and infant disturbance.* San Francisco: Jossey-Bass.

Vaccari, C., & Marschark, M. (1997). Communication between parents and deaf children: Implications for social-emotional development. *Journal of Child Psychology and Psychiatry, 18*(7), 793–801.

VanDam, M., Ambrose, S., & Moeller, M. P. (2012). Quantity of parental language in the home environments of hard-of-hearing two-year-olds. *Journal of Deaf Studies and Deaf Education, 17*(4), 402–420.

vanIJzendoorn, M. H., Goldberg, S., Kroonenberg, P. M., & Frenkel, O. J. (1992). The relative effects of maternal and child problems on the quality of attachment: A meta-analysis of attachment in clinical samples. *Child Development, 63,* 840–858.

Vihman, M. M. (1993). Variable paths of early word production. *Journal of Phonetics, 21,* 61–82.

Vohr, B., Carty, L., Moore, P., & Letourneau, K. (1998). The Rhode Island hearing assessment program: Experience with statewide hearing screening (1993–1996). *Journal of Pediatrics, 128,* 710–714.

Vygotsky, L. (1967). Play and its role in the mental development of the child. *Soviet Psychology, 5*, 6–18.

Vygotsky, L. (1978). *Mind in society: The development of higher psychological processes.* Cambridge, MA: Harvard University Press.

Waxman, R. P., & Spencer, P. E. (1997). What mothers do to support infant visual attention: Sensitivities to age and hearing status. *Journal of Deaf Studies and Deaf Education, 2*, 104–114.

Weir, R. H. (1962). *Language in the crib.* The Hague: Mouton.

Weisel, A., Most, T., & Efron, C. (2005). Initiations of social interactions by young hearing impaired preschoolers. *Journal of Deaf Studies and Deaf Education, 10*(2), 162–170.

Wood, D., Wood, H., Griffith, A., & Howarth, I. (1986). *Teaching and talking with deaf children.* New York: Wiley.

Wood, H., Wood, D., & Kingsmill, M. (1991). Signed English in the classroom: Structural and pragmatic aspects of teachers' speech and sign. *First Language, 11*, 301–325.

Woolfe, T., Herman, R., Roy, P., &Woll, B. (2010). Early lexical development in native signers: A BSL adaptation of the CDI. *Journal of Child Psychology and Psychiatry, 51*(3), 322–331.

Wynn, K. (2000). Addition and subtraction by human infants. In D. Muir & A. Slater (Eds.), *Infant development: The essential readings* (pp. 185–191). Oxford: Blackwell Publishers.

Yoshinaga-Itano, C. (1992). Predictors of successful outcomes of deaf and hard-of-hearing children. *Volta Review, 94*, 107–129.

Yoshinaga-Itano, C. (2003). From screening to early identification and intervention: Discovering predictors to successful outcomes for children with significant hearing loss. *Journal of Deaf Studies and Deaf Education, 8*, 11–30.

Yoshinaga-Itano, C. (2006). Early identification, communication modality, and the development of speech and spoken language skills: Patterns and considerations. In M. Marschark & P.E. Spencer (Eds.), *Advances in the spoken language of deaf and hard-of-hearing children* (pp. 298–327). New York: Oxford University Press.

Yoshinaga-Itano, C., Sedey, A., Coulter, D., & Mehl, A. (1998). Language of early—and later-identified children with hearing loss. *Pediatrics, 102*, 1161–1171.

Young, A., & Tattersall, H. (2005). Parents of deaf children's evaluative accounts of the process and practice of universal newborn hearing screening. *Journal of Deaf Studies and Deaf Education, 10*, 134–145.

Young A., & Tattersall, H. (2007). Universal newborn hearing screening and early identification of deafness: Parents' responses to knowing early and their expectations of child communication development. *Journal of Deaf Studies and Deaf Education, 12,* 209–220.

Zimmerman-Phillips, S., Osberger, M., & Robbins, A. (1997). *Infant-Toddler Meaningful Auditory Integration Scale (IT-MAIS).* Sylmar CA: Advanced Bionics.

Zimmerman, I. L., Steiner, V. G., & Pond, R. E. (2011). *Preschool language scales,* 5th ed. Upper Saddle River, NJ: Pearson Education.

INDEX

DISCARD
Porter County
Library System

DISCARD
Porter County
Library System